BRITISH SOCIALIST FICTION, 1884–1914

CONTENTS OF THE EDITION

VOLUME 1
General Introduction
1884–1891

VOLUME 2
1892–1900

VOLUME 3
1901–1906

VOLUME 4
1907–1910

VOLUME 5
1911–1914

BRITISH SOCIALIST FICTION, 1884–1914

Volume 5
1911–1914

Edited by
Deborah Mutch

PICKERING & CHATTO
2013

Published by Pickering & Chatto (Publishers) Limited
21 Bloomsbury Way, London WC1A 2TH

2252 Ridge Road, Brookfield, Vermont 05036-9704, USA

www.pickeringchatto.com

All rights reserved.
No part of this publication may be reproduced,
stored in a retrieval system, or transmitted in any form or by any means,
electronic, mechanical, photocopying, recording, or otherwise
without prior permission of the publisher.

Copyright © Pickering & Chatto (Publishers) Limited 2013
Copyright © Editorial material Deborah Mutch 2013

To the best of the Publisher's knowledge every effort has been made to contact
relevant copyright holders and to clear any relevant copyright issues.
Any omissions that come to their attention will be remedied in future editions.

BRITISH LIBRARY CATALOGUING IN PUBLICATION DATA

British socialist fiction, 1884–1914.
1. Political fiction, English – 19th century. 2. Political fiction, English – 20th century. 3. Socialism – Fiction.
I. Mutch, Deborah, 1965– editor of compilation.
823.8'0803581-dc23

ISBN-13: 9781848933576

This publication is printed on acid-free paper that conforms to the American
National Standard for the Permanence of Paper for Printed Library Materials.

Typeset by Pickering & Chatto (Publishers) Limited
Printed and bound in the United Kingdom by Berforts Information Press

CONTENTS

Introduction	vii
Clarion	1
J. Cartmel, 'Jeshurun's Great Kick' (1911)	3
Robert Blatchford, 'The Perpendicular Recruit' (1911)	9
A. Neil Lyons, 'Unearned Increment' (1912)	15
R. B. Suthers, 'A Coster's Funeral' (1913)	19
Daily Citizen	23
W. C. Anderson, 'Who Killed Downie? An Aberdeen Legend' (1912)	25
Frank Dilnot, 'The Public Spirit of Mr. Josiah Grub' (1913)	29
Frank Starr, 'The Aerial Armada. What Took Place in A.D. 2000' (1913)	35
Hugh Derrick, 'The Making of a Red' (1913–14)	39
'Pat', 'Living Retired. An Unconscious Tragedy' (1914)	251
W. O. Pitt, 'The Last Dinner' (1914)	255
Justice	257
Tom Quelch, 'His Reward' (1911)	259
Victor Grayson, 'The Lost Vision. A Spring Fantasy' (1912)	263
Edward Hartley, 'Mr. Prowser-Wowser' (1913)	267
Edward Meyer, 'It Can't be Done! A History of Impossibilities' (1914)	273
Labour Leader	277
J. Keir Hardie, 'Nellie' (1911)	279
I. O. Ford, 'In the "Good Old Times"' (1911)	283
Herbert Morrison, 'Lord Santa Claus, G.E.R., M.P. A Drama in Ten Minutes' (1911)	289
Herbert Morrison, 'The Weaker Vessel and the Strike' (1912)	293
J. Zimmerman, 'Stitch, Stitch, Stitch' (1913)	297
'Casey', 'Alice in Sunderland. A Baffling Mystery' (1914)	301
Social Democrat	305
'Optimus', 'The May-Day Festival in the Year 1970' (1911)	307
May Westoby, 'Shamed' (1912)	311
Schalom Asch, 'Behind the Wall' (1913)	317

Socialist	321
Eugene Sue, '"Stop Thief!" The Proletariat and Slummery (An Incident of the Revolution of 1848, told by Eugene Sue)' (1911)	323
Tom Anderson, 'Mary Davis; or the Fate of a Proletarian Family. A Lesson Given to the Glasgow S.L.P. Socialist Sunday School' (1912)	327
Socialist Review	337
D. C. Parker, 'Elsie's Day' (1911)	339
R. C. G., 'The Patriots' (1912)	343
Eileen Hynes, 'Barky: A Sketch' (1913)	347
Editorial Notes	351
Silent Corrections	371

INTRODUCTION

The final volume in this collection covers both a period of industrial unrest and one of literary change, as retrospectively designated by Virginia Woolf. In 'Mr. Bennett and Mrs. Brown' (1924), Woolf semi-seriously, semi-humorously pinpoints December 1910 as the precise point of change in British literature. The new period, which she termed 'Georgian' in contrast to the former 'Edwardian' era, was the point at which Edwardian authors, represented by Galsworthy, Wells and Bennett, lost control of British fiction and metaphorically handed the pen over to Georgian authors, represented by Strachey, Lawrence, Eliot, Joyce and Forster.[1] These, and others, she asserts, are the authors of a new age of fiction, authors who will take a different perspective on their characters. Woolf uses 'Mrs. Brown', travelling in her railway carriage, as an example of the changing attitudes:

> With all his powers of observation, which are marvellous, with all his sympathy and humanity, which are great, Mr. Bennett has never once looked at Mrs. Brown in her corner. There she sits in the corner of the carriage – that carriage which is travelling, not from Richmond to Waterloo, but from one age of English literature to the next, for Mrs. Brown is eternal. Mrs. Brown is human nature, Mrs. Brown changes only on the surface, it is the novelists who get in and out – there she sits and not one of the Edwardian writers has so much as looked at her. They have looked very powerfully, searchingly, and sympathetically out of the window; at factories, at Utopias, even at the decoration and upholstery of the carriage; but never at her, never at life, never at human nature.[2]

Of the fiction in this volume, Woolf might have recognized Hugh Derrick's 'The Making of a Red' (1913–14) as nearer to her own ideal of 'looking' at a character. Derrick's story of the journalist Majority Gaunt's conversion from 'Authoritarian' to 'Red' politics is not 'modernist' in the sense of, say, James Joyce's range of interiorities in *Ulysses* (1922) or Woolf's expansion and compression of time in *To the Lighthouse* (1927); instead it is closer to D. H. Lawrence's straddling of Victorian and modernist literatures. But Derrick's fiction differs from earlier socialist fictions as it shifts its perspective towards an 'interiority' of Gaunt and his attitudes, a perspective that was to become associated with later modernist fiction.

Previous changes of heart or mind in the more realist-oriented serials were understandable, if rather sudden (Jim Campbell's instant conversion to socialism in 'The Red Flag', *Justice*, Volume 4), or necessary for plot development and conclusion (Nigel Grey and Constance Compton's journey to mutual ideological ground in 'Nigel Grey', *Labour Leader*, Volume 2). A failure to change has similarly been understandable to the reader, as, for instance, is Frank Wilson's desire to remain anonymous in 'A Working Class Tragedy', *Justice*, Volume 1. Nevertheless, while the reader understands Wilson's reticence to become involved in the socialist movement, the external forces that impose a barrier to change are the primary focus, and there is very little examination of Wilson's own feelings about his situation. Similarly, Jim Campbell's relief at being rescued from destitution by the socialist Joe Summerfield is understandable, but his acceptance of socialist politics is the result of a series of visions and dreams over the course of a single night. Derrick's fiction, on the other hand, gives a much more detailed and nuanced account of a change of political allegiance.

In 'The Making of a Red', the reader is shown Gaunt's experiences of socialism and working-class life through his own eyes and his internal debates, vacillations and resistance to the morality of socialist politics. Gaunt is not an innocent hero-in-waiting who simply needed to be enlightened about socialism, nor is he given an epiphanic moment of conversion. He is, rather, a hard-nosed, well-paid journalist who, for the duration of the fiction, works to undermine 'Progressive' and 'Red' political ideology through the paper he is employed to write for, the *Daily Light*. Through a series of experiences, Gaunt begins to question his political stance: his meetings with the socialist politician Raston Path convince him of Path's sincerity; his investigative journalism, undertaken to prove there is abundant employment in London, reveals to him the trap of unemployment and removes his complacency about finding work; and his affair with Viola Cartlet opens his eyes to the selfishness and vacuity of entrenched 'Authoritarian' ideology. His political change of heart is similar to Katherine Mansfield's characterization of the effects of 'different impulses' on the subject, as described by Dominic Head: '[t]hese points of conflict reveal a complicated view of personality, a stress on impersonal identity, determined by a variety of social forces'.[3] It is this sense of his internal political turmoil, provoked by external events, that draws the character of Gaunt closer to Woolf's 'Mrs. Brown' than to the older authors' descriptions of the surrounding upholstery.

Woolf designated December 1910 as the turning point in English literature to make her point, rather than from a conviction that literary change can be dated. As discussed in the General Introduction, modernism was not a uniquely new literary form but one that utilized earlier literary techniques and brought a new sexual openness to British literature. This openness about sexual relationships is evident in the fiction included in the volumes of this collection: A. Gilbert Katte's 'The Whip Hand' (*To-Day*, Volume 1) presents Sir Reginald

Hastie's mistress as the heroine of the story, since she gives him the means by which he can prevent his wife from exposing their relationship, in turn allowing them to continue their affair without public knowledge; John Law's [Margaret Harkness's] 'Connie' (*Labour Elector*, Volume 2) describes a loving and happy cohabitation between the eponymous character and her aristocratic lover. Both Katte and Harkness use the extramarital sexual relationship to bring their true lovers together, as Hastie carries on his relationship with the woman he loves while maintaining a façade of marriage to pander to the social demand for 'respectability'. Harkness's incomplete fiction leaves the reader only with a sense of a possible happy ending, but provides a clear, non-judgmental and in some ways positive depiction of women and sex, including prostitution. Derrick's fiction takes a position that is simultaneously more 'modernist' in its approach to sex and ultimately harks back to more 'Victorian' attitudes.

The relationship between Majority Gaunt and Viola Cartlet is one of mutual attraction and therefore conforms to previous literary standards. As they attend a political meeting together, their emotions are initially described in very traditional terms: Gaunt 'felt his heart beat a little quicker as he watched her talking to friends with the knowledge that she was coming to sit by him presently'; Viola 'was thinking of him all the time ... her departure from him, her conversation with others, were labour to her, that she sought nothing but to sit by him, near him' (p. 81). Yet as they sit next to each other on the platform of the meeting, the couple's relationship moves away from this modest literary description. Here there is a clear indication of the future physical relationship between them, as the contact of their knees is described in highly charged language: 'Accidentally their knees touched. He felt the pulsing of her blood, and she was all a tremble with the warmth of him. He allowed the side of his hand to touch the side of hers, and she did not move' (p. 82). The physicality of their relationship draws the fiction towards naturalism and is similar to that of Katte and Harkness, while Viola's married status further aligns Derrick's fiction with that of Katte. Where the fiction appears to move closer to the attitudes of the modernist authors, particularly Lawrence, is in the morality of the relationship. Like in Lawrence's *Sons and Lovers* (published in 1913, the year Derrick's fiction began its serialization), marriage is not the full-stop happy ending for Viola, who, despite her authentic feelings for Gaunt, remains married to her husband and conducts a flirtation with Gaunt's employer, Archibald Lodden. Nor does the blame lie solely with Viola; although there is no suggestion that her husband is similarly unfaithful, he chaffs her about her 'lovers' and therefore appears to be aware of her serial infidelities, and Gaunt is unconcerned about her marital status or her husband's feelings. Thus the fiction takes an unflinching look at sex, marriage and fidelity in ways not dissimilar to the relationship between Paul Morel and the separated Clara Dawes in Lawrence's novel.

Where Derrick's fiction deviates from that of Lawrence in terms of sexual relationships is the way each tale concludes. The death of Morel's mother leads him to the realization that no woman will live up to her place in his life; but Gaunt, through his change of political ideology, wins his soul mate, and the fiction ends with the traditional conclusion of marriage. Gaunt's fidelity to his new wife, Nancy Kirk, former secretary to the Progressive's chief agent, is suggested through his ending of the relationship with Viola, his confession of love for Nancy and their establishment in a coastal town away from the temptations and deviancies of the city. Viola's marital infidelities appear to continue as her husband again teases her about her admirers, but even Viola is drawn into the traditional ending as her feelings for Gaunt are secretly maintained and the end of their relationship privately mourned. Thus the freer attitudes to sexuality raised during the fiction are gathered up and re-bound to return it to the conclusions of an earlier era.

The tidy conclusion was not the only technique in Derrick's fiction that was drawn from earlier literary methods. As much as Woolf would like to imagine a clear break between 'Edwardians' and 'Georgians', between Victorian realism and modernism, the continuum between the two is evident. As Jessica R. Feldman argues, 'the Victorian period and the Modern period, each so complex as to resist intellectual containment almost successfully, may be studied fruitfully as one continuous period'.[4] In Derrick's fiction, there is a clear and cohesive structure that moves to a recognizable conclusion – the lost beginning, middle and end that Thomas Hardy lamented of modernist fiction;[5] there is an omniscient narrator giving the reader descriptions and histories of secondary characters; and there is the romance of Gaunt and Nancy Kirk threaded through the fiction to achieve coherence and conclusion. Modernists, it has been argued recently, did not leave realism behind as conclusively as they would have liked history to believe. As Liesl Olsen states, 'Modernism is still generally committed to modes of realism and coherence that could be called an aesthetic order'.[6]

Derrick's fiction, and much of the short fiction published during this period, had a strong basis in realism. In Derrick's case, even what appears to be a fanciful narrative tool, designed to raise excitement and provide drama as the fiction moves towards its conclusion, finds a counterpart in reality. The plot to kidnap five Irish MPs as they travel to the House of Commons for a crucial vote, organized by Archibald Lodden, proprietor of the *Daily Light*, along with some Authoritarian MPs, seems far-fetched. This part of the fiction might be accused of being poor literature, as the use of the *deus ex machina* had brought the same accusation to earlier working-class and Chartist fiction.[7] Nevertheless, this was very close to the experience of Victor Grayson, the socialist loose cannon who represented Colne Valley as a Labour MP and who was renowned for his fondness for alcohol. At the Labour Party conference in Portsmouth in January 1909,

Grayson 'was kidnapped by local Conservatives who drove him into the countryside where they plied him with alcohol'.[8]

Realism might still be considered a necessary genre, for voters were still in need of convincing about the necessity of socialism and a truly independent Labour Party. The two elections of 1910, caused by the Lords' rejection of the Liberal 'Peoples' Budget', made it clear that the Labour Party had made little progress since 1906; Labour fought seventy-six seats in the January election, which were reduced to fifty-six in the December election at the suggestion of the party's agent, an increase of six from the number standing in 1906.[9] The difficulties for Labour and socialists were twofold. First, the drift of the Labour Party towards the Liberals would be difficult to extricate from because the Liberal Party had hijacked some of the socialist aims, and opposition to the Liberals would mean opposition to Asquith's proposals for non-contributory pensions, minimum wage, municipal labour exchanges and Lords reform. Second, there was no increase in support for the socialist groups or for socialism generally, and therefore no foundation for political independence. Modernism – as the momentum of progress, the journey from the old to the (better) new – seemed to be taking a different direction, or appeared to be journeying towards a different destination, from that which socialists had anticipated at the start of parliamentary socialism and the founding of the Independent Labour Party (ILP) and the Labour Representation Committee (LRC); it was certainly different from the revolutionary socialism of the Social Democratic Federation (SDF) or the Socialist League.

The ease of organizing and maintaining socialist groups appeared to be no easier in 1906, when Robert Noonan and his friends joined the fluctuating body of the Hastings SDF,[10] than it had been in the early days of the group. There were attempts to unify the socialist societies in this part of the country as there were nationally, and, as also happened nationally, there was no permanency in the union. Nevertheless, there was a desire for an alternative way of ordering things, and this resulted in the backlash against parliamentary representation and the rise of industrial action after 1910. As Labour had not made a visible improvement in the lives of workers, there was less confidence in parliamentary methods of change and a corresponding rise in syndicalism, and industrial unionism saw workers take issues into their own hands.[11] There was also the Unity Conference of 1911, where the British Socialist Party was formed out of 'an amalgamation of seventy-seven SDF branches, thirty Clarion clubs and thirty-six ILP branches'.[12] Nevertheless, there was a sense that there was still work to do to convince the majority, and realist literature was one of the most useful tools of persuasion.

The most famous socialist fiction was written during this period, published in 1914 in an abridged form that seriously skewed the original story and not published in its complete form until 1955. *The Ragged Trousered Philanthropists* by Robert Tressell, the pseudonym of the Hasting SDF's Robert Noonan, has been dubbed the first 'working class' novel and follows the fortunes of painter and decorator Frank Owen, his work colleagues, his family and his employers. Raymond Williams noted the amalgamation of traditional 'working class' forms – 'the family novel, the family novel partly extended to a class, and the novel written from a conscious class perspective'[13] – that created a novel of broad perspectives. The political basis for the novel is presented directly as the reader, along with Frank's colleagues, is given lessons in socialist economics and ideology. As Ian Haywood explains, Tressell's novel is an 'experimental juxtaposition of styles ranging from allegorical satire to long disquisitions on socialist economic theory' and is scathing in 'its ... condemnation of working-class servility and benightedness'.[14]

The short fiction of the socialist periodicals took a similar approach to Tressell, who uses the amalgamation of genre evident in earlier working-class fictions. For instance, the issue of poverty in old age is tragically described in both Tressell's character Jack Linden and Eileen Hynes's Barky in 'Barky: A Sketch', published in 1913 in the *Socialist Review*. Both men had worked all their lives; both were still looking for work in their advanced years, when a civilized society would have wanted to give them rest after their lifetime of labour; and both were edged out of the system by dint of their age. The difference between Tressell's and Hynes's workers is their eventual end: while Tressell leaves Linden entering the workhouse, where he will stay until death, Barky takes action to ensure that Linden's fate – and that of many, many others – is not his own. The methods may be different, but both authors cannot envisage an alternative, positive end within the system as it stands. And it is not only men who suffer such a fate. A similar outcome awaits Tom Anderson's eponymous protagonist in 'Mary Davis; or the Fate of a Proletarian Family' (*Socialist Monthly*, 1912), a woman who has worked all her life and who is left without work as she ages and is injured by her employment in a laundry. Like Barky and Linden, there is only the choice between a long, drawn-out death through starvation or in the workhouse and a quick end to the long years of suffering.

Meanwhile Herbert Morrison's 'The Weaker Vessel and the Strike' (*Labour Leader*, 1912) gives two perspectives of the female attitude towards industrial action. Like Tressell's Frank Owen, who, under the pressure of underemployment, became 'tired of impotently watching the sufferings of his wife',[15] Morrison's working men are aware of their responsibilities for their wife and children, and both are striking for the eventual betterment of their existence. The necessity of the strike is a given; no working-class person – man or woman – looks forward to an old age of the type experienced by Linden, Barky or Mary. The importance of a class standing united against the might of capitalism is the basis for the two contrasting stories in Morrison's tale: Bill Wright's wife can only see the short-term privations arising from strike action, but Jack Robins's wife is able to see the long-term benefits of winning the strike – and the battle against capitalist power – as she persuades her husband to join the strike and cease strike-breaking on their behalf. His concern about the children and the effect the strike will have on them materially is countered by his wife's consideration of the long-term effect on the children of having a blackleg father:

> I been thinking about them, and I see it this way. All being well, those kids'll grow up; they'll know more than what we know, Jack – they come along later ... When they grow up, the likes of us won't put up with the rotten time we're putting up with; they'll kick against it! And our kids'll be among the kickers – I'm seeing to that. Do you think it'll please them to remember that their ole man was a blackleg? ... They'll cuss the likes of you; they'll feel you've put a blot on their characters; they'll say you wasn't a good father, 'cos you never joined your mates to get more wages, so that they could be brought up better. (p. 294)

One might argue that Morrison imposes a patriarchal hierarchy on the family and positions the female role as merely child-bearer and help-meet for the male, but it could also be claimed that a united stance at home will make a united stance in industry.

Unity will bring benefits for all workers, regardless of gender; the stories of Linden, Barky and Mary remind the reader that poverty does not discriminate between the sexes. But what we have at the end of the period covered by this volume is a unity within the parliamentary Labour Party and a waning of the power, voices and periodicals of the independent socialists. As the Labour Party moved on to power and government during the twentieth century, alternative voices were either ignored into silence – Blatchford, who lived until 1943, faded away – or demonized by association, as the Communist Party of Great Britain suffered through connections with the Soviet Union.

Notes

1. V. Woolf, 'Mr. Bennett and Mrs. Brown', in M. J. Hoffman and P. D. Murphy (eds), *Essentials of the Theory of Fiction* (Durham, NC: Duke University Press, 2005), pp. 21–34, on p. 22.
2. Ibid., p. 28.
3. D. Head, *The Modernist Short Story: A Study in Theory and Practice* (Cambridge: Cambridge University Press, 1992), p. 33.
4. J. R. Feldman, *Victorian Modernism: Pragmatism and the Varieties of Aesthetic Experience* (Cambridge: Cambridge University Press, 2002), p. 3.
5. T. Hardy, quoted R. Stevenson, *Modernist Fiction: An Introduction* (Lexington, KY: University Press of Kentucky, 1992), p. 4.
6. L. Olson, *Modernism and the Ordinary* (Oxford: Oxford University Press, 2009), p. 5.
7. R. Breton, 'Ghosts in the Machina: Plotting in Chartist and Working-Class Fiction', *Victorian Studies* (2005), pp. 557–75.
8. M. Pugh, *Speak for Britain! A New History of the Labour Party* (London: Vintage, 2011), p. 77.

9. Ibid., pp. 78–9.
10. D. Harker, *Tressell: The Real Story of the Ragged Trousered Philanthropists* (London and New York: Zed Books, 2003), p. 30.
11. M. Crick, *The History of the Social-Democratic Federation* (Keele: Keele University Press, 1994), pp. 229–30.
12. Pugh, *Speak for Britain!*, p. 78.
13. R. Williams, *Writing in Society* (London and New York: Verso, 1991), p. 243.
14. I. Haywood, *Working-Class Fiction from Chartism to Trainspotting* (Plymouth: Northcote House, 1997), p. 22.
15. R. Tressell, *The Ragged Trousered Philanthropists* (1914, 1955; London: HarperCollins, 1993), p. 66.

CLARION

J. Cartmel, 'Jeshurun's Great Kick', *Clarion*, 13 January 1911, p. 1.

Robert Blatchford, 'The Perpendicular Recruit', *Clarion*, 2 February 1911, p. 1.[1]

A. Neil Lyons, 'Unearned Increment', *Clarion*, 27 September 1912, p. 1.

R. B. Suthers, 'A Coster's Funeral', *Clarion*, 6 June 1913, p. 1.

Robert Blatchford (1851–1943) had passed the editorship of the *Clarion* (1891–1935) to his daughter Winifred when he withdrew in 1910, but he returned to edit the paper briefly in 1913 before handing Winnie permanent control. Nevertheless, he continued to write articles for the *Clarion* while employed by other newspapers. R. B. Suthers (1870–1950) had left the *Clarion* in 1910 to become editor of Edward Hulton's (1869–1925) *Ideas* in 1910. When Blatchford returned in 1913 he asked Suthers to re-join him; Suthers did so and remained with the paper until 1925, after which he continued as a freelance contributor. A. M. Thompson (1861–1948) similarly remained with the *Clarion*, but his attention had turned to the writing of plays. The power of the *Clarion* and the Clarion group would never again reach the heights of the 1890s and 1900s despite the periodical's continuation into the 1930s.

The *Clarion* maintained its commitment to bringing socialism to the reader in an entertaining manner. Blatchford had generally ceased writing fiction in 1909 to concentrate on his warnings of the German threat, but the *Clarion* continued to publish fiction, including one of Blatchford's many army tales; for Blatchford's biographical details, see the headnote for the *Clarion* in Volume 2, p. 3. A. Neil Lyons's long serialization 'Simple Simon: The History of a Fool' was the most sustained piece of the period covered by this volume, and it was published between 3 March and 18 December 1911. There were other, shorter serials also published, and all the serial fiction at this point was authored by Lyons, whose biographical details can be found in the headnote for the *Clarion* in Volume 3, pp. 2–3, along with the biographical details for R. B. Suthers. The only author not already included in the selections for this collection is the Reverend J. Cartmel Robinson (n.d.). He was one of the founding members of the Clarion cyclists and was a regular *Clarion* contributor of short stories and poetry.

Notes

1. 'The Perpendicular Recruit' consists of two chapters from Blatchford's book *My Life in the Army* – Chapter XIV, 'No. 3 Mess', and Chapter XV, 'Human Documents'. These stories of army life were first published as a series of articles in the *Sunday Chronicle* in 1889.

J. Cartmel, 'Jeshurun's Great Kick' (1911)

"Ah! Rabbuts are funny things, mister," said old Sumpton, the verger, as he sat down on an oak log outside the belfry and rubbed his hand over the roof of his skull, from which the thatch had long since disappeared. "Folk ut live in towns, and have only seen dead uns, think they're all fools. As if anybody could look their best hung up at a poulterer's by their heels to roast or boil. Whey, ye can't tell a rabbut frae a cat wi' its napper[1] off. But a real live rabbut is one o' the wonders o' the brute creation. Even a rabbut reared in a hutch isn't gradely rabbut 'ceptin' it has favourable conditions. They are maistly like humans; they don't develop and become proper sort o' rabbuts in a one-roomed tenement; they want plenty o' space to fling about in and larn things. Why, I've known rabbuts with half a chance o' disguisin' theirselves kick up the devil's own dordums,[2] and show as much wickedness as a goat or a Chinee pirate."

"Have you read 'Brer Rabbit,'[3] Peter?" I inquired.

"Have I not?" he replied. "And what a skep full o' wisdom and craft he was. Why, he could throw away points to Mister Rennard, the fox, and them make him chew his own tail with envy."

"But he was an imaginary rabbit, Peter. The real rabbit is silly."

"Now, look you here, Mister: folk who say rabbuts are silly know nowt at all about them. Just look at them in Australia. Think what they've achieved. Why, they've conker'd the country and taken possession. Like ten million bum-bailiffs[4] there they are eatin' and drinkin', reapin' where they have not sown, and no man to shift 'em. In spite of poisun and traps and weasels and wire nets, and attempts to destroy their constitutions by incubatin', there they are, defyin' the whole world,[5] and then tell me rabbuts is silly! Why, it's a – well, it's an error o' judgment."

"You once saw a rabbit's ghost, didn't you, Peter?"

"Well, it was that or a phenomenon. She was a grey rabbut, and had her hole under the parson's wood stack. When I was a bit of a striplin' I went to the Bible Class. She was the only grey rabbut I ivver see in these parts as hadn't a white scut[6] on to the end of her. I knew her, d'ye see, for I spent the whole o' one blessed Sunday mornin' huntin' her alongside of Wullie Spender, the rector's son, him ut went to college and some did say got hanged, but as it turned out after, got a snek[7] to his name, and hanged other folk instead. I remember that mornin' well, for we should ha' been at church, when the rector comes peedlin' round the stack, and catches us doin' it, and he sez in a solemn voice, just at if he was givin' out the lesson at the goose,[8] he sez: 'now, then, none o' that. No rabbutin' o' Sundays. How dar you breek the Sabbath?' And then the rabbut, it runs out, and the rector he shouts, 'Hi, hi,' not mindin' it was the Sabbath – not when he seed the rabbut, for he was a sportin' man down to his stockin's, only his father made him a parson. Well, when I seed her ghost it was more or fifty years later, when I was a grown man. She –"

"You say *she*, Peter. How did you know she was a doe?"

"Well, I nivver! There's a question. How do I know you're the son o' your mother? I was goin' to say ut that rabbut knowed a Sabbath day better nor any man i' the parish, and would sken at ye bold as one o' them gargles[9] on the church when she knowed you hadn't got no dog nor gun. Ah, and I've seen her sitting up combin' her whiskers while the bells was ringin' to church just like a mortal Christian. It was said she knowed the difference when a grandsire or a triple[10] was rung as well as most folk, but that isn't sayin' much, and besides I have no sarten knowledge mysel."

"Did nobody ever put a ferret in to her, Peter, or shoot her?"

"Not ut I knowed on. As the Rector said o' Mister Jobson at the Bone Manure Works when he stood for Parliament, and they threw bad eggs, 'He has made for hisself a sangchooery in the hearts of the people which will be a defence unto him.' And it wus the same with that there rabbut."

"But what became of her?"

"Well, she disappeared, and no mortal man ever seed her again until New Year's Eve afore last, when I was choppin' wood at the stack and I seed her. It was her right enough – the identical. I knowed her by her scut. Look here, mister, if you've ever thowt about it, why shouldn't a rabbut have a ghost as well as a human?"

"I have not thought much about it, Peter, and yet is strikes me as an eminently reasonable claim. There seems to be a considerable assortment of ghosts about just now, and a disembodied rabbit should meet with favour."

I thought I had said rather a clever thing, but Peter looked at me doubtfully, and said, "Ye know nowt about it." Then, meditatively: "I expect you've heard tell of Jeshurun[11] – the kicker. An' he *was* a wild rabbut ut we dug out."

"Why did you call him Jeshurun?"

"Well, ye see, mister, it was a Scripture name. When we'd had him a bit, and he got into good fettle, he took to kickin' like his namesake, so we called him Jeshurun – Joss for short. They say Jimmy Denny[12] can kick main hard at football when his dander's up, but if my Jeshurun had laked at that game he's ha' kicked the football clean out o' the field and t'other side efter it, for he nivver could bide no opposition."

"How did he take to kicking?"

"Nay, it comes nat-ral to a rabbut, but some's worse nor others. We kept him in a sugar hogshead,[13] ye must know, me and Maister Wullie Spender, for we was partners; and that rabbut when he wanted anything to eat would bang away at the flure of his hogshead like a drummer.

"But he nivver was like any other rabbut I ivver seed. He could do owt but talk, and he made up for that by squeakin'. What wi' squeakin' and drummin' there was nivver a neighbor all round ast didn't know when he wanted summat to eat.

"Then he started breakin' out o' bounds, for he's two pairs o' scizors 'ut would go through a boiler plate a'most, and so he took the run o' the yard. In less for a week he was monarch of all he surveyed, like Alexander Selkirk.[14] Nivver a cat went near him – not knowingly; he'd a wiped his feet on 'em same as ye do ona dure mat; and as for the fowls and ducks, he hunted 'em all over t' shop, and nipped 'em that hard they fair squarked again; besides bitin' their tails off. No fowls in the yard ivver wore a tail. They were out o' fashion in those days. Joss he seemed to object to cockerels wearin' a tail moren' most things.

"There was no feathered fowl as could stand again' him – but the ravel and a ravel is not a fowl. It's a black boggart wi'out conscience or honor. Joss had no truck wi' him. He knowed him too well for a child of the divil. So they had to respect one another like folk does when they're flat o' one another.

"A sight o' visitors came to see Joss. Some would handle him and guess his weight and age, or talk about rabbuts they had known, and say they couldn't see no difference form other rabbuts mebbe, 'ceptin' ut Joss had a flap ear which he had through fitin' a tortoise-shell cat from the bakehouse. Now, one o' the curious points about that rabbut was he couldn't abide any mention o' that flap ear, seein' how he got it; and as sure as anybody touched it he'd bit his scizors into 'em awful. Mister, you wouldn't believe what that rabbut could bite through 'ceptin' you touched his ear."

"Didn't he fight several battles with ferrets?"

"No, he nivver fowt no ferrets as I saw. He leathered them without feightin'.

"I mind me once as we advertised for two ferrets, and put at the bottom, 'good-pluck'd uns; must not be afraid of rabbuts; on approval.' There were several answers, but we fixed on Young Strickland frae Backburrow for the plant, as he had a prize-breed, very large and fierce. Well, he fetch'd them with him on the coach, and Wullie Spender he does the talkin'; he was one o' them you wouldn't think butter would melt in his mouth. A few o' th' neighbours was admitted privately through bein' interested in Joss and lettin' Wullie have things on tick[15] at their shops, and when my young gentleman from college comes into the yard we all looks down our noses as if we didn't know nowt.

"'Where's the rabbits,' he sez, 'for to try the ferrets?'

"'One o' them 's in the hogshead,' sez Maister Spender, casual like.

"'O, indeed. Shall we put a ferret in the drive him out? Ah, ah! I see he's a tame brute. Mebbe he'll refuse to be driven, and in that case the ferret will make cats' meat of him where he is. You don't mind, eh!'

"'Well, he is a favourite of mamma's,' sez Wullie Spender; 'but, if he is killed, I hope he'll agree with the cats better'n when he was alive, or he'll make some of 'em sick.'

"At this sally our party sniggered a bit, but Mister Strickland he takes out a ferret, and sez, 'You really don't mind, eh?' Maister Spender he sez, 'No, he's rather largish; but never mind' makin' believe he would try and bear it if the rabbut got killed. Then they puts the ferret in, and the band plays, so to speak, and the show begins. The ferret he crouches down on to his white belly and looks about careful, like one o' our chaps when the team goes to play a league match. Joss he never moves a whisker, but just cocks his right ear a bit, and gazes about as if he was thinking deeply whether the earth was flat or round, and couldn't make up his mind. After a bit the ferret begins to slither along towards him, and gets within the range which Joss had marked out afore with his eye. Then, while you could say Jack Robinson, that there Joss steadies hisself, and delivers a stroke with his back legs as sent the ferret flyin' up again the staves, flop. Down he falls all of a heap like a puddin' cloth and never moves, while Joss sits down again and looks up as much as to say, 'Next, please!' I never seed him perform better. Generally he had finished wi' them after twice or three times, but that was a big ferret, and I expect it fell heavy.

"Mister Strickland he sez, 'O Jerusalem!' when he seed it, but I told him the rabbut's name were Jeshurun, which was similar, only we called it Joss for short.

"'Would you like to try the other ferret?' sez Wullie Spender. 'That one wasn't a good driver, was he?'

"'Go on,' sez Mr Strickland, 'you've had me. 'Fore George, the game's against me. But look here, I'll put the other in if you'll place a kicking strap[16] on that rabbut. 'Fore George, he kicks pile drivin'. No I won't. Look here, I'll give you – yes, I'll give a soveran for the rabbut.'

"Just then, I mind, Judith the cook comes out, and hears some one say ut he's dead – meaning the ferret. But she runs in and tells Mrs. Spender ut Joss is dead. Then the fat was in the fire, I can tell ye. Out rushes Mrs. Spender in a tantrum, and gives Mister Strickland a bit of her mind. 'You cruel man,' she sez, 'to come here and kill a poor tame rabbut. How dare you, and your father a justice o' the peace? O, you naughty, cruel, wanting reprobate,' with a lot more such like, and put him out, lockin' the yard dure on him afore he knew where he was.

"I hided mysel' in the toolhouse till she'd gone – Mister Strickland searin' outside dreadful all the time, and sayin' he'd fetch a ferret as would lick that rabbut yet."

"Then the rabbit finished the battle at one stroke, Peter?"

"That's so. He was a wonder. And yet, mind you, mister, for all he was so clever and tricky, he never gave hisself airs or thought hisself better'n other rabbuts, 's far as I could see.

"Was he never licked, then?"

"No, never. Young Strickland, he did fetch a ferret once, but when we put it in the tub I seed there was something wrong with Joss, for he waggled his head and listed over to one side when he shifted, like a man as has had too much ale into him. So I takes him out and I says: 'Joss, thou'rt drunk. Thou has been gotten at and hocussed.' But I sed nowt to t'others just then, only as he was poorly and couldn't feight. If there was one thing that rabbut liked better'n another, it was grain steeped in liquor, and that's what he'd ha. Well, ivverybody has some weakness, so he was no worse nor a human; but excuse me, mister, the funeral's comin', and I mun toll the bell.

Robert Blatchford, 'The Perpendicular Recruit' (1911)

I was standing outside a shop in Hunstanton[1] the other day when I heard a man ask his friend to "come and have a liquor." Instantly I was back in the Ramchunders,[2] in the summer of 1871, and the "Perpendicular Recruit" was making the same proposal to me. Oh, what a man he was; and what men they were. To begin with there were the men of my own room: No. 3 Mess.

We had twelve men and a corporal in No. 3 Mess of F Company, and a weird baker's dozen of human documents we were. First of all there was Matty Mains, the corporal in charge. Matty was a kindly, easy-going fellow, and beautiful penman, and good accountant. His ruling passion was beer.

Then we had four recruits. There was George Dedman, a simple Hampshire peasant, who was ugly, illiterate, and innocent, and for whom I used to write love-letters to a girl named Minnie. I met Minnie later, and found her very pretty, and dainty and treacherous and vain. Another recruit was a stout and swarthy Londoner named Burridge, who sang music-hall songs and was always hungry, as most of us youngsters were. Burridge was very good-humoured, and full of boyish mischief. The fourth recruit was a smart, good looking young Londoner named Wilsher, who was one of the first to get the corporal's stripes, and one of the first to lose them. He was a simple, well-meaning lad, and had nice eyes.

Of the elder hands, the most noteworthy were Augustus Cashman, known as Mad Gustus; Charles Pride, alias Pompey the Pirate; Larry Dolan, alias Trunkey (so called from his large and peculiar nose); Old Tim Doyle (who was not more than twenty-eight); William Ryan, alias Ryan the Beauty; Peter Nevins, and Johnny Peters.

Johnny Peters was a short, square, powerful Irish navy; Nevins was a tall Irishman, with a jolly face and a mild blue eye. This man used to write notes for the negotiation of loans as: "Dere Comradd will ye lend me the loan of the price of a pot till the end of the munth for the love of God, me been on a penny a day, and I will pay ye back plaze God Pat Nevins." He always promised to pay "please God"; but it never pleased God within my experience.

Peters and Nevins were clean, smart soldiers. Their ruling passion was beer.

Tim Doyle was a burly Irishman, with a heavy, good-humoured face, a chin like the toe of a boot, and a slow, wise smile. He was an excellent chap, and his ruling passion was politics.

Larry Dolan was a thing of beauty and a joy for ever.[3] He was one of the most comic soldiers I ever met, and that is saying much. He was short, and lean, with large feet and hands; and his small, dim eyes, his small and flexible nose gave him a strange look of wistful doubt and surprise. He was Tim Doyle's cot-mate and friend, and he loved beer as much as Tim loved politics.

Hour after hour Trunkey Dolan and Tim would sit side by side and "chew the rag." I think of them now, after thirty-eight years, with gratitude and joy. I laugh all over myself, when I recall their names. They were *lovely*.

"Look at here, Larry, avic," old Tim would say, in his deep bass growl, "'tis no use talkin' to the amadhauns[4] in this pultan,[5] but be the seven shores iv Cork, bedad, the Rooshians an' the Prooshians 'll be the full o' ther eye. D'ye moind me, Larry. Wid the French all bruises an' stickin' plaister, an' the divil a British fleet in the Adriathic, the good Lord Himself only knows what thim Russians and Prooshians do be after!"

"An' phwat the divil *do* they be afther, Tim?" Larry would inquire; and then the basso hum would begin again about the Rooshians and Prooshians.

But no one ever got the glimmer of an idea what the black intrigues and diabolic alliances of the Rooshians and Prooshians might potent, for when we pressed Tim he scowled darkly, and muttered and stammered that the Rooshians and the Prooshians were at the back of something not named, or at the bottom of something still in embryo, and would ultimately be the full of the eye of some person or persons whose identity was mysteriously veiled by the pronoun "they."

When Larry was, so to speak, "fed up" with the two stealthy and terrible allies, he would break suddenly into the conversation with one of his amazing stories. When Larry told a story, he "conducted' it, as one might say, with his wonderful nose, which he could at will cause to travel about his face in a manner at once alarming and delightful. To see his small mouth curl itself into a peerless Irish grin, while his nose twisted itself nearly under his right ear, and to hear the sound, between a sniff and a whistle, with which this action was "pointed," was to lose oneself in admiration.

"Och! The Prooshisans, the curse iv Cromwell on thim, they're as deep as a bog-hole, an as tricherous, Tim. Bad end to em! Last night as I was comin' along the Cowes Road, who the divil should I meet but Andy White, of H Company; be the token I had not a trauneen in me kick, an' me wid the thirst o' the ages upon me; and says he: 'Larry Doonlan, be jabbers,' says he, 'an' me lookin' for a pal,' says he. 'What for?' says I. An' och, Tim me jool." Here Larry's nose curled under his ear and one eye closed and the other squinted. "An' och, Tim, me jool, if ye'll believe me, he was afther findin' a sailor!"

At the word "sailor" Tim's face would flush, his eyes would sparkle, and he would say with emotion:

"Howly saints, Larry, what is ut ye're tellin' me?"

"'Tis the honest trut," Larry would answer, "an' we had the *great* time. Comin' back across the drill field at First Post, be jabbers, I saw three moons dancin' in the sky; an' I passed the sintry walkin' on a golden cloud o' glory."

Tim would regard his friend with deep earnestness, and inquire:

"Larry, man, is there any pickin's left, honey?"

Larry would curl his nose again, and with a wink and a sniff would answer:

"Whist! To-night, at the Anchor Brewery!"

Then Tim would rise up, pull off his tunic, reach down his soap and towel, and start for the lavatory without a word.

A "sailor" was the slang term for any person whose nature was so generous, and whose finances so sound, as to allow of the quaffing of many cups at his personal charge. A "sailor" was to a thirsty Ramchunder what a carcase is to the eagles. No Ramchunder worthy of his corps ever wasted a "sailor." With a "sailor" in the offing, even politics had to wait; for the Rooshions and the Prooshions were always with us,[6] but a "sailor" was the gift of Fate.

One does not often meet such a character as Private Augustus Cashman outside the covers of a romance. He was a sparely built man, of five-feet-nine, with rather crooked legs. He had regular features, good teeth, black hair, and grey eyes, one of which had a strong squint. His voice was remarkable – a soft, caressing tenor. He was a most harmless and amiable fellow; but quite mad.

Now a mad Irishman is a being full of bewildering possibilities. Cashman loved big words, and use them prodigally. He sang strange Irish ballads as only an Irishman could sing them. He performed quaint gymnastic antics, and danced grotesque jigs, and when the moon was propitious he prayed weird prayers, in a mad blend of Erse,[7] English and Latin.

It was said of "Gustas" that out in India he had been made a prisoner for making love to the colonel's daughter, whose pony he kissed one day on the grand parade.

On moonlight nights he had been known to go into the field or the forest and pray, having first lighted all round him a circle of wax vestas[8] stuck in the earth.

I have myself seen him open a barrack-room window, kneel upon the window-sill in his shirt, and pray to the moon.

It was told of him one day, when the tea was too sweet, he reported it to the orderly officer in his best language, and that the officer asked the colour-sergeant to translate.

Orderly Officer: "Any complaints?"

Private Cashman: "Yes, sir."

Orderly Officer: "What is wrong?"

Private Cashman: "If you plase, sorr, the superfluity of the sugar destroys the flavourality of the tay, and renders it obnoxious to the human palate."

Orderly Office: "Colour-Sergeant Saunders, what does he mean?"

The Colour-Sergeant: "He's a fool, sir."

Orderly Officer: "Take his name down."

Cashman being what he was, and our two London recruits being what they were, relations were soon strained. The recruits roasted Cashman, and Cashman reviled the recruits. Cashman's oaths were peculiar, his denunciations picturesque. The recruits – were from London.

Cashman would mount to the bread-shelf to search for a piece of bread which he had left, or pretended he had left, for tea. He would glare round the room and ask: "Which of you voracious and dishonourable ring-tailed[9] varmints has devoured me tay bread?"

Wilsher would open the ball.

"Why, you pigeon-nosed, hungry Irish beastie, you scoffed it yourself."

"See, see, see!" Cashman would splutter. "By the holy, flying, jumping, tearing, whipping cripple, if I detect any gramnivourous Cockney rodent in the act of abstracting sustenance from my accumulation, I'll peel the hide off him. I swear it by King Corney Cass me ancestor."

This would fetch Burridge, who would ask the constellations to listen to this Irish goat with a face like Sweeny Todd.

Gustus would spring to the floor and dance a war dance. "See, see, see," he would shout, "you million times accursed black pig of Beelzebub; you shameless product of seven generations of infamy; you mangy loot wollah[10] born on a dunghill, you have robbed Augustus Cashman of his tay bread; and you shall die."

"Gar on, Jack Shepherd," Wilsher would strike in. "You go and chuck yerself out o' winder and say 'Ere goes nothink."

"Don't talk to the animal," Burridge would say; "he's always savage when he's lost his bone."

"See here, you pusillanimous pariah dogs," Cashman would reply. "I'm the smartest man in your regiment; and the sergeants know it, and the officers know it, and the colonel's daughter was in love with me in Morar."[11]

"Liar!" would be Wilsher's comment; and then Cashman would throw a boot at his head, and Burridge would answer with a pipeclay-box;[12] and the two recruits would break into a chant: "Who kissed the nose of the pony of the daughter of the colonel of the regiment on the parade of the Governor-General of *Bom*bay?"

At this point I would interfere to prevent bloodshed, for it was a fact that Cashman, who hated recruits in the general, had a particular liking for me in particular.

Cashman's ally in his war with the "ring-tails" was his countryman, William Ryan, known as Ryan the Beauty. Ryan was a curious human document. When sober he was melancholy, almost morose, and would sit and read a dog-eared volume of Irish ballads, or croon a mournful song:

Oh, what will ye do, love, when I am goin'
Wid white sail flowin', the seas beyond?[13]

But after a visit to the canteen he was translated. Then he would burst suddenly into the barrack-room with a yell: "Yeho! Here's Bill Ryan, yeho! Here's Bill Ryan the Beauty, yeho! Why don't yez turn out the guard?"

In this mood he would often throw the tea basins into the coal-box, dance a jig on the table, challenge any six Saxon Salpeens[14] to "stand fornnist"[15] him, and conclude the exhibition by bursting into tears.

Then there was the "Perpendicular Recruit."

It was while listening to the band one fine moonlight night that I first made the acquaintance of Johnson, "the perpendicular recruit." Johnson was lean and tall and rigidly upright; hence the nickname. It was rumoured that he had once served in the Mexican cavalry, and that he had been an officer. He was a very gentlemanly fellow, and eccentric enough to be noticeable even among so many eccentric characters.

"I have noticed you before," said Johnson, "listening to the band. You are fond of music."

I said I was very fond of music.

"I notice, also," said Johnson, "that you look at the moon."

"Don't you?" I asked.

"Of course I do," he answered; "but hardly anybody else does. Don't you remark that, Blatchford? If you hung up a halfpenny Chinese lantern on a pole the whole regiment would stand and stare at it. But never a man looks up at the moon. Damme, they don't know it's there!"

"I believe you are right," I said.

"I am right. A few nights ago I was looking out of the window at the moon, when one of the men asked me what I was staring at. When I told him, he thought I was mad. If, my dear chap, I had been looking at the disgusting pictures in a French journal, the whole barrack-room would have crowded round and been ready to fight for the paper."

"Yes, yes!" I said.

"Poor fools," said Johnson, "they imagine they are sane."

"Do you ever talk to them like this?" I asked.

Johnson shook his head. "No," he said; "if you talked sense or culture to these animals it would end in a fight. They have no soul for anything but beer. By the way, talking of beer, come and have a liquor."

When Johnson asked a man to "Come and have a liquor" he was transfigured. I have never seen another person put such a poetry of expression into so trite a speech. He stood very upright, closed his heels, raised his right hand gracefully, as if to suggest the quaffing of nectar from a golden chalice, and smiled the smile beautiful.

But I was a strict abstainer, and I told him so. He dropped his eloquent hand, shook his head sadly, and said: "That, if you will pardon my saying so, is a mistake, Blatchford."

"You think so?" said I.

"Yes," he said, smoothing his long, silky moustache, "it is a mistake, amigo. Take the good the gods bestow. The moon, the music, and the beer. Woman is good, and wine is good; but the combination! Ah, Blatchford, come and have a liquor!"

I declined gently, but firmly, at which he sighed, and, sitting down upon a form, began to roll himself a cigarette.

"Have you ever had a romance?" he asked me.

"I don't know," I said, feeling shy. "Don't you call this a romance?"

Johnson jumped up and laid his hand upon my shoulder.

"A true remark, Blatchford," he said, "a devilish true remark! Everything in life is a romance. The music and the moonlight and the beefy troopers are romances. They are, by Heaven. The goose-step[16] is a romance, in a way. *Won't you come and have a liquor?*"

I shook my head.

"You have been abroad, Johnson," I suggested.

"Don't," said Johnson. "The word has no meaning. Was I more abroad in Texas or in China than I am here in Parkhurst Barracks? Are you abroad now? Or do you feel at home, comrade?"

I admitted that the whole life seemed strange and foreign to me.

"Ah, so it is, so it is," said he. "I am a stranger here; heaven is my home. Eh? That's the idea, Blatchford. And I would to Heaven I could convince you, my dear fellow, of the merits of the course I just now invited you to pursue. Are you quite sure, Blatchford, that you will not come and have a liquor?"

I was quite sure, and at that we left it. But who would expect in the British Army to meet such a man as the perpendicular recruit? The fact is, one need never be surprised by any character one meets in that rendezvous of the unusual.

A. Neil Lyons, 'Unearned Increment' (1912)

Somewhere upon the road between Brede and Rye, in Sussex there exists a small farmhouse, which is most aptly situated for the sale of milk and eggs. And, in an upper window of this farmhouse, facing the flagged path which leads to the dairy door, there sits and dithers a very old maundering man, having in his beard the moth and dust of ages. This old man was blowing about in the window-opening when I went up the path, and he shook his old head at me and spoke. He said:

"Hulloa! Hulloa! God bless moi soul! Good arternoon. How *be* you?"

I told the old man that I was very well, and ventured to hope that he also was free from ill. He nodded.

"I beant never no ways out o' gear," he said, "on'y exceptin' the *old* trouble. Ha' ye seen Fred?"

Not only had I not seen Fred, but, to all human knowledge I was utterly unacquainted with Fred. I had never seen this territory before, much less this old man, much less Fred. But one humours aged folk; and so I simply told my veteran that I had not seen Fred.

"You beant come from chapel, then?" demanded the old man.

I sadly confessed to the old man that I had come from somewhere quite secular.

"Ha' ye brart me anything to read then?" he continued.

I put down my milk can and examined my pockets, in which I found some literature: the sort of literature which we Bohemians do carry about with us, a copy of the "Christian Commonwealth," a copy of the "Pelican," and two back numbers of the "Gasfitter's Gazette."[1] These I gave to the old man, who thanked me with emotion. "'Tis a pity you aren't seen Fred," he remarked. "He's got a noo walking stick what he won at the ploughing. Ha' ye come round here to look for 'im, then?"

"No," I answered with frank simplicity, "I have come round her to look for milk."

"Milk!" exclaimed the old man. "Oah! – Milk. You'll ha' to see Mary about milk. Hareunt you sin Mary, then?"

I confessed that Mary had escaped my observation.

"You'd better look for Mary, then, if 'tis milk as you be wantin'," quoth the aged one. "You'll find her in the Tenter Mead, shouldn't wonder or else you might look down there t' other side o' Goddard's Place. 'Tennerate, you be bound see William, and William 'll set ye straight for Mary. Step along, now, 'fore it git darker. You look for William; unless you find Mary."

"Yes, I'll look for William," I said, by way of appearing not to notice the old gentleman's insanity. I felt sure that he *was* insane.

"And look a-here," he said, suddenly becoming more insane than ever, "Don't you mind naarthun about speakin' to oold William. He's a bit cross-grained, so to speak, the way he act and talk, but that don't signify naarthun, not wuth oold William. Ye needn't speak about The Past, nor ye needn't fear as he will speak about The Past. You onnerstand my meanin'? What's past is past. Lat it goo at that. Now run off."

"Yes, sir," I assented, "I will now run off."

I accordingly began to run, but my progress was arrested by the old man, who called me back to utter further maunderings. "You better arst 'em to give you a few apple," he said. "I dessay you would relish a apple, arter – arter your – your visit to Devonsheer. I'll be bound as they didn't give ye a great lot o' apple t'eat down there in – Devonsheer. They did'nt give ye much t' eat at all: what? Ha! Ha! Well, never mind. Run along to Mary. She'll find ye a apple, shouldn't wonder."

The old man then allowed me to go quite away from him, which I did with great rapidity, wondering at his great folly. I came to a wicket gate and opened it and found before me a darkling expanse of chilly grass, which, I supposed, must be the Tenter Mead. At the far corner of this enclosure I found another old man, who looked all dim and misty in the twi-fog.

He was an old man of similar aspect to my other old man, and was evidently nearly related to that Patriarch. But his beard was cleaner and he had a sterner eye. He spoke to me saying:

"If 'tis moi sister you be lookin' for you'll find her down in the Piece."

"If your sister's name is Mary, then it is your sister I'm looking for," I answered.

"Certainly her name is Mary. You know that as well as what I do," replied the old man, putting his stern eye close up to me. He was also mad, I perceived.

"I don't want to say naarthun out of place," continued this second old gentleman, "but that don't seem's if they taught you a great deal o' sense down – down where you come from. No 'arm said, I 'ope?"

"Not at all," I answered, wondering whether by any chance I had found my way into a Rest Cure establishment.[2]

"What's past is past," continued the old gentleman. "So we won't say any more about it. Run along down to the Piece, now, and find Mary. 'Tis 'er you gotter look for if you wanteth milk. I dessay Mary'll find you a quart or two of apple. You could eat a apple, shouldn't wonder – what? They didn't give you a lot of apple down – down where you come from. What?"

"No," I answered, striving to fall in with his humour. "They gave me anchovies and artichokes and aeroplanes, but not apples. How cold the wind blows. There are chilblains about, I think."

With this I left him. He superintended my departure with an open mouth and a tremor of the eyelid. Evidently he did not relish the competition.

I then groped my way into a further pasture where – God be thanked! – I found Mary. Mary was also old; but she had no beard at all. And when she saw me, she said, "Good God!"

"Have ye seen Tom and William?" she added.

I replied that I had certainly seen William, and if Tom was an elderly person who sat in an upper window, rearing moths, then I had seen him also.

"Of course that be Tom," exclaimed Mary. "That don't seem's if they taught you a lot o' knowledge down in – in: down at Dartymoor."

Mary likewise repeated that somewhat stale "gag" about The Past being past. But she gave me my pennyworth of milk, and likewise about three shillingsworth of apples, for which she would take no payment. She also took my hand and patted it with evident pleasure and emotion.

I drank the milk that night, in my little tent on the roadside. I also ate a number of apples. Yesterday I ate more apples; and to-day I have eaten the last of them. It now occurs to me that they were not my apples at all. They belonged quite certainly to some young gentleman whom I have the honour to resemble in bodily charm: some young gentleman who has recently emerged from a period of solitude in – on Dartmoor.

I wonder what I ought to do about it. I can't return the apples because I have eaten them. I suppose that I shall have to go to Dartmoor, too, and earn my apples.

R. B. Suthers, 'A Coster's Funeral' (1913)

I stood in Piccadilly Circus on Monday wondering which of the social functions I should favour with my condescension when I was bumped into by a motor 'bus. Turning round to apologise the sign on the back caught my eye. It said "To Plumstead"[1] – and there came into my mind a paragraph I had read in the papers a day or two before. As swift as thought I stepped aboard and enquired of the conductor if he went near the Plumstead Cemetery.

"I don't know no cemetery," he answered.

Feeling sure I was on the right track, I mounted to the top and took a back seat, hoping thus to escape some of the nerve-wracking thrills which a clear view of the route force on the attention of the front-seaters in these days of swift locomotion.

It was a glorious morning and the joy of life was rampant even in the faces of the dead-beats we passed in Trafalgar Square. A moment or two later I thought my last had come.

Just as we swept past the Horse Guards in Whitehall, with a clear course in front of us, which I could see owing to the lack of passengers, a misbegotten knave in a motor car coming in the opposite direction suddenly turned at right angles and wheeled into our track. There was ample room for him to turn and run along *with* us, but he appeared to be unconscious of our existence, and seemed intent on crossing the full extent of the road. Our driver, naturally expecting him to turn off sharp, kept his pace.

A collision was inevitable. The blood rushed to my fingers and I turned over my money and wished. That saved us. I don't know how it was done, but we came to a dead stop with an electric standard at one side and the motor car on the other, and you couldn't have put a Cabinet Minister's Marconi explanation[2] between us.

I leaned back and pondered on the strange difference between coming to a dead stop and coming to a stop dead. I had mounted that 'bus with the fell purpose of attending funeral at Plumstead. Phew!

After an hour's drive through some of the most interesting architecture in the Metropolis, I arrived safely at the Plumstead Cemetery. One of the advantages of motoring is being able to pay lightning visits to about a score of historic and otherwise famous places in the twinkling of an eyelid. Going from Piccadilly to Plumstead you get pin-prick views, for instance of Trafalgar Square, Whitehall and the Horse Guards, the Government offices, the Duke of Cambridge, Disraeli, the Houses of Parliament, St. Thomas' Hospital, the river and the Embankment, the Elephant and Castle, the Old Kent Road, Mrs. 'Enery 'Awkins,[3] Greenwich Hospital, Observatory, and Park, Woolwich, Arsenal, and Plumstead Cemetrery. Not to mention what you miss.

It is remarkable, too, what you can miss. The end of our journey was the cemetery at Plumstead. A very suitable ending for a journey, too. It was the terminus for that 'bus. Yet the conductor had apparently never seen it. He didn't know where the cemetery was. But he must have seen *something*. What did he take it for? I turned back to ask him, but he had vanished. I was going to tell him he had made a grave mistake.

A very grave mistake, for the place was packed with tombstones. I found an old man solitary sitting on one, and I asked him if there was any more room.

"Oh, yes," he answered, "there's a buryin' here this afternoon."

"Is it the 'Coster Queen'?" I asked.

"That's her," he replied. "Ninety years of age, she was. She'd 26 children, 48 grandchildren and 26 great-grandchildren. They'll all be there. It'll be a lovely funeral."

I had never seen a coster's funeral. I have been told that next to the funeral of royalty they are the most gorgeous affairs in the way of furnishing to be seen in Christendom.

Having an hour or so to spare, I strolled into Woolwich,[4] and in a busy shopping street found a crowd clustered round a shuttered shop. The door was open and there stood a man in shirt sleeves. Behind him could be seen stacks of beautiful wreaths. This was the home of the "Coster Queen," whose relatives are all in the fruit and flower trade.

Every few minutes someone pushed through with an enormous box, or an unpacked wreath, and handed it over the heads of the people to the man in charge. For the onlookers it was quite an afternoon out. All the wives of the Arsenal men[5] were there with their babies. The public-house next door but one was festooned with weary-looking women drinking glasses of stout. Unemployed dockers, shopmen, sailors, soldiers, errand boys, giddy girls, and a sprinkling of Woolwich West-Enders all gossiping in the blazing sun, suggested a crowd round a park band rather than a funeral. It was uncommonly lively. There were few black bonnets here and there, but they only served to make the colour more conspicuous. Yet behind those shutters were sorrowing women and men and tear-stained cheeks. How true it is that in the midst of death we are in life![6]

"And what d'yer think she ses? She ses to me, she ses, let's go and 'ave a drink, she ses, an' 'er not twenty-four, mind you. Yes, she ses, I know you like a drop, the hussy. And *I* do, she ses."

"An' did yer?"

"Well, what can yer say? Of course –" Thus one old lady to another. On the other side of me a giddy young girl.

"Oh, I told 'im off. I says, dear Mister Sim, I hope you enjoyed yourself last night same as I did because I went to the Empire with mother, an' I signed it yours ever, no I didn't I put yours sincerely, an' then after the letter I put, some fellers seem to think every girl's a go-along, but I'm not one of that sort. Why, I once went out with a feller for nine months. Just because I gave him the glad eye! Oh, did I tell you about our Jennie? She's got a game on with a gentleman in the City. Oh, it *was* funny! You know she was going from Algit Station[7] and she asks the porter is this right for Commercial Road, and he says yes, jump in quick; so in she 'ops, and of course, it was all a game. You know these trains just go round and round, and in about five minutes she was back again at Algit an' the porter larfin' at 'er. He' done it o' purpose, the saucy devil, an' while she was jawin' 'im up come this gentleman an' says were you wanting Commercial Road? I'm going that way; would you mind accompanying me? An' she did, an' she's met 'im, again. Oh, 'ere comes the' earse."

The crowd by this time was large, and the street was lined several deep all the way. The hearse came along, and I opened my eyes to note the gorgeous trappings and the weird accouterments which I had been led to expect. But I have been deceived. There was nothing *outré*. There were certainly brushes on the heads of the horses, but otherwise the whole turnout was of the ordinary kind, and I turned away and sought more thrills on the top of a West-bound motor 'bus.

DAILY CITIZEN

W. C. Anderson, 'Who Killed Downie? An Aberdeen Legend', *Daily Citizen*, 8 October 1912, p. 6.

Frank Dilnot, 'The Public Spirit of Mr. Josiah Grub', *Daily Citizen*, 24 February 1913, p. 7.

Frank Starr, 'The Aerial Armada. What Took Place in A.D. 2000', *Daily Citizen*, 10 April 1913, p. 7.

Hugh Derrick, 'The Making of a Red', *Daily Citizen*, Prologue and Chapter I, 17 November 1913, p. 8; Chapter II, 18 November 1913, p. 8; Chapter II (continued), 19 November 1913, p. 8; Chapter III, 20 November 1913, p. 8; Chapter III (continued), 21 November 1913, p. 8; Chapter III (continued), 22 November 1913, p. 8; Chapter IV, 24 November 1913, p. 8; Chapter IV (continued), 25 November 1913, p. 8; Chapter IV (continued), 26 November 1913, p. 7; Chapter V, 27 November 1913, p. 8; Chapter VI, 28 November 1913, p. 8; Chapter VI (continued), 29 November 1913, p. 8; Chapter VII, 1 December 1913, p. 8; Chapter VII (continued), 2 December 1913, p. 8; Chapter VII (continued) and Chapter VIII, 3 December 1913, p. 7; Chapter VIII (continued), 4 December 1913, p. 8; Chapter IX, 5 December 1913, p. 8; Chapter IX (continued), 6 December 1913, p. 8; Chapter IX (continued), 8 December 1913, p. 8; Chapter X, 9 December 1913, p. 8; Chapter X (continued), 10 December 1913, p. 8; Chapter XI, 11 December 1913, p. 8; Chapter XI (continued), 12 December 1913, p. 8; Chapter XII, 13 December 1913, p. 8; Chapter XII (continued), 15 December 1913, p. 8; Chapter XIII, 16 December 1913, p. 8; Chapter XIII (continued), 17 December 1913, p. 8; Chapter XIV, 18 December 1913, p. 8; Chapter XIV (continued), 19 December 1913, p. 8; Chapter XIV (continued), 20 December 1913, p. 8; Chapter XIV (continued), 22 December 1913, p. 8; Chapter XV, 23 December 1913, p. 8; Chapter XV (continued), 24 December 1913, p. 8; Chapter XVI, 26 December 1913, p. 8; Chapter XVI (continued), 27 December 1913, p. 8; Chapter XVII, 29 December 1913, p. 8; Chapter XVIII, 30 December 1913, p. 8; Chapter XIX, 1 January 1914, p. 8; Chapter XIX [continued], 2 January 1914, p. 8; Chapter XIX (continued), 3 January 1914, p. 8; Chapter XX, 5 January 1914, p. 8; Chapter XX (continued), 6 January 1914, p. 8; Chapter XXI, 7 January 1914, p. 8; Chapter XXII, 8 January 1914, p. 8; Chapter XXII (continued), 9 January 1914, p. 8; Chapter XXIII, 10 January 1914, p. 8; Chapter XXIII (continued), 12 January 1914, p. 8; Chapter XXIV, 13 January 1914, p. 8; Chapter XXIV (continued), 14 January 1914, p. 8; Chapter XXV, 15 January 1914, p. 8; Chapter XXV (continued), 16 January 1914, p. 8.

'Pat', 'Living Retired. An Unconscious Tragedy', *Daily Citizen*, 20 January 1914, p. 8.

W. O. Pitt, 'The Last Dinner', *Daily Citizen*, 25 August 1914, p. 2.

The *Daily Citizen* (1912–15) was the first official daily newspaper of the Labour Party and the Trades Union Congress, both of which co-owned the paper. It was published in Manchester by Labour Newspapers Ltd, selling for a halfpenny, and was edited by Frank Dilnot (1875–1946). In 1913 the *Daily Citizen* attempted to boost sales by including horseracing coverage, and this resulted in the resignation of W. C. Anderson (1877–1919) and Arthur Henderson (1863–1935) from its board of directors in protest at what they saw as the encouragement of gambling. It ceased publication on 5 June 1915, unable to compete with its rival, the *Daily Herald*. The *Daily Citizen* had aimed to be the first British socialist daily newspaper, but it was beaten to that title by the launch of the more successful *Daily Herald*, which was first published in April 1912 and continued until it was renamed the *Sun* in 1964. The *Sun* was sold to Rupert Murdoch in 1969 and continues today.

The *Daily Citizen* regularly included short stories, a daily poem and serial fiction by authors such as Richard Starr, Blanche Eardsley and the editor, Frank Dilnot, whose short story 'The Public Spirit of Mr. Josiah Grub' is included in this selection. Dilnot was an author and journalist who had previously worked for the *Central News* in London and for Alfred Harmsworth's *Daily Mail*. When the *Daily Citizen* ceased publication, Dilnot became president of the Association of Foreign Correspondents in America, formed during the First World War, while working for the *Daily Express*. Later he was editor of the *Globe*, and he was chairman of the London Press Club between 1928 and 1929. His books include *The Adventures of a Newspaper Man* (1913) and *Lloyd George: The Man and his Story* (1917).

Biographical and further publishing details have not been discovered for either Hugh Derrick or 'Pat', but information on W. C. Anderson is presented in the headnote for *Justice* in Volume 4, pp. 136–7. Frank Starr was also the author of 'Electric Jimmy' (*Daily Citizen*, 4 March 1913) and 'A Woman and a Vote' (*Daily Citizen*, 12 March 1913), as well as publishing stories in the *Labour Leader* and *Teddy Ashton's Northern Weekly*, two of which are included in Volume 3. W. O. Pitt was also the author of *Italy and the Unholy Alliance* (1915).

W. C. Anderson, 'Who Killed Downie? An Aberdeen Legend' (1912)

When I was an industrious Aberdeen apprentice, many years ago now, I often heard a saying which I daresay is still in vogue. When a number of men had done something which required their sticking together, one would say to the others, "We're a' airt and pairt in Downie's slaughter." When a student in cap and gown, striding proudly along the street, swept some ragged urchin from his path, the outraged boy would round promptly, and shout, "Fa killed Downie?" Then the lad would go back to his play feeing he was quits with cap and gown.

Now it is clear from this that Downie must have achieved fame of some sort, either in his life or his death. Latter-day historians, it must be admitted, say that Downie never lived, and so could not possibly have died. But no great importance need be attached to modern historians. If they are to be believed, it is very doubtful whether anybody really lived more than three hundred years ago, and the saintly personages and dramatic heroes whom we venerated in our green and unsophisticated youth are but historic myths.

Downie was sacristan[1] at King's College, Aberdeen, toward the latter end of the eighteenth century. He was a sour, harsh man, with none of the milk of human kindness. The students hated him, and cursed him with curses not loud but deep. It brought a stern joy to his heart to find them in some fault and report them to the Regents and Principals.

At night some of the students would wander by the wooded banks of Don, avowedly to study astronomy and hold high converse regarding Mars and Jupiter and Saturn, but actually to hold sweet and idle dalliance with the flirtatious mill lassies of the ancient town. The lynx and puritanical eye of Downie was ever upon them, and sometimes he would drive them toward the college with an oak cudgel threatening their backs. Sometimes a breathless student would rush up to the gates a moment after they had closed for the night, but Downie would not by a hairsbreadth relax his discipline. The laggard had to climb into college by some surreptitious way, with the certainty of getting a severe moral lecture from a Principal next day.

The wrath of the students burned hot and fierce against their too officious sacristan, but for a long time revenge was out of the question, because the students could not trust each other, and feared expulsion. But at length an action of Downie's, more oppressive even than usual, brought matters to a head, and the anger of the students fell upon him like a thunderstorm.

It was a day when His Majesty's Judges were visiting Aberdeen to hold their sessional courts and punish wrong-doers. The magistrates, proud but uncomfortable in their gold braid and their cocked hats, rode out to meet them, and all the city was alive with expectation. Ruthless men of blood and iron most of these old Scotch judges were. Without the slightest compunction they would send a man to death or banishment for long years of penal servitude for crimes which to-day seem trivial enough. "Ye're an ill'lookin' rascal," remarked one of them to his prisoner. "I'm thinki' ye'll be a lot the better for a gude hangin'," "He's ane o' thae reformers," snapped another judge in reference to a man found guilty of agitating for the vote "Yes, that's true," pleaded the man's counsel, "but remember, my lord, that some of the greatest men in history were reformers. Jesus Himself was a reformer." "Aye, He was that," came the sour retort," and a lot o' gude His reformin; did Him. Did thy no hang Him?"

After the judges had spent the day in making the punishment fit or exceed the crime, it was the custom to spend the evening at a feast where many capons and much salmon and beef and whiskey and port were provided in the interest of public justice at the public expense. It was a feast, therefore, which the high dignitaries of the city were nothing loth to attend, and the Principals of the University were as eager as any to enjoy. On the evening in the question the Principals and Professors had left in a body to be present at the hospital junketing, and they had no sooner taken their departure from the quadrangle than a strange scene began to be enacted.

Six strong men arrested Downie, and carried him, despite his loud protests and threats of vengeance, to a large room decked with all the paraphernalia of a court of justice. There sat the stern-visaged judge in wig and ermine; the jury were ready and alert; counsel for the prosecution and defence busied themselves over their briefs. The whole room was draped in black – black hangings, black curtains, black carpets. It looked like a chamber of death. The court was crowded, and there was a rustle of expectation when Downie was forced forward and placed in the dock.

Downie was at first inclined to treat the whole thing as an untimely and outrageous joke. He denounced judge and jury and audience, and threatened them with direst pains and penalties. But his counsel spoke quietly to him, warning him that the proceedings were real enough, that life or death was in the balance. Counsel urged Downie to remain cool and quiet, and promised to fight hard to get him free.

Then the trial began. A long indictment was read, charging Downie with lying and treachery against the students, with suppression of their rights and privileges, and with general tyranny and oppression.

Counsel on both sides argued and pleaded. Witnesses gave evidence and were cross-examined. The case lasted for two hours, and through it all sat Downie, getting more and more nervous and alarmed, the danger and horror of his position slowly dawning upon him. At last the judge summed up, and, though fair and impartial, his summing up was on the whole against the prisoner. The jury retired to consider their verdict, and Downie waited in an agony of vague apprehension, great beads of sweat standing out on his brow. After a short absence the jury returned, and announced to a hushed and breathless court that they found the prisoner guilty of the various crimes charged against him.

The judge put on the black cap, and looking sternly at Downie, whose knees by this time had begun to shake, enumerated the crimes of which he had been found guilty, and announced that these crimes merited and would receive the extreme penalty of the law. Downie was condemned to death.

The Court rose, and the unhappy wretch was half dragged, half carried into an adjoining room, where his terrified eyes rested upon a block and a tall, strong headsman wearing a mask, was fingering the edge of a bright axe. Terror stricken, he sobbed and cried for mercy, but was reminded that never once in his life had he shown mercy to others.

The hands of the clock pointed ten minutes short of the hour, and he was told he would be granted this brief respite so as to receive the administration of a clergyman, and prepare himself for death. At this point a clergyman entered singing a hymn and reading a service. Downie, beside himself with panic, groveled at the clergyman's feet, beseeching his intervention confessing his own many sins, including those against the students, and begging forgiveness. The headsman brought in a tub of water, and began to scatter sawdust round the block.

The hour struck, Downie's shirt was unfastened, and his throat made bare. He was blindfolded, and carried to the block on which his head was laid. Then the headsman, with a broad grin, put aside his axe, and dipping a towel in the cold water, brought it down sharply on Downie's neck.

A peal of laugher followed, for the grim farce was at an end. The thirst for revenge had been quenched. The were even prepared to deal kindly with the sacristan upon whom they had inflicted such acute suffering. They lifted the cloth from his face, and asked him to get up.

But Downie did not move. He lay limp and still, his head resting on the block, his hard face white and set. A student stepped forward, looked closely at Downie, and kneeling down, felt for the beating of his heart. Then the student looked up in a strange way at the others. No need to speak. They all knew that Downie was dead.

They gathered round in dull amaze, and for a time gazed silently and stupidly at the dead man who had been their bane in life and seemed likely to remain so in death. Then the consequences of their deed began to dawn upon them. They joined hands, and solemnly swore to be loyal to each other, not to divulge a word of what had happened, but zealously to guard their secret till their death. They were "a' airt and pairt in Downie's slaughter," and safety lay in silence.

When the Principals returned to the college, feeling merry and at peace with the world – had they not been looking on the wine when it was red? – court and black hangings and axe and block had faded like an insubstantial pageant. There was only a dead man lying in an empty room – a dead man on whose face was written fear and dread, though no wound or mark of violence was found upon him, and his keys had not been taken from his pocket.

Frank Dilnot, 'The Public Spirit of Mr. Josiah Grub' (1913)

Josiah Grub, the builder at North Hyben,[1] lived what he called the "upright life," and in view of the fact that in these days honesty is not always financially profitable, it is pleasant to note that Josiah, in the course of some forty years, had amassed a more than comfortable competence. Placid, slow of speech, with a deliberately-expressed contempt for people who drank too much or beat their wives, or descended to the tricks of trade. Josiah, in his quiet way, made himself a pillar of the more conventional virtues. He pretended to none of the great, high-minded qualities of the oral enthusiast, and with it all he recognised, with the philosophy of the simple mind, that the very honesty of his life would make him disliked, and that detractors would spring up. "There are," he remarked, "as many evil-seekers to be found here in Hyben as in the New Kent-road,[2] but I don't take any notice of them – not me."

He would fill his pipe afresh and smoke away in peaceful content.

Really some of the Hybenites said extremely nasty things of Josiah. They said he was avaricious, and some of the more malignant said he was a hypocrite. Josiah shook his head in gentle resignation. People referred to the restoration of the chancel of Hyben Church, which Josiah had offered to carry out for the mere cost of the material. They said Josiah was able to build his new outhouses and piggeries from the profits of restoring that chancel. They further made remarks about the fact that within two years the mortar which Josiah had used proved to be so bad that the church had once more to be given into the hands of the builders.

Then there was the case of Josiah's brother Daniel. Of course, everybody knew that Daniel was a drunken ne'er-do-well, who came to sponge on his village friends when he was particularly hard up. But in spite of that they said it was a shame when his father, old Grub, died and left £800 to be divided between the two brothers that Josiah should in some devious way have acquired the control of Daniel's share and used it for Daniel's advantage in building cottages that belonged to him, Josiah.

But Josiah would not answer these calumnies, which, to tell the truth, were not uttered in his hearing, but were repeated secondhand.

"People here," he said, "are a suspicious, evil-thinking lot that they simply don't understand a man who tries to lead a simple, honest life. I won't argue with them; it only encourages them."

He would say this as he leaned against his garden-gate in the twilight of a summer evening, smoking a pipe after the labours of the day. He said he realised how hard it was for an ordinary man to live a decent and unobtrusive life of principle in a country village where jealous back biting was so much more prominent than in town. He fully realised the difficulties of his position, but no amount of ill-natured gossip should make him defend himself or retaliate on those who maligned him, and he treated the people who talked about him with good-natured indifference.

Now there had cropped up a matter which Josiah was fully convinced would lead to further abuse of himself. It was a matter in which he felt bound to take a hand, but which he was certain would cause trouble to others, especially to the rival builders of the district. "It's not a profitable job," said Josiah to Mrs. Grub, "and I have a jolly good mind to wash my hands of it altogether."

Mrs. Grub went on with her ironing and did not answer. As a matter of fact Josiah did not look for an answer; he was merely talking to himself, as she knew quite well.

"If I let things take their course," he said, "I shall do grave injury to the other builders. And yet if I say anything to warn them I shall be told I am only trying to feather my own nest." Josiah smoked a pipe in silence. "It is a hard choice," he said at length – "a hard choice."

It was late on the same evening that Daniel Grub looked in to see his brother after an absence of three months.

"I hope," said Josiah, "you haven't been up to any mischief while you've been away?"

"A fat lot you'd care if I had," said Daniel. "What do my doings matter to you? You're a blooming old hypocrite, Josiah, and you know it. It's all very well to other people, but it won't do in front of me."

"I could put up with your laziness," said Josiah, "I could even sometimes excuse your dishonesty, because of your poverty, but I never can stomach your bad language."

Josiah looked at his brother with an air of placid regard. "You were always coarse, as long as I can remember," said he, "but I really do wish you would moderate your talk when you are in this house."

"I don't know as ever I saw anybody as could carry it off as well as you."

"I am not moved by your coarseness," said Josiah, philosophically. "As a matter of fact, I can't see you go without shelter to-night. I am going to give you a supper and offer you a bed."

"What do you want me to do for it?" asked the suspicious Daniel.

"You're a bad lot," said the elder brother, with a trace of sudden ill-humour – "you're a bad lot, Daniel."

It was after supper that Daniel, having been stimulated by four glasses of beer, listened to the quiet talk of his elder brother with some amount of interest.

"Between you and me, Daniel," said Josiah, "I don't quite know what to do about this new infirmary at Harton."

"What about it? You'll be sure to do the other builders down, whatever happens."

"Don't be rude," snapped Josiah. "I'm in a difficulty, and it's just for once because I want to do the other builders of the place a good turn. Hang it all, man, I'm after the money as keen as anybody, but I don't like to see any one of the other chaps made bankrupt just because I wouldn't say a word, especially when that word wouldn't cost me anything."

"There spake Josiah, but let's have the story."

"It's quite simple," said Josiah. "You know that all of us builders are tendering for the job of putting up the new infirmary, and that the tenders are to be sent in to-morrow. The Guardians have for some reason or other made it a condition that a large amount of greystone shall be used in the building. To-day it comes to me through Bilton's traveller[3] that a big strike is just going to begin in the greystone quarries, and that for months to come greystone will fetch double its usual price. Now, if these other fellows, Brown and Softley and Jebb, go and tender, reckoning on the ordinary figure, why the job will burst up the one who gets it."

"I shouldn't tell 'em," said Daniel, doggedly; "let 'em find it out."

"That's all very well, but then they'll tender at a price that will knock me out."

When Daniel had gone to bed Josiah leaned back in his chair, and with the aid of his pipe studied the affair in all its bearings.

"Daniel," he said to himself, "I don't like to judge you, but I'm positive that during to-morrow you will go round to Brown and Softley and Jebb respectively, on the chance of getting a glass of beer for the news."

Josiah smoked steadily for five minutes.

"Well, perhaps it's best," he said.

The next evening Josiah called on Brown, the most prosperous and at the same time the worst-tempered of all the local builders. Josiah told him about the strike.

Now Brown never liked to appear at a disadvantage, and he received Josiah's information with no appearance of surprise.

"Yes," he said, "I know. I had it over a week ago from a Welsh firm, so you needn't have troubled."

"I thought it only neighbourly to drop in about it. What about letting the others know."

"They've had a hint," replied Brown, "and I'm sending round this morning to let them know. We shall all be in the same boat."

Josiah took his departure, knowing for certain that Daniel had visited the builders. As for Mr. Brown, he remarked to himself as Josiah disappeared, "I was just wondering if I could trust what Daniel said, but this puts it beyond a doubt."

He altered the figures of his estimate considerably. Josiah had foreseen this. Josiah had also foreseen that Softley and Jebb would do the same.

Three days later the Guardians were to give their decision, and at the appointed time Brown, Softley and Jebb were waiting in the public gallery to see who gained the contract. Josiah was not present at first, but he turned up later while the trio were discussing matters of business.

"'Taint a bit of use," Softley was saying, "making the price too little. You can't put in the best of workmanship; you spoil the game for the rest of the trade, and it's kind of blackguardly all round."

"Well, I won't go as far as that," said Jebb, " but these 'ere democratic boards nowadays thinks a lot of trade unions, and you can't pay trade union rates unless you makes the contract a fair figure."

"Cutting under is a game any man ought to be ashamed of," said Brown; "but, besides that, it don't pay. Anyone who has been in business knows that."

"I don't want to set myself up above anyone else," put in Josiah, quietly, "but I take a stand on higher ground. What I say is this; that any man who undertakes to put up a public building is doing a public duty – yes, a public duty. A person who tries to make money out of a public duty is a scoundrel. Pay your hands good wages, do the work properly, and be content with the smallest margin for yourself. That's what I say. A quiet conscience is better than two thousand in the bank."

The other contractors became very silent after that, for they were smitten with a sudden apprehension of what Josiah's theories might have led him to do. Their fears were well grounded.

But even though they were prepared for a surprise, they were not quite prepared for the actual facts disclosed when the clerk read out the figures. The sealed envelopes containing the tenders were opened, and the names with the amounts were then announced.

"Softley," said the clerk, "£10,000."

Brown and Josiah looked on unmoved, while Jebb frowned.

"Jebb, £11,000."

Softley smiled, but became grave as the clerk proceeded.

"Brown, £9,800."

There was a moment's delay while the last envelope was opened, and then the board as well as the spectators heard with surprise the words, "Grubb, £7,000."

In spite of their surprise, the Guardians wasted no time in closing with the offer of Josiah. Softley, Jebb and Brown were bewildered. Bewilderment gave place to suspicion. Softley and Jebb looked at Brown and agreed that it was "cursed curious." When they turned to go and Brown offered to shake hands with them, they wagged their heads and said, "No; they preferred not to just yet."

After they had gone Brown turned to Josiah who had been leaning against the stair-rails, pipe in mouth, watching the proceedings.

"Don't know what's huffed them, I'm sure," said Brown; "disappointed, I suppose. Strikes me you'll have more cause to be disappointed than they before you've done, Josiah. How the devil are you going to make the thing pay?"

"I don't look for a great deal of profit," said Josiah, stopping to return a smile of recognition from the rector, who was passing, "but still I think I shall be fairly recompensed."

"Well, I don't know how you're going to do it with this strike on and all."

"Strike!" said Josiah, mildly. "What strike?"

"Why, the strike in the greystone works."

"Strike in the greystone works?" repeated Josiah, thoughtfully. "I hadn't heard of it."

"Hang it all, weren't we talking about it the other day?"

"I don't know what you mean."

"Do you mean to tell me," said Brown, striving to speak calmly, "that you have never told me about a strike in the greystone trade?"

"Never," said Josiah. "Whatever put such an idea in your head?"

For the moment Brown was overcome. "You blackguard," he spluttered, "you miserable, dirty hypocrite!"

By this time the pair had reached the street, and there was a group of people round them.

"Brown," said Josiah, sorrowfully, "you have been drinking. The best thing you can do is to get home as soon as you can."

"You lying toad, you."

"Hush, hush! said Josiah, soothingly, "for the sake of your family, if for nothing else."

In answer Brown ran at him with uplifted hand, but a constable who had come up saved Josiah from assault, and then with friendly force guided Brown in the direction of his house.

"A man in that condition is the saddest sight I can imagine," said Josiah. "For myself I have belonged to the Band of Hope[4] this twenty years."

Josiah is now doing well. His fellow-builders, however, will have nothing to say to him – a fact which Josiah often remarks upon regretfully. "There is," he says, "More jealousy in the building trade than any other calling I know."

Frank Starr, 'The Aerial Armada. What Took Place in A.D. 2000' (1913)

"Grandfather, will you tell me the story of the Armada?"

"The Armada, sonny; why, certainly I will. You mean the Armada of the Air, of course. Well, it was on July 29, 1938, that the events I am about to recount took place. It was rather odd that the Morgulian Admiral of the Air should have chosen the three hundred and fiftieth anniversary of the Spanish Armada disaster for his aerial invasion of England. But in selecting the date he was guided by the fact that all the junior officers of the Army and Navy would be at Goodwood,[1] and all the senior members of the service, to a man, would be at an Alhambra matinée, at which a ballet of the Maud Allen species[2] was to be produced. By directing his airships first to Goodwood and dropping a few hundredweight of bombs on the grandstand and the paddock, and then flying off to London and removing Leicester-square,[3] he calculated upon paralyzing the whole of the services, including their flying wings.

"But the Admiral reckoned without Captain Stedison, the commander of No. 49 Aeroplane Squadron, whose size in field service caps told that he possessed more brains than the average army officer.

"On the morning of July 29, Captain Stedison had tethered his tiny visiting biplane to the hitching-post in the roof garden of the Caravanserai, a huge hotel which used to stand on the site of Charing Water-Gardens, and which commanded a view of the Thames from Vauxhall to the old Tower. Stedison was in the Caravanserai billiard-room playing a thousand up with one of the half-dozen professionals kept on the premises, when his squadron sergeant-major, who had just flown from the Nore observation station,[4] entered excitedly.

"Saluting his superior officer, the sergeant-major gasped, 'I have just received information that the Morgulian dirigible[5] fleet is preparing to start from Bluephalia. Air Scout 2579 brought the news, and her observation officer reports that the fleet is ten times as large as we have ever imagined; that its battle "dirries," with manœuvring distance between each, extend for eight miles in two parallel lines; and that they are followed by clouds of smaller craft; I have wirelessed to every station along the coast and there is not a single air-pilot on duty. What shall we do? They will be here in six hours.'

"The commissioned officer bit off a fresh supply of chewing-gum[6] (smoking was forbidden to flying-men, and in those days, when six out of seven civilians were professional footballers, everybody chewing-gummed). Then with the nonchalance of Ouida's guardsman[7] he said:

"'Tut-tut, Marshman, have you got the jumps? What do the papers prophesy regarding the weather?'

"'The *Daily Wail* and the *Daily Distress* both predict continued east wind and fine weather, sir.'

"'And the *Morning Toast*?'

"'That says the same.'

"'With such unanimity then we may undoubtedly expect a change within a few hours. I shall therefore finish my game at bowls – I mean billiards.[8] We have plenty of time for the Spaniards – I should say the Morgulians. Meanwhile wire to the headquarters of the United Longshoremen these three words: "Prepare to charge," and then return to duty.'

"Three hours later Stedison was opening the door of his own private hangar, whose secret till then had been his alone.

"There stood the darling of his heart, his own invention: a gigantic monoplane, four times as big as anything in the service, driven by a 2,000 h.p. motor, and bristling all along the edges of its planes with long razor-edged blades like a steel-quilled porcupine.

"'There is plenty of time, Marshman,' said the Captain, as he climbed into the pilot-seat. 'Send an orderly with another wire to the United Longshoremen telling them to charge for all they are worth.'

"Within five minutes this command had been executed, and the sergeant-major was in the observer's seat behind his captain. Stedison touched a button. In a second the machine was off the ground. In 60 seconds she was a mile in the air and speeding at the rate of eight miles a minute towards the drawling fleet of dirigibles, whose greatest pace was 70 miles an hour.

"Soon they were a speck in the air three miles above the great airships, whereon, as Stedison knew beforehand from his spies, were to be found not only the Great Morgul himself, but all the finaniers and Bourse thieves[9] from Morgulia; for the expedition to England had been long planned and they intended to be on hand when the loot commenced.

"The British coastline was but two miles distant when, like a stone, Stedison's craft dropped to the level of the huge envelopes.

"It was all over in two minutes. Racing along the line of balloons at eight miles a minute the razor-edges of the monoplane cut through the silken fabric of the dirigibles with a noise so like the tearing of calico that Marshman, who abandoned a drapery counter for the Army, had murmured, 'And the next article, please, Madam,' before he realised what was actually happening.

"As they turned at the end of their eight-mile run and commenced to slit the parallel line of gas bags, the sergeant-major saw the balloons – dirigible no longer – sinking, flapping and sagging, to the sea level.

"Then he understood his captain's message to the longshoremen. From the beach flew boats by the hundred – motor boats, sailing yachts, rowing skiffs – everything, in fact, that would float.

"The deflated envelopes had drifted to within three-quarters of a mile of the shore, so that the boats soon reached the slowly submerging cars.

"'For the shore, sir; for the shore. Anybody going ashore?' shouted the boatmen in chorus, as they lay on their oars and watched the water creep up from button to button of their victim's waistcoats.

"'Yes, oh, yes,' cried the Morgulian raiders. 'Save us, oh, noble seafarers.'

"'Charge for all they are worth,' rang the clarion tones of Stedison from his megaphone above their heads.

"'Right-ho, guvner!' answered the boatmen; and then, to the sinking Morgulians: 'Two hundred thousand pounds a piece for putting you ashore, gentlemen.'

"The sinking men raved, but when the water reached their collar studs they capitulated with curses in 15 modern languages.

"But they were not yet out of the wood. At the pierhead they were charged £200,000 per head as landing dues; the bandsmen in the pavilion made a gold collection; the skating rink attendants sold them skates at £50 a pair; so that by the time they were clear of the pier-gates the whole lot of them were not worth a promissory note[10] for the price of a drink.

"They reckoned, however, on being able to repudiate their liabilities once they regained their ancestral halls in Morgulia. But they had counted without Baron Isascstein. That worthy scion of a fine old English house was cruising off the coast in his steam yacht when the Armarda was shattered and his instinct prompted him to do a little bit of business on his own. He recognised the Great Morgul on one of the sinking dirigibles, and cutting the car adrift he towed it another two miles out to sea before he persuaded the G.M. to surrender his sovereignty as the price of a ride to shore and safety.

"Isaacstein was no fool. He had the transfer of the monarchy to himself drawn out in *propria forma*[11] before he parted with his royal prisoner. Once installed on his regal throne as the Great Morgul, Isaacstein discounted the whole of the longshoreman's bills at 50 per cent. and collected the debts himself."

"And what happened to the shoal of little air-craft that you mentioned, grandpa?"

"Oh, the newspaper weather forecasts were, as usual, incorrect. The wind swung round to the south-west, a storm sprang up, and the rest of the fleet was blown away North. It was thought that the crews perished; but the discovery of a new race of white Esquimaux recently has rather modified that theory."

"Grandfather, shall I tell you a story, now?"

"Why, certainly, my lad, I shall be delighted."

"Once upon a time there was a little boy named George Washing—"

"What do you mean, you young scamp? You get off to bed at once."

Hugh Derrick, 'The Making of a Red' (1913–14)

[17 November 1913]

To The Reader By Way of Prologue.

You are to be the witness in this story of many strange shifts, but mainly of a cool, calculated, but nevertheless fierce conflict between two men of outstanding personality and equal determination. One of them is Archibald Lodden, whom you will like to read about but would be nervous to meet, and the other is Raston Path, a young Progressive statesman, occupying the post of Home Secretary, in whose efforts to ameliorate the conditions of life among poorer folks you are sure to be interested.

They interested Lodden, to the point of provoking him to a dreadful decision, and that was to break Raston Path politically – and personally, if need be. How could he achieve his purpose? Well, he was the controller of a great daily newspaper, and the man who finds himself the victim of a newspaper campaign has a battle to fight in which he cannot possibly gauge the strength of the combining forces against him. You will see how Raston Path met this terrible onslaught.

Of course, a struggle such as this inevitably draws into the vortex a number of lesser people, who, willingly or otherwise, consciously or the reverse, play their parts. There are Lodden's men, for instance, good journalists every one, who find themselves being sucked into the whirlpool fight against the Home Secretary. There is Majority Gaunt, the reporter, on whose shoulders falls the task of carrying out all sorts of difficult and delicate missions connected with the attack on Raston Path. When he boldly calls on the Home Secretary himself with a view to being let into a secret which is only known to the Cabinet, one's feelings respond to this journalism of the "Daily Light" school. When in the momentary absence of Path from the room, Gaunt sees the very information he seeks lying before him in typescript, one appreciates his tremendous difficulty. Shall he copy the coveted document? What a moment of temptation! Could it be a trap deliberately laid for him by Path? You shall see what a far-reaching effect that little incident was to have on the fortunes of the fight.

It may sound a little strange that because of the enmity between the politician and the newspaper owner a third man should have to become an out-of-work for a few weeks and live from hand to mouth amid the squalor of London's by-streets; yet this was another of the difficult tasks that fell to Majority Gaunt. Lodden's idea was to disprove Raston Path's contention that the man who is willing to work with his hands has often the utmost difficulty in earning even a few coppers a day, hence Gaunt was given a shilling or two and cut off from his ordinary life, so that he might fend himself in the role of out-of-work. You will follow him through his experiences as a casual labourer, and you will hear the rebuffs he met with. You are sure to enjoy his advent into the oyster business, that was a choice adventure, when he tried to create a taste of Portuguese and Blue Point oysters in the vicinity of Seven Sisters-road.[1]

Though the experiment in trade was not encouraging, it was yet fraught with consequences that he dreamed not of: it brought him into a midnight episode of the most mysterious kind, and one with such a direct bearing on the Lodden and Path struggle that you almost tremble with apprehension. It was by far the most important result of Gaunt's poverty investigations.

It has already been shown that Gaunt came into this drama of human wills purely by professional accident. Very different were the motive influences in the cases of others whom you will meet. Take Viola Cartlet, that young married woman of puzzling temperament, who could lend her name to the attack on her brother-in-law, the Home Secretary. Was it because he was only amused by her weighty political opinions that she grasped at the opportunity for a little bit of personal revenge? This is a question that will occur to you, friend the reader, in connection with Viola Cartlet. And you will not find it surprising, when she crosses his path, if Gaunt responds to the call of her, for she is an adorable and spirited creature.

And then, Nancy Kirk, the pretty young typist in the Progressive office, striving after refinement and respectability in spite of her sordid home surroundings in the Borough – what a malicious manœuvre of fate it was that first of all dropped Gaunt into her home and then put her in possession of a private story concerning Raston Path, which was sufficient, had she known how to use it, to wreck the "Daily Light" campaign and carry the Home Secretary on the crest of a wave of popular feeling into a position where even Lodden could not reach him with his barbed shafts. By what a thread does our destiny hang!

Nancy Kirk, unlike her jollier sister Nellie, had an antipathy to Gaunt, which no one regretted more than he. Why this was so you have to decide for yourself. It may have been instinctive, one cannot know for certain, but one can easily sympathise with Gaunt in his earnest efforts to break it down. There was something almost spiritual in Nancy Kirk that greatly attracted him; even to see her was comforting. Viola Cartlet, again, had but to smile, or stand near him, to raise a storm of passion in his veins. Each of these women, so different in temperament and outlook, influenced Gaunt – which of them, do you think, brought him to journey's end? Ring up the curtain!

Chapter I.
Archibald Lodden's Impulse.

The exact cause which led Archibald Lodden, the millionaire newspaper proprietor, to bring a campaign against the Home Secretary has never been known with any certainty even by those who had a hand in the fight. Beneath all speculations was the assumption that Lodden had the direct and narrow vision of a middling kind of person, and that some secret and terrible motive lay behind the project. Of course, no big person is built that way.

A man of the world was Archibald Lodden – 39 years of age, boyish in his manners, possessing an impressionableness which in one who had made a fortune was attractive and unusual – but he was more than a mere man of the world, and the range of his nature would have permitted many and various descriptions. Whatever his qualities, it is certain that will power and an innate energy were among his weapons; he was angry with failure even in small things, and he had a brain which flickered like lightning through his working hours, and sometimes through his sleep as well. All business men who are very successful are perhaps like this, but there were special points about Lodden. Intuition is possessed by some women to an extraordinary degree, and Lodden had intuition more certain than any woman's, and more rapid, and just as unconscious. What he thought about a certain course of business action was pretty well always right, even though at the time it appeared to be in conflict with the judgment of experienced men. This always puzzled people at first, and those who had just begun to know Lodden called him "lucky"; but the people who had been in touch with him for any length of time did not use the word "lucky." They knew that success sprang from the soul of the man – though there were differences of opinion as to whether it was a good soul or a bad soul.

What was he like to look at? There was really nothing very extraordinary about him. He was of middle height, with just the slightest bend in his heavy shoulders, and he was kept from the commonplace by a swarthy complexion, wavy black hair, and a small trim beard which, instead of being pointed, was square-cut.[2] His blue eyes were a little bulging, and had a strained expression which made him seem worried even when he was perfectly comfortable in mind. One did not feel that he had power in him till after some conversation; and the only traces of his energy were the quickness of his words, whether in friendly talk or in anger, and the nervous movements of his hands and the quickness of his short footsteps. He was not, therefore, very different from a thousand others – mediocrities or silly failures.

At 17 years of age he had started a little weekly paper for the sewing-machine business, and at 39 he was the principal shareholder in the greatest newspaper concern in the world, and the virtual owner of the *Daily Light*. By the time he had reached 35, Archibald Lodden, owing to his journalistic conquests, was being talked of all over the country, and on the whole it is not surprising that he was sometimes appraised quite wrongly, and was very generally deprecated. This success embittered many and confused many. People shrugged their shoulders at his achievements, and the latter were sometimes put down to chance and sometimes to unscrupulousness. Very likely there was a touch of truth in both these suggestions, but they were carried too far. Lodden's success was in his bones, and he worked as a natural force – occasionally almost blindly – carrying his projects to culmination as a bee makes honey.

He was not an inscrutable Napoleon; he had some little human ambitions, and when they leaked out in various directions he was not specially hurt that they should be known. He wanted to win the America Cup[3] with his own yacht; he wanted to become a Privy Councillor;[4] he had a whim to possess Trendane Castle in Sussex,[5] which the Duke of Kallorye obstinately refused to sell at any price.

It is easy to see some of the reasons why Archibald Lodden was misjudged. To sycophants he was a perfectly maddening problem. One never knew the way the man would turn. It was disappointing and dangerous to one's self-respect to indulge in admiration for him, shattering to one's discernment to affect disgust. He was week by week overturning the calculations of acquaintances. There was the case of the paper mills at Shoreham. Everyone knows the Shoreham Paper Mills, producing something like a quarter of the paper in use in the British newspaper world. The importance of the business was great, but its potentiality was far greater, and the small syndicate of owners, hampered by lack of capital and prejudiced against modern innovations, had steadily dropped back to where profit finishes, and on this borderline had remained almost stationary for some years. With the increase of competition, due to the growth of newspapers, they had to confess a dismal future prospect, but though they might have sold the business they hung on with a kind of grim, old-fashioned reluctance to part with something which had almost an historic touch about it. At last, however, the outlook was so black that they allowed themselves to enter into negotiations with a combination of the three principal newspaper proprietors (apart from Archibald Lodden) and a purchase of an extensive price was somewhat hurriedly discussed. The old paper manufacturers had strange, unbusinesslike aversions from the up-to-date men with whom they were dealing, and it was with irritated feelings that they found themselves sliding into a bargain which would take from them and their families the control of the undertaking. There was no help for it – though the sellers rather disdained the purchasers.

While negotiations were delicately poised, Archibald Lodden heard of the matter. He saw at once that it was a thing which would be a feature of the *Daily Light*, because, as he explained to the managing editor, the public always liked to read of these big financial stories. The hundreds of thousands of pounds in the balance give people not very rich a pleasant exhilaration. Lodden pointed this out to the managing editor, and urged the advantage of securing an exclusive story. The result was that Primrose, a trusted and tactful member of the staff, conveyed to Sir Henry Lyn, chief of the purchasing group, the compliments of Mr. Lodden on the acquisition of the paper mills with a request for a short interview in which the fact of the purchase could be announced, and an indication given of the general scope of the work before the mills. Now Sir Henry Lyn (in spite of the fact that he assumed contempt for Lodden) was a little flattered by the message and by the request for an interview and all it implied, and he rose to the occasion and told Primrose the outline of the negotiations, gave him to understand that sweeping changes would be made in the production of paper in this country, and generally let himself go. Sir Henry Lyn felt that for once he had beaten Archibald Lodden (to whom the paper supply could not be a matter of indifference) and he was rather glad to let the world know it in the columns of the *Daily Light*.

The sight of the *Daily Light* next morning must have warmed his heart, for not only was his interview given prominence, but there was a special leading article apparently written at the instruction of Lodden, in which the congratulations of the journal were offered to the newspaper proprietors (especially to Sir Henry Lyn), who had "by bold and determined action secured a great business, and who (as is evidenced by the interview in another column) intended to remodel it in accordance with plans for a wide-spread undertaking."

Rarely does a story get such headlines as this story of the paper mills received in the *Light*. So obtrusive was it that Sir Henry Lyn's utterances seemed in the light of day to be really very boastful indeed. If they appeared like that to the ordinary reader, conceive the impression they made on the proud old Shoreham syndicate. Horror but faintly mirrors their feelings. To them Sir Henry's words were the extreme of bumptious audacity, an outrageous attempt to precipitate them into a bargain on which they had been hesitating. There was a meeting at which it was decided to break off at once the bargaining. Whatever betide, they would get clear of these vulgar hucksters and their offensive blustering. So the Shoreham paper mills purchase fell through.

One need not enter into the reflections of Sir Henry Lyn; the man with whom we are concerned is Archibald Lodden, and he heard what had occurred with a shrug of the shoulders and a passing comment of regret at Sir Henry's impetuous words in the interview. What happened after the breaking off of the business is not very clearly defined, but certain is it that the angry syndicate were quickly approached by a City financier, who offered to buy out the mills at the sellers' own price, and under conditions which would allow the principal vendors to retain a share in the direction of the business. The price asked was enormous, but it was paid over in two days, and within a week the paper mills had passed into the possession of a company which was purely nominal and which had as its head and driving force Archibald Lodden. He frankly owned to the managing editor afterwards that the possession of the paper mills was of much importance to the *Daily Light* and he remarked that it was a lucky chance which caused him to send and get that interview with Sir Henry Lyn.

Here is another instance of Archibald Lodden: George Pryor, a reporter five years on the *Light*, died after two days' pneumonia, and, as is the custom with any working journalists, left his wife unprovided for either by way of insurance or any kind of property. She had about £30 in cash and a child 18 months old. Lodden was coldly blasphemous about it. "I pay my men the best newspaper salaries in the world, and this is what comes of it. Did good work? Of course he did good work. He was paid to do it. Well, his wife must suffer, that's all about it. I hope he'll be able to see his wife suffering."

The foreign editor, who overheard the remark, said that Lodden was a beast, selfish and coarse to the soul of him. But even foreign editors are sometimes wrong.

The day after the funeral Lodden went down to Beckenham,[6] where the young widow was living, and with a kindliness of manners which she always remembered told how sorry he was for her, and left her with documentary assurances that she should have through her life a pension of £100 per year.

In order to explain the beginning of the attack on the Home Secretary, it is necessary to refer to the politics of Archibald Lodden and the politics of the *Daily Light*, a newspaper which owed some part of its success to a recognition of the fact that however lively and otherwise admirable a modern newspaper may be, however smart, vivid, brilliant, it is certainly most essential that that paper should possess a set of sober, serious State opinions. From the time he began his rocket-like course Archibald Lodden had had few illusions on the matter, and had steadily and firmly bent politics to the use of his journalistic projects. He realised that a very large number of people in this country were in earnest about politics, and, indeed, could well understand that, because he retained memories of the Authoritarian atmosphere in which he had been brought up as a boy, and which still to his amazement sometimes coloured his vision. But when he definitely fixed the grade of politics for the *Daily Light*, enthusiasm in politics was as far from the mind of Lodden as enthusiasm for Confucianism or Theosophy.[7] Here were the cardinal points for his news columns: –

Youth to be given prominence: the success of young men, the romance of young women.

Personality to be dominant over all theories.

Women's interests always to be kept in view (because prosperous daily papers are largely made by women readers).

The upper and middle classes always to be supported against the working and poorer classes, whenever differences arise between them.

A zeal for the common good to be always the note of the principal contents of the paper.

Sometimes Archibald Lodden would permit himself to explain in his frank, quick way why the last rule but one was necessary. "The men on this paper," he would say to the managing editor, "never seem properly to understand the importance and influence of the instrument they have helped to make. The *Daily Light*, with its circulation of a million a day, is perhaps the greatest individual force in the life of this country at the present time. Everyone vaguely realises that it has power, but no one knows how really great and potent is that power. That is what I complain about in the foreign editor and the news editor: they never seem properly to comprehend the magnitude of the weapon they handle. Do you know we could make war with Germany if we liked to set ourselves to the task? That we could break up the understanding with France? What's more, we could stop a war if we bestirred ourselves. We have practically relieved a famine, and we have raised an army – you'll remember how we got together 12,000 men in a fortnight for the Southern Counties Militia.[8] And remember, too, we mould day by day, to some extent at any rate, the minds of all our readers, and allowing on an average four readers for every copy of the paper sold, we help to form the opinions of four millions of people daily. That means we are part of the life of the nation. We have got to keep that nation together. We have got to maintain the balance of wealth-producing and prosperity-producing minds against the big mass of ordinary people. We've got to keep this Socialistic nonsense down. Hardships for many there must be, and yet on the whole ours is the best country in the world. Yes, yes, it is no use talking. The merchants, the scholars, the financiers, the dramatists and authors – some of them have had advantages and some have not, but when it comes to the point you find that practically all are keeping in front by brains or will denied to others. Don't forget this, too, that while their energies benefit themselves a good deal they also benefit circles around them. We are held together by network, and it is only the one-idea people who want to pull it to pieces. The *Daily Light* has done good work for poor people, but when it comes to a fight between the educated and successful part of the community on the one side, and on the other those who work with their muscles, well, then, of course there can be no mistake about the line one must take. With the increased extent and power of the trade unions, and with the general way in which legislation has been going of late, there's no chance of the working classes being oppressed at all; and we must not allow spasms of discontent to lead to disastrous strikes putting a stop to our industries. Sometimes, no doubt, we feel sympathy with sections of these people, but we must not be frightened by their sufferings any more than we must be frightened by the sight of a surgeon's knife. Things will slowly right themselves."

Archibald Lodden would deliver this lecture on the policy of his newspaper in sudden, quick gasps of a few sentences at a time and though sometimes it varied a little its tenor was always the same. The managing editor would lean with his elbow on the mantelpiece, smoking a cigarette and apparently listening thoughtfully. Lodden sometimes dived forward as though to thrust some of his sentences down his listener's neck; at other times would sink into his chair and shake a nervous forefinger at his lieutenant. All the time conviction bubbled from his words. A stranger, knowing the prejudices outside, would have been a good deal surprised at Lodden, would have felt that the man was sincere, would probably have acknowledged on the spot that there was a good deal in what Lodden said.

Archibald Lodden's spirit, of course, found its reflection in the columns of his paper. He meant that it should. The hearts of Authoritarians through the country responded daily, and the *Daily Light* (though perhaps smilingly deprecated) was more or less of an oracle among the middle classes and the upper classes.

Most people bought the *Daily Light*, and even those who read the *Times* bought the *Light* as well; its safe and sound political views took it into practically every well-to-do home. This was a fact that advertisers were not slow to notice, and as more than half the revenue from a successful newspaper is derived from its advertisements the value from the proprietor's point of view is easily to be understood. So it was a good thing for Archibald Lodden financially that his earnestness was directed towards Authoritarian ideals; and it shows that virtue is not always unrewarded that his devotion to public duty had much to do with the multiplication of the dividends derived from the *Daily Light*. A glimpse of the man is given in the fact that not a member of the staff ever denied in the most scurrilous of moments that Archibald Lodden was a firm politician.

On the day that the attack on the Home Secretary had its beginning, Archibald Lodden reached his office without any antagonism in his heart; indeed, without so much as a flicker of thought concerning the Home Office; and up to lunch time he was deeply engaged with the help of two secretaries and occasional interviews with chiefs of departments in finding out why the sale of two of his weekly magazines had dropped 40,000 in the preceding fortnight; in making further steps towards the publication of a new monthly review; in flashing off answers to a score of letters; in adjusting the finances of one of his newspaper companies, the annual meeting of which was due in a month's time. Impressions and reflections on extraneous matters came and went in the interstices of his settled work; and by the time he set out for lunch he had stored in his memory a dozen different criticisms and suggestions with reference to the contents of the *Daily Light* that morning. He had, moreover, within his consciousness the seed of a decision which was to produce a great harvest of consequences.

That morning there had appeared in the *Light* a short leading article mildly commendatory of the Home Secretary in relation to his administration of the new Children Act[9] – a little deviation from partisanship by which the *Light* sought to show occasionally that it was big enough to appreciate merit wherever it was found. Once in a way these friendly articles would give piquant surprise to the readers of the *Light*.

"Accuracy," said Archibald Lodden to his staff, "is the thing principally to be striven for, but of almost equal value in a good newspaper is freshness of outlook. Do not carry the principle too far; ordinary people won't stand it. But within the limits it is stimulative."

A few days before Lodden had suffered a passing rudeness – or what might have been a rudeness – at the hands of the Home Secretary when they met at a dinner party, and this friendly article was – apart from general newspaper consideration – a little bit of personal revenge. Archibald Lodden had permitted himself to a moment's smile at the thought of Path reading the approving patronage of the *Daily Light*. Now within about nine hours of the appearance of the article, Archibald Lodden had forgotten the motives which inspired it, and within him there were impulses, half-formed, sub-consciously gathering force with every minute, concentrating on a course of action which it was meant should agitate the whole of the newspaper reading public.

Archibald Lodden was a creature of impulse; where he differed from most was in the fact that the impulses were generally right. That strange, sweeping tide of influence which, with all its mysterious currents and concealed harbours we call fate, had him on the move, and he was bearing surely and with increasing swiftness for the unknown seas.

Raston Path, the Home Secretary, young for a statesman, amazingly successful, famous already through many civilised countries, was hated thoroughly by his opponents. You must feel that hate to know it. He was in various ways altering the traditional trend of events in the history of the country. He was hastening on changes dear to the heart of Progressives, hateful to true Authoritarians. His effectiveness, his vividness, roused rebellions, even passion, in the breasts of the majority of the Authoritarians. It is no exaggeration to say that thousands of God-fearing people wished him dead. He was soon to introduce another of his revolutionary measures; and already the rumblings of his coming action were noticeable to the political atmosphere.

The decision of Archibald Lodden at lunch time was this: To break Raston Path; to break him politically and for ever; to wreck him personally, if need be, but in any case to injure him so that during the rest of his life he should be of no account in public affairs. "I shall take the conference myself this afternoon," he said to his secretary, St. Just, when he came in from lunch.

Among the causes of Archibald Lodden's decision the big, overmastering one seemed to have been purely journalistic, the desire to give the *Daily Light* one of those occasional and tremendous fillips which kept it on the lips of all and maintained it as the greatest newspaper of the age. Letters had been pouring in to the editor charged with all kinds of argumentative venom against Raston Path and his proposed new legislation, and it may well have been that Lodden got an insight into the depth and extent of the feeling against the Home Secretary from one particular communication selected for his perusal by the managing editor, a communication which, intended for publication, called on all and sundry to stop the mad and seething movement about to be set up by the Home Secretary. That communication was signed by a relation of Raston Path, Mrs. Viola Cartlet, his sister-in-law. If a woman so related will go thus far to show the strength and bitterness of her feelings, there certainly must be swirling up and down the country extraordinary gusts of passion against the man. Perhaps that letter of Viola Carlet's gave the finishing touch to a rapidly formed opinion. After all, the fact which really mattered was that Archibald Lodden heard the mysterious voices from wherever they came, and in full confidence rushed, as he always did, to obey their wordless and inexplainable behests.

(*The characters in "The Daily Citizen" serial story are entirely fictitious, and the names used do not refer to any living persons.*)[10]

[18 November 1913]

Chapter II.
Skirmishers at Work.

It was really no a matter for surprise that within a day or two Lodden's project found its way to Whitehall. Though outsiders had been told nothing of the scheme and the other newspapers were quite unsuspicious, the Home Secretary had learned the news within 48 hours of Lodden's decision. A secret which is shared by four or five is always on the brink of exposure, and where that secret is a comprehensive plan of attack, in which the help of subordinates has to be organised, there is almost a certainty that some knowledge of affairs will get through to the enemy.

Fore, the news editor, knew of the project; Wansmuth, the managing editor; Majority Gaunt, the reporter; Lumley, the foreign editor; Lodden's secretary, St Just; and his lady stenographer; and of these, certainly two or three were engaged in preparing letters bearing on all parts of the proposed organisation. There were as a result a hundred crevices through which the news might drift, and useless would it be to follow with detailed surmise the means by which the course of things was outlined to one or two of the principal members of the Cabinet. Even now, after the passage of years, it is not at all certain whether an indiscreet word from St. Just in the hearing of his brother, an Admiralty clerk or the direct treachery of the ambitious young Oxford man serving as Wansmuth's secretary, was responsible for the Cabinet's foreknowledge. The latter was under notice to leave just at the time and resentment as well as hope of profit might have influenced him. It is hardly fair to say that, however, because nothing has ever been proved; and possibly it was neither through this man nor through St. Just that the leakage occurred. Anyway, it does not affect matters seriously. At this distance one can but record the leakage.

Raston Path and Sir Harry Venture, the Secretary for Foreign Affairs, were talking about Lodden's new move two days after the campaign was decided on.

"Has the paper any real influence?" asked the Foreign Minister. "If one can ignore it, 'tis by far the better way."

"Yes, I know, but it's only affectation for us to pretend to ignore the *Light*. Excepting the stalwarts, pretty well every elector comes under its influence to some extent. You can't ignore a paper like the *Light*."

Raston Path sat on the edge of his big writing table. Eagerness lighted his pale features, and he was strung up with that boyish alertness which always marked him in time of interest and perplexity, for worry was not a depressant to the Home Secretary but a stimulant, and the darting electricity of his mind brought to the surface a vivacity which had the semblance of lightheartedness. His face, feminine in its features, possessed the smoothness of youth, and when he spoke tiny criss-cross wrinkles came to sight, telling of age, experience, and a thousand emotions. How much was boy and how much was man in Raston Path always puzzled those who did not know him very well. He was, so to speak, a picture of himself this afternoon, as he sat gripping the edges of the table, sliding backwards and forwards on the slippery mahogany and addressing the Secretary for Foreign Affairs. The latter was standing with his shoulders against the chimneypiece, his hands in his trousers pockets.

The two men were in happy contrast. Sir Harry Venture was tall and athletic, with raven hair and classic features, immobile and serious in expression, carrying over all a reserve and dignity as impregnable as it was natural. It has often been said that dignity was in the blood of the Ventures. The first of the line served in the Government of the elder Pitt,[11] and the second of note was he who with Lord Grey went to force through the Reform Bill[12] against the wishes of the King and peers. Statecraft was born in all the family, but it did not make itself manifest in every generation, and 80 years had passed after the Reform Bill episode[13] before the ability and strength of a Venture again made it impossible to keep his hereditary talent out of the government of the country. Sir Harry Venture, handsome, distinguished-looking, was reputed to be cold, but to counterbalance this, at least as far as externals were concerned, he had a mellow, clear voice, which was like music. I have often thought that it was his calm, deep, passionless tone more than his words which impressed the House of Commons and impressed popular crowds, and was responsible for the unshakeable consciousness that what Sir Harry Venture said was right, always right and true. His power of speech being what it was, his looks helped him. The clear-cut aristocrat with the melancholy eyes was instinctively trusted by English people, and even his opponents had a grudging good word for him, and the latter made much of his gifts when they wanted to compare him with that scoundrel-demagogue Raston Path, whom they bitterly referred to as "a son of the people."

There grew up the delusion that in the Government Sir Harry Venture and Raston Path were opposed to each other, that it was Venture who sought to curb Raston Path's wild schemes that there was the prospect of a sensational break between them, and that presently Sir Harry would leave the cabinet and later on join the Authoritarians with whom he was at heart in sympathy. This rumour had spread far and wide, and Sir Harry Venture was much too scornful a person to contradict it even to his friends, and Raston Path on his part was quite delighted to see his enemies digging a pit for themselves. Far indeed was rumour from touching the truth. Not only was there no opposition between the two men but, as a matter of fact, it was Sir Harry Venture who in the privacy of Cabinet Councils backed up Raston Path with cold insistence and who had made it quite clear that he shared the ideal of the fervid Home Secretary. Partly as a result of this, partly because they were mutually attracted by each other's personality, they had become, if not intimate, at least close friends understanding each other very well.

Ministers are frequently to be found in the departments of their colleagues for the purpose of talking over Government matters, or, it may be, personal affairs, and no two members of the Government visited each other more often than did Venture and Path. Their offices were in the same great quadrangle.

"Of course, it's temporary," said Path, "but that doesn't make it the less serious."

"First, it's you, but the Government as well."

"Yes. He'll lay himself out for the Bill.[14] He knows it's in preparation and when it's introduced he'll smash away as hard as he can."

"Shall we do anything?"

"I think we had better wait on events. But it won't do to miscalculate Lodden. When he's on the warpath he doesn't think of past civility. He means to get there, and he usually does get there."

"I suppose he really has got some political beliefs?"

"Who knows? I dare say he has leanings. I doubt any great missionary motives. His newspapers and business first, but, of course, there is the knowledge of his power and the satisfaction of using it on what he thinks is the right side. A wonderful man, that's all we've got to think about. He'll stand at nothing. Threatening appeals, and distortion of facts, they'll be the commonplaces."

"He has begun the foreign side already," said Sir Harry, with a glint of a smile.

"Yes?"

"That is to say he has begun at me. I had a visit yesterday from one of his men; his foreign editor. He's a stout, blusterous, bombastic fellow. Lumley is his name. He seems to have had some trouble in trying to get at me at the Foreign Office, the attendants and the office keeper refusing to take his card beyond Johnson. Johnson thought fit not to bother me with the man, with the consequence that he was refused. Mr. Lumley was annoyed, even indignant. He treated the men with scorn, then he abused them. Finally they had practically to force him down the steps and out of the office. You miss the point if you haven't seen him – big, important, dignified, and, above all, with an Irishman's temper. On reflection I rather like him. He came afterwards to my house in Berkeley-square to see me in the evening, and though I at first refused to see him, yet when he sent in that he had important news received by cable which he wished to tell me before publication, I thought it best to break my rule and have him in. Sometimes the papers get cables through before we do.

"'You will forgive me for disturbing you at home, I am sure,' he said, 'but where matters of importance to the State are concerned I have always thought it best not to stand too much on ceremony.'

"I expressed my acknowledgements, and he then assured me that though he, having a deep and wide experience of foreign affairs, might have taken upon himself the responsibility of disturbing me with the cables that had come to hand during the day, his decision had been ratified by the definite suggestion of Mr. Lodden that he should come straight to the Foreign Office with the news. In the course of conversation he said that I might give you these messages with his compliments, together with the guarantee that nothing of them should appear in the *Light* if publication should be opposed to your wishes. While he was talking like this I was wondering where the deuce in the world the trouble had broken out. 'It's a serious matter, is it?' said I. 'Very serious indeed.' He dived slowly into the breast pocket of his overcoat to get out three or four foreign telegrams, and as he handed them over he said, 'There, Sir Harry, you will find information about the most serious situation that this country has ever been called upon to face.'

I made him sit down, and took the telegrams to the table, where the light was better. I read them through. I need not have worried about Russia. What I was called upon to deal with was the fact that there was grave and increasing dissatisfaction abroad with the present action and future policy in this country of the right Honourable Raston Path, his Majesty's Secretary of State for the Home Department. What do you think of that?"

Path's face had softened into a comprehensive smile.

"To find out how I stood with you?"

"I read the dispatches through three times with, I hope, some signs of a reflective mood. The places drawn upon were Paris, Madrid, St. Petersburg, and Berlin. The messages were quite vague. For instance, the Paris one, signed by the resident Paris correspondent of the *Light*, ran something like this: 'I learn that in Government circles there is much misgiving as to the activities of Raston Path. The growing power of the Red statesman, the character of the legislation he has succeeded in forcing through, the mystery of his revolutionary plans for the future, are factors in a situation which has its obvious dangers for all civilised countries. The stability of society will be shaken in many parts of the world if he obtains more power. The leader of the Moderates, who will certainly hold high office at the next change of Ministry, tells me that he regards Raston Path as a danger to Europe.' The other telegrams were on the same lines. They had apparently been arranged for from the London office, and though, of course, not fictitious in the shape of being manufactured out of nothing, are pretty much as valueless as if they had been."

Raston Path twisted a pencil between his lips thoughtfully.

"And the delightful Lumley?"

"He was quite a serious man. He waited for my opinion with the composure of a person who has been the bearer of unpleasant information. As I said, I read the messages through two or three times, and he must have seen that I was not in the least disposed to scoff. 'I've brought these telegrams up for your personal guidance,' he said 'and whether you think there is any importance in them or not we should not proceed to print them at present if your wishes are not in that direction.' I replied that though I could not say anything about a colleague of mine in the Ministry – he would see that that was quite impossible – I was free to say I found some significance in his telegrams."

"Was he convinced?"

"Without saying so he gave me to understand that he knew my difficulties. 'If this Government ever became unpopular,' he said, 'there is one man who will stand firm with the whole country, Sir Harry and that is yourself.' After that I had to let him go."

"I wonder if they'll be deceived. Loddon is not a dull person."

There was a knock at the door and an attendant entered with a card for Path. He looked at it and, chuckling, extended it to the Foreign Secretary. "My turn now," he said. Sir Harry glanced at the card and saw on it, "Mr. Majority Gaunt, *Daily Light*, London, E.C."

[19 November 1913]

Chapter II – Continued.
A Tempting Opportunity.

"I think I'll see him." Path turned to the attendant. "Show the gentleman into Mr. Brown's room; I'll be with him shortly."

"Is it wise?" asked Sir Harry, when the man had gone.

"It's just as well to learn what we can."

"You know what they are. Keep your eye on the young man."

"Ay, ay."

Gaunt will never forget the first sight he had of Raston Path, because it was so vividly different from the picture he had carried in his mind. He found Path not to be the scornful, nervous, person he had imagined, found no probing intensity in his eyes, no sneer round the corners of his mouth. The man who smiled a quick welcome at him from his chair in front of the writing table was a placid, businesslike individual whose delicate features showed no trace of worry or past passion, and who carried an air of pleasant wonderment at an unexpected visit, together with a kind of humorous but not unfriendly surmise. In that revealment which comes to all in the first few moments of a new meeting with a personality he realised that he would always be unable to dislike Raston Path. The Home Secretary rose to his feet with two or three sheets of foolscap[15] in his hand.

"I suppose there are some men who are clever enough to keep clear of the *Daily Light*, but I don't seem to be one of them. What is it now?"

"I have come to talk to you for a minute or two on political matters – that is if you can spare me a minute or two. I have come up really for news and do not, of course, want to quote you in the sense of an interview."

"Won't you sit down?" said Path, providing the example and dropping into a big armchair on the side of the table.

Gaunt found himself another chair, and sat down with his bowler hat and walking stick in his hand.

"A Cabinet Minister is not generally the best person to come to for political news," said Path. "What's the idea?"

"I am out to find what can be found about your new Bill. I have come straight to you because it is possible you might like to have a direct statement made about it. All kinds of rumours and discussions are abroad, and a good many of them are hostile. Would it not be well to have a plain statement of facts given to the public?"

"A plain statement of facts. What direction do you propose the statement should take?"

"An outline of the main provisions of the Bill; failing that, a definite announcement as to its purport, and an indication of when it is to be brought in and the course of procedure in Parliament with regard to it."

"That's a pretty good sweep, isn't it?"

"I know it seems a lot to ask, but what was in my mind was that you yourself might think it well to get a correct idea of your plan known quite early. There is no newspaper and not even any combination of newspapers, which can approach the *Daily Light* in circulation, and as you know, it goes everywhere and is read by all sides. To get your plans published even through a paper with opposite opinions might suit your purpose."

"You are not out to attack the scheme?"

"I am out for news."

"Yes; but there's news and news. I've spent a good deal of my life fighting against news of some newspapers."

"So far as this interview is concerned, I can assure you that I don't intend to print anything except the information with regard to the Bill."

Path's hand roamed thoughtfully among the documents on the table in front of him, and then, as though suddenly gripped by a new idea, he said: "Perhaps you are in the journalistic fashion and are one of those young Reds who have to earn their living from the Authoritarian newspapers?"

There was nothing offensive in the question, and it was thrown out in a conversational way which bespoke friendliness, rather than suspicion. But Gaunt stiffened himself. "On the contrary, I am dead against all the Red beliefs, and I think Authoritarianism is the only sane and wholesome creed."

"Sorry! We know where we stand."

A pleasant frankness was in Path's grey eyes, but Gaunt was somehow not comfortable, and began to know that the Home Secretary was talking on the surface. Gaunt could not take his measure. There was something intimately appealing about him, and it was an influence that must affect more or less everyone who came within his range. But Gaunt was vaguely conscious of purpose and hardness covered up by that natural attractiveness. As one who had previously despised Path, he had his first glint of the man's danger.

"One has always to be on guard against you newspaper men, but I can see that your mission is a perfectly frank one, and that you desire to do nothing more than to put the *Daily Light* in front, as it so often is with big news. But I don't know about this. I have to consider."

A tap at the door interrupted him and an attendant came in with a card which he carried to the Home Secretary. Path looked at it thoughtfully.

"Would you excuse me for two or three minutes?" he said, and then, turning to the attendant, "Show his lordship into my small room."

Gaunt left alone had time for thought; and his calloused journalistic conscience suffered no smart from the Home Secretary's trust in his good faith and straight intentions. Indeed, such trivial considerations were far from Gaunt's mind. Far more important things occupied him. He was glowing with the success of his tactics. Whatever the artfulness and designs hidden behind the charming frankness of the Home Secretary it was pretty certain he knew nothing of the coming campaign. All Gaunt's mental energies were now centered in the determination to procure some hint about the coming Bill. He seemed on the track. It was evident that Path, no doubt for his own purpose, was inclined to consider the suggestions put forward, and it was within the measure of possibility that he might go far as to indicate the actual provisions. Gaunt bent himself to the task of devising arguments to influence the Minister. Then his eyes fell on some typewritten foolscap sheets lying on Path's table in front of his chair.

I make no excuse for the action of Gaunt. But it is necessary for full understanding that the bare facts should be stated. Gaunt, like all the more effective of his colleagues, was just a privateer. The opponents of his newspaper were fair and proper prey. It mattered not who they were nor what they were; so long as they were enemies, they were all subject to attack. The more unscrupulous that attack the more likely it was to be successful, and Majority Gaunt was a very successful reporter.

From his sideways position Gaunt made out that the upper sheet of foolscap on Path's desk wore the title "Road of Life Bill."

In a flash it came upon him that this must be a draft of the measure, apparently the latest draft, because Path had it before him for examination. This Bill, Gaunt knew, was a very short one, and these two or three quarto sheets might well contain the words of the Government's sensational proposals. He gave a travelling glance at the door by which Raston Path had gone out a minute before, and then, rising from his chair, stepped forward. Five seconds showed him that he had made no mistake. On the top of the first page were the words "New Methods Bill," and beneath on the same page Clause 1, and farther down the commencement of Clause 2, and on the next two pages were Clauses 3, 4, and 5, while the final page was blank except for the words "Machinery Clauses." With eagle eagerness Gaunt extracted the gist from each clause, rapidly transferring sentences with his stubby pencil to the folded sheets of copy paper he had drawn from one of the outside pockets of his coat. He was at high pressure and he had finished in three minutes. During that time one of the things he noticed was that no formal preamble to the Bill existed and that the missing machinery clauses were those which would have given the method for putting the Bill into operation. What he had secured from the typewritten sheets was the general principle of the measure – exactly what he had sought for, for herein lay the heart of the Government's proposals, the secret so closely guarded.

Gaunt's face was calm, but excitement was in his veins as he settled himself in his old place and took up the *Times* and turned an unseeing eye on the first leading article, and he was still hot with exultation when, after another five minutes Path came in, with a word of quick apology and a manner which showed to Gaunt that other affairs were close pressing and that his welcome was at an end. "I'm sorry," he said: "a caller on business that could not be delayed." He remained standing as he went on to say rapidly: "Mr. Gaunt I have turned your proposals over in my mind, and have come to the decision that it is not possible for me to do what you desire. To give away the Government's plan now would be simply to open the gates to our enemies, and I do not think would serve any useful purpose at all."

"You can't say anything about the procedure to Parliament?"

"I think not. What statement there is will be made in the King's Speech. Until that is delivered I must ask the *Daily Light* to wait and see."

"I can get nothing from you, then?"

"If you like to put it in that way." They were across the room together by this time, and when they reached the door Path opened it for the departure of his visitor.

"I am much obliged for your kindness in seeing me," said Gaunt, and as he went out he unconsciously half raised his hand to take that of the Home Secretary, but the latter did not appear to see it, and said coldly, "Good bye."

Gaunt went back to the office, pondering as to how much of his work he might reveal to Lodden.

[20 November 1913]

Chapter III.
The Adventures of Room 54.

Inkstained deal desks, paper-strewn floor, dusty blue-books on the long window-ledges, hats and coats flung pell-mell on the middle table, and a general air of hurried untidiness gave to expectant visitors an unsatisfying and disillusioning impression of the reporters' room of the *Daily Light*.

This, as they had been led to expect, was the rallying place of the group of men each of whom, as occasion demanded, would go forth to hunt down a murderer, to interview a princess, to extract secrets from the Foreign Office, or dash off at three hours' notice to join a battlefield half-way across the world; it was, so they had been told, the home of wit and adventure. And with these thoughts painting a highly-coloured picture, they would be introduced to a dull, begrimed, and littered room with commonplace written all over it.

When the door of the room was opened and visitors looked in, a dull-eyed, clean-shaven young man seated near the fire might look up from the evening newspaper with a glance entirely barren of expression and then go on reading again, as though the door had not been opened. Quite obviously uninterested and uninteresting, he would give an additional touch of dullness to the place. People always went away with the idea that the room was very much over-rated, and that there was really very little to see in it. Sometimes reporters would laugh to themselves about all this.

The work of the reporters united them in a singular, cheerful comradeship, and they made up a group which would have puzzled outsiders, for they carried beneath a certain rollicksomeness of demeanour many secret and tenacious aims. Frankness, coarseness, gibes for pretentiousness were to be found among them, and an unselfishness of which they were not in the least ashamed; and in their labours they exercised a levity which well-ordered people, regular subscribers to the *Daily Light*, would certainly have looked upon as reprehensible. It was impossible to make them really respectful, and those who were specially gifted with audacity used it always with a certain disturbing deliberateness. None of the reporters ever made the mistake of taking himself too seriously.

Rufton, after a hard day's work interviewing city stockbrokers, was in the middle of dinner one evening at a restaurant half-way down Fleet-street when he was fetched back to the office to write into a connected whole telegraphic fragments arriving from the north-east coast with regard to the distress among the workpeople springing from a Labour dispute. Rufton cursed violently when he got the message. He went back to the office, and learning that a long dramatic story was needed from him, sneered at the suggestion to the news editor's assistant, who had called him in.

"These local correspondents trying to make lineage, that's all it is. There's no story in it. Who did the damn fool idea come from? The chief sub-editor? I thought so. The wooden-headed automaton; just as a fellow is in the middle of his grub, too."

However, he took the pile of telegrams retired to the reporters' room and proceeded in a bad temper and with many mental wrestlings to turn out the column story required. That column, powerful and appealing, backed up by a leading article, subsequently brought in from all over the country £1,700 in unasked subscriptions from people who had been touched by it. But Rufton sent in his copy to the chief sub-editor with venomous maledictions, and he went back to the restaurant and was extremely nasty to the waiter because there was no Camembert cheese to finish up the second half of his belated dinner.

Young Adam was playing snooker-pool[16] at the club one evening when a peremptory telephone message from the *Light* took him over to do a personal sketch of the notorious American financier, P. W. Sluzerpump, who was arriving at Liverpool the next day. The office library provided him with cuttings about Mr. Sluzerpump's history, personal and financial, and also provided him with an excellent photograph. Guided by the cuttings and the picture, he turned out a character-analysis implying all that he dared not state, but making it clear that P. W. Sluzerpump was an unprincipled desperado of fabulous riches whose mission to this country was bound up with the project of extracting additional millions from a credulous public. That article, with its touch of exaggeration, was interesting reading, and the circulation of the *Light* took it into practically every home and office in the land. The result was that the financial operations of Sluzerpump in this country, despite excellent organisation and unstinted capital, did not run at all smoothly, and though he made a lot of money it was not nearly so much as he had determined upon. Mr. Sluzerpump had no misconception as to the origin of his failure. He estimated the loss resulting from the *Light*'s hostility at three-quarters of a million pounds.

After writing the article which set the campaign in motion young Adam went back to the club to continue his snooker-pool, and next day was very resentful. "I had won 15s. when they rang me up," he said, "and hang me when I went back I had lost the run somehow and couldn't put a ball down to save my life, and the result was that at half-past eleven, when I went to get my train I was 13s. out."

The barrack-like apartments of the reporters was on the second floor of the *Light*'s building, and the windows, which filled nearly the whole of one side of it, opened on to a rectangular courtyard whence arose all day the hoarse shouts of newsboys, the rattle of vans, and the snorting of motors – all engaged in the distribution of the *Evening Beacon*, the subsidiary organ of the *Light*, and published at intervals throughout the day. At the time of publication papers came flying out in thousands over the counters on the ground floor to a struggling, shouting brigade of boys and men, and for minutes at a time the courtyard would be like a pandemonium.

When to these noises was added the vibration of the printing presses at work in the basement beneath the building it is easy to understand that the reporters' room was not an ideal place for sustained and concentrated intellectual effort; and even the most hardened of the reporters permitted themselves a groan of rebellion at times – though they got through their work noise or no noise. The room itself was no more inspiring than its outlook; it measured about 25 feet by 20 feet, and was entered by a door on the other side from the windows. Five flat-topped bare desks were ranged along under the line of windows, two others were side by side in the corner of the room to the right of the door, and one was in the other corner on the left of the door. In the middle of the apartment was a big square table with polished surface, laden with coats and hats mixed up with walking-sticks and gloves – because the use of pegs was a lengthy operation only to entered upon on leisure occasions. If you had removed the higgledy-piggledy heap of coats and sticks from the table you would have found the surface scored with lines and circular marks which indicated a new game of shove ha'penny (improved from the regulation shove ha'penny) with which the members of the staff provided casual enjoyment for themselves during times of enforced idle waiting.

On the ledge above the fireplace was a narrow row of letter-boxes bearing the names of the reporters, and above this was a big green baize notice-board, on which appeared the general announcements of the news editor – bordered by cartoons and epithets. The walls, painted a pale and dirty blue, were variegated here and there with a railway map fastened up by stamp paper. Add the fact that the desks were always in littered confusion, with half-written copy, flimsy, pamphlets, unused letters from correspondents, and blank sheets of copy paper; that the floor was always carpeted with unused editions of the day's journals, and you have some idea of the room in which eight bright young men of the *Daily Light* brought most of their adventures to a culmination.

It was to this room that Majority Gaunt returned after his interview with the Home Secretary.

Gaunt was chief among the reporters, although he carried no distinctive title and although his salary was the same as that of two of his principal colleagues. He was 27, squarely built, with a face which was commonplace till you looked at it twice. Wavy chestnut hair, parted in the middle, surmounted a broad and bumpy forehead. His chin was firm, but his mouth was on the edge of weakness, rather loose, perhaps sensual. The best part of him was to be found in his eyes, which were clear grey (not blue), steady and reflective, with a latent humour in them. As he walked his head was canted a little forward, a habit of which he had in vain striven to correct himself. In his lazy periods, and they were very frequent, he was uninteresting; stir him to action, and you found why he was sent out by the *Daily Light* on the big emergencies.

An explanation should come here of one or two things in Majority Gaunt's personality; not that they were so markedly strange, but because they helped the development of events which will afterwards have to be chronicled. When not under the harrow of *Daily Light* worry, Gaunt had a mellow humour and a kindly sensitiveness which endeared him to many men and to nearly all women. He could be quickly moved, and if you had wiped away occasional outbreaks of selfish irritability he would have been summed up by the majority of his acquaintances as a man of much human attractiveness. "He can understand one so quickly," said Lady Brave, who was organising a charity sale, and her remark conveys a pretty good idea about Majority Gaunt. Of course, such a temperament was impressionable, and despite his busy life the flutter of a pretty woman's skirt was to him a flag of battle, and if one half-year found him engaged in an innocent but cruel flirtation, the next found him in a desperate intrigue which would have shaken the courage of more than one of his not too particular colleagues. In the course of time he obtained a reputation as a Lothario, but it was a Lothario of differing calibre and intensity.

This, then, was the man who spent a striving life for the *Daily Light*, and whose faults, what ever they may have been, were at any rate subordinate to his work.

When Gaunt hustled into the reporters' room the stout, red-faced Butler, with eye glasses balanced on the bottom of his nose, was writing industriously at the desk in the right hand corner and Wrightson, who, despite his untidiness, always wore a frock coat, was throwing a model aeroplane across the room in an endeavour to make it fly. Primrose, the gentle-mannered expert on criminal matters, sat on the left of the fireplace, with a glass of whisky and water by his side, and in his mouth a cigarette the end of which he had chewed to a pulp in his efforts to think out a form of words which would give to the public a secret which he had just received from Scotland Yard without letting the public know that it was Scotland Yard which had imparted it.

The door of the reporters' room was suddenly opened, and a boy looked in and glared round to see what reporters were present, and went out again.

"What was the meaning of that performance?" asked Butler.

"The meaning," said Wrightson, sententiously, as he dropped his magazine and disentangled his hat and coat from the heap on the table, "is that Dunlop, being in charge while Fore is engaged in the conference is suffering worry from callers as usual, and in accordance with custom he is seeking relief in the reporters' room. One of us has now got to see a bore of some description to get rid of him. I'm off."

Wrightson was barely away before the boy was back again. This time he came on and addressed Gaunt. "Please, sir. Mr. Dunlop says would you see this lady, Miss Carlisle, and if she's got nothing to say get rid of her, because she wants to talk politics." He held out the printed slip which all visitors have to sign before gaining access to any department in the *Daily Light*.

Gaunt glanced at the slip, saw that she business of the lady was 'political meeting,' sighed deeply, and said, "All right sonny; bring her up." He threw his cigarette into the fire and pulled out Wrightson's chair for easy access. Butler and Primrose turned themselves steadily to their work.

[21 November 1913]
Chapter III – Continued.
Enter Viola Cartlet.

Reporters' manners vary in the reception of strangers, and they adapt themselves intuitively to the call of the moment. When the boy came back and showed in an erect and graceful lady in autumn tweeds, Gaunt reared himself to the alertness of a man receiving gracious favours. Some message in the visitor's face and form and movement came home to him with swiftness. She might have been 28. She was slim and tall, the plainness of her dress suggesting rather than expressing her girlish figure, and her face, with squareness in it, was lighted with shining brown eyes, half inquiring, half wistful, as though a little doubtful of surroundings. She was not pretty, but her dark hair and dark complexion helped to make up a physical harmony. Without youth, she had yet some of the attributes of youth; and there was the call of beauty in her body. Gaunt was content with the knowledge that she was in communication with him, and within a second or two (so swift are the impulses of the feminist[17]) he found himself surmising as to whether at last he had met the one woman.

Pleasant courtesy was in his tone as he stepped forward to meet her with the usual falsehood. "I am sorry the editor is not in, but I am able to deal with any ordinary business that is required with regard to the news side of the paper. Perhaps you will be able to give me some indication –"

"It's a political matter I wanted to see him about. First of all, I wanted to let him know about a meeting." She unfastened her handbag in order to extract a leaflet.

"Won't you sit down?" said Gaunt, sweeping Wrighton's chair towards her. With a smile of thanks she accepted the offer and handed him the printed slip. It was about a meeting of protest against the Government's new activities.

She leaned forward with the colour rising in her cheeks, and Gaunt realised the exquisite texture of her skin. Life glowed through her soft features.

"We shall be in the thick of the fight," he said. "Of course, I can't commit the paper on details –"

"But what of this article of yours this morning? We can't understand it. We are all so keen on the *Light*, and we do so hope and pray for its help against the deadly ideas of the Government, and we are all so surprised this morning at your praise for Mr. Path. With this dreadful Bill coming we are all so anxious that he shouldn't be strengthened in the country, and it was because we feel so strongly on the whole thing that I came to tell you of our meeting, and to try and get your aid in making it into a really big affair. Really, I think it is sure to be that."

"We cannot condemn a man personally because of his political views or activities," said Gaunt, with an assumption of high calm judgment, "and this morning's article –"

"But it gave quite the wrong impression of Mr. Path. I assure you it did. Everybody knows he is really wrong. Whatever he does or says shows it."

"I am rather inclined to agree with you about this morning's article, but I don't think you need have any fear about the line we're going to take. As for your meeting, we shall certainly give it a good show. I can't very well say anything about booming it without consulting the editor, but I'll see him as soon as he comes in. I'll write you if you'll let me have your address."

Gaunt thought this a rather ingenious way of securing further communication with the lady, but he need not have bothered, because the lady herself had decided on a somewhat similar plan of action long before.

Of course, Gaunt had no intention of speaking to the editor. It would indeed have been disregarding duty to bother the great man about an enthusiastic lady. In the circumstances he might, however, go as far as to speak to the news editor about the political meeting, for the sake of an official assurance that a man would be sent to it.

"My address is 4, Cowdray-gardens, Hampstead.[18] From whom shall I expect to hear? The editor?"

"I think I'd better give you my card," said Gaunt, with an air of consideration. He produced his case and handed over a card, which the recipient, with a word of thanks, placed in her bag.

"I had thought of trying to see Mr. Lodden, but I know he is one of those great men who are protected by an army of secretaries, and I fear the editor would be almost an equally impossible person."

Gaunt never failed when evasion was required. "I'm afraid it's a poor compliment that you've been shown into the most untidy and dirty room in the office."

"All parts of a newspaper office are extremely interesting, I think," said the visitor, as she rose to go. "I have often thought I should like to see the interior of one."

"This is but a dirty corner of the workshop. If anyone is sufficiently keen we are always pleased to show what there is to be seen through out the building."

Gaunt was plunging into deep water, for among the many tasks of the reporters was that of avoiding requests from visitors to be allowed to see the office. Butler turned a quick sideways glance at the lady. There was expectancy and pleasure in her face. "I should love to see it. May I come some day?"

"Delighted if you would let me know any day."

Gaunt went with her along the passage to the left and on the way explained how it was best to come during the evening, for then it was that the machinery of organisation was in full swing. He had rung the bell for the lift, and it was ascending towards them when she said: "My husband will be so interested in this visit. You know he did not quite approve of my coming."

"Oh, yes."

Married, was she? Tricked and cornered, Gaunt had to bring an effort of will into play to preserve a pleasant, interested face.

"He though it unwise that I should write to Mr. Lodden the other day to use the *Daily Light* against Mr. Path's schemes. He was of the same opinion to-day about my calling on the editor. But if one feels very strongly about a thing I don't think relations ought to stand in the way."

"Yes, I quite understand," said Gaunt, grasping blindly for her meaning.

The lift was waiting and she stepped into it. She put out her hand. "Thank you so much for your kindness."

Gaunt went back to the reporters' room and after suffering a mild joke from Butler secured from his desk a slip of paper bearing the visitor's name. On it was written, "Mrs. Cartlet."

"All through that stupid Dunlop. Does 'Mrs. Cartlet' look like 'Miss Carlisle'?" He strode out to tell Dunlop about the result of his carelessness, and on his way down the corridor he overtook the news editor, who had just emerged from the conference.

"I've just had a lady up here entreating us to do justice to a Hampstead political meeting that's coming on."

"Hampstead? That's where some of Raston Path's people live."

They had reached the news editor's room by this time, and Dunlop, as they came in, looked up from his desk.

"Got rid of the lady politician, Gaunt?"

"Yes; but a pretty mess you made of it. Sent her in to me as Miss Carlisle, and I go and talk to her as a pleasant, attractive maiden, and find that she is a determined, married woman."

"What a funny chap you must be not to look at her name," said Dunlop. "I sent it in."

"I don't call that a really good defence."

"What's the trouble?" asked Fore.

"Oh, nothing," said Gaunt, "only my Hampstead lady was married instead of single, as I had been led to believe."

"Let's look at her name."

Gaunt handed over the slip, and Fore with a glance at it smiled rather unpleasantly.

"And neither of you recognised Mrs. Cartlet?"

"Mrs. Cartlet? Who's she?" asked Gaunt.

"She happens to be the sister-in-law of Raston Path, the Home Secretary."

"Oh, lummy; oh lor."

Fore went on turning over a pile of manuscript on his desk as though the announcement was of little or no interest. "Yes, that's all."

"Well, I'm hanged if I ever noticed her name," said Dunlop.

Gaunt rubbed his eyebrow with a finger. "But what does it mean? She may be a very bitter politician, and all that, and when people get carried away by their feelings they do startling things, but I should have thought no one who had a Cabinet Minister for a relation would have gone out of the way to run him down or to do him an injury."

"A simple mind is a great possession, unless you are in newspaper work," said Fore. "How would it strike you if you learned she had come here, not against her brother-in-law, but on his behalf?"

"Don't believe it."

"The trusting faith of a susceptible man has always been a barrier to truth. Why should she not come here to learn from the editor all there is to be known about the *Light*'s campaign against her brother-in-law? She asked to see the editor. Why did she not ask to see Archie? I know they have met, because I heard him say so a week or so ago, and they got on very well together. He, apparently, likes her. They were introduced at some reception or other. Now she comes here and asks for the editor. No, no; there is more in heaven and earth than is dreamed of in the reporters' room."[19]

[22 November 1913]

Chapter III – Continued.
Lodden's Methods.

It was unusual for a subordinate to seek the chief in his room, and only the push of great matters justified it; but Gaunt realised he had no choice this afternoon, and went down to the first floor to give Lodden some of the news of the day.

Fore shrugged his shoulders as Gaunt disappeared.

"Old Man's pretty rampageous this afternoon. Gaunt may catch it in the neck."

"Oh, Gaunt'll be all right," said Dunlop; "the Old Man likes him just now. He's in the midst of a little burst of favour."

"You never can tell," said Fore, with memories of his voice.

As a matter of fact, Gaunt had no trouble, for Lodden met him with a quick, cheery word, offered him a cigarette, and took a place with him in the big comfortable window seat.

"We've got a good deal of material already, Gaunt, but we've got to get more before we start. These extracts from Path's speeches during the war[20] are just the thing. We'll have them all printed again. There is some stuff coming in from abroad – not very strong but all in our line. Rayburn going around the clubs has got hold of some information about squabbles in the Cabinet. Path seems continually to be setting them by the ears, and some of them will be very glad to get rid of him. Lumley has seen Venture. Says he has found out Venture is against Path, but I am not sure. I almost wish I hadn't sent sent him. He's a pretty sharp man, Lumley, and the best foreign editor in London, and yet he is so full of bombast and talk about himself that he is dangerous in some things. What do you think of Lumley?"

"He's a man who ought to tread carefully among these Cabinet Ministers."

"Yes. I don't think he can do much harm, though. He is no fool."

"I've come down to tell you I've seen Path to-day."

"Path, eh?"

"Tried him on the straight line of giving us an idea of his new Bill. He wouldn't hear of it."

"I cannot understand that," said Lodden pleasantly.

"He would not be persuaded at all. He was very kindly and nice to me."

Lodden lowered his brows a little.

"Be very careful with the man. Don't you let Path's civility get in your way."

"I don't think there's any fear."

"Don't you underrate Path, like a good many people do. He's pretty well a genius. We are hard up against him now, and he will know that soon, even if he does not already, and his civility is never thrown away. Let me tell you that."

Gaunt nodded his head assentingly at this little outburst, and then he said, "I've got the new Bill."

"How much of it?" snapped Lodden.

"The whole." He rapidly ran off the main points.

Lodden's head was thrust eagerly forward. "That finishes him. We have him now." He stopped to think for a second. "Does he know you've got the thing?"

"Not a suspicion."

"I thought you told me he refused?"

"So he did, but I had a chance –"

"Wait a minute. I don't think I want to hear particulars of your work."

He sprang up and walked quickly and heavily over to the chimney-piece and rested his arm on it, and then surveyed Gaunt as though to get a bird's-eye view of him. His manner was severe.

"I must warn you against anything underhanded. Follow me? The paper must not be prejudiced. I won't tolerate anything, mind you."

His chin was thrust forward bullyingly. He had suddenly become the accuser.

"There must be none of that. Anything you do you must stand by. I should disclaim you publicly if serious actions came to light which showed you had behaved wrongly."

"I understand that perfectly."

Lodden relaxed again. "I cannot afford any other kind of arrangements, you know."

Gaunt was a little disturbed at this repudiation, and wondered what would come of it. But he put the thing from him for a moment, and passed on to his fresh news for Lodden.

"Mrs. Cartlet called here this afternoon."

Lodden lifted his head and opened his eyes wide.

"Mrs. Cartlet?"

"Yes, she came here about a big political meeting to-morrow up at Hampstead. She's interested in it and wants us to give it a boom. She's very bitter against her brother-in-law."

"Why was I not informed?" asked Lodden harshly.

Gaunt was surprised at his tone, and explained that he had seen the lady, and treated her request sympathetically, and had promised to do what he could.

"Of course you did. That is only politeness to Mrs. Cartlet. But why was I not told she was here? Why was she not brought down to me?"

"I had no impression that you –"

"What, the sister-in-law of the Home Secretary! Mrs. Cartlet, who is fighting against him! She is brave enough to come here about it, and then you do not show her the compliment of telling me, or letting me know she is here and bringing her down to me. Can't you see the importance of it? Can't you see what we have missed?"

The words cascaded from him. He did not gesticulate, but the forward poise of his body and the swiftness with which he spoke gave the impression that he might even strike Gaunt.

Gaunt cut in determinedly. "She told me she had written you a few days ago, and that you had not answered her letter. That was a pretty plain indication. In the face of it I thought I ought not to bother you with her."

"Written me?"

"Yes: wrote you on the same thing."

"I have had no letter."

"She said it was two or three days ago."

Lodden pressed an electric bell, and St. Just, one of his two secretaries, came in from the adjoining room.

"Do you remember a letter coming from Mrs. Cartlet a few days ago?"

St. Just thought for a moment. "Yes," he said, "yesterday morning. I put it with the others. There are so many of them begging political help that I don't trouble you with them unless they are very special."

"Not answered?"

"It isn't possible to answer them all."

"Do you realise who Mrs. Cartlet is?"

"She is some relation of Raston Path, I think."
"Oh, you know that, do you? Do you understand what that means?"
St. Just looked up full of inquiry.
"It means that she is a very important political person. You have snubbed Mrs. Cartlet. The thing is almost inconceivable, but that's what you have done."
"I am very sorry if –"
"Fetch in Brown."

Brown was St. Just's colleague in secretarial work, a young man of quiet manners and deferential aspect. He came in wonderingly.

"Brown," said the Chief, "St. Just has ignored a letter received yesterday from Mrs. Cartlet. Passed it over as of no account, and told me nothing about it. That means he is quite lacking in judgment. This is so grave a break that I shan't feel safe with him here any longer. From to-day you will take over his duties. Make out a cheque to St. Just for £150 – that is three months' salary – and he can leave at once. St. Just, you had better take a long holiday and brace yourself up again. Now, all of you go."

He drove all of them out of the room with a gesture suggesting the hurrying of fowls out of a garden. When he was alone he took some of his private dainty notepaper from a drawer and wrote a short letter to Mrs. Cartlet. This, one may suppose, was the right thing to do after a breach of etiquette. Later a boy came in to collect the letters for the post and took up the one addressed to Mrs. Cartlet. "Leave that," said Lodden, "I'll post it myself."

[24 November 1913]

Chapter IV.
Two of the Fighters.

The dominance of great souls will always be one of the fascinating mysteries for us. Certain men flash before their generation like passing meteors in the sky, coming from one knows not where, and disappearing into outer darkness perhaps to startle fresh ages. They are always potent for good or evil, these men, and they attract and disturb to a degree disproportionate to their seen energies; and within them are subtle motive forces unknown to themselves. Their aims are often not clear, and it is safe to say that in the storm of intense feeling which they arouse, and which envelope them, there is always an apparent preponderance of hate. Raston Path at forty-two was one of these man-forces.

A bright boy of sixteen, Raston Path had been articled to a firm of highly respectable solicitors in the City of London, and in between the times he was lapping up the knowledge necessary for his examination he was feasting eagerly on books in general. Ardent as well as keen, young Path found his work but a daily incident, and his heart and mind were always panting for fresh kingdoms.

Such a young fellow could hardly escape an interest in politics, and soon he was busy in social study. His focus point rapidly became the joylessness and struggles of the poor and the semi-poor. With the quick eye of imagination he perceived that background of dull labour and sordidness, with the deeper shadows of suffering, which lay spread behind the more endurable life of the minority.

As knowledge grew upon him he became touched with a burning impatience, with the sting of anger. Then he set himself steadily and arduously to understand things. He strove for an acquaintance with the actuality of poverty. He saturated himself in Local Government Blue Books, worked during night in the slums, secured invitations to workhouses, attended London police courts, visited Salvation Army[21] shelters, and made night tours along the Thames Embankment. The work became a passion. The outline of formal political economy had been his from boyhood, and a devotion to modern history and the biographies of the last two hundred years had given him a certain bookish basis of understanding. He became engrossed by the human side of study. Faced as he was by those flesh-and-blood problems which shake the faith of so many young persons in Christianity, make the wage-earner callous to all but the requirements of the week, and lead the comfortable middle-class to the placid and settled assertion that the poor we have always with us,[22] Path was very soon in the thick of political discussion. His youthful scorn of the comfortably placed in life, his white-hot sympathy for the undertrodden millions made him a firebrand, and his name began to be mentioned frequently in the newspapers. Then his employers began to protest against his vagaries. The concluding period in the city office was a stormy time for Path; life in its fullness was coming upon him like a vision, and he knew himself to be at the entrance of a field of activity whence came an irresistible call. Many people were already interested in him. His gifts had lifted him into a public man before he was yet at a man's legal age.

When Path was out of his articles, his brother, a mild-mannered man ten years his senior, who was himself a solicitor, offered him a salaried position, and Raston accepted it, and for nearly a couple of years devoted a strenuous energy to his brother's work, in which his touch of genius served well and profitably. For a time he dropped public speaking, and gave his spare hours to reading and presently to the formation of practical schemes for the relief of some of the evils which are the curse of the poor in town life – sketchy outlines, with many practical defects, but bold and sweeping in conception, and of a kind to make the moderate reformer's hair stand on end.

It is not possible to know with certainty, but it may be guessed that during this period Path began to nurse the idea of getting into Parliament. Probably he had dreams, and saw himself engaged in a lifelong fight at Westminster against the triple-headed foe of arrogance, self-contentment, and officialdom. It is not likely that his ambitions were very definite, because up to a certain period he was quite single-minded, fanatical if you like, but entirely without the taint of self-seeking or the desire for personal advancement except as machinery for promoting his ideas.

Even without the irruption of the Roumanian War,[23] it is certain that he would have emerged sooner or later, because it is now quite obvious that short of physical dissolution nothing could have prevented Raston Path coming out before his fellows. The war, however, was the first means of bringing his personality to general notice. It proved the turning point, perhaps it would be more correct to say the starting point, of his life.

The passion that swept the country at the time of the Roumanian War will never be forgotten by those who lived through the period, because modern opportunities for expression (due to the spread of elementary education and the popularising of the Press) gave facilities hitherto unknown for the manifestation of the war spirit. The merits and mistakes of our statesmen, the wisdom or folly, the morality or immorality of the campaign, all went for nothing as soon as the country was face to face with an enemy in the field. All consideration of policy or party politics were swept from the mind of the common people as they saw regiment after regiment of stalwart, high-spirited young fellows marching through London streets to Waterloo Station on their way to Southampton, going to fight their country's battle in a foreign land. The casual labourer from slumland, the city clerk, the wife of the working man, the schoolboy, the man who tended cows and horses on the farm, the prosperous barrister, the indolent son of a wealthy family, one and all were carried along in this great tide of feeling. Over every part of the land the war flamed. The newspapers fanned it, public meetings added fuel, and in exaltation men came forward in their hundreds and thousands to shoot and ride, to toil, to suffer wounds and die. There was something at once frightening and elemental about the feeling which enveloped town and countryside. One could no more argue against it than one could argue against the ebb and flow of tides.

Raston Path, prejudiced by a belief built up by newspaper study in the months of the negotiations, decided that there had been arrogance in the hearts of British statesmen, that the fierce, encroaching attitude of our Foreign Office was due to the realisation of our overwhelming power against a few thousands of people, and was convinced that ethically the Roumanians had the right of the dispute. He thrilled at the thought of a great nation like Britain establishing injustice by force. It was poison to him that the natural patriotism of the multitude would be stirred by a wicked cause, and the fact that no one to speak of should trouble to understand things set his nerves on edge. And thus it came about that he stood apart from the crowd and looked on at the state of England with something like fury. He girded himself for a task. Throwing up his legal work and his chance of a business career, content in the knowledge of a small private income of £200, he went forth to meet the whirlwind. He quickly joined himself in the protests of the scattered few, moved by his own beliefs, who were proclaiming their horror at the prevalent enthusiasm, and denouncing the war as oppressing, cowardly, wicked, who scoffed at the watchword, "My country, right or wrong."[24]

Raston Path's wanderings, his scarifying eloquence, his reckless charges, are now more or less a matter of history. Within a few moths he was leader of the Anti-War party, and he made himself execrated throughout the length and breadth of the land. His meetings were broken up, he was mobbed many times, and on one occasion was thrown down and trampled on in the street. He gloried in the hatred, and something of the madness of the martyr laid ahold upon him. Here and there he found frenzied support, but the people were a hundred to one against him, and eventually rage reached such a pitch that it was with difficulty he could say half a dozen words on a public platform.[25]

Thereupon he took to appearing at meetings where he had not been previously announced, preached his doctrines in the parks and at street corners, and by means of lurid letters sent to the papers.

With all and through all, hounded, detested, loathed, he could not be ignored. He had that gift of searing words and a ruthless disregard for consequences which always play their part in keeping a man in the forefront. Before the war was over he was a public character. In times to come, when the campaign was being written of in history books, people recalled the fact that Raston Path in his advocacy of peace had succeeded in proving himself the bitterest and most relentless of fighters. Unknown to himself, those years of turmoil; and struggle of heavy blows unflinchingly received and as cruelly returned, of that dare-devil pleading for peace against the religious upholding of the war, Raston Path was in himself proving that the ability to fight is the ability to govern, and the ability to live. During that terrible two and a half years he spared neither friend nor foe, and succeeded in laying the foundation of his subsequent position. His gifts were developed and he brought to a fine edge a native persistence and a savage gift of exposition in the face of the enemy; barbed repartee hung ever on his tongue. And in soft moments before calmer audiences he perfected that swift, low-voiced, human appeal which a quarter of a century later was still one of his greatest instruments. The experiences he went through would have crushed most enthusiasts, but there was something stronger and harder in Raston Path than finds expression in the public emotionalist, and the rebuffs and denunciations with which he was assaulted politically and personally helped to harden and solidify subtle qualities – which in any case would never have been entirely repressed while his physical life persisted. He emerged from the conflict a stronger, steadier man, armed for the great occasions.

Contempt and hate and scorn surged round the mention of Path towards the end of the war, and when the campaign was brought to a successful conclusion nine-tenths of the electors would have judged him a foolish extremist who would never be heard of again. Very wrong would they have been in this judgment. He had become, willy-nilly, the most prominent of that little band of Reds – doctrinaires, faddists, and young spirits who are always to be found the extremest critics of moderate forces of progress and who court unpopularity like a mistress. How much bigger was Raston Path than his friends and colleagues was to be shown later, when he sought public favour as deliberately and ruthlessly as he had faced public hatred for the promotion of his ideals.

The greater the soul of the man, the more complex its operations, the more difficult it is to analyse or define; and it is impossible to say when ambition for power began to mingle in the thoughts and aspirations of Raston Path. Long, long before he had seen visions and dreamed dreams of great changes in the life of the common people, and now that he had come to know dominance, of his ability to sway his associates with vitalizing persuasion, he could not possibly fail to see that opening out before him were great avenues of achievement. In a word, Raston Path was feeling himself. By the time public attention was directed toward him he had his gaze on vistas which would have caused even his associates bewilderment. When, therefore at a by-election in the remote north of Scotland a little band of Reds put him forward as a candidate in opposition to the wealthy Authoritarian who represented the Government, he calmly but quickly accepted the invitation. The Authoritarians claimed that the moderate Progressive usually opposed to the Government would on this occasion support the Government's candidate against the furious young Red, anti-patriot and reckless breaker-down of institutions. To the general surprise, Raston Path was returned by a large majority, and for the first time gave evidence to those who did not appreciate him previously of the personal driving force which was in him.

"They say I do not love my country," he cried to the exultant crowd roaring their joy at his return outside the Town Hall, where the figures were announced. "I love my country better than those who would send her poorest sons to fight and suffer and then, on their return, allow them to starve in the streets or the garret."

[25 November 1913]

Chapter IV – Continued.
Battles in Parliament.

In the House of Commons Raston Path had his place below the gangway[26] on the Progressive side, and within a week of entry into Parliament was making a reputation.

From the first he set himself to learn all the forms and ceremonies, and, as others had done before him, he rapidly forged them into a weapon of attack. His deference to precedent and regulation was but the House of Commons cover for the most dare-devil defiance that ever livened up the floor of Parliament.

He assailed the Government leaders and the Opposition leaders on small matters and great, on points of order, at question time, and in set debate. Always was he in his place in the corner seat below the gangway, always ready with vitriolic comment or stabbing suggestion. Many times was he howled down in the House, and his rebuffs were so severe that to a man thinking only of self-advancement they would have been deadly. But it was Path's strength that insults and epithets left him unstaggered and generally untouched so long as he was making his protest on behalf of the beliefs which possessed him. His natural gifts lent him weapons available equally for offence and defence, and very soon he was standing up without fear to veteran statesmen a great part of whose life had been spent in acquiring the power of trampling down inconvenient friends and enemies.

Extreme was the delight of the Reds at the presence and action of this young politician – and there were always a dozen or so to shout their joy when Path was baiting a Minister and, where possible under the rules of the House, covertly insulting him.

The little band of political desperadoes cheered him loudest of all when, as sometimes happened, he was argumentatively crushed and derided and held up to Parliamentary ridicule, when he was shown to be wrong in his facts, mistaken in his ethics, unreliable in his conclusion. Always Raston Path pushed on. With an overriding passion on behalf of the poorer classes, a withering hatred of the complacency among the upper sections of society, he united an unfailing bitterness about the recent war. After a time it began to be easier for him to gain a hearing on the campaign and he did not fail to turn the fact to account. Some young members are afraid to play the part of gladiator early in Parliamentary life, but Raston Path allowed no such mistake to mar him.

From the first he flung himself body and soul into conflict; he made a dead set at the strongest man in Parliament, Jasper Bolum, the Foreign Secretary, whose negotiations had led up to the war, who had prosecuted it with so much vigour, and who had defended his action in Parliament and out of Parliament with a sardonic ability which had lifted him to a place prominent in modern political history. Bolum's cold, clean-shaven face reflected power. In the House of Commons he was feared as well as respected. He had been known to bring down without mercy his own Ministerial colleagues; to cause the political ruin of a minor opponent was no more to him than the shooting of a rabbit.

This was the man on whom Path fixed with a strange mixture of idealistic revenge, ambition, and hatred. Quickly Bolum tried to crush presumption; and twice in one week he turned savagely on Path and held the young man up to ridicule. Raston Path hung on to him undeterred. Bolum, after this whenever he could spare a few sentences for scornful asides, made clear Raston's womanish spite, his hatred of his own country, and his unceasing desire for notoriety. Raston Path still hung to his quarry. Bolum used to lean back on the Treasury Bench when Raston Path was speaking, and his eyes would behalf-closed, with not a trace of interest in his face, and his whole attitude that of one who is tired with a minor bore.

One night he lay like this while Path accused him of a hundred faults and wickednesses in connection with the war, charged him with self-seeking, even charged him with prolonging the war for the purpose of profiting his own family, who were manufacturers of war munitions. Later in the debate Bolum spoke.

"There is some difficulty," he said with slow, intense disgust, "in comprehending the kind of mind a man must have in order to charge a statesman of the British empire with carrying on a war for the sake of the pockets of his relatives. But that type of mind does exist. The hon. member who sits below the gangway has that type of mind."

The words had to be heard to get the full measure of contempt that lay in them, and a singing hiss of approval went up from the ranks of Authoritarians behind him. "I now propose," said Bolum, in a tone of mingled scorn and dignity, "to tell the full story in connection with the war."

"For the first time," jeered Raston Path.

The audacity was so colossal that just for a moment the usually unshaken composure of Bolum was overthrown.

"You cad," he said sharply.

Gone henceforth was the air of boredom, of indifference to insults. The episode made Raston Path an interesting man in all newspapers, and set members of the house discussing him in the Lobbies as a person who could dare deliberately to shake his fist at the Foreign Secretary.

When the Progressives came into power five years later the pawky[27] Scotsman who formed the government dared not leave off his list the brilliant, eloquent, and regardless young Red below the gangway, and Raston Path accepted the subordinate post of Under-Secretary for the Colonies. He soon made the position an important one. Sometimes he joined in debate when he was not expected to do so, and he upheld the side of the Government with the same power and ferocity with which he had in past years on occasion attacked it.

Under-Secretaries are expected to hold their tongues except on allotted occasions, but Raston Path did not keep the rule. True, he used some discretion, but his was not the nature to be diverted to the mere answering of Parliamentary questions for ten minutes each day; and the Prime Minister, quick to recognise talent which would not be repressed, set him from time to time to the task of defending the Government in debate on matters of principle. Path always filled the House, and his reputation increased swiftly.

At a critical period of unpopularity of the Government he toured the Northern counties with withering speeches against the Authoritarians, with impassioned argument for Progressives, especially the extreme Progressives. He pursued his travels along a trail of excitement. A storm of mingled acclamation and fury heralded his arrival at any centre, and his departure left behind a leaping fervour on the one side and something like virulence on the other. With his increasing power had come a deepening of the note of hostility on the part of the Authoritarians, and he had reached a point when, though only an Under-Secretary he was the most-abused politician of the day. Such a man could not long be kept out of the Cabinet, and on the death of Sir Charles Brunnen, President of the Board of Trade, he was given the post.

From now onwards Raston Path was the moving spirit of the Government, and it says much for the strength of his ideals, as well as for his personal power, that they gave him tenacity to force onwards so strongly the more moderate elements in the Cabinet. That he did so was evident from the measures which began to be pressed from that time forward. Raston Path would not have been human if a sense of ambition had not been mingling in his strangely composite impulses, and with all his boyish exultation over immediate ends he had his eye on the acquisition of power – and still more power.

Such a personality as that of Path was necessarily at times a trouble and a deterrent, as well as an inspiration, to a Cabinet of 20, which included strong-headed and stout-hearted men who had themselves proved their stiffness by an upward lifelong fight. But the flashing genius of Raston Path could not be kept under. Rapidly the time arrived when in a rearrangement of Cabinet posts he was offered the important portfolio of the Home Office by the Prime Minister. He had been Home-Secretary for about a year when Archibald Lodden decided on his campaign.

Path's elder brother, a successful man of business with no deep interest in politics, was in general sympathy with Raston's humanitarian ideals, and it was with him and his wife that the young politician found the peace and comfort of a home in the intervals of his early warfare. Mrs. Path was a delicate woman with white face, small features, and black hair, who said very little, who understood a good deal, and had the gift of getting her own way unsuspected by those who loved her. Behind a deep placidity she had the intensest sympathies. She was proud of Raston and his progress and his thoughts and his aims in a way she had never put into words. She had mothered him, sometimes stimulated him, and never failed in troublous times with soft and almost silent sympathy. Raston was deeply grateful then and throughout his life, and Hilda Path to him was at once all that was gracious and sweet and helpful in mother and sister.

In view of this affectionate relationship and all it meant to Raston Path, it is of more than passing interest that Hilda's younger sister, Viola, disliked him, and had an aversion to him which grew as time went on. No deep reason or formal cause lay behind the antipathy, and any close acquaintance of Path and his younger sister-in-law would have been able to forecast the sentiments of both when they came into contact, would have known of Raston's indifference and Viola's innocent pique and not very serious prejudice. It may be doubted, however, whether the most sympathetic and far-seeing of friends would have anticipated the strength of Viola's ultimate anger and how far she would be carried in the field of protest.

[26 November 1913]

Chapter IV – Continued.
A Woman of Prejudice.

Viola was a dozen years younger than her sister Hilda, and possessing something of her charm, together with a more aggressive physical fascination of her own, had, besides, a vivacity and a dominating temperament which occasionally brought her little humiliations as well as a great amount of admiring deference. She had not been carried into touch with Raston until comparatively late in his career, when he was a member of the Government, and she had worked herself up to a state of lively curiosity beforehand.

Drawn from a well-to-do middle-class family, the head of which, after making money by the establishment of a wholesale tea business, had given himself up to the promotion of legitimate and successful companies. Viola had acquired in what she would have called the better-class circles of Hampstead, a horror of anything that was low or "bad form," and under the ban of her disdain quite naturally fell those whose politics were not of the gentlemanly kind. While a Progressive was not considered a worthy person at all, a Red was just an uneducated, violent individual, who had no real place in social comity. With as little knowledge of books as of life she would treasure up stray comments from sympathetic acquaintances, and hurl them with a delightful air of finality at anyone who ventured to suggest such a stupid doctrine as that which assumed that the physical life of the family who supported life on 30s. a week might be harder than the life of the family supported on £80 a week, or assumed that there was at least some doubt as to the advantages of a prepondering power in hereditary government.

"Read the History of Rome,"[28] she would say. "That is what I would seriously advise you to do. You'll see things clearer then."

She had married an accountant in the City, a kindly man inclined to stoutness, who loved a peaceful life above all things, with but the scantiest feeling for politics – though his preferences, as was to be expected, were on the side of the Authoritarians. He used to smile at his wife's enthusiasm, indulge her many whims, and by the time Raston Path took office had humorously threatened her with an introduction to her raging brother-in-law. She began to desire it presently.

After all, he was something of a celebrity, and there could be no doubt that he was personally acquainted with those who were really great, such as the leading dukes, and he must occasionally be asked to royal functions, even if it were only by virtue of his official position. There could be no doubt either that he was a very interesting man personally, and she began to be certain that she would like to meet him. And so, presently, with the help of Hilda, who smiled at learning her sister's desire, Raston was brought within the orbit of the Cartlets.

It has to be chronicled that Raston was not at all interested in the fact that the Cartlets were interested in him, and he treated Viola with that exact degree of courteous friendliness becoming to their relationship.

Vaguely, deep within her, Viola was disturbed, although she could not have told the reason even to herself just then. Curiosity and annoyance were all commingled within her, and in order to talk with Raston she began to listen with more attention still to the political comments of her friends and tried to get a grip of their opinions. After this, as occasion offered, she laid some of her views before Raston, and she succeeded in rousing him from a certain abstraction to mild amusement. These statements of hers were delivered with all the conviction of profound, unshakeable judgments. They were the currency of the suburban train passenger.

"Ah, if our principal opponents would argue like you," said Raston, once with genuine wish in his tone.

That was in the initial period, when Viola saw in his remark nothing but a pleasant compliment.

"It seems to me," she would say with seriousness and much feeling, "that all Progressive legislation leads to one end, the destruction of the monarchy."

"It is difficult to judge these things with any certainty," said the polite Under-Secretary.

"The pampering of the lower classes," she would remark, "is destroying the fibre of the nation. They think it wrong to pay respect to their superiors now. That is surely a sign we are going down."

"There is perhaps something in what you say," mildly commented Raston. A second's pause, during which Viola would try to read the thoughts of the Under-Secretary, and then Raston would say, "May I trouble you for another cup of tea?" a request which would be followed by a little laugh from Hilda.

It was not long before Viola began to understand the position she occupied in Raston's outlook, and to see how much weight he attached to her political reflections. Dislike is somewhat too crude a word to express the feeling which sprung up, but she had a certain unpleasant nagging fear that she did not understand him. That fear is an awful thing to a high-spirited woman who is dealing with a man. And thus it happened that Viola Carlet, expressing repeated and vehement verdicts on Raston's opinions to her husband, began to dread meeting him as much as she had once looked forward to it. She made politics into a minor passion. She began to frequent the society of those more capable than herself of putting Authoritarian beliefs into words, and became a member of the local Authoritarian Society. Raston, who was in blank forgetfulness of Mrs. Cartlet directly he was out of her presence, laughed wholeheartedly when Hilda told him of these things.

"You have made yourself a real enemy there," she said.

"Alas, alas," he said, with a deep sigh, "another is added to the list."

It was all very well for the Under-Secretary to treat the matter thus lightly, but to Viola it was a very real thing indeed.

[27 November 1913]

Chapter V.
The Moods of Viola.

Viola Cartlet went home to Hampstead after her visit to the *Daily Light* office stimulated by her new experience and with a vague sense that she had accomplished something. She hummed a song to herself as she went up to her room to change her dress for the more or less informal dinner – which was always ready fifteen minutes after her husband's return from business in the evening. He was not yet in. Viola looked from her windows along the country-like, tree-lined suburban road, and felt very nearly content with her lot in life. She wondered why she was so happy. Elation was hers.

When George Cartlet came in, she began to tell him about her journey to Fleet-street as soon as she had helped him to take off his overcoat. At dinner-time she was filled with the subject.

"I suppose he was a sub-editor, or something of that kind, but he was very interesting. They are going to send up to the meeting. I am so glad! Somehow I feel as if I were in league with the paper, and it's such a nice, powerful kind of feeling. I'll show Raston Path we're not to be despised."

"You'll make him dislike you if you're not careful."

"He knows very well I hate him, and I don't care a bit. Everyone can see perfectly well that he's trying to ruin the country. What I'm so glad about is that the *Light* is taking it up. Would you mind if I asked that sub-editor here sometimes?"

"As you please, my girl. Don't expect too much from him, that's all. These newspaper men are bound to be pleasant, but they haven't always the power of doing things. Of course, he had to be nice to you."

"Oh, but he's not an ordinary man at all. You don't a bit understand. I shall ask him over one Sunday afternoon. Then you'll see."

"All right. I'll have a look at him."

"I've got a presentiment, and my presentiments always come true – you say so yourself. I believe that man is going to be a good deal mixed up in my life. I believe it's fate."

"What another of them!" George Carlet proceeded to turn over the evening paper to find out the progress of the billiard match between Stevenson and Gray.[29]

After dinner he spent an hour with his paper and a French novel in the snug little room he called his study, and Viola left him to go to the drawing-room, and there, seated at the piano, she crooned to herself a sentimental little song called "Waiting."

Undisciplined except by the convenances, impatient for approval, with the currents of passion running strong within her, Viola Cartlet waded deep in sentiment. Children might have saved her, but she had no children; serious trouble might have saved her, but she had not that either. She looked eagerly for great experiences – and she was ready attuned for the heaven she had hitherto missed. She had married at 20 under the pressure of Cartlet's desire and her family's preference, but she had never loved her husband in the romantic way, though she had tried to think she had, and his cheery take-it-for-granted manner was gall to her. When he laughed at some flicker of her sentimental imaginings she told herself he did not understand, and resumed her search into the unknown.

She was 28, and in the course of her married life had amassed tendernesses for several men, and had been prepared to dwell much on one or two of them in memory till Majority Gaunt came her way.

She had a real uplifting at the sight of Gaunt; he touched some elemental chord in her – perhaps some part of them had met in previous ages, she said to herself, but it was only a part. She answered the call gladly, joyfully, and revelled in the freshness and originality of Gaunt, in the vigour that lay with him; at the first meeting she had seen more of the man than he ever knew.

Her eyes were on vacancy as she touched the keys of the piano and sung her ditty, and she gave a little shudder as the sharp ring of the door-bell told of the postman delivering the last letters. A maid came in with an envelope on a tray, and Viola felt her heart jumping quickly as she saw that the letter was addressed in strange writing. She almost snatched at it. Down with a plunge into depression she went as she found it was a courteous note of apology from Archibald Lodden with regard to her call at the office of his newspaper; she was to be sure if ever she came again to ask for him; he was distressed at the fact that he was not informed of her presence that afternoon, and assured her that if the paper could give any assistance in her political work he should be very pleased.

At any other time Viola Cartlet would have been glad and a little flattered by such a letter, but now she was in the deeps of disappointment. She rang for the maid.

"Was that all, Parker?"

"There was a letter for Mr. Cartlet."

The maid had hardly spoken before Cartlet came in, pipe in mouth, carrying a letter in his hand.

"Here is something from Hilda. It is for you, not me. Parker thought 'Mrs.' was 'Mr.' Lucky it was none of your secrets."

He smiled as he held out the letter.

Viola was disappointed, but a touch of interest came into her eyes as she read: –

> My dear Viola, – This is just a private word to tell you not to become too closely mixed up with political things just for the moment. There is going to be unpleasantness for everybody, and it is just as well you and I should keep out of it. You are so impetuous, dear, and knowing how keen you are against Raston I do not want you to be led into any active part just now. I have been told in confidence – and you must not let a word of this get round – that Archibald Lodden is setting out on a desperate fight to ruin Raston, and has already got a little army of men at work trying to rake up things to injure him. Of course, I do not know, but I feel sure Raston will certainly make some kind of an attempt to expose Lodden, for he is not Christian enough to turn the other cheek to the smiter.[30] I dare say there will be all kinds of scandal getting about, so do please, Viola, keep your enthusiasm down for a little. I am so afraid of your becoming mixed up in these things. This afternoon I heard about your Authoritarian meeting at Hampstead, and I am told that in connection with it there will be a lot of excitement. Lodden is going to make it the opening of his campaign, and Raston has already laid a trap for him there ... Keep clear of these politics for a while, there's a dear. You will guess how serious it all is when I tell you that Raston regards Lodden as a danger to the country, and is going to try and stop him, whatever that may mean. Charlie says it will be a real big fight between them ... Can you come over to tea with George on Sunday afternoon? ... Is the cold better now? Baby has been troublesome to-day – I think it is another tooth.
>
> All my love, dear, – Yours,   Hilda
>
> P.S. – Please don't go to that meeting to-morrow night at all.

"Hilda seems frightened about nothing," said Viola.

"I don't know about that."

"What nonsense about not going to that meeting! Of course I shall go."

"There's something in it. Of course, really what she says comes from Raston Path himself – just a friendly word of caution."

"Raston Path – what right has he to interfere? I never heard such a thing."

"But there is no harm."

"No harm? I assure you I don't intend that he shall dictate what I shall do or what I shall not do. Why, you don't want that, George, do you?"

Cartlet shrugged his shoulders good-humouredly.

"Please yourself," he said. "I should go slow if I were you. There's trouble brewing, that's plain."

"Oh, but I am not going to cut off all my friends and interests. I have just got an awfully nice letter from Lodden. Look here."

She held it out to him.

"That's very decent."

"I certainly don't intend to be frightened by Hilda."

Cartlet handed the letter back.

"My word, old girl, you do attract all of them, don't you?"

"All of them?"

"Well, all except, of course, Raston Path."

"Oh, he doesn't count!" she said seriously.

Viola went to bed filled with the thought of the Authoritarian meeting, and of the fact that Majority Gaunt was coming to it.

The political meeting on which Viola Cartlet had spent so much enthusiasm beforehand was really nothing out of the common, and the audience who cheered the prospective candidate, and the prospective candidate who addressed his partisan hearers with fluent, fetish phrases, were not very stimulating to a man like Gaunt, who knew public meetings by heart.

Gaunt's thoughts had been following the great scoop of the day and the methods by which it would be followed up to-morrow, and so far as he could see the only topical interest of the Hampstead meeting lay in the references made to the *Daily Light* and its work. Apart from and beyond the work of his paper he had a pleasant tingling in him at the thought of meeting Mrs. Cartlet, for he knew quite well that she was looking forward to the encounter.

Viola, indeed, was expectant, but how much she was expectant she herself would have found difficult to say. That she would see this young man from Fleet-street was, as she quite frankly explained to her husband, a point with her, because, after all, she met so few interesting people. And as an acquaintance he really was interesting, but her feelings went very much further than she acknowledged even to herself, and she really had almost forgotten the order of the proceedings which she had helped to arrange – first of all, the speech from the chairman; then the "few words" from Mrs. Lumley Thornton-Thornton, the authoress, and after that the candidate. At one time she had been feverishly concerned with the whole business and particularly anxious that Mrs. Thornton-Thornton should have the opportunity to discharge some of her sharpened epigrams into the thick hide of the Home Secretary. Now that the evening of the meeting was here she had somehow lost her enthusiasm. Well for her that none of her suburban friends could know her mind or realise her happy thoughts and inclinations.

Majority Gaunt came in while the people were gathering and Viola at once led him from the little table where several local reporters were placed and gave him a chair on the platform. He insisted on being at the back, so she arranged for him to have a seat on the third row and asked him to guard the next chair because she wanted to come and sit beside him to see how "a real newspaper man actually did his work." She had a gracious appeal about her. Colour was high in her cheeks. The mass of her glossy hair reflected the electric light. She moved with a quick little stride of decision and grace. Foolish Majority Gaunt felt his heart beat a little quicker as he watched her talking to friends with the knowledge that she was coming to sit by him presently. What would have been his feelings had he known that she was thinking of him all the time – that her departure from him, her conversation with others, were labour to her, that she sought nothing but to sit by him, near him.

It was five minutes to eight when she came up with a smile and took the chair next to him, and it was eight o'clock when the chairman rose to open the meeting. Two or three people were on each side of them, but as they were in the third row of the platform none was behind them. Perhaps this was fortunate on the whole, because it would have been impossible to conceal the fact that their minds were but spasmodically and at forced intervals on the speeches. There was a little whispered conversation at first on general topics, but both were quickly on friendly personal terms and were not amazed at it. They talked of their relations even. The speakers droned on, and for minutes at a time Gaunt and Viola Cartlet seemed to be listening, and occasionally one or other or both would join in the periodical clapping. All the while new sensations held them. Gaunt was quite without compunction.

Viola drifted along on clouds. Her spirit had gone out of her. She had the feeling that the man was at one with her. Nothing mattered. She was exhilarated, bewildered.

Viola Cartlet was a woman with a strong sense of right and wrong. She went to church pretty regularly, because it made her feel good, and she said her prayers and felt them every night at her bedside. But she had no hesitation now about this new, unsought-for glow of passion which was racing through her. She had a tumultuous feeling that it was her fate; that she had reached the summit of her experiences. If she had permitted herself to analyse her feelings she would certainly have said that it would be wickedness to shut out from her soul this long-delayed thrilling contentment.

The happy-go-lucky Gaunt, ever a woman hunter, would have been shamed had he not responded to a far less emotional invitation, and he had realised the call of Viola Carlet's individuality from the first. And now, to-night, shining with beauty as she was, with eyes alight, she was irresistible, and in the delight of it all he would freely have declared to himself that he was in love with her. He had no thought of wrong-doing. The vision was before him, and he held out his arms to grasp it. What is known as morality did not appeal to Majority Gaunt. The fact that the woman beside him was the wife of another man troubled him not at all. He sailed easily, delightedly, into the welter of feeling.

Through all the two preserved an appearance of attention to the speakers, and Gaunt now and again wrote a sentence in shorthand, although what was going on in front was extremely unimportant.

"You will come up and see us soon?" she asked. "We seem to have known each other quite a long time."

"Yes, I should like to come."

"You speak a little slowly, as if you were doubtful."

"I hesitate a little."

"But why do you hesitate?" She spoke in a half-rallying way, a suggestion of pique about her.

Gaunt did not look at her, but kept his gaze fixed ahead. "I hesitate because I do not think it would be possible for me to stay away – after to-night."

Neither of them said anything after this for a little while. What thoughts were rushing between them were incoherent and violent. Presently they steadied themselves. Accidentally their knees touched. He felt the pulsing of her blood, and she was all a tremble with the warmth of him. He allowed the side of his hand to touch the side of hers, and she did not move. They both avoided looking at each other and kept their gaze in front of them. Happiness thrilled through all the being of Viola Cartlet, and she wanted nothing more on earth.

As the two sat together in silence with unnoticing neighbours on each side and in front of the respectable gathering in the body of the hall cheering from time to time, a telegraph messenger, mounted noisily at the back of the platform with a red envelope in his hand. The platform people turned to look at him. He showed the telegram to someone at the end of the row, and half a minute late it had found its way to Gaunt. On it was the address, "Gaunt, *Daily Light* reporter, South Hall, Hampstead." His thoughts came back to earth with a bound. He opened the envelope and read this message.

"Return immediately to office, sensational disclosure involving yourself made by Raston Path at his meeting to-night. Lodden wants you here. – Wansmuth."

[28 November 1913]

Chapter VI.
First Blood.

The morning on which a newspaper publishes an important exclusive story has exhilarations all its own for the chief men of the paper, for they feel they have justified themselves to the world. Accomplishment is theirs; they have shown their rivals that brains and energy tell; they pride themselves that by intelligence, or money, or luck, or by the three together, they have got ahead, and if luck happens to be the principal factor, they point out that good fortune is the handmaid of enterprise; altogether it is a sunny morning when a newspaper gets a real big story to itself. The satisfaction is deepened when the news published is connected with a campaign of any sort; then, for instance, it opens an attack on the hostile political camp.

Then, if ever, a paper chortles in its glee, calls attention to what it has unmasked, appeals openly for admiration in the execution of a public duty – and good, honest, intelligent people all over the country read the journal's tribute to itself, and say what a wonderful paper it is, and how there is absolutely nothing hidden from it. To produce this frame of mind is the delight of newspaper proprietors and editors.

Satisfaction was in Archibald Lodden as he glanced at the morning's scoop of the *Daily Light* while at breakfast in his Mount-street[31] flat and saw Gaunt's article with its headlines and saw the short leading article referring to it. Much consultation had been given to the form in which Gaunt's material should appear, and it had finally been decided by Lodden that while the statement should go in as the "splash" – that is, the most prominent article of the day – it should not have any sensational introduction, nor any embellishment in the form of interviews or comment in defamatory headlines. The information obtained by Gaunt should, it was decided, be boldly and clearly given, but without any straining of emphasis. The facts in themselves were staggering, and a plain statement would go much further than a display of strong adjectives. Political circles would certainly be amazed at the proposals of the Home Secretary and there would be set up the first eddies in a great storm of hostility. Lodden knew this directly he saw Gaunt's material, for he had the touch of the public pulse to the nicety.

This was the article as it appeared with headings: –

MR. PATH'S NEW MOVE.
STRIKING PROJECT.
BILL TO ABOLISH POVERTY.
LEVELLING DOWN AND LEVELLING UP.
ACTUAL PROPOSALS.

We are enabled to-day to give details of the new scheme which Mr. Raston Path will shortly lay before Parliament. He is proceeding on lines very different from those which have been freely spoken of during the last few weeks. It will be seen that what the Home Secretary proposes to do is simply to take away from the rich and give to the poor. We await with interest the country's opinion of the measure. The following are the main proposals: –

1. – That on and after January 1, 1920, any man or woman having worked for a period of not less than 48 hours in one week shall receive for that week's work a sum of not less than thirty shillings.

2. – A Board of Commissioners appointed by Parliament shall in cases of appeal from special trades or professions make recommendation to Parliament with a view to the granting of votes of money sufficient to increase the wages in heavily burdened industries up to the maximum of 30s. a week.

3. – We are in a position to state how the sum of money will be raised – perhaps the most important part of the whole proposal. It will be the business of the Chancellor of the Exchequer in presenting his Budget to show the taxes necessary to meet the new demands of the Home Secretary, and in view of the colossal sum required it is not surprising that methods hitherto unknown in this or any other country will be introduced. To put the matter in an nutshell, it is suggested that three-quarters of the income of a very rich man shall be taken away from him, and that half the income of a man less rich shall be available. This is the rough scale in view: –

> The sum required by the Imperial Exchequer to meet the demands of the 30s. minimum shall be obtained by assessing the income tax as 75 per cent. of a person's income for all incomes of £5,000 a year and upwards, with a graduated scale for incomes of less than £5,000 down to incomes of £1,000, which would be assessed at 50 per cent. of the total each year.

The first leading article of the *Daily Light* dealt with the matter in this way: –

> The public cannot fail to be interested in the news in this issue of the *Daily Light* about the coming revolution in social life. It is nothing but a revolution. The outline of the new plan of the Home Secretary will be found on another page. If the spirit of the British people can be stirred it will be stirred by this announcement. Under the guise of humanitarianism it is designed to take away the possessions which the law has hitherto protected and entrenched in the possession of the owner. There are 50,000,000 people in this country, and the great majority of them must necessarily be humble workers with their hands and among them will be found hundreds of thousands unfitted for other occupations, as well as hundreds of thousands of slackers and inefficients and hundreds of thousands who see no reason to look forward to next week as long as they can get beer and tobacco for this week; and it is to give these people comparative comfort that the Home Secretary proposes to break up estates and homes, disturb thriving businesses, and plunder the intellect and ability of the nation. We have an idea that his scheme will not get very far even in the field of discussion. The light of day will quickly have an effect on it. Possibly the author may find himself destroyed by his project. In any case, we are glad it has fallen to the *Daily Light* to strike the first blow in this decisive battle for public sanity and political morality."

As was to be expected, there was a stir in the evening paper offices on the *Daily Light* announcement, and reporters were sent off pell-mell before the midday editions were issued to get confirmations or contradictions. The prejudice against the *Light* and its early reputation for sensationalism steadied the evening papers for an hour, but nevertheless the statement had the ring of fact about it, and certain it was that the *Light* would not print such an announcement without being pretty sure of the position. To fall down on a statement of this kind would be a heavy blow to any paper, and the majority of the newspaper men in Fleet-street felt in their hearts that the *Light* had once again done a good thing for itself.

[29 November 1913]

Chapter VI. – Continued.
A Blow for the "Daily Light."

The reporters went hurrying forth to attack the Government offices and the residences of Cabinet Ministers, and between 9 o'clock and 12 o'clock they were at work like a swarm of bees. One or two Ministers were seen. Secretaries were drawn forth and questioned, the organising party chiefs were examined and cross-examined. Out of all their inquiry, it would seem to the outsider that something must emerge with regard to the plans of Raston Path – new features, a hint as to modifications, even a denial as to parts of the scheme. But as a matter of fact nothing of the kind was forthcoming. Raston Path had locked his secrets up very securely. The party organisers admitted themselves as staggered by the *Daily Light* announcement as the ordinary public; Secretaries in Whitehall emphatically denied all knowledge of Path's measure, and the one or two Cabinet Ministers who were secured declined to say a word either in the shape of comment or confirmation. To this, it should be added, there was one small exception. The Lobby correspondent of the Press Association, paying a visit to the Foreign Office, had the good luck to meet Sir Harry Venture in the quadrangle. "A most serious announcement," he said, "but I cannot say anything for publication."

Raston Path himself was seen by a representative of the *Charing Cross Gazette*. "I have no comment at all to make for the moment. I do not choose to dispute the *Daily Light* statement: I do not choose to accept it. There is nothing to be said just now. As you know, I am addressing a public meeting at the Holborn Town Hall this evening and I shall then take the opportunity of handling the matter and explaining the situation to the public."

The evening papers did their best with the scanty fresh material to hand, and they felt justified in their lack of confirmation in giving prominence to the *Daily Light* scoop. The morning's inquiries conveyed the impression that the *Light*'s information was true, that Ministers were annoyed at the news leaking out, and that their plans were temporarily disturbed by the disclosure. That was good enough for the newspapers, and they let themselves go.

Lodden was very pleased about this whole thing. He knew that the *Light*'s exclusive would be used in every town in the kingdom, not merely by his own paper, but by other papers, and that the *Daily Light*'s name would be used with it – not from benevolence, but as a safeguard. This was really good business.

"Gaunt, we must run the thing harder to-night. The Opposition Leader must give us his opinion. I'll try to fix that up myself. You set to work and have the big business chiefs interviewed, members of the House of Lords, and some big religious men who are on our side. I will be seeing Lumley in a minute, and we must get opinions from abroad. We'll have a leader note to-night with more vitriol in it. We must not forget it will take the people two or three days to realise what this proposal of Path's means, but as soon as they do you will see how everybody will be in a roar. This is a big thing for us. We must push it through."

"If I was not booked for that meeting of Mrs. Cartlet I would go up and see what Path has to say at the Holborn Town Hall to-night."

"Oh, there will be a shorthand report of that. He's sure to be abusive. Just a good report. You go up to Hampstead – give a nice little show to that meeting. We must keep in with these people. They can help us a lot."

The great triumphant shout of the *Daily Light* was in preparation throughout the evening. With interviews, arguments, denunciations, and a sprinkling of facts, it was to take up three and a half columns on the main page, and the fourth column was to be completed by extracts from the speech of Raston Path. That he would lacerate the *Daily Light* no one doubted, and least of all Archibald Lodden.

"The more venomous he is, the better it will be," he said. "Give all he says about us. The more he abuses us the more he condemns himself. I can see if we only do this thing properly we get the Government out of office and we give the first real hard knock to Path."

Before Lodden went home to dinner he had a consultation with Wansmuth about the placard for next day's issue. The red and white bills of the *Light* were famed throughout the length and breadth of the land, and the legend they bore each day might be taken as the epitome of the day's news – from the *Light*'s point of view. This was the bill devised by Lodden and Wansmuth: –

<pre>
            FINISH
              OF
            RASTON
             PATH.
</pre>

It was with a feeling of real triumph that Wansmuth returned to the office at nine o'clock after dinner for his accustomed task of looking at the principal proofs. A boy brought in the letters from the last post, together with a batch of proofs.

"Please, sir, can the chief sub-editor see you for a moment? He has got something he wants to show you off the tape."

The electric tape machines ticking out their news day and night from the various agencies often brought the first indication of important happenings, which might disturb the make-up of the paper; and it was the practice on very startling occasions to consult the managing editor himself if the tape should be telling of something very significant.

"Tell Mr. Duden I will see him at once," said Wansmuth.

The chief sub-editor came in with some scraps of typewritten tape in his hand.

"Thought you had better see this," he said; "it's about Path's meeting."

"Eh!"

Wansmuth reached from his chair, took the slips from Duden, and began with a glimpse at the first of them: –

> "8.50 – Mr. Raston Path to-night addressed a mass meeting at the Holborn Town Hall. The building was crowded in every part. Tremendous enthusiasm was manifested when the Home Secretary rose to speak. Mr. Path thanked the audience for their kindly reception, and said they were gathered there that night –."

Wansmuth dropped one slip and took up the next and his practised eye skimmed rapidly the first few lines, then the name *Daily Light* occurred, and what he saw set him reading carefully and closely. He read 20 lines, perhaps, and then looked up.

"This is a pretty thing."

There was a tense five seconds during which Wansmuth gazed fixedly at the chief sub-editor in concentrated thought.

"Kill the make-up for page 5," he said suddenly. "Take Path out and make the German Emperor's visit to Paris the splash. Fill up with other stuff. Leave a top half-column open for material to come."

Wansmuth was a person of quick decision and action. His finger was on the electric bell as he spoke. A boy came hurrying in.

"Get Mr. Lodden on the telephone at his private house. I want to speak to him. Duden, kill the leader on Raston Path and send the leader writer in to me. We must have something on the German Emperor."

Durden hurried out, and as he did so Wasmuth's telephone bell rang.

"Is that you, Mr. Lodden?" said Wansmuth. "Sorry to have to call you up. Path's speech to-night – not over the telephone? Oh, all right. Very strong, it has caused me to kill all the stuff we prepared and fix up a new splash. Sensational? Yes, that's the word. You'll come down? All right. I'll see you directly you come in."

He snapped the telephone down, and rang for a boy again.

"Take this down to Mr. Brown," he said; and he rapidly scribbled on a piece of paper: "Kill placard, 'Finish of Raston Path.'" As he gave the paper over he said, "Let me know directly Mr. Lodden arrives."

When the boy had gone Wansmuth muttered to himself, "First blood to Mr. Raston Path. But we are not finished yet."

[1 December 1913]

Chapter VII.
Lodden's Way Out.

When Archibald Lodden arrived in his motor at the *Daily Light* office Wansmuth had ready for him the agency report of Raston Path's speech, completed since the telephone conversation.

"This is an interesting business," he said, as he flung his hat and coat on to the seat and took the tape machine slips to read them.

"Throws us down completely," said Wansmuth. Lodden read on growlingly. There were the essential parts of the report before him: –

> After dealing with the general political situation, Mr. Path spoke of the good work of the Government, and said that he had a Bill in preparation which would undoubtedly be fiercely opposed, but which would make for a high ideal and help in the succour of the undertrodden and the poor. He was not at liberty to reveal the nature of the Bill, except in so far as to say that it punished idle privilege and would make certain that the day-by-day workers of the country would have to be the foremost consideration in the mind of the Government of the day. (Loud cheers.) In connection with their new proposal he must say a word about the scandalous and wicked story which had appeared that morning in a widely-read newspaper – he meant the *Daily Light*. Distinguished from its birth for unscrupulousness and sensationalism, the *Daily Light* had outdistanced all its previous efforts. With every sign of circumstantial investigation this journal published to-day a statement purporting to give the Government intentions about the new Bill. With the utmost assurance and definiteness it drew an outline of the measure, giving the scope and operation and told exactly its provisions. That was what the *Daily Light* did. Well, every one of the so-called facts was wrong. In the whole of he article there was no trace of truth. From first to last the thing was a fabrication, without any foundation whatever. Ladies and gentlemen, that shows what democracy has to fight against in the capitalist Press: wilful and deliberate lies carefully framed to deceive the vast public which reads the paper. (Shame.) Are there any ordinary political terms which will serve on this occasion? There are none. It is a time for straight speaking on the personal side. The owner of the *Daily Light* is a man who has made a colossal fortune. His eyes are on the future of his paper and the acquisition of more money. He is on the safe side in politics: the side which keeps the workers in their place. (Shame.) Yes, and what does he do to help his side? He forges a malignant plot and puts in his paper a bogus Government measure with the view of prejudicing the Government and prejudicing the Minister principally concerned. And they talk of the uprightness of the British newspapers and the honour of public life. This man, with all his vast possessions, without the excuse of the worst burglar in prison, sets out to mislead and delude a million people. He is without mercy and without conscience. He publishes broadcast a calculated and poisonous lie. He makes up a Parliamentary proposal and presents it to the world as mine, and then condemns me for that proposal which he and his men have produced. (Tremendous cheers and cries of 'Shame,' 'Shame.') This, then, is the kind of thing that democracy has to face. I challenge Archibald Lodden to announce the source of his information. I challenge him to prove it is anything beyond a plain falsehood from start to finish. Let him answer if he dare. (Loud and tumultuous cheers.)"

Archibald Lodden raised his eyes and said thoughtfully, "He's clever." Then he changed his tone. "Where's Gaunt?"

"He has just come in. I sent for him."

"Tell him to come up."

Wansmuth went to Lodden's writing table and telephoned down to the reporters' room. Gaunt had been in five minutes and was waiting the summons, for he was anxious to be at the battle, knowing that startling times were ahead for him, for Archibald Lodden was at his worst with a man who had put the paper in a difficulty. Storm and fury were before Gaunt, and he knew it well. He listened with a pleasant face to the comments of Wrightson.

"It's a devil of a throw down, but most likely Path is lying. May be Archie'll be all right about it."

"We'll soon see."

"I should tell him straight out how and where you got the stuff."

"I think he pretty well knows."

"Oh, oh." Wrightson turned to his work again.

When Gaunt received the telegram at Hampstead he had an instant idea of what had occurred, and on his way to the City squared himself for the worst. A burst of passion, dismissal with three months' salary, and a statement in to-morrow's paper of how an unscrupulous reporter had been sent to the right-about;[32] that was the way he figured his prospects. And knowing the *Light*'s methods he had a reasonable basis for the belief.

"Mr. Lodden wants to see you, sir." A boy burst into the room and delivered the message with the rush characteristic of the *Light* staff.

"Right-ho."

"Good-bye," said Wrightson.

"No flowers," laughed Gaunt, as he swung out of the door and into the corridor. For Lodden had little mercy for those who gambled in his services and lost, and they were tossed aside as discreditables – and if their departure could be made to appear as part of a necessary discipline of a paper of tone and character – well, so much the better. It would really seem, even to those who knew Lodden best, that his indignation was sincere. He would appear to feel the slur on the paper, and his direct instructions against anything that could rightly be called "underhand" were unequivocal and smashing.

Conceive, therefore, the surprise of Gaunt when he learned that Lodden did not intend to attack him. True, the famous scowl sat across his brow, but his tone was quite friendly when he looked upon the reporter's entry.

"What are we going to do about this Gaunt?"

"I really don't know."

Gaunt had come down prepared to make no excuse, and he was very much surprised at his chief's mildness. He stood with his hand resting on the writing table, on the other side of which sat Lodden leaning back with reflectiveness in his eyes. Wansmuth by the window rubbed his upper lip with his first finger and realised for the hundredth time that one never knew what Archie Lodden would do.

"I suppose it was a deliberate trick of Path's? He got this draft into Gaunt's hands somehow," said Wansmuth.

Lodden looked up with placid inquiry in is eyes.

"He went out of the room," said Gaunt, "and left on his table a draft of the Bill. I copied the memorandum of it."

Lodden looked at Gaunt coldly.

"Obviously a plot," said Wansmuth. "Why not show it up?"

"That means that I must be fired out," said Gaunt. "All right, I'm ready."

"You would have no option if it were necessary for you to be fired," said Lodden. "You would not be consulted. I don't intend that you shall go – at least, not yet."

Gaunt reddened.

"I am inclined to think that it was no trick, but that the draft Gaunt saw was the real thing, though very much in the rough; a draft which had not been submitted to the other members of the Cabinet. And this has had the result that Path is able to change his plans and declare our story a myth. You will see that later he will bring in a Bill somewhat on these lines in spite of all he has said tonight. He will disguise it, of course."

"Stick to our guns, then," said Wansmuth.

Lodden did not answer, and Gaunt also was silent.

Presently Lodden said, "Any fresh suggestions, Gaunt?"

"No, I don't see any other way out."

"Very well, then, I have it."

"Wansmuth, scrap all the stuff you have prepared and in place of it give one column in which will be summarised Raston Path's speech and our comments on it. The tone of our reply is that the early revelation of his plans has inconvenienced him, and that they will be changed. That is the note. We have frightened and angered him, and he is revengefully contradicting us. We reply by a considered and dignified adherence to our original statement and advise the public to wait and see."

Lodden's tone was explanatory. He spoke as one who after thought had found out Path's secret.

"Of course, we must not descend to his level in abuse and we must say so. We leave that method of public controversy to the Home Secretary. We must be cold and clear – that is the line."

"Yes," said Wansmuth, "but in his next speech he will say that our dignity is all bluff."

"I hope so. Other papers must take some notice of his attacks, and all this is to the good. And there is one thing you seem to have forgotten, Wansmuth. Path makes one of his virulent speeches occasionally. We go on giving our views of the facts day after day."

[2 December 1913]

Chapter VII. – Continued.
The Foreign Editor in Action.

But notwithstanding the ingenuity and audacity of the *Light* in meeting the occasion, Raston Path's speech was a heavy blow. It was given full publicity in the other papers, and the two Progressive journals had leader notes pointing out the malignity and unscrupulousness of a paper which would descend to the methods so exposed by the Home Secretary.

A good deal of talk about the matter arose in the Lobby of the House of Commons, and the one or two politicians on Path's side who were addressing public meetings in various parts pressed home the moral of the whole thing. Truly this was an advertisement for the *Daily Light*, but it was not the kind of advertisement which would do the paper any good. And what was more, Lodden knew it, but he permitted himself no outburst and went on with his plans steadily.

Path had made his thrust with calculation; his indictment of the *Daily Light* told against the reliability of the journal throughout the country, deposed it at least temporarily into an organ of sensationalism, and at the same time discounted in advance future attacks. Whatever the *Light* did now for a time would be all too plainly out of revenge, so Lodden held his hand, preparing and making ready. But venomousness was behind his quiet, and Raston Path had made his dangerous enemy still more dangerous. Paragraphs from Path's speeches in days gone by were typed out and kept in readiness to be used against him, and inquiries were set on foot with regard to his private life. In these days of energetic making-ready Lodden showed no special excitement, but the fires were burning underneath, and just once they blazed forth. Gaunt came up to report some small development, and Lodden, having heard him out, suddenly barked at him furiously.

"Mind you, the thing has got to be done thoroughly. No more bungling. You've had a great fall, Gaunt. Through you the paper has had its biggest blow for years. Oh, yes, I haven't said anything about it and you mustn't think I've been indifferent. What is more, you nearly brought the paper into criminal disgrace. Of course, I couldn't save you if it were known how you got those papers; of course, I couldn't save you. Not the slightest doubt but what you'd have to go to prison."

But this was just one of Lodden's lapses, and for the most part he was placidly encouraging towards the general work. Reporters and other members of the staff were steadily engaged on different parts of the campaign.

Gaunt, chastened and depressed, turned himself principally to the library, where he found much to occupy him in compilation. The Parliamentary correspondent, the society correspondent, the principal leader-writer – each had a section of the campaign in hand apart from the day's routine work.

Particularly busy was Lumley, the foreign editor, and he fully enjoyed himself. He was always a genial, important soul, and now a fresh arrogance bloomed on him, and he talked with politicians and under-secretaries with the quietly confident air of one within the inner circle. His swagger did not make Lumley a fool, and as a widely-travelled man with weight beneath his touch of bombast and a irrepressible generous strain he had a picturesqueness about him. You must add to this the fact that no journalist had a better nose for "big" news, that he really understood the convulsions of international politics, that he was swift with devices for getting foreign information which Governments sought to hide, and it will be seen that Lumley's Gallic touch was but so incidental; it made him interesting, it added soul to his ability. He had a sudden audacious temper which at times was terrorising, and if there was something of the Frenchman in him, there was also something of the Irishman. A burly man approaching 50, with heavy shoulders, a drooping grey moustache, and a dainty imperial,[33] he was always exquisitely dressed and carried his huge body with the poise of a commander. He had a pleasant face, and manners *do bon ton*,[34] and was popular with men, and even those who suffered from the slash of his ready tongue carried no ill-will toward him. He cultivated fierceness where he was opposed, and would shout down a bully and was quite ready to chastise an offender with his fists. Many tales were told of his early political adventures. He had no idea that his colleagues laughed at his little vanities. If he had suspected it he would probably have set himself the task of thrashing them one by one until they had repented.

Full blooded was his way of recounting his troubles and accomplishments. But he could always hold his hearers. Now and again he came a cropper, but not often. He was proud of having languages in his grip, and proud of his journeyings and his acquaintances, and all those who knew him were frequently reminded of his experiences. He knew French and German and Italian, and was perfectly well up in Spanish. "Used to live in Spain. Knew Don Alfonso.[35] Yes, quite a nice fellow. Used to meet me in the morning sometimes and say 'Good morning, Mr. Lumley,' and I would answer, 'Good morning, Don Alfonso.' Oh, yes; knew him quite well." This particular recital became almost a chorus to some of Lumley's more intimate acquaintances. One day he was walking along Whitehall with Charlock, of the *St. George's Gazette*, and saw Sorel, of the P.A.,[36] approaching. "Introduce me to Sorel," said Lumley, "I have heard of him often." Charlock pulled himself together for the task. He stopped Sorel.

"Sorel, will you let me make you acquainted with Mr. Lumley? Mr. Lumley is of the *Daily Light*. Speaks French, German, and Spanish; particularly good in Spanish. Used to live in Spain. Knew Don Alfonso. Met the Don every morning, and used to say 'Good morning, Don,' and the other used to reply –"

But Charlock did not get any further, though he had rushed his words together to get as much out as possible, for the blood was in Lumley's face and he had burst out with a roar and advanced a threatening step. "You scoundrel, you impudent scoundrel, you whipper-snapper. Don't laugh at me, I tell you. I'll tear out your throat and poison a dog with it."

People were gathering round on the pavement by this time, but to Lumley they did not exist, and there was murder in his eye. Swiftly Sorel drew Charlock through the crowd to escape the vengeance. Lumley, bewildered as well as angered at the thought that such discourtesy was possible in a friend, stood for a moment gazing after them and muttering. And then, turning sharply to walk in the other direction, found his way impeded by a small boy. He hit him smartly on the back with his walking-stick. He felt better after that.

You would hardly know this Lumley as the man who went into the headquarters' office of the Progressives in Whitehall one afternoon to learn what he could about Progressive activity on the organising side, and to get to know if there was any thought of a coming General Election. Urbane was the word for Lumley on such an occasion, and he carried a man-of-the-world graciousness which fitted him like a glove. Lumley was always important-looking, whatever his mood, and this somehow added to the effect of his suavity when he chose to be suave. Difficult was the task this afternoon, and his tact was indeed needed.

All good Progressives dislike the *Daily Light*, and the dislike was naturally acute in the organising headquarters of the party. On the other hand, organisations are brought into touch with all the papers, and, unless for some very special reason, give what information they have for publicity without distinction, knowing that it cannot very well be garbled, and that an announcement in a hostile print is sometimes very useful. So to start with Lumley was all right. He had to get into conversation on some general political matter, and after establishing a chatty intercourse to extract as tactfully as might be any news on his particular subject. He sent in his card to Sir Robert Furley, the chief agent of the party, because it is always advisable in these cases to ask for the top man. Not that Lumley wanted to see Sir Robert – far from it, and he had chosen a time when the chief agent, he knew, would be out at lunch. As it happened his second in command was also out.

"You can see Mr. Thompson, sir," said the office boy.

"Who is Mr. Thompson?"

"He is in charge of the publication and reports department, and answers all inquiries."

"Very well. Just tell him I'm here."

The boy took Lumley into a room wherein a wide counter separated callers from the space occupied by the clerks. The staff were out at lunch just now except Mr. Thompson, who sat at a desk in the middle of the room. He was a middle-aged man with red hair, close-cropped moustache, and a perpetual frown. The boy left Lumley at the counter and took his card to Mr. Thompson. Now Mr. Thompson was the worst possible man for Lumley to approach, for he was not only cantankerous by habit, being barely civil to friendly callers, but he reserved a special nastiness for people connected with papers like the *Daily Light*. He glanced at the card and, without even turning his head to see Lumley, snapped out "Nothing to say," and went on writing.

"Will you pardon me?" said Lumley, in a pleasant grandiloquent way, as though he had not heard the reply, "I am here on a special mission for Mr. Archibald Lodden. Perhaps you will be good enough to spare me a minute?"

Mr. Thompson looked up at this in a quick way, shook his head sourly, and repeated: "Nothing to say; nothing to say."

But if Mr. Thompson thought he could dismiss Lumley as he would dismiss a junior reporter from the *Star* or *Evening News* he was mistaken. His demeanour had roused Lumley, who was rapidly forgetting the object of his visit. Lumley put his hand behind his ear and leaned forward slightly over the counter.

"I beg your pardon?"

"I have nothing to say," shouted Mr. Thompson.

"I am extremely sorry," said Lumley, with apologetic self-deprecation, "but my hearing is so bad, and it is such an important matter. I would be much obliged if you would come a little closer."

Mr. Thompson glared at this pertinacious nuisance of a man, and for a moment he hesitated and it seemed he was going to ring the bell for a messenger again; then he grudgingly paid a tribute to Lumley's dignified bearing by shuffling off his chair and crossing the room to the counter, and as he walked he began "I tell you I have no news or information of any kind, and –"

Lumley, leaning forward anxious to hear, Mr. Thompson had to approach quite close to the counter. Then was Lumley's opportunity, and, drawing himself back a trifle, he launched his fist at Mr. Thompson's jaw, shouting, "Well, take that, you blasted scoundrel, and when a gentleman addresses you learn to answer him properly!"

Mr. Thompson avoided the full strength of the blow by a quick twist, but he had a heavy whack in the neck which unbalanced him and sent him to the floor.

"I'll teach you," roared Lumley, "I'll teach you." His blood was sizzling. One word of protest from the bewildered Mr. Thompson would have sent Lumley over the counter to complete the thrashing, but the assaulted man had risen to his knees and was brushing the dust off himself without a word. It was while matters were at this point that the door or the inner office, and a young girl, Sir Richard Furley's secretary, came hurrying out to find out what was causing the commotion. She was fair, with hair that shone, and she was short but of graceful figure, with rather a broad nose, an exquisite complexion, and deep blue eyes which gave one the impression that she understood things perfectly. This was Miss Nancy Kirk. Wonderment was on her face now.

"Why, Mr. Thompson?" she said.

Lumley cut in from the other side of the counter; his hat was in his hand and his manner was courtly. "I hope you have not been startled. Mr. Thompson was rude and I had to correct him."

Miss Kirk's eyes as she looked at Lumley were cold and non-committal, and then she turned to Mr. Thompson.

"Can I do anything, Mr. Thompson?"

"This man has committed an assault on me."

"It will be repeated in five seconds if you are impudent," said Lumley.

"Shall I fetch anyone?" asked the girl.

"Perhaps we had better have a policeman –"

"Yes, and I'll see to you before he comes," said Lumley, preparing to vault over the counter.

[3 December 1913]

Chapter VII – Continued.
Gaunt's meeting with Nancy Kirk.

It was two hours later when Majority Gaunt, debonair and courteous, came up to the Progressive headquarters on his errand of peace. He asked to see Sir Robert's secretary on a private matter, and gave his name without reference to the paper. Nancy Kirk came out to him and Gaunt, notwithstanding that his business lay heavy on him, was suddenly touched by her looks. He realised her delicacy, her self-determination, the steady poise that stood reflected in her face, and felt the effect of a strange new beauty. Mrs. Cartlet was forgotten; a thousand miles away were her charms. The fineness and sweetness in this little stranger uplifted Gaunt. Gallantry surged within him.

"I am sorry Sir Robert is engaged," he said thoughtfully, "because my business is rather important."

"Any matter with regard to newspapers I can deal with for Sir Robert. You are from the *Daily Light*?"

"Well, yes, but I am not here on an ordinary inquiry. We came up about some unfortunate incident here earlier in the afternoon."

"A bullying man came in and struck one of our staff. He was from the *Daily Light*, I think."

Gaunt had a feeling that he was making no progress.

"Well, I came up to say that there had been some wretched misunderstanding. Of course, we have to fight against Progressive politics, but we don't send up men to batter the staff at the central office. Mr. Lumley is a distinguished journalist and a well-known man, and he says he was deliberately affronted by a clerk and lost patience with him. He thinks now he went too far."

"He seemed to want to do more than he did."

"Well, we came up to say we would not have let this happen for worlds, and to offer Sir Robert a very sincere apology. I can't do more than that, can I?"

Gaunt half shrugged his shoulders at the way his overtures were received, and he saw signs of softening, for he had a certain frank air and a look in his eyes which appealed for fair play.

"I'll tell Sir Robert. I don't know what action he's going to take."

"Please say that Mr. Lodden is very much concerned about the thing, and that Mr. Lumley will not again call at this office. That has been arranged."

Gaunt managed to convey the effect that Lumley was in disgrace for his behaviour.

"Your friend seems to have acted like a madman," said the girl, "and why he should have attacked Mr. Thompson none of us can tell."

"Well, Mr. Lumley said he had great provocation, and I cannot carry it any farther."

His alertness and boyish way of explaining, together with his self-restraint, had their effect on Nancy Kirk.

"I'll tell Sir Robert all you have said."

"It's a jolly nuisance all this business." Gaunt, with his walking-stick hooked on his arm, was drawing on his glove, and there was a confidential note in his voice. "I suppose you don't know anything about the *affairs* of the office?"

"No," cooed the girl with half a smile. "I am not a politician at all."

"Pity the poor Pressmen," he said. "Well, I'll go on over to Downing-street to see what I can pick up in the shape of news." He was speaking like an old friend now. "But I must have a cup of tea first. I suppose you never have tea in the afternoon?"

The door of the inner room of the office opened as he spoke, and a thin-lipped clerk put his head through and said: "Sir Robert is asking for you, Miss Kirk."

"I'm coming now."

Gaunt had to depart. The girl went back to the inner office, where she told Sir Robert Furley all that had happened. Among the communications which it was her duty to take down in shorthand was the following addressed to Lodden: –

"Sir Robert Furley presents his compliments to Mr. Archibald Lodden, and begs to inform him that this afternoon a representative of the *Daily Light* visited this office, assaulted a member of the staff, and that later another representative of the *Daily Light* came to the office and tried to extract information from a lady secretary. In view of these occurrences, Sir Robert Furley has to ask that no representative of the *Daily Light* calls here again."

In the early evening Archibald Lodden had Lumley and Gaunt before him, and hissed his contempt for their blundering. Disappointment was mixed with his rage in connection with Gaunt; he made allowance, he said, for bursts of stupidity on the part of Lumley.

"His heavy-footed blundering is what I expect, but Gaunt's behaviour has upset me. I was going to play golf to-morrow, and now I simply cannot do it. He has put me off my game completely. He has spoilt a day for me."

The strange thing about it all was that Majority Gaunt had been pleasant to the girl secretary with no idea of getting information for the *Light*, but only because he was fascinated by her pretty face. That is the worst of being a Lothario. You are so apt to be misunderstood.

Chapter VIII.
The Fight Thickens.

It was not a matter of surprise to Wansmuth and Gaunt that Archibald Lodden very soon put himself on visiting terms with the Cartlets out at Hampstead, because the help to be obtained indirectly from hostile relatives of Path would certainly be of particular value to the *Daily Light*.

To a man like Lodden the making of acquaintanceship was a trifle, and whereas he had commenced his move by his letter to Viola Cartlet he had completed it by making sure that the business manager of one of his subordinate companies (connected with the publication of the *Weekly Novelette* and *Feminine Companion*) secured the services of Viola's husband as accountant in connection with the company's figures. From this latter move came the necessity before very long for an interview between Lodden and Cartlet in connection with an approaching shareholders' meeting, and Lodden at once frankly said that he had looked forward to meeting Cartlet apart from business urgencies in order to apologise personally for what might have seemed a discourtesy to Mrs. Cartlet a week or two back.

The two men went out to lunch together, and from that time the path was easy. Of course, Viola was pleased when Archibald Lodden came to Hampstead with her husband one evening, and the quick way Lodden made himself at home with them was a very nice sensation to her. For, after all, a millionaire newspaper proprietor is not an everyday acquaintance. She made him promise to come up again. He said he would be delighted, and Viola proceeded to map out in her mind the two or three local friends whom she had decided should be present on the same occasion.

The men went into Cartlet's little smoking room after dinner, and Viola came in and joined them, and they talked away in a free and easy fashion which the Carlets would not have thought possible on their first meeting with a man like Lodden. As a matter of fact, Lodden laid himself out to be agreeable. After he had gone, Viola said: "I shall get to like that man quite well, I believe."

"He's not bad, and quite different from the usual kind of money-maker. It's a bit sudden, though, this."

"Sudden?"

"Yes, it is, coming up here and being so friendly right away. I don't know whether it is you or me he has taken a fancy to."

She laughed.

"Oh, really, you are not so thick as all that, George. Just as if we mattered anything to him. He's making friends with us so that he can glean all he can about Raston Path. You can see that."

"He didn't mention his name to-night."

"Well, the man's not a fool."

"He cannot find out much from me, that's one thing."

"No, I suppose not, really; though, of course, there are a lot of little things we've heard from Hilda."

"But, really, we couldn't repeat family gossip like that. I should hate –"

"Oh, I would never dream of repeating anything untrue, but of course, Raston Path is a public man, and I don't see why his life should not be scrutinised. He is very fond of criticising the other people. I don't blame the *Daily Light* for trying to find out anything that it can. Look what he said about the *Light* – it was scandalous. Majority Gaunt told me all about the thing Path absolutely laid a trap for him. It was wicked, wicked. It might have ruined him. It was despicable, and mean, and cunning."

"Well, I don't know the facts, but I don't think Lodden or any of his men would stand on ceremony if they saw a chance of getting an advantage."

"I was told in confidence, so I cannot repeat what Gaunt told me, but the trick was too abominable for words."

Cartlet shrugged his shoulders and reached over to the writing table for his tin of tobacco and his pipe. "Don't get yourself into a mess over it, that's all."

"I should like to get him into a mess. He's a beast."

Then Viola went off to the room to write some letters. The first she wrote, and the longest, was to Majority Gaunt, a friendly invitation to tea on the following Sunday, and an account of the first visit of Archibald Lodden; how he was coming again and all about him.

That after all this Cartlet himself, well meaning and devoid of offence, should have been the means of giving the key of an attack to the *Daily Light* is just one of those curious happenings that always occur in big complicated battles. In a conversation with Lodden in the course of the following week Raston Path's name came up, and Cartlet shrugged his shoulders good-humouredly at the Home Secretary's "attacks on property and his denunciation of those who made large sums of money and supported legislation for the well-to-do against poorer people."

"Well, well," said Lodden, "it is the nature of the beast, and we are on his track now."

"You know he has got an income of £200 a year of his own."

"I knew he had some small amount, but I didn't know what it was. If it were larger he probably wouldn't be so fond of abusing people with property."

"The funny thing is his shares have gone up lately?"

"Shares?"

"Yes; he holds shares in the Newcastle and Scottish Shipbuilding Company Syndicate. I was hearing about it from a friend of mine in the City the other day."

"It's news to me," said Lodden, "but they don't amount to very much after all."

"No, I think they were left to him by his father. It is quite a good thing, because they are one of the soundest shipbuilding concerns in the country, and within the last year or two they have got hold of the patents of this new oil-combustion engine for ships, and with oil fuel coming along it has been a good thing for the company."

"He is a bit of a financier himself, then?" said Lodden unconcernedly.

"In his way, yes. But you won't be able to attack him on that."

"No, no," said Lodden; "not much chance there. We'll have to get him on bigger things than the holding of a few shares. Still, it's as well to know of these things."

"I suppose I ought not to say too much," said Cartlet, "because I'm by way of being a relative of his, or at least a connection, and it doesn't look very well for me to talk about him behind his back."

"Ever met him," asked Lodden.

"Once or twice. Just a how-do-you-do acquaintance. Nothing more than that. He's a keen chap."

"Yes," said Lodden, thoughtfully; "he's very keen."

The innocent Cartlet went away quite unaware that he had laid a train, and he would have been very surprised to know that during the afternoon Archibald Lodden spent half a hour in consultation with the financial editor, together with Wansmuth and Gaunt, in regard to the information which had come to hand in the conversation.

[4 December 1913]
Chapter VIII – Continued.
Staggering Announcement.

In a newspaper campaign you cannot afford to despise any weapon for the sake of squeamishness – that is, if the fight is important enough; and this fight had become very important to Archibald Lodden. He had found it good business, for one thing, in spite of the blow to the reputation of the *Light*. The knowledge of its deliberate battle with Path had sent up its circulation all over the country, and the figures were nearly a hundred thousand a day above the normal.

There would certainly be still further increases by a continuance of the battle, and it is a principle in the newspaper world that if you can get a big boom in circulation over some special topic you will retain some of the new readers as permanent subscribers.

Besides the business incentive there were other spurs to action, for Lodden had permitted himself to take a personal interest in the fight now, and though it was certain he would not allow it to over-run commercial consideration, he nevertheless felt a flicker of personal animosity within himself. He was interested to find that the lust of battle was touching him. He began to want to crush Path as a personal satisfaction as well as a business achievement. It was curious, this, because as a rule Lodden knew that apart from a day's annoyance or a passing spasm of contempt or dislike he was not moved to injure individuals by a personal resentment. He only crushed them for the sake of the paper – its circulation and its advertisement revenue. That, to him, was virtue, consequently, he was almost amused at his growing feeling against Path. As this coincided with other things it would have been easy to foretell that a vigorous period was ahead for the *Daily Light*. All kinds of inquiries had already been set on foot with a view to the ultimate injury of the Home Secretary, and it was not likely that Lodden would pass over the possible chance revealed in the talk of Cartlet. Poor Cartlet's puny scruples had not even raised a smile from Lodden.

Consultation with Wansmuth, Gaunt, and the Financial Editor, and they were all scattered on lines of action sketched out for them by Lodden. The Financial Editor had to make inquiries in the City; Wansmuth had to arrange the make-up of the paper and to fix the headings for a special article, and Gaunt had to delve into the library records and to get facts to supplement the researches of the financial man. It was one of those dashing little mid-way attacks so characteristic of the *Daily Light*.

"Mind your facts, mind your facts."

These were the last words of Lodden as he dismissed the three men. He spoke threateningly. Before this he had been encouraging and exhilarating. He meant that now there should be no mistakes.

Ever since Path's attack on the *Daily Light*, and his revelation of the inaccuracy and sensationalism there had been much talk in political circles about the whole affair. Authoritarians pursed up their lips and suggested that there was more in the thing than met the eye, and that "Path had been up to his tricks again." Still, they were careful not to associate themselves with the *Light*. On the other hand, the Reds and Progressives were wrathfully joyous over the downfall of the *Light*, and they poured contumely upon it and everyone connected with it. The *Light* Lobby correspondent at Westminster had a hard time. Some members of the House, hard-shelled Progressives, simply refused to talk to him at all, and cut short attempts with abuse or a sneer. Others, and these made up the majority, civilly said they could not give the *Light* any information or express any opinion for publication in its columns after what had occurred. And there were a few who did not mind being interviewed as of yore because the *Daily Light* was a very widely read and popular newspaper. The Lobby man, too, had to put up with a good deal of chaffing from the Authoritarian members, and he had a little sympathy also from some of them, which was equally hard to bear. The Progressive papers did not fail continually to rub in the salt. They said, if the *Light* would do a thing on one occasion, why should it not do it continually on all manner of subjects.

The word had gone forth from the Progressive headquarters that the *Daily Light* lie should be exposed on all the Progressive platforms throughout the country whenever an opportunity offered, and the consequence was that the paper was denounced whenever a chance occurred. This was a two-edged weapon because it gave the *Light* a kind of advertisement, but nevertheless Path felt that it would operate in the long run in the right direction. What the out-and-out adherents of the *Light* thought was not of much consequence, because their opinions could not be affected in any circumstance whatever. But the protestations of the *Light*, if sufficiently plausible, might set tongues going among those who were not hard-and-fast politicians, although they had preferences one way or the other. It would kill the influences of the paper as far as possible among the moderate men. And so the word went out for speakers to deal with the situation whenever they could.

It came about that, coincidentally with the advertisement for the *Light* and its largely increased circulation, a strong hostile opinion began to mass itself in the great towns against the paper, and Progressives were from this cause alone more strongly than ever in support of the Home Secretary. The deliberateness and thoroughness of the attack upon him all helped to raise the enthusiasm of the Progressives, and the result was that after a week or so the Progressive part of the electorate was more thoroughly devoted to Path than ever before.

This was the position of affairs when the *Daily Light* came out with the statement about Path's investments, and the way he had utilised Government influence to secure a rise in the price of stock he held.[37] It was indeed a thrill for the evening papers. Such a staggering announcement was it that on the morning it appeared in the columns of the *Light* the Progressive leaders were dumfounded.

Sir Harry Venture, lunching with the Prime Minister, asked his chief if he had seen the article.

"Yes," said the Prime Minister, "it's a great nuisance."

The way he said it prevented Sir Harry from making any comment, but he saw that Lodden's latest stroke had not been without effect, and if it affected the frigid head of the government it could not be without an effect on others more impressionable.

The Progressive organisation headquarters determined to hold their hands for the moment and refused to make any statements to worrying Pressmen. Progressive evening papers were also reticent and sought vainly to interview Raston Path and get him to throw down the story. It happened that he was away, staying at the country house of a friend in Scotland and was not accessible, a fact which went to disturb further the perturbed Progressive papers and Progressive leaders.

The statement of the *Daily Light* was to this effect, that Raston Path had shares to the nominal value of £5,000 in the Newcastle and Scottish Shipbuilding Company, and that these shares had increased in value to something like £6,500 during the past six months owing to the fact that the Government had made contracts with the company for the construction of new internal-combustion engines to be fitted to a proportion of the smaller warships in the Navy, with the contingent proviso that if satisfactory the company should have the opportunity of making the first tender for the same work in connection with a widening circle of the larger ships of the navy as they continued to be built. This had been a great stroke for the Newcastle Company, and the shares had gone up steadily since.

It was nothing to the *Daily Light* that the shares had been left to Raston Path by his father many years before, and had brought him in a settled income from the time that he was 21. What the *Light* was concerned to point out was that the Home Secretary had been benefited by the action of his Cabinet colleagues, the First Lord of the Admiralty; that this was the first occasion on which the Newcastle Company had received any government contract; and it was plainly suggested, moreover, that Path's position in the Cabinet was certainly no hindrance to the company's business with Government.

"It is time for the country to understand the situation," said the *Daily Light*. "Here is Raston Path, the financial purist, the man who is always declaiming against the wicked rich who grind down the faces of the miserable poor – here is the man profiting by the action of his Cabinet colleague in giving national business to a firm in which he is a proprietor. The matter must certainly be raised in Parliament. We cannot conceive that the bulk of Mr. Path's colleagues on the

Progressive side will feel proud of this new revelation. We are not charging Mr. Path with corruption as it is usually understood, but it cannot be denied that there has been a substantial increase in the value of his property, and that the increase has been brought about by the action of the Government. If Mr. Path challenges our statement we are willing to stand by it and have the whole matter investigated in the proper way."

This was a defiance to a libel action, and all the public wondered what would happen. A coldness clutched the hearts of the Progressives when Raston Path let it be known indirectly that he intended to take no action, and that he had decided to make no reference in public to what the *Light* had said. If the charges were brought against him in the House of Commons he would defend himself, but not till then. Rapidly all the facts became known, and they were substantially as stated by the *Light*, with this important exception, that Path had not known that the contract was going to the shipping company, that no reference to the business of the company had ever passed between him and any of his Cabinet colleagues, and finally that the First Lord of the Admiralty in acting on the advice of his departmental chiefs about the contracts had no knowledge at all that Raston Path possessed shared in the Newcastle and Scottish Shipbuilding Company. But what mattered all this to the *Daily Light* and its huge body of readers? What mattered it to the rank and file of the Authoritarians? Here was a point in the armour of the enemy. High and low was spread the cry that Raston Path had been speculating on the strength of Government knowledge; that he was amassing money which was actually drawn from the tax-payers.

The *Daily Light* put on still another fifty thousand to its circulation. Its readers gloried over the denouncing headlines and the bitter words in its news columns. Every little commonplace fact with regard to the investment was served up. One day details would be given as to how many years the Home Secretary had been receiving dividends from the company, and how much they all amounted to. Another day dates would be given on which the dividends were payable, and the prospects of the company in the future; and on still another day the names of all the directors, and description of the work carried on by the firm, and hints as to its future developments. Placards were made to match. "More About Raston Path's Money" was one, and another "Has Raston Path Some More Secret Investments?"

Raston Path kept himself more or less in retirement, and the Progressives squirmed and said bitter things about "calumny" and "poisonous weapons," but for all that they knew that the *Light* campaign was helping the cause of their opponents throughout the country. Half-and-half people would shake their heads and say: "Well, there must be something in it, though it cannot be so bad as they say." And so it happened that Raston Path was vilified throughout the length and breadth of the country, and had no opportunity of meeting his opponents. His plain statement of the facts made in the course of an interview with a *Times* representative was treated with contumely. "Miserable subterfuge," exclaimed the *Daily Light*, "fails by its very contrast with the swashbuckling bravado which he usually employs. When will the Government drop him!"

It was in the thick of this cloud of public comment that the Home Secretary was steadily pushing along with his new Bill; building it up after consultation with local administrators, Treasury experts, and Cabinet colleagues. The Prime Minister, who was intensely loyal to the members of his Cabinet, went out of his way to show his friendship and admiration for Raston Path; for the Prime Minister knew how much depended on his new measure, and saw the advantage of encouraging Path. He realised the injury that was being done to the party by the attack on the Home Secretary, but the latest Bill was so important, so far-reaching, that no interruptions must be allowed to prevent its introduction or the carrying of it to a successful issue. He set himself to hearten Path. He need not have troubled. Path would have pushed on, Prime Minister or no Prime Minister. The vilification throughout the country had only stiffened his back. But Sir Harry Venture and a few of his intimate friends knew that for all his silence every fibre of his body was strung with rage against his assailants, and that when the time came he would as nearly as might be rend them limb from limb. Path, though a pacifist in politics was a rare good fighter in actual life. He lay low for the moment, but he was pushing on with his Bill and it was a Bill in which he believed with all his soul – and incidentally knew the Bill would save the Government if it could be carried through.

Meanwhile, he cared not whether the Cabinet supported him or not. If the far-fetched suggestion that he should leave the Government came into effect, well, then, he would go to the country on his own account and carry the flaming torch as he had done in time gone by. That he could get hundreds of thousands throughout the country to follow him he had good reason for believing, but if he couldn't get hundreds of thousands he would be content with thousands. That was the mood of Raston Path. It will be seen that he was working himself up for his new Bill. It is pretty certain that the outside turmoil round his name strengthened his fervour.

This was the state of affairs when on a memorable Monday morning the *Daily Light* came out with this announcement: –

> "A further exposure in the life of one of our public men will be made in these columns to-morrow. We have felt it our duty to explain the financial position of Mr. Raston Path, the Home Secretary, because we thought his connection with trade was not such as to add to the dignity and reputation which British statesmanship had hitherto enjoyed. To-morrow we are going a step farther. We believe that Mr. Raston Path is unfitted to be one of his Majesty's Ministers of State, and our belief is based on vari-

ous grounds. We shall to-morrow publish the full story of a romance in the early life of Mr. Raston Path, and we make no excuse for the personal nature of the revelation. A man who behaved as Mr. Raston Path behaved in the episode which it will be our painful duty to relate is no fit man to follow in the footsteps of honourable men like Gladstone, Beaconsfield, Salisbury, and Asquith."[38]

"He's really a devil, Viola – this man, Lodden," said Cartlet that evening.
"Oh, I don't know."

[5 December 1913]

Chapter IX.
Raston Path's Romance.

The ingenious deviser of human happenings; he who plans the mysteries, big or little, arranges for some to be revealed and some never to be revealed; has a frequent trick of dropping into a life a disturbing fact, some glowing incident which long after it has been forgotten is resuscitated to fill in a plot or round off a story. Sometimes it provides a tragic finish, and sometimes rounds off a series of happenings in true novelette style.

Disturbing, indeed, are these resuscitations from the past. They are like a message from the dead. The individuality who works out these involved groupings with their final solutions is no reporter of the feelings of his puppets. He had his unknowable purposes to fulfil, and they seem sometimes to be quite cruel purposes and sometimes benevolent purposes. A forgotten sin to give a touch of happiness; a forgotten folly to stir someone into further folly, a mad action to harass and perhaps to destroy domestic happiness two generations later. In the piecing together of sections of the game there seems a steady and intentional hand, and that is all we can say.

The impulses which linked together the lives of Path and Lodden, Viola and Cartlet and Gaunt, and a number of others, might well seem to the imaginative mind to have sprung from some single general purpose; and the events which I am trying to record are but visible fragments of a complex whole. The blind motives of Lodden and Path respectively, and the fight which arose from the proper mingling of elements; this fascinating influence of Gaunt over Viola Cartlet; the conventional relationship between the Cartlets and Path, were all parts of the general scheme. There were many other persons and events to come in before the story was to be taken towards its conclusion. Meanwhile Fate, the planner, was putting in events to help on the development.

Some among the simple-minded readers of the *Daily Light* exclaimed with relief it was the doing of Providence that Raston Path should be revealed as he was before he did any more injury to the community. The great mass of the respectable people – and these provided the bulk of the readers of the *Daily*

Light – were very pleased at the attack on Path in reference to his investments, and although some of them deprecatingly shrugged their shoulders over the announcement as to the coming revelation of a hidden romance, they nevertheless were very glad and thankful in their hearts about it, and the devouter of them, especially the middle-aged ladies with property, saw in it the hand of heaven. At last he was to be curbed. Of course, this feeling was nothing like so prominent or widespread as the curiosity set up by the advertisements, but it went to swell the volume of expectation.

Orders poured in to the newsagents for the *Daily Light*. Lodden and his business staff had a fierce 12 hours of preparation for printing an unexampled number for one issue.

It was a daring move, this of the *Daily Light*. Hitherto all papers had made it their ostensible practice not to touch the private lives of Ministers or ex-Ministers except in so far as they were made known by Parliamentary proceedings, or occasionally by happenings in the courts of law. Journalistic traditions and public traditions were thus broken by Lodden's action, but he had carefully considered the cost and had taken all the circumstances into account. The worst that could happen would be a big libel action, and this he was prepared to meet to any amount of money. On the other hand he would certainly gain enormously for his paper; it would have an advertisement such as had never been available for any journal published in the British Isles. Questions of good taste or common humanity did not influence Lodden, were not thought of by him. His object was to benefit the *Daily Light*, and also to achieve that which he had set his hand to, namely, the ruin of Path. It was perhaps more important for him now to bring about the latter than to pile fresh success on to the already-successful *Daily Light* for he was a man who had a feverish loathing of failure; he hated himself for failure; and frequently lost sleep over projects, comparatively small ones, which he had been unable to carry to fruition. Now, with all the world aware that he had set out to smash Path, there could be no turning back, no hesitancy, in the use of his weapons. This was a far more important factor than his personal desire to crush this obstinate opponent.

As I have said, a certain resentment had grown up within him.

Well hated already, Lodden had nothing to lose in the shape of personal regard by the desperateness of his venture. And this desperateness thrilled him. The preliminary set-backs he had experienced at the hands of Path stimulated him for further encounter.

The *Daily Light*'s narration of the episode in Raston Path's life was a great success from the journalistic point of view. Practically all the evening papers in the country copied it. The circulation of the *Light* that day, for the first time in its history, touched two millions. It was a genuine triumph for Lodden. He had done great things for himself in a business way by this stroke, and had, moreover, given an uplift to the Authoritarians such as they had not had since they went out of office. If a General Election would have been forced it is certain that the story as to Raston Path, whether true or not, would have been sufficient to turn the balance against the Government.

While all the Progressive papers fiercely proclaimed the *Daily Light* story a libel, no statement about it could be obtained from Path himself. He did not reply to any of the telegrams which were addressed to him in Scotland. "Possibly," said the *Westminster Gazette*, "he thinks the malignant assertions are unworthy of serious notice." But the public, which dearly loves a bit of scandal about a prominent man, gave a great deal of notice to the story. It was the topic of conversation everywhere. And if ever politicians gloated it was the Authoritarians.

What, then, was the story in the *Light*? It was not very long, and can thus be reproduced exactly as it appeared. This was the story: –

> RASTON PATH AS LOVER.
> FORGOTTEN INCIDENT IN HOME SECRETARY'S LIFE.
> WHERE IS THE GIRL!
> POLITICIAN AND A ROMANTIC MYSTERY.
>
> We are able to give publicity to-day to an interesting incident of the past life of Mr. Raston Path, the Home Secretary, the most prominent member of the Progressive Administration. Interest in Mr. Path's personality has always been great, and it will be increased by the knowledge that he was one of the principal figures in a romance which is now, unhappily, extinguished.
>
> A few months before Mr. Path was invited to become the Red candidate for the northern constituency which first elected him to Parliament he had an acquaintance with a lady which, after his return to the House of Commons, was somewhat abruptly broken. Young as he was Mr. Path was a well-known speaker before he received the Parliamentary invitation, and he was, perhaps, more careful then than now, and always, where possible, prepared his longer speeches in advance and made elaborate notes. For the preparation of these notes Mr. Path used to go to the office of the Misses Denver, of 1,001, Victoria-street. His letter, too, and the frequent articles for the newspapers which he wrote were also dictated at this typewriting office. He became acquainted at the Misses Denver's establishment with a young lady of 20, the daughter of a clergyman in Warwickshire, who had come to London to earn her living, and was in the service of the typewriting firm. Like most other people who dictate material he had a preference for one operator, and this lady, Miss Croxten, did practically all Mr. Path's work.
>
> The business acquaintanceship developed into friendship, and there could be no doubt that Mr. Path found in Miss Croxten interesting personal traits, even as she did in him. We are in a position to state that Mr. Path subsequently developed a great friendship for Miss Croxten, made her his companion on frequent occasions outside of business, took her to lunch, entertained her at theatres, and on more than one occasion made a day excursion up the river with her.
>
> We can carry the story a step farther. An intimate personal friend of Miss Croxten tells us of how that lady regarded herself as the future wife of the present Home

Secretary. She was only a woman clerk, she said, but she knew that that would make no difference with Raston Path. He loved her far too well to allow ambition for his future or enthusiasm for the cause in which he was engaged to stand in the way of his union with her. But there must have been a mistake somewhere. We are credibly informed that the acquaintanceship came to a sudden end. The rupture was not due to Miss Croxten's initiative. It is, perhaps, merely a coincidence that it took place about the time that Mr. Raston Path was expecting the honour of an invitation to contest his first constituency for Parliament.

That, then was the story of the *Light*. It was supplemented by a short leading article, which carried mock modesty, mock dignity, and mock moderation throughout.

"We have presented the story of Mr. Path's past adventure without any desire to attract the vulgar attention of the seeker-after-the-curious in the lives of well-known men. We have presented it because we feel that it is not an episode of which any honourable man would be proud, and not an episode which any right-thinking citizen would like to belong to the history of one of our leading politicians. Before now we have criticised Mr. Path on grounds of his political policy. But every public man owes a debt of private honour to the State.

"There may be nothing specially blameworthy in Mr. Path's action. We set out the facts for what they are worth. But we may be permitted the observation that the story which we give to the country this morning is not one which we should like to be associated with the character of a public man who is attempting with some determination to remould our social life."

[6 December 1913]

Chapter IX – Continued.
Conflicting Opinions.

It does not require much imagination to conceive the storm which the publication of the two articles in the *Daily Light* aroused in political circles all over the country. People asked where the facts had been obtained. Miss Denver's office in Victoria-street had been closed for years and Miss Denver had retired with a comfortable competence, and her staff had been scattered to the winds. That was rapidly ascertained by the other papers which sought to glean confirmation or contradiction from 1,001 Victoria-street.

It was to be supposed, therefore, that the devastating energy of the *Light* had unearthed in some direction or other someone who had been employed with Miss Croxten at the office. The searches for Miss Croxten herself were equally unsuccessful. Her father, a widower at the time, had been dead some years, and no immediate relatives were to be found. Given time, of course, the matter might be elucidated, but in the pressure of a few hours, a few days, even a week or so, there was nothing to be discovered.

Raston Path came back from Scotland 24 hours after the publication of this story, but he declined to make any statement, and indeed shut himself in his office in Whitehall and devoted himself steadily to the preparation of this new Bill. The only Cabinet colleague he saw for a few days was Sir Harry Venture, with whom he had a private talk.

Hardened as he was, Majority Gaunt had some misgivings about the story when he saw it in print, for, in spite of Path's trick on him, he could not shake himself free from that instinctive personal touch of liking inspired by his first meeting. This personal story about the Home Secretary's past made him feel rather low and sordid. True, the story had been obtained practically without his help, but that did not affect his feelings. Sentimentalism ran through Gaunt like a white streak, and somehow he felt queer.

He knew how innocently sometimes men get mixed up with women, and how in the cold light of subsequent days their behaviour looks beastly. And he was quite prepared to find excuses for Raston Path, even if the story was true. He was not certain that it was true, in all its details. Still there must be some foundation for it. And he realised with what cold unscrupulousness it had been sought for and set out on behalf of the inquisitive and curious public. His standard of journalistic behaviour was not high, but he was half inclined to agree with Wrightson, who, in the reporters' room, declared that "Archie was playing it low down on Path." All he said, however, was: "Serve him right. Shouldn't go into public life if he has got these things back in his private days."

"All that be jiggered," said Burton, "who hasn't got 'em back in his private days? What about Archie himself; do you think he is a blessed saint?"

"Oh, Archie – but I'm not talking about him. I mean the really respectable people. Those high and mighty respectable kind of chaps. There's the Prime Minister – highly dignified and a pattern to the world, according to the papers. Do you think he's got nothing back which he wouldn't mind becoming public? Don't be a durned fool."

"Well, he takes the chance of it coming out."

"So does everybody else. Look at Fortesque, the novelist, who's got that castle in the North of England. He preaches all about deserted women and starving girls, and heaven for the blessed, and all that sort of thing in his novels, and as a result of it his last book went through sixteen editions. They say he has done more good for the morals of the nation than all the popular preachers of the last ten years put together."

"Probably he has."

"The funny thing is, he was a devil of a chap with the women. From what I can hear, too, he's got an eye for a pretty girl now."

"That's all right," cut in Burton. "What are his little personal peccadilloes compared with the good he is doing to the rising community by his sloppy goodness in his books? Probably kept many a girl on the right path."

Gaunt drew a copy-pad in front of him, frowned, and set to work to do a bit of writing. "Oh, well," he said, "Path's able to bear all the blame you're able to load on him."

"He's a bit nippy," said Wrightson. "He'll probably get back yet."

"I've an idea this will do for him," said Gaunt. "I think he is down and out over this business."

"He hasn't made any statement up till now," said Burton, "and very likely he'll come along and deny the whole thing. Another bit of the *Daily Light*'s flapdoodle!"[39]

"It's a blooming fine look-out," said Gaunt. "Wouldn't that please the 'old man'? But I think we've got him this time, right enough."

But for all his words Gaunt was not particularly happy about the matter, and when he went up that evening to see the Carltets, Violas' joy over the revelation grated on him a little.

"Isn't it beastly," she said, "having to be connected by family with such a man? He seems to be really a low man altogether, apart from his politics."

"I hadn't anything to do with the story," said Gaunt; "but you know how sometimes these things get exaggerated. I don't know that he's so bad as all that."

"You could tell he was low," said Viola; "you could tell it by his manners and the way he talks about other people. Think of all those vulgar speeches he made. You remember what he said about the Lords, and how rich people are always wicked and poor people are always good."

"Not quite that," said Gaunt, smiling.

"Oh, but he did. Have you ever read any of his speeches? You should study them. Of course it is all artfulness on his part, pretending to look after the poor people and all that; of course, it is only his way of getting popularity for himself."

"I don't agree with him," said Gaunt, "with his politics, but I think he is a bigger man than you make out. He's sincere –"

"Sincere!" cried Viola. "Great Heavens! What do you think he is doing all this for?"

"I think he is carried away by his sentimental regard for the wretched sections of the population, and that there is a good deal of ambition –"

"That's just it. Now you have hit it. Don't talk to me about his sincerity. He's looking out for himself."

"But what do you think he could get out of it? He is probably the most important member of the Cabinet, more important really than the Prime Minister, and to that extent he has more to say in the Government of this country than any other single person."

"You don't understand," said Viola; "you don't understand. Do you know what he is trying for? He's trying to get a baronetcy. He wants a title. That's all it is."

Gaunt looked at her blankly, and then he tried to smile. "A baronetcy?" he said. "Politicians like Path give those away to successful merchants and financiers. They don't –"

"Oh, that shows how little you understand Raston Path. It's a title he's been trying for all this time."

Poor Gaunt gave it up then and tried to turn the conversation. "Yes. I suppose there will be a terrible hullabaloo about this romantic story."

Viola would not be put off. "You don't really believe that working people are hard done by, do you, and all these things that people say, like Raston Path?"

Gaunt was a wee bit obstinate. "There's a good deal of poverty and misery which we know nothing about," he said.

"But they deserve it. They are not the same as we are. The people of that kind have always been poor; they are brought up poor, and they don't feel things like we do."

"We all get hungry the same."

"Do you mean that these people feel just like we do? Don't you think it hurts a well-bred person to be poor more than some of those workmen who have been in different conditions all their lives? Of course, it isn't the same thing. Do you think that if a fine lady is suddenly reduced to hardship she doesn't feel it any more than a factory woman?"

"She's lucky ever to have had a time of refinement and luxury."

"Don't be stupid. They are a different class of people altogether. And look at those workmen. Look at those plumbers we had in the other day – lazy and cross people. There was a leak, and they actually wouldn't stop to see to it after 12 o'clock on Saturday. Said their time was up. One of them was swearing like anything because he had to carry some piping in from outside. Said some other man ought to have done it. There was another of them spitting about all over the place. Disgusting. You don't mean to say that these people are just the same as we are?"

Gaunt shrugged his shoulders.

[8 December 1913]

Chapter IX – Continued.
"A Sign of Good Friendship."

"Of course, politicians and people like that – they don't know about the working classes," said Viola. "My father had a factory, and I know them well. I know about them exactly. When you have had experience of it of that kind you don't believe in the sentimental nonsense talked by Raston Path and others. Look how the servants treat you. I found my biscuits in the drawing-room gone the other day. I laid a trap for one of the girls; counted the biscuits in the biscuit-box on the sideboard; made sure that only Parker, the maid, went into the room, because I was in the kitchen with cook the whole time – so cook couldn't have done it. Then I went into the drawing-room afterwards and found that four of the biscuits were missing. Parker outfaced me, but when I told her that I had counted the biscuits she had to confess, and cried like anything. Of course, that didn't get over me. No; they are a deceiving lot. Don't talk to me about the working classes. No; the more you do for them the more ungrateful they are. My mother and people live in the country now and devote themselves to parish work and so on, and the way the cottagers scandalise about them is something atrocious. You have only got to know of these things and then never talk about the poor, hard-done-by working class."

Viola had worked the colour into her cheeks with her emphasis, and she was in no mood to stand contradiction. Gaunt was not interested enough to argue with her. They were walking up and down the garden together, waiting for George Cartlet to come home to dinner, and Gaunt bent to smell a rose.

"All this talk about democracy," said Viola.

"Rotten," said Gaunt.

"Do you know, I think you are a bit of a Red yourself, Marjorie," she said.

Gaunt felt a little thrill run all through him, but he still bent over the rose, as though intent on inhaling al the sweetness that he could. The thrill was due to the fact that he had called him by a common abbreviation of his Christian name. It was the first time.

"I a Red!" he said, straightening himself up slightly. "What nonsense."

"Oh, you think a good deal of Raston Path. I can tell that."

"Doing my best to knock him out," said Gaunt.

"Yes, and he did his best to knock you out, didn't he, when he played that trick on you about the Bill!"

"All in the game," said Gaunt.

Then they heard George Cartlet coming in at the front door, and they went through the house to meet him.

Gaunt was inclined to think that his name had slipped out unconsciously, and that Viola was unaware of it, but at dinner he was put straight on this. Towards the end of the meal she looked up and said, in reference to nothing in particular –

"We are such good friends, now, Mr. Gaunt, that I am going to ask you to call me Viola; that's my Christian name, you know; and I am sure George would like you to call him by his Christian name; wouldn't you, George?"

For the fraction of a second George seemed to hesitate, but he swallowed the dose quickly, and muttered, "Yes, yes, certainly."

"There you are," said Viola, "there you are. And I am going to call you Marjorie: that's short for Majority. You don't mind?"

"Delighted," said Gaunt, though for once the callous young man was not quite comfortable.

It was all so unexpected and sudden. And yet he had known that it must come. It was the outward symbol of an intimacy which they had long understood without words. Poor George Cartlet was the sufferer. It all seemed very amusing to Gaunt, and yet at the same time quite reasonable and natural. Six weeks before he would have snorted with scorn at the idea that a married lady of great personal charm and irreproachable manners and standing would be calling him by his Christian name before her husband and claiming her husband's endorsement of the familiarity. Gaunt felt his breath coming and going a little quicker over the whole business. Momentary embarrassment for himself and the husband was not the thing that stirred him, but the portent for the future. Gaunt felt himself in the midst of a swiftly-moving current. He did not try to reach the bank.

All three of them went into the drawing-room afterwards, and Viola played a little music, and Gaunt sang that robust little song of Conan Doyle's, "The Song of the Bow."[40] And then, presently, after some desultory chat George Cartlet went upstairs to develop some photographs.

"It's really only an excuse," he said. "It's because I want to have a pipe, and Viola won't let me smoke in the drawing-room. You stay here and have some more music."

He seemed quite pleased that Viola should have found a congenial companion, and Gaunt had a momentary glimpse of the tacit domination exercised by Viola.

They did not have any more music after George Cartlet had gone upstairs to the back room on the first floor to develop photographs, because Viola said she wanted to hear Gaunt talk about his journalistic experiences. And so they sat together on the settee and Gaunt told her some of his amusing adventures.

Once or twice he was a little startled by the lack of interest in her eyes, and he had an uncanny feeling that she had no sense of humour, because she did not seem to appreciate the point of some of his narratives. He wondered about it at the time. Afterwards, some time afterwards, she told him it was because she was interested in him more than in his stories, and she liked to watch him talk and hear his voice, and to notice his gestures, and to feel his personality; she was not particularly interested in what he had to say – a confession which somewhat hurt Gaunt at the time. It is to his credit that he would rather have had her interested in what he was saying than in himself. But as he sat by her side he was only faintly conscious that there was something wrong in her listening, because he had had many good listeners in his time. Their knees did not touch to-night. They took care of that. They sat diagonally on the settee, half facing each other. Presently some incident from him caused them to drop into conversation and Viola told of her deep and passionate belief in the existence of the soul. Gaunt felt a little uncomfortable about these things. She had vague and wondrous longings for soul companionship in eternity. "That was the be-all and end-all of love affinities on earth," she said. "There is no greater motive power, nor could there be any," and all the nice things in the universe were but subsidiary to this grand summit of emotion which reached through life and beyond death when two people really loved each other.

Gaunt had become the silent one now. He said "Yes' or "No," or "I suppose so" with the taciturnity of a man beyond his depths. It seemed a little morbid to him. And yet, as he looked at her, her brown eyes brimming, her hair glistening, her cheeks imbued with the deep red, rich colour, her head thrust forward towards him in her eagerness, her neck most beautifully fair, her body eloquent in its lines of sinuous grace, he could feel himself yielding to some of her vague imaginations.

"Do you ever go to church?" she said, as she came a little nearer to him.

"Afraid not," he said, "unless I get an assignment from the office."

"Do come one night; come one Sunday night when you are over here."

She was nearer him now. Upstairs they could hear George Cartlet rattling some tin dishes as he went on developing his photographs. Away outside from one of the main suburban streets they could hear the faint rattle of a cart. Somewhere in the distance a dog barked faintly but continually. Long afterwards Gaunt remembered all these things. Presently, when there was a pause, he said, "After your kindness to-night at dinner I have got to try to call you by your Christian name."

"Didn't you know that you had already done so?" she asked.

"Good heavens, no."

"You did it unconsciously the day before yesterday when we were talking together, and I felt then that it was a sign of good friendship. I told George that I should call you by your Christian name."

"So it was not new to him to-night?"

"Not exactly. I told him I was going to do it. I am sure we are going to be mixed up together a lot, because we understand each other, and I never met anyone who could understand me before."

Gaunt was no hero and certainly no saint, and he put out his hand and touched the back of hers gently, and said: "I am sure we shall."

She did not take her hand away. He took her fingers in his own, and then they sat there together with out saying anything for two or three minutes. George

Cartlet came downstairs noisily, and before he reached the drawing-room door Viola and Gaunt had unclasped hands, and were talking about the result of the *Light*'s disclosure and the future of Raston Path.

[9 December 1913]

Chapter X.
Secrets Past and Present.

The Chief Whip of the Progressive Party could not fail to be concerned about the reports from constituencies as to the campaign of the *Daily Light* against Raston Path. It was not altogether what the paper had said, although that was serious enough, but the fact that the story was laden with innuendo and built up into quite a disgraceful charge.

"Of course they meant that," said the Chief Whip, "and it has come off. All the *Daily Light* has got to do now is to report references to the Home Secretary at meetings."

The Prime Minister pursed his lips in customary fashion, but was quite calm.

"Do us a lot of harm," he said; "but we shall pick up again."

"Jolly awkward if we got a by-election just now."

"The thing will have faded a bit by the time we start on the new Bill."

"What about the Bill? Do you think it wise for Path to handle it, in all the circumstances?"

"Oh, yes, he must. We can't take it out of his hands."

"And he lies low for the present?"

"It's his own choice; he has reasons, he says. Meanwhile he is getting on with the Bill."

"The *Light*'s articles are simply disgraceful, of course; they are scandalous. I am telling all our men to rub it in at every meeting throughout the country, and, whether Path likes it or not, I am telling them to say the thing is a scoundrelly, cunning move."

"There will be a rebound presently against the *Light*, if they abuse Path enough."

"Yes, I am looking for that. And I am pretty sure he'll break out himself a little later on, although he doesn't say anything just now. Something in it about this girl, I suppose?"

"I suppose so."

Then they went off into a discussion of the Parliamentary arrangements for the following week, and forgot all about Path for the moment.

Path used to go down to the House every day to answer questions or to take part in a debate, and showed no special sign of resentment towards the *Daily Light*. Members who discussed the whole thing freely enough in the lobbies said nothing about it in the House itself – at least, for the present. There was a kind of feeling of outrage about it all; even the most venomous opponents of Path had a sneaking feeling that the *Light* had overdone it. On a knife-edge expectancy of future developments the most unscrupulous politicians among them dared not make a reference in debate.

That time would come, perhaps. For the moment there was hesitancy, partly from insecurity in the *Light*'s information, partly from a sense of nicety. If there should be any mistake with regard to facts they were quite sure that Path would turn on them like a tiger and not fail to score an advantage for himself in the country at the accusations. And, moreover, among the more thoughtful of the Authoritarian group there were real scruples about attacking a man on such a personal matter. With all its much-advertised drawbacks the House of Commons is a very human place.

Those members whose business it was to see Path, either in his room or in the Lobby, to talk about public affairs with him, carefully avoided the subject – unless, indeed, they happened to be personal friends, when there would be a bitter word from them about the *Light*, and a responding shrug of the shoulders from Path. He would, perhaps agree that it was a scandalous outrage.

"But you know what this blessed paper is; there are no bounds to its fables."

So there grew up among his intimate friendly acquaintances the knowledge that there was really nothing in this *Daily Light* story. True, in the smoke-room those who hated him were not afraid to suggest the worst against him. And it is also true that in the Progressive ranks once in a way you found a congenial soul who said: "Well, you never can tell. Even the best of men have their lapses."

On the whole, however it may be assumed that, so far as Parliament was concerned, Path was acquitted by his friends and was condemned whole-heartedly by only a section of his opponents. Some there were, of course, who held themselves in suspense ready to stab him if the opportunity should come along, and ready also to take no side if further evidence against him was not forthcoming.

In the country, however, the position was different, for here among the Authoritarian ranks there were no two opinions about his guilt – if guilt is the word to use with regard to the incident related by the *Daily Light* – and there was also no doubt about it in the minds of the enthusiastic Progressives as to his entire innocence. But evil communications find easy channels, and it is much more interesting to believe a piece of calumny than to disbelieve it. The result was that a good many thousands of people – perhaps a good many thousands who had no particular interest in politics, but who were familiar with the names of public men – accepted in effect the *Daily Light*'s story. Raston Path, it seemed, had been revealed as a trifler; perhaps as something worse; and it was all very interesting and very wonderful to talk about. To many a country rectory the story was a godsend. Authoritarian landowners in the Southern and Western counties, and rich men who had made great fortunes out of trade in the Midlands and the North, smacked their lips over the story.

"You have only got to look at his picture," they said, "to see what kind of a man he is. Talk about these new taxes on incomes, and nationalisation of railways. He's the kind of man who always talks about those things. Character? The man hasn't got a shred of character. And that's the kind of fellow we're governed by these days. Thank Heavens, there's a General Election coming along. We shall see, then, what the people think."

It is not to be imagined that that troublous spirit Raston Path was unmoved by the stream of abuse and comment which were sweeping up and down the country. Quietly enough he pursued his particular duties, and his answers to questions lacked some of that acerbity and stabbing cleverness which were characteristic of him. But this may have been partly due to the fact that the questions were not specially provocative. Perhaps it was as well that no big acrimonious opportunities were offered him during the debates mentioned. He was not called upon for dashing efforts of attack, and his subordinate, the quiet-mannered Financial Secretary to the Treasury, conducted in the Commons most of the routine business appertaining to his office. To the world at large Raston Path, scornfully ignoring all abuse and innuendo, was planning out his great Bill – the Bill on which the Government was to sail into a fresh sea of popularity.

But while to all appearances calm and careless of the all the buffeting, Raston Path was very angry at the outcry, and sometimes when he read the papers he was almost burning over with resentment at the malicious *Daily Light*.

Who can tell all his thoughts? He was stirred, of course, because his Parliamentary work was necessarily interfered with. His aims, sincerely directed to humane ends, would certainly be, to some extent, deflected, and some of the achievement he had set himself in his great passion of politics were certain to be delayed, and he was a man who did not easily endure delay. His spirit was too ardent, his desires too fervid, and the more he was kept back from his efforts the more intensely did he feel the wrongs and inequalities he sought to deal with. Of course, there was egotism in this. The wrongs and inequalities, if they existed, were no greater because he was hindered for a time. That there should be obstacles in the course of his conquering ardour was at times almost intolerable to him. He chafed under it. Back to him came the old rebellious heart he had in the time of the war, when he stood up against popular inclinations and gloried in fighting street corner crowds. There had, however, been a change since those days, for he had tasted of power. He had learned how his fierce persuasive will could triumph over those less persuasive, and in him was the automatic accretion of dominance of the almost vicious confidence which comes to a man who knows how to trample down obstacles in spite of suffering to himself. Unconsciously, he did not take opposition as such a matter of course now, and somewhere within him was a feeling that his great position in the State ought to be recognised even by those who vilified him.

There can be no doubt, also, that he was influenced, perhaps sub-consciously, by the knowledge that the remarks and reports about him would injure his personal career and would tend against his good name as a high officer of State. Raston Path had, perhaps, aims as impersonal as any statesman ever had, and yet he would have been too much of an angel if there had not come to him sometimes the thought that his destination was Prime Minister of this country. If such a thought flitted across him occasionally, it was accompanied by the knowledge that he would have still more power – and if some critical archangel had challenged him with pride, Path would swiftly and genuinely have retorted that he sought more power for the sake of pushing on still more strongly with the work he was now engaged upon. True, indeed, would this have been, and yet at the same time, whether Path recognised it or not, there was a personal vanity in him; the intuitive strivings for more eminence and still more eminence. So it was that he set his teeth hard, sometimes panted his fury at the *Daily Light*.

It will be seen at once that Path was holding his hand for some purpose, keeping himself in for some effort. The silence of Raston Path in such a case did not spring from benevolent motives. He was not an altruist where his enemies were concerned. Why he was waiting was not clear even to colleagues of his in the Cabinet, but it was pretty generally felt that he was feeling his way towards an effective retort and undoubtedly seeking to find means to counteract the energy of the *Light*.

While he did not say very much about the attacks on himself he endorsed the platform campaign in his defence which had been set going by the Whips. He thought it a good move, he said. His own opinion was, however, that this calumny would pretty soon die out. The best way to meet it was to produce a feeling of confidence in the new legislation put forward by the Government, and to make the Bill upon which they were now engaged such a measure of reform that these personal squabbles would be drowned and swept from sight. Though he said all this his friends knew perfectly well that no day passed without careful scrutiny as to methods of dealing with the *Light* and its propriety. The Home Secretary, they knew well, was not a Christian who turned his other cheek to the smiter. So everybody waited on the certain knowledge that there would be a good deal of interest yet in the fight that was going on.

[10 December 1913]

Chapter X – Continued.
An Episode at Hampstead.

It was on the day the *Light* published the story that Hilda Cartlet said to Path: "Was there ever such a girl? I don't remember her."

"Yes," said Raston, "there was such a girl. She did act as my typist."

Hilda waited for him to go on, but he seemed to be thinking to himself as to how much he should tell her.

"Does that mean –"

"I don't think I can tell you everything now, Hilda, but you know you will be the first person to hear the truth. It is rather a staggerer, this thing. I must have an hour or two to think over it."

The next day he told Hilda all the truth, and she did not repeat it to anyone – even to her husband. She did not know, and her husband did not tell her, that as a good, faithful brother he had known of the incident in Path's life at the time. He was inclined to smile at the memory though he told Raston as they talked about it that the *Light*'s action was a "dirty and disgusting piece of business."

There was one other man who was apprised of the facts, and that was Sir Harry Venture. And he took it upon himself to tell the other members of the Cabinet that the story was one which Raston Path could not be expected to enter into, and that his colleagues must take his honour for granted. If they did not choose to do so – well, their blood be upon their own heads.

In a body of eighteen men, however friendly they may be together, there are bound to be some who would privately find cause for suspicion in circumstances such as those I have described; and here and there a head was shaken and an eyebrow tilted at the silence of Raston Path. The Home Secretary took no notice. He went on with his ordinary business.

Viola Cartlet was much stimulated by the revelation, and she told her husband that she had been quite certain from the start that Raston Path was a bad man. "He is just one of those sharp, cunning men that get on, and he is selfish, too, or he would have got married before now."

"Nothing is too bad for him in your eyes, Viola. You overdo it a bit, you know. You would never convince anyone that he is really a rotter."

"Oh, he's not clever enough to deceive me. You can trust a woman in these things. I knew there was something crooked in him directly I saw him."

She wrote to Gaunt that night and asked him to come and spend the following week-end with them. This was her letter: –

My dear Marjorie, –
George and I want you to come over and spend Saturday and Sunday with us. Do please come. I know you can manage it if you want to. George doesn't get home till the afternoon, but you come along in the morning if you can, because I want to have a long talk with you about a lot of things. What an extraordinary story that is about Raston Path. Did you have anything to do with it? I am just dying to know how you got the news. Nobody seems to know anything about it in the family. Hilda won't say a word. I think she's cross with me because I don't like Raston. I can't help it. I can't possibly disguise my feelings. I dare say the man has got some good points, but I simply loathe him. Do bring up the first three chapters of your story. I am just dying to read them. I am sure it is going to be a great success. Let me give you whatever help

I can – that is, if you don't mind me seeing your material before it is made public. You know I should treat it in confidence. You will have to have it typed two or three times, I am told. Would you let me help you with it? It would be rather fun for me. I should just love it. If you will, I shall begin to take typewriting lessons next week. Don't forget next Saturday. I know it is your week-end off, because I have been keeping count. If you can get here about eleven I will meet you at the station.

    Yours as usual, Viola.

Things had gone so far with Gaunt that such an invitation was impossible for him to refuse, and, indeed, was such as to set him eager for the Saturday. True it was that in the coming weekend he was free. The knowledge that Viola Cartlet had remembered this was pleasant. It was equally pleasant, though one fears not at all right, to know that she expected him in the morning before her husband returned. Gaunt was not the man to hesitate under such provocativeness. He was at Hampstead by the selected train, and there at the station was Viola, spick and span,[41] her face glowing with healthy pleasure.

Instead of walking to the left, down towards Cowdray Gardens, they turned to the right, up towards the Heath. Viola was full of lively talk, high spirits were in her eyes, and Gaunt thought he had never seen a more virile, graceful type of womanhood. It was a joy to walk by her side. They talked intimately on small things until they reached the Pond and began the dip in the grass towards the lanes through the undergrowth.

"Do you know," said Gaunt suddenly, "we look rather like two sweethearts out for the afternoon."

"Oh, I say, that's a little vulgar, isn't it?"

"Yes, perhaps it is."

They covered another fifty yards before anything more was said, and then her hand touched his and he tried to hold it. She took it away determinedly and increased her pace a little, and conversation fell. Presently they reached a gate overlooking a meadow, and against this they came to a halt, leaning on it and making passing comments on the prettiness of the scene. She was resting on the gate, with her arms folded on the top rail, and he, by her side, presently put his hand on her shoulder and talked to her. She did not draw away. Presently a man and two boys came along, and she shifted hastily away from Gaunt. There was another little silence, and the Gaunt said: –

"I suppose many men fall in love with you?"

She looked up at him without surprise, and said: "No. Why should they?"

They looked at each other in the eyes for a few seconds, and then Gaunt said slowly: –

"You know that I'm in love with you now?"

"I have wondered sometimes if you were," she said.

He tied to slip his arm through hers, but she would not have it.

"On, no," she said, and looked round fearingly for passers-by. No man could have been more encouraged than Gaunt.

"Let us go back," she said.

Gaunt, with his heart beating pell-mell, tried to talk about other things on their way to the house, but his words were often almost mechanical. Excitement was all in his veins; he travelled on air. All sign of emotion that Viola gave was in the deep flush on her face, which had not left her. Gaunt knew that he was not repulsed, but wondered if she were playing with him for vanity's sake. Some young married women, perfectly faithful to their husbands in big things, take a delight in the flirtatious homage of the young men whom they attract, and they carry the thing to the danger point – danger for the men, not danger for themselves. Gaunt knew this quite well, and in his excitation wondered if he was permitting himself to be a victim of this dalliance. At any rate, it was very luxurious. No thought of morality or immorality entered his head.

They went back to the house and had lunch with George Cartlet and a friend of his who had come in; and a very jolly quartet they were. Viola, not often touched with humour, said sparkling things, and George Cartlet and his friend were also lively and in high spirits. Gaunt was a little quieter than usual. Viola directed most of her talk to her husband's friend, a solicitor in the City. He was an old acquaintance of the family and treated pretty much like an indulged and indulgent brother. A flush was on her face all the time. Gaunt once came swiftly to the decision that it was vanity in her and that she had no real feeling for him, but then he changed again as he remembered the unspoken communion which had been established between them. He thought he realised, however, that she did not intend to let him go farther in his declaration.

They went out into the garden after lunch and sat in deck-chairs, so that the men might smoke at ease. While they were making themselves comfortable Viola called Gaunt to adjust her chair for her, and then she managed that her hand fell on his out of sight of the others. She pressed it warmly.

[11 December 1913]

Chapter XI.
The "Daily Light's" New Move.

The encircling cord, unseen and widely looped, was drawing in and bringing closer together those who were to play their part. What would Viola Cartlet have felt had she realised that the little typist, Nancy Kirk, was to be brought into the current of her life? Viola would have regarded it in the same way as a suggestion that her parlourmaid and she should share the relations of life; for human experiences never taught Viola any of the great lessons. The incoming of Nancy Kirk was to be a shock, a humiliation, and a continual amusement. To this there only remains to be added the fact that it was in the office of the *Daily Light* that the development of affairs put Viola and Nancy Kirk on the road towards each other.

The country was still talking of the revelations about Path when Lodden had Wansmuth and Gaunt up in his room for a talk.

"The paper's going strong," he said, "but we're failing."

"Failing!" said Wansmuth.

"Yes." Lodden walked across to the mantlepiece to get a match for his cigarette. The other two waited in silence for his explanation.

"Do you mean to say you haven't realised that! Good heavens, where are your eyes? Yes, I know we have set the country talking, and I know we have put a hundred and fifty thousand on a day. I know all about that. But what about smashing Raston Path? We're pretty near a bad break. That's what it is. Path is right up in the air. What I hoped was we should set the Moderate people in his own party against him. If we could have made the sober-sided Progressives think that he was a bit of a scamp as well as an adventurer, the thing was done. To show him up so that his own side would talk about him in private, and some of the other Cabinet Ministers talk abut him among themselves – that was the great thing. It hasn't come off."

"Well, I don't know," said Wansmuth. "There was never a man so much abused."

"Of course, of course, but who is it? It is just our own people and a fringe of noodles who don't matter. All our people are glad to get a stick to beat the man with, and we've given them several sticks, and I dare say we've done him a tremendous lot of harm among our own Moderate people who flatter themselves that they are tolerant. But are there any signs of "rattling" on the other side? Do any of the local Progressives pour resolutions against Path? Do any of them write letters to us telling of their discussions? Is any sign of members of the Cabinet giving him the cold shoulder? There's nothing of the kind. We've had a big boom for the fight, but we haven't killed Raston Path. We've got to kill him. Now, mind this, if Path takes his party into power again at the next election the *Daily Light* has scored the biggest failure of its life. The whole country will laugh at us. He's got to go under. Let's have no mistake about that."

"We can only keep it up at full pressure," said Wansmuth.

"We must do more than that. We must prepare for the future."

"Make ready to meet his next move?" said Gaunt.

"Eh? Oh, you're here," said Lodden, rudely, as he snatched a passing glance on Gaunt. "We have shown that Path as a man is a bit askew, now we have got to convince people that his opinions and views and feelings are all wrong. See? If we can get the *Light* on that line the other things will help us. It will all count. Of course, we can't do this with the dull leading articles Bellow writes for us every night. They're no good. We want something harder and better."

Lodden handed his cigarette box to the two men, and that was the beginning of the discussion as to the planning of the new campaign.

"Yes," he said, at the end of half an hour's talk, "we'll splash the facts as we see them. Our special commissioners will investigate the conditions of the poor thoroughly. There must be a real examination of poverty. No nonsense, no cant. We must get down to it. Sympathy with suffering will run though all we publish, but the facts will have to be stated plainly. The causes of poverty and all the evils that spring from it, together with suggestions for bettering matters.[42] We must be careful and thorough, and then we shall be able to show up the uselessness and injury of the spasmodic sentimentality of Path. This series of articles will do the paper good. But the principal thing will be to expose this silly, dangerous plan by which Path snatches a handful of gold from the rich to throw to the poor. If we get this well rammed home in the next month or two we shall have taken the sting out of Path's coming work in Parliament. Very likely we shall win the next election."

"Seems good," said Wansmuth.

"A man for Scotland and the North, a man for the Midlands, and Gaunt to tackle London. Yes, I think that that will do."

Lodden swiftly preparing his scheme, was speaking almost to himself.

After the consultation Gaunt went down to the library and set about preparing a list of works dealing with social conditions, so that he might master what might be called the "official facts" in the course of the following week or two. He was going over books four or five months old when there came a telephone message from Lodden. Gaunt went up to him.

"Get on to this box-makers' strike in Southwark,"[43] he said. "See that." He handed over a cutting from an evening paper wherein it was stated that 150 girls employed in a card-box manufactury had struck work for more wages. "It looks like one of those cases that might have real human interest, and if you think the facts justify it we might take the girls' side. They seem pretty badly paid. Don't blackguard the employers, but show a bit of feeing for the girls. The sooner we get on to this kind of thing the better, and this is just the beginning in a small way."

Gaunt went off down to Southwark and soon leaned the facts. They were simple enough. At the office of the employers he was told "No information can be given to the Press," but a carman coming out of the works gate directed him to a neighbouring coffee house where five or six of the girls were having some tea, and here Gaunt was right in the thick of the matter at once. The girls were at first a little quiet and distrustful, but when they heard that he had been rebuffed at the office they were communicative enough. It seems that Messrs. Brimmingstone, their employers, had paid piece rates for box-making which brought in a remuneration of 7s. 6d. to 10s. a week for six days of 12 hours a day. A rearrangement of the prices had now cut the wages down by about 1s. 6d. a week. The girls, stimulated by a ringleader known as "Nellie," had rebelled, had seen the manager, and had been told that if they did not like to accept the revised rates they could get out. There was an excited meeting of the girls outside the works, and "Nellie" had made what was perhaps her first speech, which was more in the nature of heated conversational phrases, with the result that the girls decided to leave the factory at once. That was the story.

Gaunt could see even among those to whom he was talking how resentment had not entirely dimmed the thought of further privation. Dull eyes there were that told of more hunger in the future, and he was shrewd enough to see that the weaker spirits had been prevailed upon by the fierceness of the leaders. He insisted on having tea with the six and ordered more tea for them and while he had a piece of buttered toast he made the girls have ham and eggs and bloaters. The reporter had many things to do to attain his ends, but perhaps a kind heart moved Gaunt as well.

He was told that above all things he must see "Nellie."

"Nellie" was the life and soul of the strike. She had gone up that afternoon to see the head of the Women's Trade Union League in Clerkenwell in order to find out if it were possible to get the girls a small allowance from any central fund in view of the fact that they had no organisation and had been compelled by the smallness of their earnings to live from hand to mouth.

"Where can I see Nellie?" asked Gaunt.

"She lives at 21b, Luton-buildings, Lant-street. She's sure to be home tonight – she and her mother and sister live there."

Later on Gaunt went to 21b, Luton-buildings, on the fourth floor of a block of model dwellings,[44] and Nellie herself opened the door to him. She was a tall girl, with heavy features, a big mouth, and exquisite fair hair. Her hair reminded him of something, but for the moment he could not remember what. Nellie was wearing a white apron, and her hands, hastily wiped before answering the door, bore traces of flour. On learning Gaunt's mission she asked him in – not too cordially, because when as a girl you have to find your own living you distrust most people out of your class – with the exception of the doctor. Gaunt found himself in a plain little kitchen with a fire burning brightly, and saw on the dresser a pudding-basin, rolling pin, and paste-board – indication of the task he had interrupted. "Nellie" told him pretty much what he had learned before, and her quiet tone and obvious inexperience in the use of words and phrases did not prevent Gaunt from getting an idea of the part she had played in the affair.

"I have been up to Miss MacDonald, of the Women's League," she said, "and she's coming down tomorrow and, if possible, will be able to arrange for the girls to have five shillings a week while the strike lasts."

"That's not much."

"It'll be enough."

And Gaunt had a sudden glimpse of economies necessary to sustain life on five shillings a week.

"I am better off than some of 'em," said "Nellie," "because my sister's in work in an office. We get along all right. We've only got a young brother of ten and my mother to look after, so we're all right."

"Can I come and see you again to-morrow, to find out how things are getting on?"

"Certainly; you'd better come tomorrow evening, I shall know then. Are you going to do what you can for us in the *Daily Light*? Perhaps it'll make the firm give in."

"I am going to take the side of the girls, but I wouldn't reckon too much on that if I were you. I know what firms are."

He rose to go, and as he did so there was a knock at the door.

"Hallo." said "Nellie," "here's my sister." She opened the door and there stepped into the kitchen Nancy Kirk, Sir Robert Furley's secretary. Gaunt was more confused than she was. He stammered "Good evening" to her and another "Good evening" to her sister, and then went out and descended the stone steps of the building to the street, feeling somehow rather like a criminal.

A characteristic of the modern journalist's life is that the work of the moment dwarfs his interests, that his concentration, necessary as it is, to some extent foreshortens his vision and makes his day's occupation the real and object of life. It is very good for his paper that it should be so, but to outsiders this state of mind is rather novel and in some cases might even be a little tiresome. Gaunt tried to interest Viola Cartlet in the struggle of the Southwark girls, but her feelings were not at all touched, and he was chilled by it. With a great store of passionate affection within her, she had none to spare for outsiders, and though she agreed that there must be individual cases of misery and suffering she found no appeal in the fight the girls were putting up.

"They'll get on all right – these people always do; and after all, Marjorie, I dare say the firm pays them as much as it can afford."

Gaunt, who was daily among the girls, had found, with their touch of bravado and occasional courseness, much unselfishness, and he realised that the thing had not been properly explained to Viola, and that when she understood her naturally sweet nature would make her feel for the girls. He put aside all question of politics, he said, to get her to listen for a while as he told the girls' tale. He told it carefully and plainly. When he spoke of Jenny Briggs, a woman of thirty, who had pawned a clock which she was lucky enough to possess and had shared the money between herself and two other girls to pay their lodging for the week, his voice grew warm, and few could have listened to him without a flash of sympathy. But Viola laughed.

"Oh, the enthusiast," she said. "You will be talking nonsense like Raston Path soon."

Gaunt was depressed, almost vexed; he came to feel that somewhere in Viola there was emptiness. The thought stabbed him. He disliked the loss of her companionship on any side, and he went off early that evening rather pensive, and he almost failed to notice the tenderness with which Viola helped him on with his overcoat, fetched his gloves from the hall-stand, and pressed his hand in both of hers as she said "Good-bye."

His ears should have burned as he went his way home to Sydenham,[45] for Viola and her husband were discussing him.

"Tried to get out of Lodden to-day how he had wind of Raston Path's romance; he wouldn't say."

"I expect it was through Majority Gaunt one way or another."

"No, he volunteered so much."

"Well, what does it matter?"

"Oh, of course, it doesn't matter, but I was curious."

"People who know we are friendly with Lodden might think he got the tip from us. They wouldn't believe we know nothing about the thing. I wonder how the deuce Lodden lighted on it."

"Stories like that come to a newspaper in all kinds of odd manners, so Gaunt says."

"Pretty much what Lodden told me this afternoon. Gaunt came to my mind at once, because he is a good deal of a ladies' man, and is just the fellow to drop on scandal."

"I don't see that at all," said Viola, "why should he be more likely than anyone else to get the story unless he set out specially on the search. I don't understand what you mean by saying he is a ladies' man, either. How is he a ladies' man?"

"Oh, Lord, you mean to say you don't know then?"

The colour mounted high in Viola's cheeks.

"He is pleasant and agreeable, certainly, but I think it is a little unfair to call him a ladies' man. One would imagine he was just a common, low person."

"Oh, come, now, do you mean that you think he is an unimpressionable, capable fellow, who wouldn't glance at the flutter of a woman's petticoat? Why, look how he's running after you."

"I don't think that's very nice of you, George."

"Well, we will forgive him that, because the temptation's so great. But you don't seem to know his reputation."

"Reputation?"

"Well, what I mean is he's got a pleasant way with women, and he doesn't forget to use it."

"You don't dislike Majority Gaunt; you haven't got a spite against him?"

"What nonsense! I like him. I thought you knew me better. What I am saying is common knowledge in his office. Why, the other day when I was down there one of his fellows was chaffing him about some girl, and this afternoon Lodden told me how they put him on to stories where women are concerned, because he is so successful."

"Oh, I dare say he is that," said Viola.

"You know this strike of girls at Southwark; there is a wonderfully pretty young girl whose sister is connected with it, and Lodden says Gaunt has got round them completely with his sympathetic ways, and he is producing most excellent and appealing stuff for the paper. He's got to be a woman's man to carry off the thing."

"It is rather horrible," said Viola.

"Oh, I don't know. I dare say he is really interested in the girls."

"Nonsense, it is blank hypocrisy."

"Well, one of these two sisters is most sweet, quite out of the common, I'm told. But look here, don't you go and say anything to him about this. That won't do."

"Good gracious, is it likely? He is entitled to make love to a dozen girls, so far as we are concerned. Still, I am very fond of him, and I don't like to think of him as common and low and foolish."

"Oh, he can look out for himself."

"I dare say. By the way, are we going to Simpson's for tennis next Saturday?"

But Viola, though she had got away from the subject, was thinking a good deal about Gaunt. During dinner and afterwards, she said she had a headache, and went to bed early. She did not sleep very well.

At breakfast next morning she was thoughtful, and between eleven and twelve o'clock, after her husband had gone to the City, she rang up the *Daily Light* office, and asked for Gaunt.

[12 December 1913]

Chapter XI – Continued.
"Viola, I Love You."

Dunlop, in the news-editor's room, said that he was gone out – down at Southwark, he could not tell exactly where he could be found. Viola pressed the matter: was there no one in the office who could give the information; she particularly anxious to speak to Mr. Gaunt?

"I'll inquire in the reporters' room, and see what can be found out," said Dunlop, and he scurried round to Room 54, and as luck had it found Wrightson and Butler in. "Anyone know where Gaunt can be found at Southwark," he demanded.

"He's scattered all over the place," said Wrightson. "Usually looks in here for an hour in the afternoon."

Butler turned round, and flung in a word. "Gets back here about half-past six, comes straight from seeing the girls' strike leader."

So Dunlop went back to his room, and told Viola over the telephone all that he had been able to gather as to Gaunt's movements. "Better ring up in the evening," he said.

"It's about the strike business. Couldn't I see him down there?"

"Can't say exactly where he may be. You might get him when he calls at Nellie Kirk's to-night."

"What is her address?"

Dunlop hastily searched the file of the paper near him and found it. "21B, Luton Buildings, Lant-street."

Very sweetly Viola thanked him for his help and rang off.

Six o'clock that evening found her in Lant-street, Borough. Fever was in her veins. She was determined to see this girl for herself – the pretty one she had heard about. The long flights of harsh stone steps leading up to the third floor of Luton buildings were not used to the delicate swish of a black silk skirt, and one woman, standing at her door, put Viola down as the new district visitor.[46] Very graceful and sweet, but breathing hard from her exercise in climbing, Viola knocked at the door of 21B. She had little notion of what she was going to say or do, but she felt she would become very excited if she did not meet Gaunt, and meet him quickly; and she must see this girl – the pretty one.

She had no thought of anything extraordinary in her action; that she should be mounting into a block of tenements occupied by the poor; that slumdom lay around her; that she was an incongruous figure in these surroundings; all the reflections that would have sprung from these facts were unknown to her. Had it been possible for her to have pictured some woman friend doing what she was doing Viola would certainly have been amazed and disgusted. It may, therefore, be regarded as wonderful that she had not a glimpsing thought of the proprieties, that the conventions were in a foreign land for her. She was focused on her object, and what people would think of her, or what she in other circumstances would have thought of herself was a thousand miles from her consciousness.

The door opened. There, with her hand on the latch, stood a clean-cut girl, with soft, fair hair that shone. Viola craned towards her in sweetly questioning manner.

"Can you tell me if Mr. Gaunt – oh, there he is."

Her gaze had wandered over Nancy Kirk's shoulder to the interior of the room. The picture within was instantly beaten deep into her, and years passed before the picture was erased. A middle-aged woman shabbily dressed was shifting a boiling kettle from the fire, and on a wooden chair at the other side of the room Majority Gaunt, with a smile on his lips, was busily writing in a notebook which he held on his knees. Facing him, half-seated on the kitchen table, which was covered with oilcloth, was a tall, rather ungainly girl, smiling apparently at some information which she had just given to Gaunt. The latter's hat and stick were on the dresser to the left, and he looked to be thoroughly at home. A single glance drove all this straight into Viola's heart, and how much it disturbed her was impossible to know from her pleasant, natural salutation.

"Oh, Mr. Gaunt, I'm very sorry to come and bother you, but can you spare me a few minutes? It's important."

Gaunt, from being the picture of domestic ease, was instantly on pins, and jumped up and thrust his book into a pocket.

"Why, Mrs. Cartlet!"

He plunged forward for his hat and stick, Viola awaiting him outside the open door, and pretending not to listen as he exclaimed a word of good-bye. When he came out, and while the door was being shut, she said, "I wanted to see you," and Gaunt had a sudden, very cold feeling. Nothing was said as they went down the long, dim stairways to the street, but on reaching the foot she said, "Can we go to some park or someplace where we can talk without being overheard?"

She seemed serious and unfriendly, and Gaunt knew there was trouble coming. He called a cab, and told the man to drive to Kennington Park.[47] On the way no word was exchanged, and it was not until they had found an unoccupied seat and had taken possession of it that she turned to him and said: "I hear that one of the reasons you have been successful in your work is that you ingratiate yourself with women."

"That's a strange –"

"Is it true or not? Don't attempt to excuse yourself. Is it true?"

Her eyes were burning.

"What a ridiculous –"

"You have played with women, and are still playing with them."

She was trembling and speaking rapidly, and Gaunt saw that she could not bear him to speak even, that she was asking him questions to express herself, and not for the replies.

"Go on."

"Yes, I intend to. You are now running after this pretty little doll who opened the door to me. Yes, you are; you have been put up to do it. Even this common little minx –"

Gaunt's resolution for silence gave out.

"You are entirely wrong, and I am going to say so," he snapped. "Don't abuse people without knowledge. The girl who opened the door to you has been in the flat on only two occasions during the time I have visited her sister, who is the leader of these strikers, and on these two occasions she has said no word to me beyond good-evening. Before that I had met her once only, and that was in an office where she was engaged. So much for your tirade. As a matter of fact, she is prejudiced against me, so I never go there, if I can help it, when she is in. She returned earlier than usual."

"A prejudice against you," sneered Viola; "no doubt you'll soon break it down. Oh, I loathe you."

'I won't listen –"

"But you shall listen. You have been a friend of George and myself, and now that we learn this of you, do you think that I am going to sit still under such a thing? The fair girl is to be your latest victim – she shan't be. I'll go and see her myself."

Words were pouring from her, and the passion of the woman made her shake like a leaf, and Gaunt was startled and a little scarified, although in all his resentment was a touch of pride. Something of abasement was in him, too; true, his communications with Nancy Kirk had been correctly described, but the revelation to him of her beauty on that first day went some way to justify Viola's outburst – he felt that and squirmed, and he experienced also a self-conscious shudder at the thought that passing favour for a chit of a fair-haired girl should alienate him from this beautiful woman, whose admiration and affection had recently come to dwarf all other personal matters.

"There is nothing to cause you to abuse me, Viola," he said in quieter tones.

"Come," she said sharply, "let us walk round the park; we can talk as we go."

As they walked he told her again in some more detail about the Kirks and the coincidence in meeting Nancy. She listened now, and grew warm as he pleaded with her. She asked him some questions and he answered them, and his reasonableness soothed her; and presently his voice took on more feeling. They stopped under an overhanging tree and stood face to face for a moment or two.

"This almost makes me hate you; it is very terrible."

He took her hand, careless whether people were passing or not. She did not stop him.

"I don't think I can stand it," she said.

"Viola, dear –"

There were on the brink of being in each other's arms.

"We talked of love once, and told each other how neither of us had been in love. That has gone by. Viola, I love you!"

She laid a trembling hand on his arm, and said, looking round, "I feel sometimes that I love you."

They walked together without saying any more to the gate of the park, and he called a cab for her. Before it came he said: "Are you angry with me now?" And she put her lips near his ear and whispered, "I am happy, happy, – oh, so happy."

While Gaunt went back to the office, hot with elation and achievement, Viola Cartlet returned to her home, full of solicitous thought for her husband. She got special asparagus for dinner because he was very fond of it, and brushed afresh his evening dress so that it should be spick and span for him. She had a soft tenderness and pity for her husband that night.

[13 December 1913]

Chapter XII.
Nancy Kirk's Fear of Gaunt.

Nancy Kirk had feared and distrusted Gaunt from the first time she saw him, and she was almost shocked when she found how accident had brought him to her home, and if she happened to be in when he called on her sister about the strike, she was coldness itself, and declined steadily his endeavours for friendly conversation. She simply did not like him. With Nellie it was different, for she was more robust in half-a-dozen ways, and after the initial hesitation talked freely to the reporter, and was glad to see him, and looked upon him as a kind of pal in the effort against her employers. It had, of course, to be known that Gaunt had the knack of making himself at home, and he soon attuned himself to Nellie's chord, and that of her mother, an uncomplaining, quiet woman, who through the efforts of her daughters was now experiencing a shade less of poverty than had been her lot since the death of her husband 10 years before. It came quite naturally to her that after a time Gaunt should take the kettle off the fire, and presently should make tea, and that one day, overtaking her on the stairs, he should insist on carrying up three loaves of bread she had in a basket on her arm.

But Nancy was always a stranger. The very smoothness and rightness of Gaunt that day at the Progressive office had set her against him. Nor was she softened by the intuitive knowledge that hidden power was somewhere within the man, and she shrank within herself; but she knew her mother and sister would not understand, and was content to let them think that she had merely a foolish fancy against the genial, good-natured young fellow. Long, long afterwards was it when she realised that they with a vision less intense had seen him nearer the truth than herself. Sometimes she was annoyed, because she was disturbed by the eruption of Gaunt into her life. But, nevertheless, the thought of him fluttered her nerves, and she would even delay her work at the office so that her tram journey from Westminster to the Obleisk[48] would land her home after his evening call. If she could have known that he occasionally tricked her on purpose by making a late visit, she would have been in open rebellion, but Gaunt had tact enough never to obtrude on her attention, and to treat all meetings as purely accidental. You are not to believe that Gaunt was without his better feelings.

Not altogether on instinct was Nancy Kirk's aversion founded, for you appraise wrongly quite a sweet girl if you think that with natural sensitiveness she had no repugnance to display her sordid surrounding to one who had spoken to her on what may be called level terms. That the secretary of Sir Robert Furley should be revealed to the *Daily Light* reporter as living in workman's dwellings in Lant-street, Borough, was gall to her; and indeed it is to be confessed that she resented (although she would hardly admit it to herself) that he should know her sister was a factory girl, and was calling to see her because she was a factory girl. Dainty, quiet-mannered Nancy Kirk had lifted herself to respectability, and she was wounded that the man who had talked to her in the office should find out she lived in the grimness and greyness of Lant-street, that except for her office hours the factory girl's atmosphere was her atmosphere. That was not very grand or noble of Nancy, but it was the fact, and perhaps Gaunt realised it.

Nancy Kirk was 20; her sister 18½. Nancy at 18 had had a start as a junior hand in the factory of Messrs. Brimmingstone, but she took there a fervid determination to leave as soon as she could manage it. She had set her heart on it, and Fate would not withstand her. When work was slack and she had to labour only nine hours a day instead to twelve, she would go to the evening continuation school to get on with shorthand and typewriting, and even when she did 12 hours in the factory she stole a tired half-an-hour before bed for practice at home. She made sacrifices, and so did the others, and while Mrs. Kirk struggled with a little blousemaking to eke things out Nellie, a big, growing girl, had to be content with two slices of bread and butter instead of three; and sometimes she only got one slice.

Their lot was hard, but no harder than most of those who lived in the buildings, and when fortune has put you into that class of life no day passes without your being hungry, and, after all, it is not much to complain about if one day you have to put up with a little more hunger than on other days. So they struggled on.

Heaven knows what inherited touch of illumination, what chance flush in book or spoken word had moved the soul of Nancy Kirk. Inspiration some would call it. At its least it was a quiet but immovable decision to escape the horror of Lant-street life, to taste some part of a different kind of life where people spoke in a different tongue, wore different clothes, and saw things and understood things from which the factory girls were struck out as though they were dead. After this you will begin to understand the feelings of Nancy Kirk at the descent of Gaunt into her life.

Conceive her sensations when she learned that Gaunt, having confided to her mother and sister that he was to spend a fortnight as an out-of-work,[49] had asked if he might have lodgings in their flat for that period. Horror uplifted her, then indignation flamed from her. She saw in his suggestion something like a deliberate insult.

"He could have the little room, and we could make up a bed," said her mother protestingly. "He only wants his breakfast here; his other meals he'll get out."

"Do you mean you have seriously discussed his coming here?"

"Why not. It will be 4s. a week for us."

"Four shillings?"

"Yes, he said he would pay just what I would charge a working chap, and I told him Mrs. Clerk on the next floor had young Burns, who works at the greengrocer's and he pays her four shillings."

"Oh, mother he pays that for a bed for one night at the hotels and places where he goes, and why should he come here and try to live with us? Mother, don't think any more about it. He is making an excuse to come here. It is strange and wrong; I couldn't bear it."

Poor Mrs. Kirk was much depressed. "It's throwing money away," she said. "His rasher of bacon and bread and butter and coffee wouldn't cost us anything like that. Our coffee would do for him and I don't suppose he would eat very much. We should feel a little help now that Nellie's out of work."

"There's no need for that, mother. I've got £2 10s. in the savings bank, and we can have that out if we want it. Don't you see how lowering it would be to have a man here as a lodger?"

"He's very nice, and I can't think why you dislike him so. He's most kind." And when Nellie came in later she was on her mother's side.

"You've got a blooming lot of fads, Nan. It wouldn't be half bad to have him here; he wants to write stuff for the paper, about how hard it is to get a living and all that. Perhaps he'll write about us."

"I'll draw any money we want out of the savings bank. Don't you see we're just the scum, and he comes to live with us because of that."

"He calls us his friends," said Mrs. Kirk.

"You area a silly kipper, Nan," said Nellie; "you get too grand, that's what it is."

Nancy shook her head; her straight little mouth was set pretty hard.

"Oh, all right, mother," said Nellie, "we'll chuck it if Nan don't like it, but I think she's silly."

Mrs. Kirk sighed. "I'll send him to Mrs. Johnston, on the next floor. I know she's got a room; since Jim's been dead she's wanted to get somebody."

So it was settled, and Gaunt found he would have to take up his task in quarters where he would not see Nancy Kirk every evening. To do him justice, he was not seeing the opportunity to philander. Scornfully would Nancy Kirk have repudiated the idea, for she had read things in his eyes and face denied to the blind and foolish. Yet, had she known it, he had no inclinations for dalliance – which was strange in Majority Gaunt. But so it was. He had some unanalysed feelings about her, but they sprang from impulses which he recognised as being good and true. This reserved and dainty young typist, with her very fair hair, her blue eyes, her trim, strong young body, with her understanding of things not often given to the young and beautiful, affected him like a shaft of sun in summer. The sight of her delighted him. He basked when he was near her, though she said nothing and was obviously cold and aversive.

Withal, he was not continually thinking of her; his work held him in willing clamps, and in the hours of less pressure there ran through him the hot claims of Viola Cartlet; the thought of her stirred passion and delirious fancy. No escape was there from the fact that Viola Cartlet held him fast, and he woke often in a dream of her, and once in a way his constant realising of her youthful beauty and abandon would leave him breathless. No one could take her place. And yet, while this passion dominated his disengaged time, while his work took draughts of energy and scheming power, there would come moments when the knowledge of Nancy Kirk would be to him a sweet, uplifting fact. That he knew her not and had nothing to gain by her favour qualified his impressions. Something impersonal hung about her for him. The serenity of those dark-blue eyes, the opalescent complexion, the reliant poise of the head and neck stirred in him no desire for possession, and yet gave him happiness.

Why, he knew not. His passions were held in other directions, and it was a practical fact, and no merit in him, that he never soiled his thoughts with so much as an association of sentimental indulgence. Nancy Kirk was to him like the music of a distant bell. He did not analyse his emotions, but he was nearer to purity and peace when he thought of her than he had been for years. Somehow he was happy beyond words in the knowledge of her existence.

He had a certain sensitiveness, too, about him, and he knew and half-feared that his living in her little home would have made him intrude on her; he was like a boy with some idealistic notion of being happy near her, and not quite knowing why. There was thus even an element of relief in his disappointment at having to take up his residence for his fortnight's poverty adventure in a neighbouring flat instead of the actual home of Nancy.

[15 December 1913]

Chapter XII – Continued.
The Adventure at the Obelisk.

The idea was that Gaunt, with five shillings in his pocket and just the clothes he stood up in – an old tweed suit, flannel shirt without collar, a well-worn pair of boots, neckerchief, and cap – should cut himself off from civilisation and friends, and live the life of a young man without work, and should try to earn enough to keep himself from hunger and in shelter. His experiences, related later in the *Daily Light* in a series of articles factfully realistic, would play their part in that wide-spread fight which Lodden was conducting against the Home Secretary.

To Mrs. Johnston Gaunt was merely a respectable young fellow from Islington who had got the chance of a job as a builder's labourer on the schools which were being put up in New Kent-road. He played the part very well. He was up at five o'clock after his first night, and had a try at the school buildings in question. Alas, he was not yet used to the game, for at a quarter to six the man in charge at the office told him that he was too late, but in an off-hand way he said he might come along two mornings later, when some fresh hands might ne needed. During the day Gaunt, sufficiently disguised by his neckerchief and his cap pulled well forward, tried to get a job at a greengrocer's in Walworth-road to push a hand-truck, clean the windows, and give a hand generally in the work about the shop. He was dismissed with a rough word by the proprietor when he hesitated about his last employment.

"Don't like the look of you, my lad," said Mr. William Guggins. "Outside."

Mr. Guggins subsequently spat viciously on the kerb as Gaunt went off, and ventured the opinion to the street in general. "The blighter's just out o' Wandsworth,[50] I suppose. I know the sort."

Gaunt made one or two other vain attempts in the course of the morning and in the early afternoon, and had the luck to earn sixpence by carrying a commercial traveller's bag from the Elephant and Castle station up to the office of a paper manufacturer in Newington-causeway.[51] His lunch had cost him ninepence at a cheap restaurant, and his tea threepence. Gaunt felt his first day had not been a success, and he began to experience a rather unpleasant sensation of helplessness and a feeling that he was not using his efforts in the right line, for he knew perfectly well that in a great city there must be ten thousand opportunities for a strong, healthy man willing to work with his hands; it was absurd to believe that a young man like that could not get work. His journey up to Newington-causeway had taken him in the direction of Lant-street, and in his tired state he had felt that it would be pleasant to see Nancy's face, and he was half inclined to go up and call on Nellie Kirk and her mother. Almost at the foot of the flats he stopped himself, and then he decided to follow along the road leading to the Obelisk, where Nancy Kirk alighted from the tram on her way home, because he knew that within half-an-hour she was due. At first Gaunt thought boldly of meeting her, but he presently put that aside and loitered about on the opposite pavement within sight of the trams. He just had an idea that he would like to see her, and was without thought of interference.

Busy and dull and spacious are the cross-roads where the new Oblisk raises itself in place of the old,[52] where the trams rattle up on their way to and from

Blackfriars Bridge and south London, with the intersecting cars from Westminster cutting across on their way to the Borough. All kinds of vehicles are hustling between the City and the southern suburbs, and the great crossing has never any respite from the tramcars, motor-omnibuses taxi-cabs, and lumbering drays.

People on the pavements pass north and south in a never-ending flow, and in the evening hours, particularly between four and seven, there is an outward flowing crowd hastening from the City to their homes after the day's work. From a hundred yards up the Borough-road, in the gathering darkness, Gaunt watched the dull liveliness of the panorama, ever changing in the degree and yet always the same. At intervals trams from Westminster pulled up on the south side of the cross-roads and allowed some of their passengers to get out, then slowly took their way across the network of metals to the side where he stood, and then proceeded to put on speed as they went by him. Nancy Kirk could have ridden on some hundreds of yards further before alighting, but by getting down at the Obelisk she saved a halfpenny fare. Tram after tram went by, and still she did not come, and Gaunt waited with growing anxiety until the mere possibility that she had already gone, that this should have chanced to be one of her early nights, became to him a misfortune, something like a catastrophe. How much the sight of her would refresh him he now was very suddenly aware, and on realising the loneliness of the day it made him hunger for a known face. That this of all nights should be one when she had gone home early was really extremely bad luck. He was discussing within himself whether, after all, he would not go round to Lant-street and call at the flat, when he saw her stepping off the tram.

He pressed himself back from the prominence of the kerb to the doorway of a shuttered shop – although there was actually no need, for as she passed on the other side of the street she did not so much as glance at him, and if she had would certainly not have distinguished him from the dozens of others strung out on the way along the pavement. Gaunt followed along as she progressed down Borough-road, noting the steady swing of her precise little body; he could imagine character radiating from her as she walked – Gaunt in some of his moments being an imaginative man. Nancy had not progressed more than 150 yards from the trams along Borough-road when an incident occurred which made the evening notable. Afterwards Gaunt was pleased to think that some special fate had caused him to go and meet her that evening, but he was deceiving himself, because on more than one occasion before Nancy had suffered rudeness and interference, her quiet beauty being a beckoning light in the byways. A fortunate chance had taken Gaunt to the Obelisk; his going was not particularly exceptional providence, but he was not to know this for some time, and he enjoyed the comforting idea for quite a period. What was far more remarkable than his presence was that Nancy should have been stopped in the early evening within so short a distance of the busy crossing at the Obelisk.

London is full of strange surprises; and you may find acts of gallantry done by dirty, slothful people in the slums – that is a commonplace of the universe; what is equally surprising is that in a big, busy street an attack can be made on a man or woman, robbery effected, or murder done, and complete escape made, notwithstanding that people are within call, perhaps within a score of yards. It is amazing to read of these occurrences, but not quite so amazing when you are on the spot.

In the case of Nancy Kirk, a brilliantly lighted tram laden with people had just passed, on the other side of the road people were moving singly or in two or threes, with intervals between them, though no part of the pavement was uncrossed for more than a few seconds at a time. It so happened that the pavement on which Nancy Kirk found herself was a little less busy than the one opposite, and when she reached the narrow little turning known as Clonmel-street there was no one near her for 30 or 40 yards in front or behind; but that was the luck of the night, and not to be reckoned on by the assailants. Two of them there were, a loutish, heavy man of 28, and a younger fellow and when they poured out of Clonmel-street straight upon her Nancy recognised the older of the two as a man who sold oilcloth from a barrow in the New Cut,[53] and who, when she was looking over a second-hand book stall one day, spoke to her and suggested they should "have a walk together." He and his pal had apparently seen her often, and they had set themselves in devilment to waylay her. Not very deep and not very dangerous was their plot. But it was one which in revealment roused Gaunt as much as an attempt to murder her. What these two intended was that each should kiss Nancy Kirk before she could prevent it or make an outcry. When the younger man, lighter than his companion, bounded forward and seized Nancy's wrists and said, "Now, give us a kiss," Gaunt saw the action if he could not hear the words, and sped across the road like bow from arrow. Before he could be half-way the man was clasping Nancy closer to him, in spite of her furious struggle. Half her words came to Gaunt in these few seconds. "Mother," she cried instinctively and piteously. The man was thrusting his face close to her, and she twisted and squirmed and wriggled deliriously.

"Curse you!" he said, as his beer-stained lips touched her little ear, and then the bigger man was on the scene.

Gaunt was three strides away, coming on like a tornado. He saw the younger man helping to hold the little, slim, wrestling figure so that the bigger man could kiss her. Gaunt was not an expert boxer, but he knew more than the elements of boxing, and among his gifts was hard-hitting power, and it served him now, for collecting his balance, even in his fury, he got a first blow into the upturned face of the big man, hitting him between the ear and jaw with a click that told of real effectiveness. Timed pretty well and with all the swinging force of a strong young body behind it the blow was sufficient to cannonade the big man free, and he collapsed and lay huddling on the pavement, which his head struck unpleasantly and sharply. With a deep breath Gaunt turned quickly to the other man, who had released the girl, and having recovered from the first shock was looking in a tense moment for the opportunity to kick or strike Gaunt before fleeing. But he had no chance. Gaunt was beyond himself in a delirium of action, and would have jumped on the man in the face of a gleaming dagger. Murder was in his eyes, and he ran at the fellow and his fury did what in other circumstances skill or science might have achieved. He got in a terrific right and left, and the man went over like a sack of wheat. I should like here to be able to chronicle that Gaunt behaved with chivalry, but he did not, being for the first time just a wild beast and nothing more. The young man showed signs of raising himself, and Gaunt seized him by the throat and hammered his head against the pavement until he was quiet. The whole operation from the time of its first impact, had not lasted more than fifteen seconds, and the people who were mildly crossing the road to see what the commotion was about had not yet reached the spot. In the spasm of breathlessness Gaunt reared himself and tried to steady his breath. The big man was wriggling, and would soon be himself again. Gaunt looked round for Nancy, but she was hurrying away in her fright and terror, as fearful of her unknown rescuer as of her assailants, possessed only of the idea to get away. Her hat was thrust back on her head, and it was only the glance of her, untidy, Gaunt had had. She looked not back, half running, half walking.

"I saw these two men assault a lady, and ran across the road to help her. I battered both of them."

Men and women who had seen the whole thing bore out Gaunt's words, and the policeman whose duty in such cases it is to be as suspicious of gallant rescuers as of others, accepted the position. He did not want the trouble of a police-court charge. The big man was struggling to his feet now, and the other was also showing signs of life.

"Now, push along. Got more than you reckoned on, didn't you? Now, push along, the pair of you, or else –"

The big man helped his friend to his feet. Blood was trickling down the latter's face and he was still dazed, but the other man helped him to walk.

"Let's hook it, Bill. As for that –" He looked at Gaunt.

"No more of it," said the constable, "or you're both coming along o' me."

They went off and the crowd melted, and Gaunt, his old reportorial practices coming back to him, slipped one of the remaining shillings into the constable's hand.

"Thank you," said the constable. Later, in consultation with a fellow officer at the Obelisk, he said: "A rum cove. Spoke like a gentleman. Hope it's all right. There's more in it than meets the eye."

"There's some queer fish about," said his friend, and then they both turned to deal with a van-driver, who, in spite of a stoppage of the traffic, had illegitimately worked his horse and van ahead of two angry taxi-drivers.

Gaunt, meanwhile, was speeding along towards Lant-street in the endeavour to see that Nancy reached home safely. He was surprised to find how glad he was that she did not know him as her protector; not for worlds would he have played the novelette hero before her; he thanked his lucky stars for the neckerchief and the drooping cap. He was within sight of her in Lant-street, and quite close as she began to climb the long stone stairs. She had straightened her hat, she walked erectly, as if nothing had happened.

"Brave little girl," said Gaunt to himself.

Then as he was close behind her he had a shock; she was crying – crying softly to herself. As she walked up the foot of the steps she stopped to wipe her eyes, and even then, as she went up the stairs, Gaunt knew she was sobbing because her body shook. She could not stop herself.

Upstairs, after she had got over the excitement a little, she told her mother and Nellie all about he adventure.

"I wish I'd been there," said the stalwart Nellie; "I'd have seen to them."

"Who was the man who came up and hit 'em?" said Mrs. Kirk.

"I think it was Mr. Gaunt. I knew him in his cap."

"Mr. Gaunt," said her mother; "then he'll be coming up here and tell us all about it."

"He's a real good chap," said Nellie.

Gaunt, however, did not go near them to tell then anything about the story, and Nellie and her mother wondered much. But Nancy understood.

[16 December 1913]

Chapter XIII.
Gaunt's meeting with Raston Path.

On the second day of his experiment Gaunt had a piece of luck, for he secured three hours' work in helping to carry furniture and fittings into a shop newly let in Newington-causeway, and earned 1s. 6d. No further success came to him that day, though he diligently presented himself at a warehouse in Bermondsey-street, where according to a placard a night-watchman was required, and also made application in a Charing Cross-road eating-house advertising for kitchen help. Some kind of previous experience was, it seemed, necessary, even for the humblest job. In the evening he walked down to the South Metropolitan Gas Works in the Old Kent-road on the chance of casual manual work, but again he was disappointed, and he went back to Lant-steet, physically tired, as well as wearied in mind, by his unaccustomed exercise.

To-night he had no adventure on behalf of Nancy Kirk to sustain him. He had resolutely cut himself off from Fleet-street and from home, for he was quite decided about living in his isolated surroundings for a period. The temptation to visit the Kirks lay in his path, but he resolutely avoided it.

The task of Gaunt grew heavier on the third day, for in the morning he learned that after all there was nothing available for him at the new schools, and all that day he could find no means of earning a penny, and when he went to bed he was depressed by the knowledge that his experiment might have to be partially abandoned for the simple reason that he might not be able to get enough to eat. That was his feeling. The little rebuffs that came to him by reason of his shabby clothes and apparent destitution, his inability to find any regular employment for his hands, and the knowledge that he had but a few pence left in his pocket gave him a sense of failure – and curiously enough it was not lessened by the fact that he was accumulated excellent material for his newspaper. True, he would not be able to prove, as he had hoped, that an able-bodied young man willing to work could get something to do whenever he seriously wanted it, but his few days of poverty would nevertheless yield a thrilling narrative in capable hands, and is certainly could be treated to suit the *Daily Light*'s purpose. Nevertheless, he was low in spirits, and half inclined to return to the office for money in the morning.

A night's sleep makes a great difference in all human depressions and when he awoke at six he found a new determination within him and something like shame at his cowardice of the night before. He realised that for the sake of his own self respect he must see the thing through, or for ever think of himself as a bit of a skulker. After a wash under the tap in the scullery he sat down at Mrs. Johnston's kitchen table for breakfast almost with buoyancy. He would go the end of his tether in the shape of endurance – that was his decision – and he knew he had the will to carry it out. He took stock of his resources; he had 5d. in his possession.

"Got anythink yet?" asked Mrs. Johnston, as she set out his breakfast.

"Nothing regular, an odd job or so."

Mrs. Johnston was a stoutish woman, rather slatternly, who sometimes took a fancy to people, and she liked Gaunt and tried to cheer him up.

"You'll be getting somethink in a day or two, you're not the kind of chap to be out o' work for long. My poor Jim, he's been out o' work for as long as seven weeks at a time. He were different to you, he liked his drop o' beer. He's dead now."

"Yes," said the sympathetic Gaunt.

"And don't you forget to tell me if you wants anythink; if you wants another slice of bread and butter, you say so."

Gaunt's breakfast consisted of two cups of tea, for the unexpected strength of which he was thankful, and four slices of bread and butter, and for this he was paying only 3s. 6d. a week, which would not permit of a rasher of bacon.

"It's very kind of you, Mrs. Johnston, and I'll ask if I want anything."

Rather heavy in spirit was Gaunt, for the sordidness of it all oppressed him and he had to stiffen himself to prepare for the continuation. On this particular morning no luck came his way. His lunch was frugal but satisfying, for by one or two experiments he had found out the purchasing potentiality of money for a hungry man. He got two stale buns for a halfpenny, and a pound of dates for threeha'pence, the dates being very sustaining and satisfying. As for drink, he made the acquaintance of a free water fountain. A good many new experiences came his way during the week that followed; on three mornings he applied for situations among the advertisements in the *Daily Chronicle* and the *Daily Telegraph* only to be defeated by a mob of others; he got the task to carry carpets into a warehouse in Cheapside for two days, and on the last night of the week he earned 1s. 6d. and his supper by acting as an assistant to a coffee stall keeper in Caledonian-road.

On the Monday morning he determined on a new course of action – he would start business for himself. Not with a coffee stall, for that required a comparatively big outlay of capital, as well as the advantage of a pitch – but as a seller of some kind of goods in the street. The thought came to him as he walked along the line of busy costermongers at Islington on Saturday night, and he ran over the various ventures with a view to selecting one suitable to his lack of experience, and finally got into conversation with an old man who sold shabby magazines and penny secondhand books at the corner.

"For my line," said the old man, "you want to 'ave been at it for years, mine's a kind of profession; yes, though if I make two shillings or three shillings I'm lucky, 'cept on Saturdays, when I 'ave made as much as five. And in these other trades you want to know a good bit, 'course you do. You couldn't start selling oilcloth from a stall, could you, and you couldn't start a vegetable and fruit stall like Jim Clark's got along there? 'Course his is a big business, him and his wife and boy they make as much as £3 a week some years … Flowers is a very good line in some places, but you've got to get the right pitch for that, and then make yourself known to regular people, that's the secret o' flowers. Ostend rabbits[54] is risky – you go and lay out a bit o' money, and if you don't sell out pretty regular, well, there you are – you can't keep Ostend rabbits for any length of time."

"There's the oyster stall – that seems to do pretty well," said Gaunt.

"Now you've hit it. The best thing to start with is oysters. I've got a son-in-law that's got a barrow down in South London, so I know what I'm talking about; and he's doing all right. The barrow costs sixpence a night to hire, then you want half-a-dozen candles, and glasses for to protect 'em, and there's your fixtures. 'Course you want a few plates and saucers and so on, but it's nothing. Go down to Billingsgate and get 100 Portuguese, costing 2s. and blue points[55] about the same, and then you sells them at 8d. a dozen, and you can see the profit you make. If you 'ave any over after the night, put them in a bucket o' water, with a handful o' salt, and they're still alive next day."

"I learned how to open oysters when I was on the coast once," said Gaunt.

"Well, there you are. Half a dozen small plates in front of your stall, and you're fixed up."

And that was how Gaunt went into the oyster line. In the lee of a railway arch at Seven Sisters-road, from seven in the evening till half an hour after midnight, with coat collar turned up and cap pulled over his eyes, he tried hard to sell his oysters to passers-by. He was not very successful, and Gaunt, who had no particular fastidiousness, needed all his will to go through with it, although he found consolation at intervals in the thought of what his fellow-reporters would think if they came across him now; and what Viola Cartlet would say or do. The memory of the latter gave him a cold little shock. He was whole worlds away from her, and he knew it would be impossible to explain to her how he could ever have tolerated the life for days, even though it were but a temporary experiment as a journalist. To her he would certainly have been lowered, he knew that; and he was rather melancholy, for he saw how she would shrink from him, not understanding. Hardly less depressed was he by the knowledge that he was now living in the atmosphere in which Nancy Kirk had existed, that the life surrounding him and touching him on all sides was the one from which she was freeing herself, but which even now prisoned her. The girl, he reflected, must be in continual revolt; she was in the coarseness, but never could be of it; and yet his common sense told him she could not have lived among the dirt and hunger without being in some degree moulded by it.

The oyster-barrow business came to a crisis with Gaunt after the third night. He found his expectations had deceived him, that oysters were not so saleable as the bookstall friend had prophesised. His capital after three days' effort consisted of 1s. 6. and 150 oysters, some of which were beginning to show signs of exhaustion after three night's exposure to the wearing atmosphere of Seven Sisters-road. Midnight was approaching, the stream of passing people had diminished to occasional stragglers, and Gaunt stood with hands thrust into his pockets, gloomily thinking of the long tram ride back to South London and of the comfortless bed which awaited him, and consoling himself much with the remembrance that one week more and his self-respect would be satisfied and his task completed. The intensity with which he looked forward to the return to his old life was a real big sensation; he wondered what was happening in the *Daily Light* office, in what ways Lodden was ripening his plans, how the other men were getting on in their poverty-investigations in the North and Midlands.

What was Viola Cartlet thinking of his failing to write to her, his deliberate avoidance of the hint as to his whereabouts? How would she welcome him back?

As he paced round his barrow in a monotonous walk to keep himself warm, Gaunt conjectured what directions his energies would take on his return to the office a week later, and what would be the phase of the conflict with Raston Path in which he would have to take his place. That Lodden must be at work with new developments he was quite sure; he was equally sure that Raston Path was planning hard, making arrangements for the opening of the fight on his side. Path was as great a force as Lodden, perhaps a greater, and Gaunt's mind flashed to the attacks which had been made upon him and his conduct under them, and especially his strange silence at the last scandal. Gaunt mildly wondered whether there was an answer to that scandal.

And then out of the murkiness of the railway arch he saw approaching Raston Path. Yes, at five minutes to twelve at night, in Seven Sisters-road, far away in the North of London, Raston Path, the Home Secretary, was walking briskly along, looking neither to the right nor to the left, and apparently thinking hard, even while he hurried. It was amazing, for the moment it was unbelievable. Gaunt had an idea that his imagination was on the jump; his thoughts had been turned towards the Home Secretary, and a chance resemblance in the dim light might have startled him into the mistake; but there was no mistake. Raston Path, in the flesh, was within a dozen yards of him; he had turned out of one of those dull, respectable little streets a stones throw away, and he was hastening along towards Gaunt and his oyster-stall, apparently on the way to the main Holloway-road. He was homeward bound to Belgravia – that was obvious. He cast his eye up once across the road, and Gaunt guessed he was looking for a cab, but there was none in sight, and with his quick, nervous stride Path went past the oyster-stall with the flickering candles, and certainly did not notice the young costermonger eyeing him from beneath his peaked cap. Gaunt waited till he was a score of paces on and then began quickly to pack up his oysters and extinguish his candles – and in five minutes he was trundling the barrow down towards the yard at the junction of Holloway-road and Seven Sisters-road in the hope of seeing the direction taken by the Home Secretary. But the operation of packing up the stall had given Path a long start, and hurry as he would Gaunt could not overtake him.

[17 December 1913]

Chapter XIII – Continued.
Near Starvation.

Gaunt lay in bed rather later than usual next morning, pondering over the sudden vision of Raston Path the night before. To what midnight mission had the Home Secretary bent his energies, what emergency had taken him into dull

North London. He could not have been playing at Haroun al Raschid,[56] for the neighbourhood of Finsbury Park is in a secluded corner; it is respectable, and although the byways have their poor people, the houses are mostly those providing a rent of from nine to fifteen shilling a week, and occupied by people who rear families on a weekly salary ranging from 30s. a week upwards. People well-to-do lived in some of the better roads away round behind the park, but even the smaller little streets were respectable; it is necessary to insist on that respectability. No, no, there was no probing of poor lives, none of the fashionable social investigation in Path's journey to North London.

The curious nature of the whole business set Gaunt's journalistic nerves tingling. A Cabinet Minister making a midnight visit afoot to a North London suburb – why, the thing smelt of mystery and sensation. What story for the *Daily Light* even as it stood; and then Gaunt reflected what a really tremendous narrative it would be if the origin and cause of the visit could be traced. What could he do? It flashed across him that this possibility was one of a series of vistas, and he had a hope; to make the discovery and reveal it to the world was worth a month of work, and for the moment he was tempted to go straight into the office and tell Wansmuth what he had seen and to devote himself to an elucidation with the help of the office resources. Then he wavered. Why not keep on to it himself? A stroke of luck might put him in the way of full revealment; the thought was almost too good to be true.

Gaunt forgot that his cash was down to 1s. 4d., 2d. having been spent for his fare home the night before, forgot his ambitions in the oyster trade, and so busy were his thoughts that his breakfast that morning was only half a slice of bread and butter and a small cup of tea. He set off on his way across London to Finsbury Park to discover things, and carrying with him an impression that the Home Secretary had emerged from a little street within 50 yards of the oyster stall he planned his initial inquiries. What hint might be found within that little street Gaunt knew not, but he knew the place must be examined, and examined well. Possibly in the daylight the scene of the night's occurrence might result in suggestions, but anyway he knew he was on the right track in going to the spot again, and going at once.

It came to pass, therefore, that for once in a way Finsbury Park knew him by day instead of by night. He went to the place where he had been standing with his oyster barrow at midnight, and thoughtfully kicked into the gutter a couple of shells which had escaped the scavenger, but he got no inspiration. He walked along to the turn from which Raston Path had come, and found it to consist of solid single-fronted little houses with bow windows. A postman delivering letters was on one pavement, and two girls with school satchels had just come out of a gate half way down; a white-bearded old gentleman, leading a Pomeranian dog, was entering the street from Seven Sisters-road, and these were the only living beings to be seen. Gaunt walked along the pavement in leisurely fashion, and found each house pretty much like each other, with six feet of court in front, with bow window and iron railing surmounting a low wall as protection against the pavement.

Gaunt was a good detective, but he could not get much out of this. He struck up conversation with the milkman, and talked to a policeman on point duty, and then confessed to himself that there was but a distant chance of making a definite discovery. But he was too old a bird to throw up a job because it looked unpromising, and quite early he had realised that although Raston Path had come out of Lamont-street – that was the name of it – it was quite possible he had been visiting some other turning altogether, and that this was merely a means of access to the main road. Accordingly he set himself to a systematic perambulation of the turnings leading to Lamont-street, though what he hoped to find he could not tell. He realised that no chance must be missed. Uneventful enough was his occupation, but he pressed steadily on, and in the end he found that all the turnings were streets like Lamont-street and finally, after some hours' work, he wearily decided he could do no more that morning. He was really very tired, and surprised was he to find how the excitement and disappointment had worked on him; he felt limp and recollecting many a strenuous buffeting of the past asked himself what was the matter.

"What I want is something to eat," he said, and it was nearer the truth than he knew. Long hours, little rest, with a minimum of food, had brought him down a good deal. On the day before, in his efforts for economy, he had gone from seven in the morning till midnight with but two scrappy meals at a total cost of threepence, and now he had had nothing since his rough makeshift of a breakfast, and two o'clock had just struck on a neighbouring church.

He waited at the gates of the park to get a tram along to Holloway-road, and as he stood on the kerb Gaunt, for the first time in his life, found himself giddy and weak; he was ashamed of himself, and fearing that people would notice it, and remembering that there were seats in the park, he turned in at the big gate and found a resting place. An effort had been necessary to reach a seat, for he had part of the sensations of a man in a dream, striving for he unreachable. On the seat he made an effort to pull himself together; then Gaunt fainted.

It was not a very serious faint, because he began coming to within a few minutes. He found that he had been stretched lengthways on the seat, and that a hard-faced park-keeper was rubbing his wrists to get back the circulation, and a bunch of school children stood by, watching the operation curiously.

"I'm all right," said Gaunt, half struggling up.

"Lie down for a bit," grunted the park-keeper, "you'll be all right then. Lets the blood to the head."

He scowled at the waiting children. "Be off, can't you, what are you waiting round here for?"

Gaunt, despite the friendly warning, struggled upright on the seat, but was still a little dazed.

"A bit of a rest, and I shall be all right," he said.

"Thought you'd been having a drop at first. When I came closer, saw you had fainted."

"You're awfully good."

"Oh, no, but I can tell a chap what's down on his luck. Ain't had much to eat this morning, I'll bet."

Gaunt was not grateful, he was humiliated by the man's pity, and he started – "Oh, I'll be all right when I get home."

The park-keeper grunted again, and started to go off, and then, having gone a dozen steps, he came back again and pushed threepence in his hand.

"Cup o' coffee and a meat pie over at Lockhart's – that'll put you right," he said, gruffly. The reporter's stammered words were lost on him, for he was striding off vengefully after the three children who were picking dandelions on the forbidden green sward. Shamefacedly, and with feebleness, Gaunt went out to the road and boarded a tram, and found a reviving breeze of wind on the top seats. He did not economise, but rode every yard to the way to St. George's Church in the Borough, which is only a few yards from Lant-street. He spent an extravagant 10d. on a meal and feeling all the better for it, went round to his room in Luton Buildings. Mrs. Johnston was surprised to see him, because Gaunt never came near his lodging in the day.

"Felt queer," he explained, "had a kind of faint up at Finsbury Park, and though I'd better come home for a rest. I'll just lie down for a little."

Mrs. Johnston, not an unkindly soul at all, had no desire to have her burdens added to by the cares of an invalid, and a bankrupt invalid at that, so she thought it her duty to go up to the Kirks' flat, and tell Mrs. Kirk about the young man she had recommended.

"If he's real bad," said Mrs. Kirk, "I'll come round a little later. I can't now. I'm just getting Nellie's tea ready, and now Nellie's at work all day again, this strike being over, she's hungry at night, and I'm just cooking her some eggs and bacon."

Nellie, who was comfortably seated at the kitchen table, preparatory to meal, said, "Look here, a half-hour won't hurt him. I'll go round after I've had a snack. I'll bring something round, too; I reckon he wants something to eat, that's what's the matter with him."

Nancy Kirk was hanging up her waterproof coat when Mrs. Johnston had entered, and she had been smoothing her hair at the looking-glass at the other end of the kitchen.

"Nancy, why don't you go round with Mrs. Johnston, and see the poor chap? It's only kindness."

"Oh, no, mother, I couldn't go. A little later won't make much difference, you know I've never cared much about him."

"Nancy's such a funny girl," said Mrs. Kirk in explanation, "she don't like this young chap at all, and yet he's very respectable. Now, Nellie rather likes him."

"He's a good sort," said Nellie, with her mouth full of eggs and bacon, "I'll be round there after tea, and see what we can do for him."

Mrs. Johnston went off comforted.

When she had gone Nancy put on her macintosh again and descended to the pavement and went across to the telephone call office in Great Dover-street, and called up the editorial office of the *Daily Light*.

She asked for the news editor and soon obtained him.

"Is that the news editor of the *Daily Light*?"

"Yes, who are you?"

"I am ringing up about a member of your staff, Mr. Majority Gaunt."

"Yes, what about him?"

"He's at 16 Luton buildings, Lant-street, Borough; he's ill – taken ill this afternoon."

"Ill? Why, what's happened? We'll send down at once."

"16 Luton buildings," said Nancy. "Don't forget."

[18 December 1913]

Chapter XIV.
Raston Path With His Back To The Wall.

In spite of daring words by the Cabinet, there was no doubt that the campaign of the *Daily Light* was having its effect in the country, and that the name of Raston Path was getting a poisoned significance in circles where hitherto it had been received only with mild hostility, or even with indifference. Raston Path knew this; no man quicker than he to know the pulse of public opinion. The protests of his friends on public platforms, the declamations of the Progressive members, were all very well, and served a purpose with ardent partisans, but among the great body of moderate people – all those whom Lodden had deliberately tried to reach – an unpleasant suspicion was trickling. Indeed, dozens of good Progressives were anxious that Path should speak out. His silence was unpleasant. As for Path himself, accustomed to vigorous fighting and enjoying it, he was disturbed by this insidious influence. At first he had hoped the affair would blow over, but as the days went on he came to see that Lodden's arrow had hit its mark, and he was not to know that at this very time Lodden was telling his subordinates that they must start an entirely new campaign. That was what was going on in the *Daily Light* office while Path was biting his lip with anger. Of course, Lodden, even while he upbraided his men, knew that the word "failure" was a comparative term, and that the scandal, while it might not ruin Path, would at least do him much harm. Lodden, however, had a rule of not relying on a single effort, and he never failed to devise new lines of attack, even when the first seemed likely to be successful. Where the issue was in some doubt, his new energies were proportionately increased. He would change his ground swiftly, and then, as new conditions arose, would just as swiftly reoccupy it. Above all that he never let the means dominate the end. This time, however, he had struck deeper than he knew when he published the story of Path's early life, but it should be added he was not more than a week behind Path in recognising that the Home Secretary's reputation had suffered a severe, perhaps irreparable injury. Steadily he went on with his preparations for attack on other ground. Already there were being prepared the articles collating the facts which were to demonstrate to sane-thinking people how much of a charlatan Path really was, how purposely shallow were his measures, how essentially false his plausibility. Meanwhile, a far less keenly perceptive man than Path would have realised the increasing feeling that his private character was not beyond dispute, that he had in early years (perhaps in later ones) departed to some extent from personal rectitude. Little more than a suspicion though it was, he knew how disastrous such a suspicion is in reference to a statesman. Let it get a proper hold, and he is damned without possibility of repair. It was his silence that was doing the mischief. He knew that.

Path pushed on, weighted with his burden, at times inclined to fear that the hindrances before him might be permanent; clearer than his colleagues he perceived the obstacles that were being raised to his political progress, and flickers of doubt touched him now and again – hitherto unknown doubts – as to success. He hustled on with his plans, was ever radiating a fighting cheerfulness, and yet there were hours when stark depression held him. He knew deep within himself that the spirit of his plans must one day, in his own time or in the generations to come, encircle human activities, that the soul of the world was progressing onwards and upwards, that he had striven with ardency and confidence for some short steps to be taken during his own period. Love of power for its own sake there must have been in him, but he hardly knew it, and if increasing influence and keenness had sapped his patience with fools, his shining convictions were still undimmed. The tricks and subterfuges of political partisanship had hardened him and taken away his lovableness, his simple soul, but his ideals were still untouched. No man was a greater master than he in the various verbal twistings of politicians' warfare, and no mercy was in him for opponents; he thrust always ruthlessly and persistently. In that surging temperament were many complemental passions, love of applause, desire for personal achievement, a fund of hot anger. Path was no meek Tolstoyan Christian,[57] and yet, withal, his eyes were on the gleaming stars.

That he should see his reputation clouded was a stunning thing to him, for the satisfactions that had grown up with his commanding position were deep-seated, and yet his chief thought was fear for the setting back of his idealistic schemes. To him was the sure certainty that in the days ahead his dreams would be commonplace materialism, but meanwhile he wanted to push the work forward a little. The puny hindrances of party malevolence seemed too silly for words; that his course should be stopped by petty personal calumny of an ephemeral newspaper was both irrelevant and stupid. His individual resentment was a matter apart from these reflections, but he was not without that individual resentment. The cold-blooded intent of Lodden shocked him – because of the smallness of the motive behind it.

"I know you are worried," said Hilda Path one morning at breakfast.

"How do you know that?" asked Raston, pausing with a piece of toast in his hand.

"Easily enough," said George Path, "you haven't spoken a single word since breakfast began; it was pretty much the same yesterday."

Hilda shook her head. "A Cabinet Minister, if so disposed, is permitted to remain silent at meals, because he is always supposed to have a lot of work and anxiety on his mind."

"Well?" said Raston, smiling.

"Yes," said Hilda, in mild though certain triumph, "but it isn't Departmental burdens that make you carelessly put on an abominable wing collar instead of the usual double collar, and make you slip the parting in your hair out of parallel from back to front."

"Oh, these women," said Raston, as he drew the marmalade towards him.

"They get there though." George Path shook his head knowingly, and went on with his paper.

"Bothered about these stories?" said Hilda.

"Well, a bit," admitted Raston. "It's a good handle for them, you see."

"It's to some intent, too," went on Raston, "that's the devil of it. I'm afraid –"

"Something will have to be said," interrupted George, looking up from his paper.

"I don't know how; I'm getting a little afraid of things in the country. It's a delicate business, and I don't see how it can be done. Two or three know the facts, of course; there's the Prime Minister and Venture, and one or two others."

Raston thoughtfully tapped the edge of his saucer with his spoon. "One thing is, whatever the explanation, hardly anyone will believe it, friends or enemies."

"A way out has got to be found, this can't go on. I bet anything the Government Whips[58] are thinking a good deal about you just now."

Raston pushed back his chair, and walked to the window, and looked into the street without answering. A minute later he turned and said; "Look here. I'm going down to Parliament-street to talk to the chief agent[59] about it."

"Going to tell him your story?"

"I suppose I'd better."

The light had gone out of Raston's eyes, and it was apparent the undertaking jarred him. Thoughtfully, he said: "He's in charge of the arrangements for the country, and he's got a right to know."

[19 December 1913]

Chapter XIV – Continued.
Raston Path's Confession.

When Raston Path made up his mind to some unpleasant course he did not hesitate in carrying it out, and so after an hour with his correspondence, that morning he put on his coat and hat and went down to the big building at the corner of Parliament-street to see Sir Robert Furley, the quiet man with the thin straight mouth and steady eyes, who constructed the electoral network for the Progressive party.

At the end of the story Sir Robert Furely said; "I can see it's impossible for you to make a statement," and as there was understanding in his words Path found himself able to elaborate the story without the distaste and repugnance he had feared.

It was through no design, but by the simplest accident that Nancy Kirk, sitting in her little nook formed by a glass partition, heard the essence of Raston Path's narration. She tried to put it out of her mind; it did not concern her; she was not meant to hear it; and yet she would have been no young woman, rich in the sense of her sex, if she had not been held by the facts. They were locked deep down in her breast. Perhaps Furley had not given her presence behind the partition more than a passing thought, owing to the trustworthiness he had found in her, and Sir Robert Furley was a keen though not a harsh judge of men and women. The secret was safe with Nancy, and she went about her work as usual after Path had gone, but in the background of her thoughts was the little drama that had been revealed to her, and mixed up with it were reflections about Gaunt and how keenly he would have seized on the story as part of his campaign, and she shivered at the bare idea that by some indiscretion, some lapse of care, she might do the work of traitor. When she went home that night she was, strangely enough, a little softened toward Gaunt in the knowledge of what she was able to keep back from him. With her native sense of distrust of him, his personality had always disturbed her, and in that fact was to be found the root of her aloofness, and now for the first time she knew that she was master of him, and it made a difference in her feelings.

Gaunt was surprised at the hint of comradely graciousness in her, and he was very happy about it, and discovered himself talking to Nancy in a quiet, brotherly way, while she listened with real comprehension. It was the first step towards a kind of friendship. Nellie and Mrs. Kirk dropped rather into the background during the three-quarters of an hour that Gaunt was present in the flat.

"That's a book I got from the public library," she said, as he took up a copy of Stevenson's "Vailima Letters"[60] from the top of the sewing machine.

"Read much?"

"Yes, a good deal. I'm very fond of books; they lift one away."

Then Gaunt talked to her of books, and had the pleasure of seeing interest mount in her face. He learned that she had read some of Dickens soon after leaving school, and that she had browsed haphazard over fiction and poetry more latterly. Thackeray's "Esmond" she liked, and Tennyson's "Idylls," which fascinated her. She had tried the "Essays of Elia" without much success, but galloped through Mrs. Henry Wood; and had begun Barrie's "Margaret Ogilvy" under the impression that it was a novel, and after that had read every line of his that she could secure. Scott she was doubtful about; she had read "Waverley," but she was afraid his other volumes were rather heavy. With much vigour Gaunt put her right, and prophesised delights for her in "Ivanhoe" and "The Fair Maid of Perth," and he quickly decided to make her a present of an edition of Scott. His eye rested for a moment on the Kirks' library in view – namely, a copy of "Pickwick," an old Whitaker's Almanack, and two paper-covered sixpenny novels which had been brought in by Nellie.[61]

"I've a few books in my room," said Nancy quickly, and Gaunt understood the reproof.

While he was exchanging a cheery sentence or two with Nellie, preparatory to leaving, he noticed that Nancy's shoelace was unfastened, and "You will stumble," he said.

She tried to get round to the other side of the table to do it up out of sight, but he was too quick for her.

"Do let me practise my gallantry." He bent as he spoke. For a fraction of space Nancy hesitated, then with the faintest touch of red in her cheek, she thrust out her shoe, and with one hand drew back her skirt tight to her leg just about her ankle, so that it should not be in his way. Gaunt tied the lace in a graceful bow with much care, then reared himself, made a quick little obeisance, and humorously scattered her embarrassments. He went away, carrying with him a picture of Nancy's erect body, perfectly moulded, in a blue serge skirt and white blouse, with shining fair hair a little ruffled over one ear. Surprised and pleased was he with her new friendliness, and Nancy, too, was softened towards the reporter by the secret she held – the secret for which he was seeking. She had made herself happier by her relaxation. A fresh claim had come on her in his homeliness and part of the old distrust of his spurious gallantry had gone, and she began to think that he would not try it with her.

Very likely Nancy's kindlier feelings would have been deflected if she had known the persistency and ingenuity with which Gaunt was seeking out the trail of Raston Path. She would certainly have shuddered at the assiduity with which he set about his task of ruining a man. Never could she have understood the up-lifting abandon which Gaunt put into his work, and the irrelevancy of the campaign would have struck her as horrible. Raston Path was a superman to Nancy, a person quite out from ordinary mortals, a man who did great things because he was fore-ordained to do them. He was gifted by Heaven. She felt this without sorting out the impression in words, and her girlish and half-ignorant reverence was not shattered by the private revealment of Path as one who had experienced ardent human affections in his youth. If he came down from among the angels sometimes, he was at least more understandable. Raston Path had never seen Nancy Kirk, and yet he had in the little fair-haired girl one who would have sacrificed much for him with no thought that he should ever know her.

You can easily understand, therefore, how it was that she, together with her mother and sister, was at the meeting addressed by Raston Path at the Surrey Theatre in Blackfriars-road a fortnight later. The meeting was the first of a series designed to rouse the country, to set up expectation, and in some measure to satisfy it with regard to coming legislation. In the course of this meeting some hints would be forthcoming on the new measure of Path's, so long talked about and feared, and possibly there might even be an outline of the measure – if not at the first meeting, then at some later ones.

All the newspapers were well represented at the gathering, about 40 reporters, sketch-writers, and leader-writers finding places at the long baize-covered table which had been specially fixed up along the front of the stage. A flash-light photographer was up in the gallery with his apparatus already fixed before the doors were opened.

The fame of Raston Path caused a tremendous rush of people, and they flocked from all parts of London in the endeavour to find a place within the building. The papers calculated next morning that over 4,000 persons were turned away from the doors after the theatre was filled. It was really full. The crowd came into the building like a sea, and the stalls, pit, and circles became a surging human surface. Some venturesome souls in the forefront of the standing crowd in the gangway climbed up over the footlights at the corners of the stage, and found places for themselves in the rear of the platform seats, only to be dispossessed by the officials ten minutes before the chairman and Raston Path and the circle of politicians came on.

The reporters sharpened their pencils, exchanging occasional sentences with each other and turning unexcited glances on the fevered mass in the theatre. It was all in the day's work for the Pressman; a speech by Raston Path, the fiery orator and leader, was always good material for the papers, and this particular evening might have more than usual interest, inasmuch as Raston Path was making his first appearance since personal charges had been made against him. He was to face the public for the first time since suspicion had been sown, and he was to stand before the excited crowd knowing that unrest was stirring about him, and that he might very well be on the downward path as a public man. Everyone realised that drama was in the air. Raston Path had to put himself right. Would he fail or succeed? A good deal depended on this night's meeting. So the reporters sharpened their pencils with leisurely interest.

The noise in the theatre increased, for most of those present were intense admirers of Path. Moderate Progressives and extravagant Reds united in common indignation at the attacks on their hero, and white heat expectation of a fighting reply fired them. Three seats back in the stalls sat Mrs. Kirk and Nancy and Nellie, and though only Nancy had any real appreciation of the position all were touched by the prevailing fever. They saw Gaunt at the reporters' table, and Nancy wondered at the unconcerned way he talked with some of those near him.

Suddenly there was a lull, for the chairman and a string of other people were coming on to the stage, and then as Raston Path came into view the people, recognising him, began to cheer. The noise swelled, and many jumped to their feet and waved their hands. Like a fire that spreads with incredible swiftness over a large area, the realisation that Path was before them swept the thousands of people in the theatre, and a great roar, varying in note, deepening in intensity, ran over the whole building, and with swift fitness took seconds to reach its climax. The audience was standing up now, waving hats and handkerchiefs. The thin tone of women could be distinguished in the uproar of a hundred ejaculations of welcome, mingled with hand-clapping, shouts of "Hurrah," and the thumping of sticks and feet on the floor. One had to be present to appreciate fully the touch of ecstasy. An answering smile was on the face of Raston Path as he took his place by the side of the chairman; and he looked fit and fresh and very unlike the man who was harassed by State cares and transactions, and was on the verge of a fight for his public life – but then a demonstration such as this was wine to Raston Path, and he was lifted beyond himself. It was one of the great moments.

The gathering cheered him again when he rose to speak, and it was a couple of minutes before the noise had fallen sufficiently for his voice to be heard. He stood a little to the left of the chairman's table, a slim figure in morning suit, his head pushed back in thoughtful poise, his rather long greying hair bursting away from his forehead and temples; in his left hand, gripped tightly, and almost hidden from sight, were two or three small pieces of paper, bearing notes of his speech – though he did not look at them once during the evening.

Complete silence filled the theatre as he began and the low note of his commencing sentences went to every corner. There was nothing sensational in his opening; he told them the story of latter-day politics, and told it simply. But within a few minutes his old strange mysterious power was seizing the people, and this notwithstanding the fact that his initial passage were but clear statements as to events, and purposely emphatic. Path was not particularly dignified physically, indeed he looked almost insignificant at times, and yet some subtle influence went out from the man, radiated from him like light. Hearers were alive to it and stimulated, and knew not why. He, no less than they, felt the union that had been established; they were together in a common medium.

[20 December 1913]

Chapter XIV – Continued.
Raston Path's Speech.

"We are on the eve of happenings," he said, "which will do much for this country, and I believe will change many lives. Alterations in the life of great communities are sometimes reached slowly, are the result of different influences, and frequently are most effective when least premeditated. The introduction of new legislation, a generation of mechanical discovery, the swift irruption in one period of divers men of genius, these things have each in turn produced tremendous changes in a nation, in the whole existing human race. Incalculable beforehand these moments of change work, some of them slowly, some of them precipitously, and only in the perspective of history can we appraise their results – sometimes to our limited vision so very good, sometimes so bad. Of all the origins of change of the conditions of life of human beings none is more potent than that accretion of feeling which through the ages has come increasingly to people, working like yeast, sometimes for scores of years, sometimes for centuries, producing at last the force of action which puts into effect aspirations which have been nurtured so long, action which rights outrageous wrongs borne patiently not by individuals, but by hundreds of thousands, aye, by millions. It happens sometimes that these changes carry with them disaster of their own, but human activities are unbalanced, and we cannot answer for the by-products of strenuous soul-forces. Does that mean that these impulses for change are not to be recorded; does it mean that we are to cultivate a cowardly quiescence in things as they are for fear that worse befall us? I need not give you an answer in this world of suffering, of wrong, of injustice.

"In these modern times it so happens that one of the instruments of change is to be found in the efforts of those who compose the legislature of the various countries. Men who have been chosen as the elected representatives have been given the power of disturbance on a colossal scale. They can make laws which can change the face of their country. We have made a good many lately, and I hope they will play their part in that change. Just at this time there are ruling in this part of the world men who are determined to bring about alterations, and I am one of them.

"The alterations on which we are determined are such as shall make different the lives of millions at present in existence, and certainly will affect the lives of hundreds of millions who are not yet born. In trying to carry out our intentions we rouse hatred as well as enthusiasm. We are denounced as scoundrels – indeed, as murderers – and we are held up to the execration of all good and honest people. Those who attack us are to be found chiefly among the best educated, the richest and most refined, and all their charges gather weight from that fact. Even among the great mass of the underworld, whom we are trying to educate and uplift, there are many who through prejudice or ignorance, or the guidance of those above them, have no faith in us, and may, indeed, help their betters to cast me out. We accept the situation. You people of this country may cast us out.

"Some of the great writers and many of the great manufacturers, nearly all rich, titled people, who won great tracts of the country, are in rebellion against what we are doing.

"These people have great position with privileges obtained from ancestors or secured to them by accident. They say in effect that by trying to change things we are going against the laws of nature, that there must always be people who work and people who don't, and that the kind heartedness and great goodness of wealthy people provide one of the proper means for the amelioration of misery.

"They do not forget to emphasise, therefore, that another and very important reform is for poor people not to be so selfish and dirty and drunken, that when they get the true Christian spirit and holiness of soul in them all will be well.

"They will then be happier in that state of life to which God has been pleased to call them."

With carefulness of diction Raston Path had philosophised, and he had been more concerned in the lucid explanation of his point of view than in any effort to arouse the emotions of his hearers. The latter were quiet and keenly attentive. As he progressed with his argument and the picture became clearer a warmth spread over the theatre. Spasmodic cheers bubbled for the from time to time. Path, too, was losing his deliberation. Words came from him with a rush. His forefinger was uplifted, and his body bent forward as the phrases burst from him. Feeling was shooting out, and his voice tensed itself to a hiss from time to time as he approached the human side of his discourse.

"The people who say these things say them not quite so crudely as I have, but nevertheless say them in effect in one form or another. They are all comfortable people – some of them have lost hundreds, some thousands a year through my taxation; when they die their heirs lose tens of thousands through my further taxation. They cry to Heaven for vengeance on the thief and the marauder. But I am sure that not one in a hundred of them – I am inclined to doubt if one single person of them – has ever through necessity known the feeling of hunger. Oh, yes, they will tell you I am material; there are more important things in the world than food. Well, I will begin to talk to the about saving souls and all the rest of it when they have been through some of the physical experiences on which they gravely sit in judgment. Meanwhile, do not forget that among these people of high position probably not one of them has known a day's real privation. Not one of them has ever known a day without food enough to eat. Bear this in mind when I recall the facts about the poorer population of this country.

"First of all, we have to realise that the United Kingdom is in a great current of prosperity, inasmuch as high incomes are better than they have ever been. That is all right, but what about the other side? Is it generally known that between 10 and 11 millions of people are in poverty, poverty so marked that they are unable to keep themselves in that standard of living which would maintain poor physical efficiency? Just let that sink in. It has been found out by diligent and persistent inquiry exactly what is the least amount of food that will keep a person just at health level without allowing that person to become weak. The cheapest food possible has been found, and the smallest amount; then a similar kind of calculation has been made with regard to clothes and also with regard to shelter. All that has been done, and there can be no doubt of the fact that fully 10 millions of our people exist below that standard of living which to quote the words of a famous investigator, is 'stringent to severity and bare of all creature comforts.'[62]

"Some of our comfortably fed friends, whose sustenance is derived from incomes of hundreds or of thousands a year, declare that it is drunkenness – it is thriftlessness – that is the cause of what poverty exists. That is a careless, inaccurate statement. A proportion of that 10 millions would just reach the physical efficiency line if the head of the family did not smoke so much, or did not drink so much, because 2s. a week makes all the difference between just being on the brink of starvation and being over the brink. Actual drunkenness does in some cases contribute, but when we think of the terrible conditions in which fellow-beings of ours live we must not be too scathing in our admonitions.

"It would also be well for us to remember that there are faults and sins among other classes, but even taking all these things into account there are at least 10 millions of people living the life I have described through no fault of their own.

"What kind of life is it? Well, let us see. I am not going to harrow the feelings of those who read any portion of this speech in the newspapers by relating the horrors of extreme poverty. I am going to give an instance or two from the life of the ordinary poor, struggling working people, who are not or heroic and not more virtuous than the wealthy people who go in for politics and read books, and yet who, properly speaking, are just as good human beings. This is a passage from the investigation of a scientific expert written a few years ago, but as true now as then. 'Practically the whole of this class – that is to say, in the extremely poor class – are living in a state of actual poverty, or so near to that state that they are liable to sink into it at any moment. By this is meant that there are people whose earnings are insufficient to supply adequate food, clothing, and shelter for the maintenance of physical health. They live constantly from hand to mouth. So long as the wage-earner is in work the family manages to get along, but a week's illness or lack of work means short rations or running into debt, or more often both. Extraordinary expenditure, such as the purchase of a piece of furniture, is met by reducing the sum spent on food. As a rule in such cases it is the wife and sometimes the children who have to forego a portion of their food – the importance of maintaining the strength of the wage-earner is reckoned with, and he obtains his ordinary share. If there is anything to buy, such as a pair of boots for one of the children, a woman told one of my investigators, "Me and the children goes without dinner, or maybe only has a cup of tea and a bit of bread, but Jim (her husband) allus takes his dinner to work, and I give it him as usual; he never knows we go without, and I never tells him.'"[63]

[22 December 1913]

Chapter XIV – Continued.
Raston Path's Great Meeting.

"Let us take the case of a woman," continued Raston Path, "whom we will call Mrs. Smith, an excellent housewife, steady husband and three children at home. Her house is scrupulously clean and tidy. Mr. Smith is in regular work, and earns 20s. a week. He gets 2s. a week for himself, and hands over 18s. to his wife. Out of his 2s. Mr. Smith spends 1d. a day on beer, 3d. a week on tobacco, puts 3d. in the children's savings-box, and clothes himself out of the remainder.

"One new dress, Mrs. Smith tells us, will last for years for everyday wear. She buys some old dress at a jumble sale for a few shillings, or some garments cast off by some wealthier female, and sometimes bought from the ragman for a few coppers; or perhaps they are not paid for in cash, and some older rags and a few pence are given in exchange for them. Garments so purchased are carefully taken to pieces, washed, and made up into clothes for the children. Mrs. Smith said she once bought a pair of old curtains from the ragman for 3d. She cut out the worn parts and then made the curtains into short blinds sufficient for all the windows in her house. She regularly pays 6d. for sick clubs, 4d. for life insurance, and 3d. per week into a clothing club. She kept detailed accounts of her income and expenditure during two months. Her 18s. is usually spent as follows: –

	s.	d.
Food for five persons	11	0
Rent	3	2
Coal and light	2	0
Soap, etc.	0	5
Life insurance	0	4
Clothing Club	0	3
	17	8

In addition, Mr. Smith spends 2s.; total 19.s 8d. It was obvious with such a close expenditure there was no appreciable sum available for extras.

"'Well, then, how do you do, Mrs. Smith,' my investigator asked, 'when you have to meet any extraordinary expenditure, such as a new dress or a new pair of boots?"

"'Well, as a rule we have to get it out of the food money and go short, and I never lets Smith suffer. He has to go to work, and be kept up, you know. And then Smith has allus been very good to me; when I want a new pair of shoes or anything he helps me out of his pocket-money, and we haven't to want food so much.'

"That little picture illustrates how millions of our people are living. They are not bad people, for you can see that. Do you wonder that in the course of years, and the natural selfishness of all of us; frail men and women that we are, there has been growing up a spirit of determination for change, a determination that in so far as we have the strength these things shall be altered. Well, I have given you only one of the pictures that influence us.

"What is the effect of life and death, of experience in these conditions? Why, say our comfortable friends, these people thrive in dirt and poverty. Are those who say this happy in their belief? If they are, their complacency must be dispelled. The death-rate among the poor is just double what it is among the rich. That is a fact worth thinking about; you are twice as likely to die if you are a poor person. And it is not only the deaths that matter, but it is the condition of the people who are left behind. It has been truly said that the record of death only registers, as it were, the wrecks which attain the shore, but it gives no account of the vessels which are tossed on the billows of sickness, stranded and maimed, as they often are, by the affects of recurring storms.

"To-night it is not necessary for me to enlarge on the things that go with poverty – the overcrowding of rooms, the deadening despair, the loosening of a dozen habits, as well as the occasional heroism; but let me give one more hard fact: Some of us are pressed by the knowledge that it is not only the grown-up people and the school children who are in the thick of these things, but also the tiny ones, babies often weak and smitten at birth through the life of their mothers and certain to be plunged into the most odious risks directly they are human beings. Unable to help themselves, they have never a chance in this life, for they are handicapped by poisonous surroundings long before they are conscious of such matters. Some grow to be healthy enough, many more to be weak, others don't grow up at all. Oh, no, I am not exaggerating; I am jut giving you a few actualities. A careful note was taken in a certain great town about the death rate, and it was found among the better-class comfortable people 94 children out of very 1,000 died before they were 12 months old; while 247 out of every 1,000 babies died in the poorer districts of the same town.[64]

In this rich and prosperous land, with its motor-cars and country houses, with its multitudes of comfortable middle-classes, there is deep down, beneath all, a seething nation of 10 million people, insufficiently fed, housed in dark squalid rooms, desperately struggling not to die. Their miseries can never be known by those who have never lived among them. The fate of being born among that 10 million is something for the imaginative soul to shudder at. And yet human beings, great numbers of them, are daily born into their midst.

"Similar conditions are to be found in other countries, but we must set ourselves to the work which lies closest to our hand. The knowledge that this great concourse of people exists has been growing in intensity for a generation, and there has sprung up one of those tremendous desires for change which break out through the centuries in various forms. We are now in the early stages of that change. That the human soul will rise to a height when it shall say: 'These things shall not be in the world,' is no more to be doubted than the rising of the sun to-morrow. Meanwhile, in our imperfect broken way, we are struggling, struggling towards the first step. Mistakes we must, and shall, make. We shall do unwise things. We are already earning the enmity of those whose comfort we slightly disturb in trying to lessen the hunger, dispel the disease, to remove the evil handicaps from little children. But all the mistakes we shall make, all the disasters we shall cause, all the hatred we shall earn are worth the task if we help some of these babies to live, if we begin to check that everlasting hunger, if we give even a fragment of a decent life to this stunted under-world.

"You know the sins of the Government of which I am a member. We have put through a lot of legislation in our short period, and have struck the first blows, and as a result we are reviled as no politicians have been reviled for sixty years[65] – and we are simply loathed by those who have five-course dinners and regard a visit to the theatre as a duty once a week.

"I have been told I am a wicked demagogue. Perhaps I am. I am on the way to breaking up the British Constitution[66] – I, a Minister of the Crown – well, I am here to say the forms of the British Constitution, valuable as I regard then in several directions, do not weigh with me at all when I think of that helpless and forsaken ten millions of people."

Throughout Path's speech mutterings and rumblings had broken on him from time to time, and now there was a great shout, scattered and broken, yet in unison. People in the circle, in the stalls, in the gallery, standing in the gangways, huddled together in confusion and discomfort, had steadily grown in excitement during the speech. The hypnotism of Path was on them. He had led up to this definite climax with unconscious skill. Sincerity and passion flared from him. His bitterest opponent would have known that he had the meeting in hand and at his mercy from this moment. That he himself was affected by the atmosphere it was plain to see. He had drifted a little to the right of the chairman's table; the original notes he carried were crushed to a ball in his left hand. He threw his shoulders back from time to time in an effort to control himself, but he quivered with intensity.

"Yes, I am a Red, if by being a Red it means that I would not hesitate to sacrifice some of the comforts of the noble for the lowly, that I would strip some of the inherited possessions from the belted earls to give food and health to even a small proportion of those babies which now are doomed. For that attitude of mine I am assailed, I am a thief, I am a reprobate. They tell you that such a man as I am cannot possibly be a decent person in private life; they have told you some stories; they will tell you others.

"Shame, shame," came from half a thousand throats. "We'll stand by you," cried a man in the first circle. A hundred voices broke into approving cheers. Path's eyes were alight.

"I have told you something of what is in my mind. I have this to add: The Government in the last two sessions has introduced legislative measures which are regarded by our foes as revolutionary, taxation and more taxation of the rich for education and health and for the cheapening of food. In the present session we shall introduce a measure on different lines, directed towards the objects of which I have spoken. The details or even the outline I do not propose to give you, but I can say this – it will be a measure framed with the idea that in the future those who are responsible for the government of this country shall be men, be they of what politics you like, whose consideration shall not be the privileges of the few, shall not be the property of the rich, but shall be human lives, especially those lives predestined to misery and poverty."

Raston Path sat down, and there was at once a great turmoil of enthusiasm in all parts of the building, waves of cheering being broken by raucous shouts of "Good old Raston!" "Don't spare 'em," "we'll stand by you," "Raston for ever." Nearly everybody had risen, and three-parts of the audience were waving hats or handkerchiefs. It was a scene which Gaunt, sitting at the reporters' table, always remembered. For five minutes, the noise continued. Raston Path gathered up his notes from the table at his side, and the flush was still on his face. The chairman said a word in his ear, and Path nodded. When a lull came, the chairman stood up. "If anybody here has got a question, Mr. Path will be pleased to answer it."

This was the formal announcement. Everyone knew that questions of a hostile nature would not be put to the Home Secretary from an audience which was wildly demonstrative in his favour.

The customary second or two of silence fell on the gathering nevertheless. Then to the general surprise, out of the silence came a voice. A man was standing in the front of the gallery and shouting a question.

"Can I ask the Home Secretary something?"

"Certainly," said the chairman; "what is it?"

"Ought not any politician who sets out on these efforts to help the poor – should he not have a good character himself?"

"I don't see much point in that," replied the chairman.

But Raston Path nodded his head assentingly to the question.

"What I want to ask is this – whether the Home Secretary did not desert a girl –"

A shout of anger went up from a hundred throats at the same tine as the chairman sprang to his feet. The questioner still tried to make himself heard amid the angry chorus, and he eventually managed to make a few more words audible. "And whether he is now paying secret midnight visits to a woman in London who –"

Lusty and determined stewards had been hurrying to him from the first, and now fell on him with a vigour and determination that brought about his rapid ejectment from the theatre within three minutes. The departing audience was in an angry uproar, but quieted down as the chairman rose to speak.

"That is the kind of calumny, that is the kind of thing our leaders have to meet. The man you have just put out, I'll warrant, was well paid for his job."

A howl of rage went up. "After him," shouted someone in the stalls. "Let's get it out of him," exclaimed another. Scores began to thrust their way to the doors in the hope of catching the questioner before he should disappear.

The meeting was practically finished now, and people came hustling forward to shake hands with Path, while those on the platform clustered round with congratulations on his speech. It was a quarter of an hour or more before he got away. He had forced back his old, quick, genial manner to meet the greetings, but the light had gone out of his eyes, and he was rather paler than usual. People said it was the reaction after his great speech.

[23 December 1913]
Chapter XV.
Path's Mysterious Visits.

The atmosphere of the meeting had affected Gaunt, as it was bound to affect an impressionable man, and unless he had been impressionable Gaunt would not have been such an excellent journalist. To picture the commonplace emotions, to be able to feel them, is necessary in the temperament of a successful newspaper man, and Gaunt, having the temperament, rarely failed to respond to influences, small or great. That such influences were but temporary, and left in most cases no lasting mark on his feelings, does not in the least take from the value of his sensitiveness from the newspaper point of view; indeed, the transitoriness was an advantage. Nevertheless, now and again things struck deep without any volition on his part. So far as Raston Path was concerned, Gaunt had certainly no desire to be impressed, and yet the speech or the meeting or the personality of Path, or all three together, had cut through his newspaper callousness, and he idly wondered as he caught a Blackfriars Bridge omnibus whether it was the reasoning of Path that had impressed him or the hypnotism of the gathering. Prejudice against the Red doctrines were high within him still, but latterly they had been less high than previously, though all his instincts ragged themselves strongly on the side of Authoritarian ideas. But, in spite of the fact that his heart remained sound, doubts had come to him on the logical side, and his brain, against his will, revolved some of the projects and ideas which had drifted to him in the course of his work in the past months. His experiences in that hard and hungry fortnight had shown him things in new lights. Now came the speech of Raston Path, and his previous experiences and his previous thoughts and doubts were stimulating subconscious appreciation of some, at least, of the things that Raston Path had said.

It should not be understood that he was giving any earnest or serious consideration to these matters when he boarded the omnibus for Fleet-street; they simply floated about in the back of his head while he bent his conscious attention on a very much more important and pressing affair. He was wondering what consequences the carefully arranged interruption of Path would lead to. That the Home Secretary was disturbed was obvious, but the purport of the question had not been to disconcert Path so much as to set up further suspicion as to his personal worth in the minds of the public and to rouse questioning and possibly to put on foot elucidations. It was also a preliminary to action which was already being arranged by Gaunt, action which might result in a sensational exposure.

Since that night when Raston Path had appeared on his homeward way in Seven Sisters-road a good many inquiries had been pushed home, a good deal of watching had been done, and rewards were on hand on some distinct discoveries. It was found out, for instance, that Raston Path always visited the Finsbury Park neighbourhood about nine o'clock on Saturday evening, and that he reached Belgravia on his return about half an hour after midnight. He visited a small thirty-pounds-a-year house[67] in a side street with carefully-kept blinds and a trim little front garden. The inquiry of the fortnight had left a good deal of mystery about the occupants of the house, and this was principally due to the fact that Gaunt and his assistants had refrained from questioning the forbidding middle-aged servant for fear of making their investigation known, and also because there was a good deal of difficulty in the little suburban street in watching a house from anywhere near at hand without being observed.

Still, some things had been discovered, and they were really important. What was now known was that a woman lived in the house, that she lived there without any family, and that her history was not known by the postmen or the milkman, of whom discreet questions had been asked. Her name, however, had come to light. And this was the most exciting discovery of the lot. The name was Croxten. The exultation of Gaunt when this name was first known communicated itself even to Lodden, who was swiftly informed of the discovery. Lodden travelled at once to a careful mental survey.

"Go steady," he said; "make no false step. Not a soul outside the office must know of our discovery for the present. We must be quite certain before we take action."

"What can we do?" asked Wansmuth.

"Do?" snapped Lodden. "A hundred things. We've got to prove the Home Secretary to be a person of low moral character, if that be the fact. Don't ask me how it is to be done; there are at least a hundred ways."

He looked at Gaunt.

"It's up to you, Gaunt. I don't want to be told what you're going to do or how you're going to do it."

"She's called Mrs. Croxten," put in Gaunt.

"He could do no less," said Lodden. "Merely a courtesy title."

"Strange he should give himself away by going to the house," said Wansmuth.

"That's just the kind of thing these clever people often do. They play straight into the hands of their enemies, they are so certain that nothing can ever be found out. Gaunt, I should get straight ahead with it. You muse devise something."

"It will be a bit venturesome," said Gaunt.

"Well, what are you here for? Mind you, there's to be no breaking the law – mind that, Gaunt. I won't have the *Daily Light* brought into disrepute. It's Raston Path that's to be brought into disrepute, not ourselves. Remember that in anything you do."

He looked at Gaunt meaningly, and the reporter's thoughts went back to a previous interview with the Home Secretary, who had on that occasion managed to damage the reputation of the *Daily Light* pretty considerably.

This time, however, there seemed hardly a way out for him.

"I will try," said Gaunt.

"Very well, start right in at once. I really don't want to hear anything more about it until the evidence is ready to publish in the paper."

Lodden swung himself into his chair as a sign of dismissal, at least for the reporter, and Gaunt went out through the secretary's room into the corridor and strolled up to the reporters' room full of thought.

All this had happened a week before Raston Path's meeting, and arrangements were now pretty well advanced for what Gaunt hoped and believed would be a great dramatic revealment. He had taken some risks, and Lodden for one knew nothing of them. Wansmuth, however, had been privately informed of what was being done, and, while not disclaiming the plot, he thrust the responsibility on to Gaunt for success or failure. And, indeed, it was quite a desperate expedient that had been devised by the reporter. Many and diverse were the devices which Gaunt had brought into action during his tenure on the *Light*, but the present was by far the most daring, for while success promised a big scoop for the paper, its failure would be very damaging. Both audacity and courage were necessary.

Gaunt, returning to the *Daily Light* office after Path's meeting, was thinking of the coming discomfiture of the Home Secretary, a discomfiture which had already been started by the questions at the meeting. The true spirit of the mercenary fighter was aroused in Gaunt. Impressions as to right and wrong in politics were mere luxuries. His was it to do the work for which he was engaged; and it was a natural ardour as well as training which set up within him an enthusiasm for the carrying out of his duty. Taken out of himself temporarily by the speech and its reception, he had been braced up by the incidents at the close and the demeanour of Path, and something of the lust of the soldier was in Gaunt as he thought over matters and proceeded to sketch the scheme of things for a few days ahead. He had to expose Path, and to expose him in such a way that there should be no escape. How the exposure was to be made had given Gaunt hours of delight and he had eventually decided that it should be dramatic as well as audacious and that no fragment of doubt should be allowed to remain as to Path's personal character.

At the same time he recognised that the reputation of the *Daily Light* had to be considered and that any action taken must be devised with that in view. As I have said, Wansmuth had been given privately an outline of Gaunt's intended plan. Two other men had to be brought in to assist in putting the thing through. These two men, Gaunt decided after careful reflection should be Wrightson and Burton. Wrightson, for all his flippancy and lack of seriousness, was a man of a thousand expedients, quick-witted, and with personal courage at a pinch. Burton, gentle-mannered, and a much older man, had a wealth of special knowledge, for as the Scotland Yard expert of the *Daily Light*, he knew all about detective methods, had more than an inkling of the law on the criminal side, and knew pretty well how far a raid on a private house might go without serious danger of criminal penalties.

[24 December 1913]

Chapter XV – Continued.
The Raid.

It was a raid that Gaunt intended.

He purposed making a descent on the house at Finsbury Park at a moment when Raston Path was inside, to enter by force or by trickery and with his two companions as fellow-witnesses to trap the Home Secretary in the company of the young woman who had been his sweetheart. That was the plot.

There were a good many practical difficulties, but Gaunt had tackled them one by one, and by the time Path's big meeting was held they had been disposed of.

The following Saturday evening was the chosen time for the adventure. On the night of Path's meeting Gaunt had a consultation with Burton and Wrightson over the form of procedure. Wrightson sat on the corner of his table smoking a cigarette, and Burton leaned against the mantelpiece near Gaunt while the latter wrote two or three pages describing the scene at the end of Path's meeting, with a little analysis of Path's feelings when the questions were put. After he had sent the copy into the chief sub-editor, he said: "You haven't said anything about this jaunt of ours to the other boys?"

"Not a word," said Wrightson.

"It's pretty risky," said Burton. "I suppose you know all three of us could be put into gaol?"

Gaunt smiled thoughtfully. "I don't think so. We've got it planned out all right."

"If the worst came to the worst it'd be a bit of sport to be charged with trying to convict the Home Secretary of an immoral life."

"We ought to be rewarded," said Wrightson cheerfully. "I'm for toleration and all that, but if I had my way all these Progressives and Reds would be burned at the sake. Give me a lord, a stupid lord, all the time."

Burton did not laugh. "That's all very well, you can be funny," he said. "I don't want to got to prison. I've got a wife and three children. You know what Lodden is if anything happens to go wrong."

"It can't go wrong," said Gaunt. "What's going to happen? We shall get into the house; we shall push through into the sitting-room or parlour, and find him having supper with this young woman, or talking to her, or whatever it may be. That will be all. There'll be a devil of a row. He'll want to know what the hell we are there for, and I shall tell him; then we shall probably all get kicked out, if there is any other man in the house to help him. We've got our story – my word what a story."

"Sounds all right," said Burton.

"The only thing is," said Wrightson, "it doesn't show him up in his true colours. I want to make him out really bad."

During the days that intervened before the Saturday the ground was visited two or three times by Gaunt and his colleagues and every preparation was made for the great night.

Raston Path usually arrived at the house at about eight o'clock, and this meant he would leave his brother's house in Belgravia about seven o'clock if he travelled by tram and omnibus as usual, or about half-past seven if he made the journey by taxi-cab, as it had been found he had done on one or two occasions.

Burton's allotted task was to watch Path's house in Belgravia from six o'clock in the evening onwards, with a private motor-car waiting out of sight in a turning, and when Path left his house it was for Burton to follow him a hundred yards or so behind. He would then have the opportunity of hastening if the Home Secretary took a taxi-cab, or of following him at leisure should he proceed by any other means.

Up at Finsbury Patrk Gaunt and Wrightson were to keep watch from half-past six onwards. Gaunt strolling up and down on one side of the street and Wrightson on the other, each prepared to join forces directly the enemy came in sight. They were not, of course, to march steadily up and down like soldiers, but were to lounge about, sometimes in doorways, sometimes smoking a cigarette leaning against the railings, and generally to pass the time as unobtrusively as possible while they waited for the appearance of Path.

Gaunt had sworn each of his friends to secrecy, and indeed for their own sakes they were careful not to allow a whisper of their plans to get abroad, even to be known in the reporters' room, while Gaunt himself, usually very open at home about his work, said nothing to his mother about the arrangement which had been so carefully made. He was on his guard all the week and was very jealous even about the interest in the office as to the progress of Lodden's campaign against Path. The merest hint he knew might be sufficient to overthrow the effort. The Cartlets, with whom he dined on two occasions during the time he was making his arrangements, knew nothing – though Viola showed a growing embitterment against Path and tried to get Gaunt to take up her arguments and share in her prejudices. Gaunt showed mild acquiescence, but did not say anything about his scheme for the approaching week-end.

Experience had shown him how emphatic was the need for caution in any daring new move. It was all the more surprising, therefore – and it was surprising to himself at the time – that, paying a visit to see the Kirks on the Friday evening before the fateful Saturday, he indicated how his duty on the next day would lead him to a startling move against Raston Path.

It was his first and only revelation, apart from talk with Wansmuth and Wrightson. He knew it would not be repeated, and knew also that not a word of his remarks could reach Path. He sat in a basket-chair before the kitchen fire talking to Mrs. Kirk and Nellie. Nancy sat at the other end of the kitchen table, studying the third regular conjugation of French verbs. She caught stray sentences of the conversation and occasionally looked up and listened.

"Got to do it," said Gaunt, as he knocked the ashes out of his pipe on the top bar of the kitchen range. "No help for it. Course, these politicians, they get over it. To be set upon and slaughtered by us newspaper men is all part of the game. They get through it all right."

"Going to see Mr. Path to-morrow, then?" said Nellie, as she peeled an orange for immediate consumption. "Going to give him a piece of lip?"

Mrs. Kirk paused in her work of making a blouse and said: "You do say things, Nellie."

"So he is; that's it, ain't it, Mr. Gaunt?"

"Don't know yet," said Gaunt. "We're going to try and lay him out to-morrow, but I can't tell you exactly the way yet. Very likely it'll all be in the paper on Monday."

Nancy looked up from her book. "You are doing something to-morrow, Mr. Gaunt?"

"Yes."

"Another bit of the fight. The paper is trying to stop Mr. Path. Have you found out the secret of his visits to North London, why he goes there?" asked Nancy.

"No; we shall probably know that to-morrow. But we have found out where he goes, and the name of the person he visits."

"It seems cruel," said Nancy, thoughtfully.

"Cruel," said Gaunt. "You don't know the story or you wouldn't say that. When you know the facts you will see that nothing we can do about it could be cruel."

"Is Mr. Path speaking somewhere to-morrow," asked Mrs. Kirk.

"No," said Gaunt. "This is a private meeting in which I am taking part. It's to-morrow evening. No one will know what has occurred till the description appears in the paper on Monday."

Gaunt went away from the Borough back to Sydenham unaware that he had fired a train. He was not to know that Nancy Kirk was in full possession of the story of which he knew but a part, and that Raston Path's romance was an open book to her, and that she knew pretty well how and why it was he was visiting the little house in North London.

Indefinite as had been Gaunt's hints she was disturbed at the thought of his action on the following evening.

At half-past five the next evening Burton had his motor-car two streets away from Path's house, having taken two whiskys and sodas instead of his tea to fortify himself against what might be a considerable period of waiting. He walked along to the corner of the street in which Raston Path lived with his brother, and had a look along its lonely and respectable length. A solitary policeman, just about to enter it from the other corner, was the only person to be seen. Burton went back and fetched his car within striking distance, and then he began his lounging vigil. Twice he walked down past the house itself, where as a reporter he had before now paid calls. Quiet and dull was the exterior of this unobtrusive Belgravia residence. It was no fitting home, thought Burton, for the turbulent spirit who was disturbing the country. A little shiver of expectation went through him as he thought of the prospects for the night, the tracking of the man, the rude bursting in upon him, the exposure of his continued association with the young woman of years gone by.

Burton had no thoughts to spare for the political results, and in these waiting minutes was not even thinking of how the story would appear in the paper on Monday; the adventure with its incidents was quite enough for him for the time being.

Once a plain-clothes detective passed him, for the house of Raston Path, in common with those of other Ministers whose campaigns aroused violence in return, was under a tacit police protection. The attitude of Scotland Yard, and indeed the necessary attitude, was that one never knows what fanatics will do, and probably all political enthusiasts are fanatics to the genially materialistic Scotland Yard.

The strolling Burton did not come in for more than a passing glance from the detective, because a strolling journalist – and a journalist the detective knew him to be – is nothing out of the common, and is not to be remarked upon in the neighbourhood of Cabinet Ministers. For half an hour or more Burton paced up and down, paying occasional visits to his motor-car to see it was in readiness. He had just scraped out his pipe preparatory to trying a new brand of tobacco recommended that day by Gaunt, when Raston Path came down the steps of his brother's house to the pavement. Burton went on scraping out his pipe. Raston Path in a bowler hat, with an overcoat buttoned round him and a walking stick in hand, walked briskly along the pavement towards Burton, passed him, emerged into the main road where the motor-car was in waiting, and set off apparently in the direction of a cab 400 yards away.

Burton gave him a minute, and then entered his car, explained carefully what was necessary to the driver, and crawled after the Home Secretary. Path took a taxi-cab from a line of waiting vehicles to which he had directed himself, then Burton quickened his pace, followed quite closely behind the taxi, and began the tracking of the Home Secretary across London. The task was an easy one by reason of the fact that the destination was in mind. Everything went as had been expected, and within 20 minutes the Holloway-road was in sight. Burton knew his two colleagues were by this time in Blackburn-road. He knew just what they were feeling, and how expectantly keen and nervy they were.

"Well, they will soon be satisfied." Burton pulled vigorously at his pipe of new tobacco and wondered what the outcome of it all would be. It surprised the philosophic Burton to find his hardened journalistic mind alive to the drama which would result form the coming together of the four of them – the two men now waiting in Blackburn-road and himself and Path now hurrying towards them.

He did not know that a fifth person was hurrying to the encounter also. Burton would certainly have been shaken from his professional melancholy calm had he realised that on a tram car which he and Path had overtaken in the Holloway-road there sat Nancy Kirk, tremulous but determined, with her mind fixed as firmly on No. 25 Blackburn-road as Path or Gaunt or Burton or Wrightson.

She was frightened but determined. Nancy knew that she had not the nerves for a heroine, but she was stirred and uplifted as well as frightened and it was in a fever of soul that she was hurrying up to North London to prevent what she thought to be a catastrophe.

Gaunt's conversation had led her to know what was afoot, and during the day she had filled in some gaps for herself. The time had been the thing – that was what had worried her; she had not been able to devise a means of getting at the time. Then, after tea, she had taken a desperate course – desperate, that is, for her. She had gone to a public telephone call-office and rung up Gaunt's home number, and under the cover of a business inquiry had learned that Gaunt had left home for the north of London, where he had an important meeting at seven o'clock.

Tremblingly she had immediately made her decision to go to Blackburn-road. Exactly what she was to do when she got there she knew not, but she realised that Raston Path must be protected. She got out at Finsbury Park Station, and two minutes later had found the beginning of Blackburn-road.

She arrived there ten minutes after Raston Path had entered No. 25, and as she got near the house she saw three men standing at the gateway apparently talking together. She was on the opposite side of the road, and when nearly abreast of them she observed Gaunt step away from his two companions towards the door and rap upon it smartly. She was horrified, all aquiver with excitement, but she could not get her courage up, and for the moment she knew not what to do. Gaunt rapped again on the door and his two companions stepped up to his side. Hardly knowing what she did, Nancy Kirk began to cross the road towards them, and it was as she was crossing the road that the door opened.

Gaunt and Wrightson and Burton were far too intent on the approach of the climax to their adventure to notice Nancy Kirk or to be conscious of the girl who was running across the road towards them. The second time that Gaunt knocked he had done with so in an imperative way, and within a few seconds he heard footsteps as of someone approaching along the passage to answer his call. Burton and Wrightson had closed up just behind him. The door opened and a tall, middle-aged, rather angular woman with a common-sense, placid face stood before them.

"I have urgent business on which to see Raston Path," said Gaunt.

"Mr. Path," said the surprised woman. "I can't –"

"I must come in at once," said Gaunt.

"You can't come in," said the offended servant. "What do you mean?"

She stood with her hand on the door.

"Come on," said Gaunt to his companion. He stepped forward, and as she was right in front of him he had to push her a little to get by. She was so taken aback that she made no real resistance. The three men rushed along the passage, at the end of which they could see the kitchen by the light of the fire. But it was obvious that it was unoccupied. On their left a streak of light came from beneath the door of the beneath the door of the back parlour. Here were probably the two people they sought.

The three young men were breathing unsteadily. They had taken the plunge, and must go on whatever happened. They did not know that Nancy Kirk had rushed in by the open door behind them and was exchanging incoherent words with the servant. Gaunt knocked smartly at the back parlour door, turned the handle and walked in, closely followed by Burton and Wrightson.

The picture they had before them was a long-remembered one. The room was small, a red-shaded electric light suspended from the ceiling gave a cosy look to what might have been regarded as a typical suburban back parlour. There were evidences of taste and comfort – a dainty bookcase reaching to the ceiling on one side of the room and a leather-covered settee which ran along another side, some statuettes on the mantel, and a couple of etchings above them. These things imprinted themselves upon the minds of the men merely as a background, and were not realised till afterwards, for all their thoughts were on the two people in front of them.

In a basket chair leaning back in an attitude of comfort was Raston Path, smoking a pipe, and on the settee near the window was a woman with snow-white hair and a gentle face lined with care as well as with age. She was doing some needlework. These were the two disclosed to the eyes of the three young men who had come so rudely into the room.

For a second there was a trance-like silence as each one strove instinctively to grasp the situation. Raston Path, with his pipe in his hand, looked round at the intruders and then flashed an inquiry at the lady opposite. She on her part was plainly bewildered, though she was not more bewildered for the moment than was Gaunt. Impetuously the latter spoke.

"Where is Miss Croxten?" he said.

Raston Path was standing up now. "Who are these men?" he asked.

The old lady had dropped her needlework. "I don't know, Raston –"

Gaunt was swinging from amazement to anger, for he saw that a trick, if not a trap, had been prepared.

"We're sorry to break in like this, Madam," he said, "but this is a public matter."

"Public matter," exclaimed Path, his face hardening.

"Yes, this can go on no longer. We are here as witnesses of one of your regular visits to this house. We are going to tell the facts as we have discovered them."

"This is very interesting," said Path. "Would you mind explaining – I think I have seen you somewhere before."

"Yes," said Gaunt, swiftly. "I am from the *Daily Light*, so are my friends here. We want to know where Miss Croxten is."

"Trailed me down," said Path, in an unpleasant tone.

"Do you mean to deny that you come here regularly, that you are here nearly every Saturday night? Do you mean to say that you have not in this house Miss Croxten, who used to be your typist years ago and whom you have continued to visit in secret?"

"The *Daily Light*?" said Path. He looked over the three men, Gaunt leaning forward, his face flushed, his fist clenched, and his arm half-raised in emphasis, and the other two silent and motionless near the door, a little embarrassed but loyal and ready to support their leader.

"You scum!"

"You won't get out if it that way," said Gaunt, and as he spoke there was a half scuffle outside the door in the passage, and Nancy's voice could be heard, a note above usual. "I will go in; I must go in."

Then the door was pushed open a little wider, and Nancy entered. She was transfigured by emotion. Her delicate complexion had lost its tint, and was dead white, but she had become entirely forgetful of herself and the hundred restraints which usually bound her hand and foot. There was no restraint about her now.

"What have you done?" she cried to Gaunt. "You must come out of here."

Gaunt looked at her like a man in a dream, and the others in the room were struck silent by this new raid. That this young girl should come rushing in after the other incursion was to Path and the old lady nothing more than part of the plot, but to Gaunt and his companions it was as great a surprise as if an angel with wings had suddenly appeared on the scene.

"I know all about it," panted Nancy to Gaunt. "You're quite wrong; you ought not to have come here, there will be terrible trouble."

For the first time cold doubt went through the heart of Majority Gaunt. Had he, after all, made some shocking mistake? He pulled himself together.

"Miss Kirk, this is no place for you. Burton, see her out."

"I won't go," she almost screamed. She thrust herself across to the other side of the room near to Path. "Tell them that it is all a mistake, Mr. Path. Tell them what I say is right."

But Path was busy ringing the bell, and in the midst of another sentence from Nancy the bewildered servant came in.

"Bridget," said Path, "go down to the police-station under the arch and tell the inspector on duty that three men have forced their way into this house and that immediate assistance is required."

The woman went out on her mission.

"As much publicity as you like, Mr. Path," said Gaunt, bravely. "I am sorry."

Path had crossed over to where the old lady was sitting, and was whispering to her, apparently in an attempt to quiet fears that had been aroused by the blustering young men.

Nancy Kirk, in an agony of spirit, appealed to Gaunt and his companions. "Don't you understand?" she said. "I tried to get here before you came in; I didn't know the time. I tried to stop you; you're all quite wrong. Miss Croxten doesn't live here."

"Oh," said Gaunt, stubbornly, "he calls her Mrs. Croxten now."

"He won't tell you. I must. His sweetheart died while he was courting her. This is her mother. He keeps her, and always has kept her, since Miss Croxten died."[68]

Then for three seconds a really shocking silence lay over the room. Raston Path looked up and turned a kindly eye on Nancy Kirk.

"This young lady seems to know a very private story," he said, quietly.

Wrightson plucked at Gaunt's coat. "Come on," he said.

"We're being bluffed," said Gaunt.

"How can we?" hissed Burton. "Come outside."

Blunderingly they found their way to the door and hustled along the passage out into the street again. They remembered afterwards they had left Nancy Kirk crying bitterly, and the last glimpse they had was of the old lady crossing the room towards her.

"We won't wait for the police," said Gaunt, as they got outside; and all three broke into a jog-trot towards the side street, where Burton's motor-car was still awaiting.

[26 December 1913]
Chapter XVI.
Gaunt's Compunction.

Lodden lounged back in the window seat, thrust his hands deep into his trousers pockets, and turned a quizzical smile on Wansmuth. "Just what I thought! Knew he'd have a way out. I suppose he didn't arrange this entertainment especially for our men?"

"No, it's genuine enough."

Lodden thought for a moment. "Bit of a nuisance just now. Can't be helped. We'll just have to drop that and go right ahead."

"Anything to be said about Saturday?"

"No, what the deuce can we say? Simply ignore it. We won't say anything more about this past romance; drop it."

"It'll come out some day that we knew the facts and didn't publish them."

"Don't look ahead for trouble. People will be thinking of other things then."

"What about Gaunt and the other two men?"

"It's a devil of a knock for Gaunt. He deserves it for not making sure about the woman before. Still, I'm sorry for him."

"Bad break."

"Yes, yes, but we all make breaks. I make breaks. That's nothing. I am not going to abuse him for this; he was right to put the thing to the test. What we lack on the paper is men of courage and grit, and I am not going to dishearten a chap like Gaunt."

"Do you want to see him?"

"No, the best thing for me is to know nothing about the affair. He and the other two chaps must be sworn to secrecy, and don't let them know it has reached me. They will feel better if they think the incident is to blow over."

"But you're forgetting Path. Do you think he is going to sit still under it?"

"Of course he'll sit still. He'd have told all we've found out long ago if he'd wanted to. If he tells it now, he's been forced into it by the *Daily Light*. 'Twould be merely an excuse to expose the impetuous action of our young men. At first he probably wanted to break their necks, but later he was sure to decide to say nothing but wait for us to make a move. We won't make any move. That'll puzzle him a little."

Wansmuth went downstairs not in entire agreement with his chief, feeling that for once in a way Lodden's judgment was in error, that Path would flaunt to the world this scandalous attack on his private life. So far as Lodden's attitude towards the members of the staff in an emergency was concerned, Wansmuth was long past wonderment; and that he should practically commend the failure of the three men instead of flinging them out into the street left him unmoved.

Wansmuth saw Gaunt, and in regretful words showed him the danger into which he had led the paper by the rash adventure on insufficient grounds, and then hinted that Lodden had been informed of the mere outline of the offence and was ignorant of its gravity and for the present might perhaps remain without knowing the details, unless indeed Raston Path should take the offensive. "In that case there will be trouble, and I expect you will have to go through it."

"You don't want me to resign," said Gaunt, thoughtfully.

"Oh, no, I expect you have had a pretty bad shake up over the whole thing. Your job now is to see that Wrightson and Burton keep their mouths tightly shut. There must be no whispering about the thing. It's just possible that Path himself may have reasons for remaining quiet and then we'll try to forget last Saturday."

Gaunt went back to the reporters' room with some of the load lifted from him, but only some of it. The raid on Mrs. Croxten's home had required for its carrying out an effort of will and a violation of some better feelings and Gaunt, with qualms growing on him, had forced the thing through with an air of audacity which was no part of him. The shock of the truth had been severe. That he should have been misled into a false belief, and that his inquiries should have lacked the thoroughness necessary to make the identity of Mrs. Croxten clear – these things stabbed his vanity. But his injured professional pride was far less than his mortification at the personal outrage of which he had been guilty. Had his worst suppositions been well based the breaking into the house might very well have led to criticism, but what was to be said of such an incursion when its victims were a distinguished public man and a lady whose age he was generously tending?

The disgust in Raston Path's voice when he summed up the *Daily Light* staff in his word "scum" was appreciated now by Gaunt. He saw how the Home Secretary must regard the paper, with its reckless and unscrupulous assertions, backed up when necessary by hooligan physical action. All through the campaign Gaunt had had the sensation that he did not dislike Raston Path, had indeed been attracted to him personally, had admired his mysterious qualities, felt the influence like a public audience did of his mesmeric emanations; and to attack him was only possible by reason of a genuine belief that he was a self-promoting politician and that his personal character was tainted. Gradually but steadily the impression of Path's political insincerity was being erased, and a close acquaintance with the doctrine of the Reds, together with his personal experiences, were producing strange and uncomfortable doubts in Gaunt's mind as to the unshakable truth of Authoritarianism. Some parts of that speech in the Surrey Theatre – a speech which it has been his duty to nullify – clung around his memory. And now in his last effort, a rash and desperate enterprise which was to prove Path a villain to all the world, he found himself held up, checkmated, scornfully impaled, as one trying to reveal a secret cad, who had brought to view a good man hiding lovable qualities from a cold world. Gaunt was almost persuaded to go and see Path. Prudence dissuaded him, and he went down to see Nancy Kirk instead.

Saturday had had its effect on Nancy as well as on Gaunt. Shaken out of her natural reserve at the time, and with trembling nervousness following her desperation, she was now wondering whether or not she had done something very wrong, even though she could not help a certain sense of comfort. Sometimes she could not realise that she had interfered in Gaunt's work, because it seemed such a tremendous thing to do. What could he think of her? What a thousand pities she had failed to catch them before he and his companions had broken into the house! She wondered how she had the courage to follow in after them.

When Gaunt went down to see her he found that much of her reserve had disappeared, that she talked with him still not very freely, but nevertheless with a gentle candour and a friendliness that were very sweet to him. She was concerned that he should not blame her, and was rather surprised that he had nothing but appreciation for her wild action, and surprised, too, that he was overshadowed by personal worry.

"There's one thing, the *Daily Light* won't go on attacking Mr. Path now. They will say how they were mistaken."

"You don't know newspapers. The *Daily Light* never apologises – that would weaken the paper. It just continues without saying anything."

"That is not honest."

"Of course not; but what does it matter? No one connected with a newspaper is honest. I, for one, certainly am not."

"But you are really; you're in the habit of saying things like that."

They had the kitchen to themselves; Mrs. Kirk and Nellie had gone to a picture palace for the evening.

Gaunt found himself talking to the girl as though she understood him like a sister.

"We're just like soldiers we reporters. We go out to hurt people, to kill people if we can, on the orders of the hour, and we do not ask whether our orders are right or wrong. Modern half-penny papers couldn't be carried on if those who built them up were allowed to have consciences. Theirs not to reason why,[69] but go and do the job they're sent on, see?"

"It is the editor who gives the order than? He is the man who has to choose."

"Yes, the editor or the man who owns the paper."

"And the reporters don't care what they do."

"They don't care very much. Of course there are limits when a man will shy at some things. Generally speaking, it is only on political matters they are supposed to have no consciences, and attacks on public men and all that. We get good money, and we've got to do the work."

"You have to be loyal to your employers, then?"

"That's what it comes to. You have heard of Martin who does those flaming cartoons for the Progressive *Daily Measure* – well, he's no Progressive at all, he's a violent Authoritarian. In our reporting room a good many chaps are Reds or semi-Reds."

"You? What are you?"

"Oh, I'm an Authoritarian more or less; really I think I'm nothing."

"It doesn't matter what you're sent on then?"

"Not much. You see what a low-down lot we are. Look at this thing last Saturday. That was my fault, but I was encouraged to go on with it. They're a pretty rotten lot, Miss Kirk."

Nancy did not reply.

"I really don't know what to do about it. At first I thought I should have to resign, but it seems for some unknown reason our blunder's to be passed over. Course I'm glad, because I can't afford to give up ten pounds a week with nothing else in prospect."

"Mr. Path didn't say anything about you on Saturday."

"He wouldn't; he knows the game we have to play. I wonder if I ought to go up and see him. It was a beastly thing for us to do."

"What can you say?"

"Tell him I'm not such a skunk as he probably thinks me, tell him I'm awfully sorry for that business on Saturday. I can't get over it. Fancy bursting in on a man with a foul word when he is only doing a kind and generous thing. After our campaign, too. I've got a jolly good mind to go up to him."

"Perhaps your paper wouldn't like it?"

"No, I dare say not. I should have to chuck them up if I went. Couldn't do that, I'm afraid; I'm not built on the heroic line."

"It is rather wicked to keep on saying things in the paper against Mr. Path if they're not true."

"There won't be anything more about him personally. With regard to this old sweetheart there can't be; but we shall go on saying things about him apart from that. He attacks other people, you know. It's all right about this affair, but he is not very particular in his language about others. He's got to stand what he gets, I suppose."

"Still, after what you've said about him –"

"Yes, I feel like a pig on the whole thing but I suppose I shall get over it."

"Can't you put something nicer in the paper about him?"

"Not we. Archie is just as keen to out him now as ever he was. Only we'll have to go on a different tack."

"He's such a good man. It seems hardly fair to hit him like that."

'Oh, he's all right in some things, but politicians are not saints; don't run away with that idea, Miss Kirk. Raston Path is no angel. All the same, I feel bad about Saturday."

"It's a good thing you know the truth about that story now."

"Yes; but, bless you, we're a shallow, callous lot. I shall probably be doing something similar next week. I'll get off now. I felt I must come and talk to you about it."

Gaunt got on a tram for the City, his spirit tossed with doubts and impulses, and yet withal there was an underlying sense of satisfaction in having talked frankly with Nancy, in having stripped some of the hypocrisy from himself, and at the same time shown that there was at least a sense of decency in him.

Strange that he knew not whither he was tending. None of us realise at the time the secret influences within us. In the midst of fighting emotions there runs a thin streak of purpose, a purpose unrecognised, but quite certainly joined up to corresponding and continuous streaks in other tempestuous souls equally unseeing. Remotely a common understanding is at work, though to what end goodness only knows. Perhaps it is just a freak for the amusement of the ghosts known as Fate.

[27 December 1913]
Chapter XVI – Continued.
The Entanglement of Lodden and Viola.

Closer and closer were coming some of the personal forces – Path, Gaunt, Viola Cartlet, Lodden, Nancy Kirk, and as yet there was but an inking in the mind of any.

Gaunt went back to the office after his talk with Nancy Kirk and arrived there about five o'clock to find Burton reading the stop-press news in the *Westminster Gazette*.[70]

"See Path is bringing in his new Bill on Monday."

"I thought it was to be a fortnight hence," said Gaunt in surprise.

"No; here you are." Burton tossed the *Westminster Gazette* across and Gaunt read the following: –

> The Prime Minister, making his customary Thursday announcement as to Parliamentary Business for the coming week, stated that on Monday next the Home Secretary would introduce his Government of the People Bill. This, of course, is the measure which has so long been the subject of speculation in the country. The Lobby was a-buzz with surmise after the Prime Minister's statement, and the terms of the new Bill are eagerly debated. It is felt by many that no question of financial rearrangement or new taxation is contemplated in the Government plan, which is said to deal rather with personalities than with fiscal matters. One generally accepted statement is to the effect that the Bill seeks to prevent the future government of the country by men who are unfitted by nature or training. What this means is not very clear. It is manifest, however, that the speech of the Home Secretary will be of a sensational nature.

We were off the line, then, about new taxation and all that?" said Gaunt.

"Yes, if this gossip is right."

"Something in it," said Gaunt; "they've got an inkling somewhere."

"The funny thing," said Burton, "is that he seems to have been able to switch the idea of the new Bill round to something quite different from his original idea."

"As a rule everybody's got some kind of a notion as to the outline of a Bill, but since the upset about our scoop it's been all vague. Neither Path nor anyone else has given an indication of the actual proposals. I should think we were pretty near the actual truth."

Gaunt shrugged his shoulders.

"It's certain we're off the line now," said Burton; "if this Lobby talk goes for anything he's got some new plan in his head."

"We'll see on Monday," said Gaunt. "I'm told these articles about poverty that we have been publishing have gone very well; people are talking about them. Adams did those Northern articles very well about –"

"The ones about life in the Lancashire towns have never been beaten. Butler wasn't as bad about the Black Country."

"What about your own?" asked Burton.

"Trash," said Gaunt. "Couldn't rise to the occasion somehow. Don't know how it was, but all the spirit had gone out of me. There was good material, too."

The others said nothing, because they knew that Gaunt was pretty well right. His articles had lacked the colour and the fire which might have given them distinction, and on the whole were a disappointment.

"This'll stir Archie up – this announcement about Path's Bill on Monday," said Burton.

"Already done," said Wrightson, "he's on the move."

"On the move?" said Gaunt. "Why, the thing's only just published in the paper."

"I expect he'd have heard of it this morning."

"Well, what's he done?"

"He's in the midst of it, whatever it is. He's got Mrs. Cartlet in his room now downstairs, and –"

"Mrs. Cartlet?" said Gaunt.

"Yes, Archie knows his way about. By the way, she's a friend of yours, isn't she?"

"I know her a little."

"Well, you'd better warn her, because Archie uses everybody without stint, and she must have been very useful to him in the past in these fights with the Home Secretary."

"Oh, nonsense," said Gaunt. "Mrs. Cartlet can look after herself."

"Well, it's a funny thing how we've had all this private information, and so on. I think Archie's been playing her up."

Gaunt felt himself getting angry, but he said in a mild way: "You're quite off the track. Don't you make any mistake about Archie being able to influence Mrs. Cartlet."

"Well, she's here a good deal," said Burton.

"I know she's been up once or twice," replied Gaunt, "but only just occasionally when some special matter has come along. Besides, her husband is one of the accountants for the firm."

"Oh, yes," said Burton, "trust Archie for that. She's been here a good deal more than once or twice. She was here last week."

"Last week?" said Gaunt.

"Yes, and a fortnight before that she had an hour with Archie here – they went out to tea together."

"I never heard of it," said Gaunt, in some surprise, thinking of his visit to the Cartlets just before the adventure in North London.

"I don't suppose Archie tells you everything," said Burton.

"Nor Mrs. Cartlet either," put in Wrightson ably.

"I don't suppose so," said Gaunt, thoughtfully.

Gaunt was more than surprised, and indeed was a little mortified, for he had been on the closest corresponding terms with Viola, and her references to Lodden had always been of the slightest, and it seemed to him that she was not so closely bound up with his life as she had indicated herself to be.

What was she doing with Lodden on these visits – intriguing against Raston Path, he supposed, conveying information that had reached her, and stimulating where she could the fight against him? It was a little unwomanly, thought Gaunt, to push the thing so hard. Why couldn't she leave such a conflict to the men? After all, she had no great grievance against Path except small political prejudices and some personal mortification at his contemptuous treatment of her. Perhaps her vanity was mixed up in it; she was, of course, gratified that she and her husband had become friends of Archibald Lodden, the proprietor of the *Daily Light*, and if Lodden, iron-hearted as he was, allowed her charms to touch him, well, then, she was not the woman to forego such an advantage. Tactfully and with all speed she would make certain that Lodden appreciated her to the uttermost, and would see, also, that he did not forget her. Reviewing her temperament Gaunt hatched out an idea of what her interviews with Lodden meant, and also her comparative silence about them. He was a little hurt, though, because she had revealed to him all kinds of private and personal things, domestic difficulties, family matters, and other subjects, many of which are only generally discussed between a man and his wife. He could have sworn there was no corner of her heart and mind unknown to him.

Even now his hand was in his coat pocket on a scented pink note from Viola which he had received that afternoon pleading with him in lover-like terms to come up and spend the week-end at Hampstead. A touch of shame had been on him when he opened the letter, but the mingled kindness, gentleness, and seductiveness had warmed him almost against his will, and he had decided on the visit.

Gaunt, standing in front of his writing table and idly moving pens and paper about on the surface pondered over the visit of Viola to Lodden. Had he sent for her? If so, why? Was it her possession of facts about the Bill which had brought her down voluntarily to see him? He was inclined to think so. Why, then, had she not come to the reporters' room, where, as she well knew, Gaunt would have been waiting eagerly. Her information would have been better in his hands than in Lodden's, because he might have secured a little credit out of it. At the back of his reflections was the stinging knowledge that she had not told him at all of her intention to come to the *Daily Light* office, and had, indeed, knowingly run the risk of meeting him accidentally and having to explain it away.

Suddenly he came to a decision – he would go down to the floor below and take his chance of meeting her near Lodden's room as she came out. Down he went to the next floor, his intention growing warmer as he neared Lodden's suite. He decided to go in to Brown, who occupied the next room to Lodden's and to be there in conversation with him as Viola came out. Afterwards he realised that this was a risky and somewhat stupid thing to do, for Lodden was not the man to be imposed upon by any surface excuses.

He entered briskly and found Brown dictating some letters to a girl typist by the side of him at his mahogany roll-top desk.

"Sorry to bother you," said Gaunt, "but I was just wondering if the chief had asked for me this afternoon about this announcement."

"What announcement?" said Brown.

"What the Prime Minister has said this afternoon about Path's Bill next Monday."

"Haven't heard of it."

"He says that Path will move the first reading of this new Bill on Monday. Something may have to be done about it, and I thought I'd just look down in case the chief had mentioned it at all."

"Hasn't said a word. As a matter of fact Mrs. Cartlet came in to see him about an hour ago and he's been with her."

"Same thing," said Gaunt. "Of course she is right with us against the Home Secretary."

"Dare say," said Brown; "she's been here a good bit lately."

"Yes, I know," said Gaunt, thoughtfully. He paused. "I wonder if I'd better wait on a bit, if you don't mind my having a look at the paper here. Perhaps the chief will be wanting something done. I shouldn't be in your way."

"Not a bit," said Brown. "Make yourself comfortable, but I don't think it's much good now. I think he's gone out with Mrs. Cartlet. Went out the other way

– you know, through Ditton's room, he can get out that way to the lift. I fancy I heard them go off about twenty minutes ago."

"Oh, Lord," said Gaunt; "that ends it then. Couldn't you just make sure whether he's gone or not?"

"I'm certain of it. But just open the door of his room quietly and look in."

"Suppose they're still there?"

"Oh, no, they're not. I think they're gone. In any case there's a screen in front of the door. Open it quietly and you'll be able to shut it again if you hear anyone talking there, and he won't know but that I'm looking in."

Gaunt crossed over, took hold of the handle of Lodden's door slowly, and quietly turned it and pushed open the door a mater of some six inches or so. The screen shut off the larger part of the room from sight, but there was a foot or more of open space though which one side could be seen. It was the side containing the window seat. Next the window seat stood the two.

The realisation that Lodden and Viola were still there was awkward, and then in the next fraction of a glance Gaunt saw that there was more than their mere presence to shock him. His first irrelevant thought coming to him in the hundredth part of a second was thankfulness at having opened the door so quietly, and the next was anxiety to get it as quietly closed. As Gaunt looked into the room Lodden's back was towards him, and Viola, standing in front of Lodden, had her face slightly away from the door so that she did not see the intruder.

Lodden had one hand of Viola's in both of his, was bending over her, and, though Gaunt could not see very plainly, seemed to be kissing it excitedly. Colour was high in Viola's cheeks, but she was not resenting it, and stood there like a blushing maiden whose youthful passion had suddenly been challenged and discovered. Her eyes were averted from the bended form of Lodden as though in timidity.

Gaunt stepped back towards Brown's desk breathing deeply.

"Still there," he said.

"Then they must have come back," said Brown. "She won't be long now."

"Don't think I'll wait," said Gaunt.

He went out and up to the reporters' room, there to write a note to Viola accepting her invitation for the week-end. He did not make any reference to what he had just seen.

[29 December 1913]

Chapter XVII.
The Crisis With Viola.

Gaunt went up to Hampstead on the following evening with his heart and mind ablaze. Gone from him was the lightning remembrance of Nancy Kirk and the despondency over Raston Path's business. Through him were running waves of anger, humiliation, and jealousy, as he travelled north by train and tram.

He had slept but brokenly in the night, and all the Saturday had paced about with broken purpose in his mind, marking the passage of the hours with scornful impatience. He waited no longer than half-past four, though his departure at this time would land him at the Cartlets' as early as six o'clock instead of seven. But every moment out of Viola's presence was now a torture. He had not settled what he should say or do, but he was possessed of a feverishness to let Viola know that he had found out the truth. So this was the woman he had allowed to fascinate him! He choked as he thought of it. And on the heels of his rage came a whirlwind of passion for her, an overwhelming desire to possess her wholly and utterly.

In spirit she was his already, she had said so in hot words. She had given him her soul – he had believed there was nothing else in earth or heaven for her but himself – and now, now he found she was a common trifler. Perhaps she laughed about her lovers with her husband. Gaunt could not bear to think of it. Then the memory of her lithe body, strong and slim and graceful, drove him almost frantic with the sense of loss.

He was calmer when he reached the house, but found as he walked up the gravel drive to the steps of the front door he had no idea as to his course of action. Hardened and flippant as he was, Gaunt found himself for once in his life quite unbalanced under emotion.

He rang the bell, there was a soft scuffle as of someone in a silk skirt running to open the door, and his heart went pit-a-pat as he remembered that whenever his characteristic ring was given Viola set the maid away and hastened to open the door herself. The door opened and she stood before him radiant. She seized him by the hand with a heartiness there was no mistaking.

"Oh, I'm so glad, so glad! I wondered if you would come early. There's no one in yet."

She was already unfastening his overcoat; he muttered some kind of greeting, but she gave no thought to his word. Swiftly she stowed his hat and coat and gloves round about the hall-stand, and then led him with a little run into the drawing-room.

"Come in here for a second. Oh, Marjorie, I must have you to myself for a moment."

She had on a shimmering skirt of pearly grey and a filmy white blouse which showed her strong and beautiful neck. Her face was flushed with excitement. Her eyes shone with tenderness and affection.

Gaunt was bewildered; he was a baby in her hands; just within the shelter of the drawing-room door she came to his arms.

"Oh, Marjorie, Marjorie! I was afraid you wouldn't come, I wanted you so much, so very much, I can't tell you."

She slipped free from him, sank into a low chair, and for a moment put her face in her hands.

Gaunt's spirit hardened. He stood in the middle of the room looking at her.

"What about Lodden?" he asked.

"Lodden?"

Apparently she misunderstood him, for she went on in the liveliest way. "Oh, he's been very nice."

"You've been going to see him a lot lately."

Gaunt was surprised that though anger was rising within him he was able to speak quite coolly.

"Of course, I have. I haven't told you anything about it, either."

"No, there are some things one finds out for themselves."

Viola looked up at him. "What's the matter, Marjorie. Have I done something wrong?"

"I don't know what you think wrong. Perhaps it's all in the game with you."

"Whatever are you talking about? Do be quick, Marjorie, and say what you mean."

"You have pretended to love me –"

"Why do you say pretended?"

"All the while you have been seeking the admiration of other men."

She looked at him in horror. "Marjorie!" she said.

He was a little taken a back at her assumption of indignation and surprise, and then he grew warm at the thought of what he had seen.

"Good heavens! You aren't going to say now that I am your only love?"

"Till you explain, Marjorie, I can't say anything. This is about Lodden, I suppose?"

"Yes, it is about Lodden."

"Well, what do you want to know?"

"Want to know? There is nothing I want to know, after what I saw yesterday."

Viola stood facing him, and her eyes were calm with no resentment in them.

"Yesterday? Of course I went to see Lodden at the *Daily Light* office yesterday – what of it?"

"I couldn't have believed it possible, Viola. No one on earth could have made me believe it, if the thing had not come before my eyes."

"What did you see?"

"Looking in at the door of Lodden's room I saw him bending over your hands, kissing them, and you didn't seem to be objecting."

"Oh!" There was relief as well as astonishment in the exclamation. "You thought I was in love with him."

"It was enough for me that he was in love with you."

"I can't help his being in love with me, Marjorie, can I?"

"You talk to me like that! You – after the words that have passed between us!"

A sudden spirit flashed into Viola.

"Why not? You don't possess me."

"No, I don't possess you." He was quieter now; he saw the woman he had to deal with. Disgust surged through him. What a fool – what a fool he had been. It was to this woman, snobbish, narrow, mad for men's admiration, that he had given hot hours and unbounded thought, a host of kindly impulses. That he should ever have treasured her regard for him was an ugly and unpleasant thought, and her present placidness was like ashes in his mouth.

A few seconds' silence lay between them, and his soul went further and further away from her. Then Viola said: –

"Marjorie, I ought really to be wild with you for your outrageous words. You will be wild with yourself when you know the truth."

His mouth was set, and his eyes were steady.

"You won't be able to deceive me," he said. "This is the love we have talked about, the love that casteth out fear,[71] the love that is filled with trust and confidence, and knows that its soulmate cannot leave it any more than a compass needle can leave the North. This is the great love we have talked about. Last night, in opening the door of Lodden's room, thinking the room was empty, I saw Lodden bending over your hands, kissing them. He was kissing them passionately. You stood, not unwillingly, permitting him – yes, you who have talked to me of everlasting love, and all that rot. There you were working the old game – oh, it nearly made me sick!"

She looked at him with staring eyes, as if for the moment she hardly understood, and then she turned away from him thoughtfully, while Gaunt, enraged as he was, wondered vaguely why she remained so unmoved beneath his abuse. He had expected a tornado, for he knew Viola very well. The few seconds she kept her gaze away from his seemed minutes, and another hot word was on his tongue when she turned and faced him with grieving eyes.

"I am a wicked woman, Marjorie, but in all things I have been faithful to you since I began to love you. That is true, notwithstanding what you saw in Lodden's room."

She spoke deliberately and with purpose, and Gaunt groped blindly for the excuse that was coming, albeit he was a little startled by her seriousness and self-possession.

"I don't think you understand what I feel towards you. Something in you appealed to me on the day we first met in the *Daily Light* office, and since then you have held me more and more. Sometimes I have had a suspicion that to you I was little more than an intoxicating pleasure. Truthfully can I say that my whole life has become wrapped up in you. I shall never forget what you have said to me to-night."

Gaunt fidgeted a little. "If you can explain –"

"If I can explain!" she flashed. "What manner of man are you?"

Gaunt shrugged his shoulders, thrust his hands deep in his trousers pockets, and leaned against the piano.

"I have been angry and heedless sometimes; but you had become the hope of my life. Everything revolved around you. Nothing else mattered. Oh, I can't tell you, because you never would understand. I wanted you to be happy. I wanted you to get on because you are so clever. I had the little blue room here fitted up for you so that you could make it your very own for writing when you came up, and I used to listen to your talk so as to learn what kind of paper and pens, and pencils you liked, and afterwards to put them in your room."

"You have always been very kind, Viola; I know that," said the uncomfortable Gaunt.

"I once spent nearly a whole day in the West End getting a dozen ties for you, ties which exactly matched your eyes, because I wanted you to look nice. I thought of no one else every day and every night I remembered you. On two wet evenings, one of them only last week, when I knew you were working late, you have wondered how it was your macintosh has been fetched up from your home, so that you should not get wet when you had finished."

"They told me somebody in the office had been sent down for the macintosh."

"It was this interfering woman who did it. I sent down, and so that you should not know I said it was the office. I have had really deep happiness and joy thinking of all the little things I could do for you. You were in my thoughts last thing at night; I never woke in the morning without thinking of you. Do you imagine I haven't thought of the future, too – sometimes when I have dared to. One day you will get married, and then I don't want to live any more. But I shall live because I haven't the courage to die. Sometimes I have tried not to have you on my mind so, but it was no good. I have thought of things I could do for you, but I have never seemed able to think of much. A month ago I made my will. There is little enough, but what there is you're to have."

'I am sorry," stammered Gaunt, "I didn't understand."

Viola looked at him sorrowfully.

"Other things have occurred to me from time to time – how you were going to rise in your work; how you were going to make a big name so that you could get that little country cottage you have set your mind on. I knew you were fitted to have a very much bigger place in the office than you hold at present. Very soon after knowing you we got to know Lodden. Latterly I have been doing what I could to influence him to make you a big man. Of course he can do it if he likes.

I have done it in a discreet way, so that he hardly knows were I am driving, but I have never failed in trying. He has got some silly feeling about me, it seems he had it even before I knew you. Marjorie, did you think I could be fond of a great, uninteresting creature like that? Oh, horrible! There is nothing in him. Of course he is very rich and very powerful, and all that; and it is always nice to know such people. I dare say I should have been stupid enough to keep up his acquaintance, even if I had not known you, but I should not have permitted a word of admiration from him. It was different, as I had you to think of. I haven't told you because I knew you would be angry and jealous. But, Marjorie, your love was in safe keeping. How could you mistrust me? Nothing mattered but you. The very breath I took into my body has been your property – yes, yes, don't stop me. I must tell you all now. Lodden began gradually but very early, and I saw the light in his eyes. Do you think I didn't know; of course I knew. Once or twice I was going to tell you, and then, thinking I might influence him, I didn't do so, because you might have done something silly. I wanted to get everything out of him I could. He hasn't pressed himself upon me, he's too clever for that, but he's never missed an opportunity for making himself agreeable and doing me any little service. He knows how I hate Raston Path, and I have helped to make him keep on the campaign, perhaps I even helped to start it. I don't know. I have kept him at length though, and he could not always content himself when he was near me. I can see what he's feeling if no one else can. George must occasionally have thought him strange, but nothing has ever been said. Once when he was staying here for the week-end I heard him tramping about his room in the night. He could not sleep, and he has told me he will never stay in the house again when I am here."

"And you let him go on like this?" said Gaunt.

"I couldn't help it. I couldn't stop him. It would mean breaking off the acquaintance to do it. Oh, my dear, you needn't have been angry or abused me. Only for your sake have I let him continue, and all the time I had your heart in my keeping. Never till yesterday has he gone so far as to kiss my hand. He did it twice yesterday, I don't know when it was you saw him, but he got up from his chair and came across to me in the window-seat, and put his hand on mine, and I drew it away and said I must be going. He pleaded with me not to go. He was very kind, Marjorie, I must say that, and told me how he would not harass me, and would not come near me if that was my wish. He may be a desperate man, but he was good and kind in all he said to me. It was just before we parted that he kissed my hands again, and I really couldn't stop him after all he had said. He told me he knew a married woman such as I was could never love him, but he asked me to be merciful to him and let him see me from time to time. I was a treacherous woman to let him go on when he was feeling so deeply. But, Marjorie, forgive me. I only did it because I wanted to help you. Now you blame me, I'll drop him; I'll forbid him the house. I will, if you want me to. I don't care for him. It was only because of you I have kept in with him. I'll write him to-night if you like, now, and tell him I can't see him again."

She bent forward, straining for an answer.

"Oh, no, no," said Gaunt. "What a cad I am!"

He stood looking at her distantly.

"My dear, dear heart," she said. The tears were in her eyes as she came towards him. He took her round the waist and seated her on a couch.

"I don't know what to say to you, Viola." He spoke softly. Her head rested on him just below the shoulder, and he felt she was breathing deeply. With his hand he caressed her face, and found it was wet. They sat thus for a minute or two, and then she sat up.

"Marjorie, it is all very wicked and terrible. What will happen to me? I shall be terribly punished one day; I know I shall, for all this. Whatever we do wrong, we are punished for in some way or other, I believe, sooner or later."

Gaunt dared not look at her, and for a few seconds she stood in silence while she tried to recover herself, and then they heard the front door open, and knew that George Cartlet had arrived home.

[30 December 1913]

Chapter XVIII.
Excitement in Parliament.

Gaunt went away from the Cartlets' house afraid of himself, afraid of his own thoughts, inclined at one moment to take blame for timorousness and the next to thank his lucky stars that he had escaped the abyss. He fled quickly to recover himself. Glad was he of the excuse that important work awaited him at the office and for the first time in his journalistic life he was genuinely pleased that Sunday was a busy day. Events had so provided that it was no mere excuse, because the introduction of Path's Bill on the following day called for a good deal of newspaper effort, for much diving and delving to get in the facts available for publication on the Monday morning. With zest Gaunt put himself into the work and was engaged for hours, afternoon and evening, at full pressure, making inquiries from the political organisers at their homes, calling on various officials, and in between whiles diligently searching the Sunday papers for fresh hints. He had to present not only some forecast of Path's proposals, vague and shadowy though that forecast must be, but also had to tell a plain tale of the actual doings on the morrow, estimate the length of the Home Secretary's speech, indicate the members who would follow him in debate, describe the probable attitude of the Opposition, make a guess at the crowded and excited scene in the House itself. Gaunt worked hard, though without a great deal of success. In the interstices came flashing thoughts, and his nerves were a-flutter when remembrance touched him.

Busy as was the day for Gaunt, it was a far heavier and more onerous day for Path, who was going through the final draft of his morrow's speech, consulting with permanent officials on various parts of it, and at intervals seeing colleagues of the Cabinet who had come down for a final word. Raston Path was used to difficult positions, and in the course of his hard-hitting life he had found exhilaration in risks and in the long chances of battle against odds. His strength had lain in the fact that he feared no results, that defeat had no terrors for him, that (almost unknown to himself) he had rejoiced in high heart at the fight itself. But he was carrying others' responsibilities now. Increasingly had the burdens of government found a place on his shoulders, and on the morrow he was to make a venture which would take the Ministry of the day to another period of office or scatter them like chaff before relentless enemies. Let the Ministry fail through this new proposal of his, let them be defeated in the country because of what would be described as hazardous experiments, and there would be dissipated not merely the immediate career of himself and his Cabinet friends, but also the prospect of administering and developing those legislative changes recently put into operation and the opportunity of carrying out still more far-reaching alterations in the direction of his visions. For a generation, perhaps, would disappear the chance of refashioning further the social government of this country, of carrying on that remoulding operation which, in spite of years of work, had only just begun.

Would this new scheme of his strike the popular imagination? Would it appeal to the sober-minded British opinion as practicable; would people have sufficient imagination to realise the ultimate results? He had to confess that the thing was not so certain as he had told himself in his more optimistic moments.

On the previous day, the Saturday, the Cabinet had met for the last time before the assembly of Parliament on the Monday, and at that meeting he had had to wrestle with some of the ministers on portions of his scheme, and all his ardour, all his fire, all his persuasiveness, and all his vehemency had been called into play during a strenuous four hours' sitting. There were faint hearts among the clever men. A good half of the Cabinet had been for some time dominated by his enthusiasm and a belief in his genius, but there were several members who to the last hour had doubts and fears and misgivings. Would it not be well to moderate this or to moderate that? He had overcome them at last, but the struggle had been tremendous, and it was a struggle the public would never know about.

His difficulties had been increased by the fact that the Bill was to reveal to the nation projects with which they were unacquainted, and here was the heart of the matter, for it was new in British politics that definite proposals placed in definite form before Parliament should be unknown in outline by people at large beforehand. For various reasons, however, it had been considered advisable that Ministers should confine themselves to a general announcement as to the purport of the Bill rather than give direct indications of what the Bill was going to do. The special character of the measure lent itself to this treatment, because it did not affect taxation, did not touch immediately the pockets or material interests of any class of the community, although at the same time its genesis was deep-rooted in the desire that the conduct of affairs of State should be so directed as to be more immediately for the benefit of the great mass of humbler souls in the country rather than for the stringent preservation of society as it existed at the moment. The effects of the Bill, in a word, would be felt increasingly by future generations rather than by the present population of these islands. Nevertheless, the fact that no indication of the actual scheme had been made public was a great handicap, and introduced into the Parliamentary proceedings a dubiety, a hazard, which the gods of chance had never possessed in modern Parliamentary times.

A great portion of the public would expect a measure somewhat on the lines of the false prophecy made by the *Daily Light* after Gaunt had stolen the contents of the fictitious Bill, and while these would be startled, it remained to be seen whether they would be startled in the right way or the wrong way. As for the great mass of Authoritarians, they, of course, would be horrified, shocked, bewildered – but withal massed together into a great army of defence and attack. Months of work were coming to a crisis in this Bill. Path knew that such is the ingratitude of the political world that, should he fail, he would be condemned by his friends almost as harshly as he would be denounced by his enemies. That did not trouble him very much, but at the same time it added to the weight he was carrying.

Raston Path went to bed early the night before parliament met, and he had cause to thank Heaven that among his possessions was the power to sleep at all times, for otherwise it must have been one of the nights in his life when a highly strung nervous system would have kept him from happy, resuscitating slumber. As it was, he slept well.

Early on the morning of the next day members of the Commons were securing their places in the House in readiness for the afternoon sitting, and the evening papers came out telling the story of how Sir James Wilkinson and Captain Dunkinburg arriving in Palace Yard at five minutes past six had a foot race across to the Members' Entrance in the effort to secure the distinction of being first in the Chamber. For the ordinary M.P. in particular, fervid for his principles, the day was to be one of exciting entertainment, one of the big rewards for weeks of dullness and duty done. The afternoon was to see the beginning of a battle, and the prospect of a contest which might mean the downfall of the Government had fascination even for the Progressive members.

The expectancy of the hour, however, was the long delayed revelation of the Government secret. The dramatic circumstances surrounding it, the battle that was to follow, the new life of the Government on the one hand or its catastrophic downfall on the other, all these things stimulated surmise and made the coming speech of the Home Secretary something which would thrill enemies and followers alike. The leaders of the Opposition had a pleasant sense of the pitfall and dangers which that day might open for the Government, and the members of the Cabinet on the other hand, even the most sanguine of them, had the feelings inseparable from great risks. Perhaps Path's measure would be their making for another period of years; it might on the other hand precipitate them from office. The long period of reform had set the pendulum swinging against the Government, and it was possible that this new expedition would increase its momentum. The brave among them said that it would be well to go down with colours flying than to drift along in power with the country steadily opposed until very shame led to withdrawal from office.

A thin string of spectators lined the kerb along by Palace Yard when at twenty minutes to three in the afternoon Raston Path and Sir Harry Venture crossed over from Downing-street on their way to the house. The pair were talking as they walked. Sir Harry Venture, immaculate as ever, was in silk hat and morning coat, and Raston Path was in jacket suit and grey Trilby hat,[72] carrying in one hand a walking-stick and in the other his leather dispatch case. The Home Secretary was braced for the occasion. His head was thrown back, he talked vivaciously, his eyes were alight. Sir Harry, on the other hand, was touched with anxiety. His face showed that the responsibilities of the afternoon lay heavy on him, and it was to be said to his credit that his anxiety was principally on account of his friend, the Home Secretary, for whom the day's speech would mean so much.

The House of Commons meets at a quarter to three, and prayers occupy a few minutes, and it is about seven minutes to three that the public proceedings begin and reporters are admitted to the Press Gallery. From that time up till quarter to four members give themselves over to questions to Ministers, questions as to administration, sometimes questions as to policy. In some respects question time is the liveliest and most interesting of Parliamentary proceedings, because all kinds of topics are dealt with, dealt with critically and with point[73] and the dialogue gives opportunity for skilful attack, no less skilful evasion, for wit, and for personal skirmishes. Even on a dull day there is usually a pretty good attendance of members at question time, although it is possible that within 10 minutes after questions are over the House may be comparatively empty. On great occasions, however, such, for instance, as Budget day, when the Chancellor reveals to an expectant House what are to be the new taxes in the coming year, question time becomes merely the preface to the real interest of the day and provides an opportunity for late-comers to throng in before the commencement of the drama.

Never has the House been more crowded than on the afternoon when Raston Path was to introduce his New Bill. Peers overflowed from the narrow pen which is set apart for the House of Lords, and the Distinguished Strangers' Gallery,[74] a narrow little enclosure, comprised four Ambassadors, five Ministers of foreign states, two reigning princes, the two best-known writers of modern English, and the ex-President of the United States. Ladies who had schemed and battled for places in the little gallery behind the grille could be faintly seen though the brass trellis work packed closer than comfort or convenience would have permitted; and while some were middle-aged and elderly, others were young; sisters, sweethearts, wives of legislators, some anxious to see this low and scurrilous Minister at an important moment; some anxious to see the greatest statesman of his time at one of the greatest moments. To those on the floor of the House or in the galleries there was a sense of shadowy romance about the occupants of the seats behind the grille, for the ladies were only dimly visible, and one caught but a passing glimpse of shimmering silk, lovely face, or diamonds in hair; and a stranger could well understand why politicians have maintained so long against political progress and common sense that mysterious haven of beauty above the Press Gallery.

The benches on the floor were packed beyond the designs of the builders, and while a good many members sat on the steps of the two gangways which bisect the benches others stood behind the Speaker's Chair, and others still stood on the open floor space behind the bar at the farther end of the House over all and through all that crowded and eager assembly there ran a ripple of excited whisper, comment, and surmise for the best part of an hour. For once in a way the members who had questions to ask of Ministers had no attention paid to them, and, indeed, could hardly make their questions heard above the prevalent murmur, and even the most important replies of Ministers had to go unrecorded in the newspapers the next day because the reporters simply could not make out the answering phrase. Once the Speaker intervened and secured a lull, but great as was his authority and his personal prestige even he could not keep under that expectant emotion which found its vent in bursts of conversation between neighbours.

It was just before the conclusion of questions that Raston Path came in with a dispatch case[75] in his hand, and he passed from behind the Speaker's Chair, stepping carefully over the feet of his colleagues on the Front Bench to his accustomed place left vacant for him by the side of the Prime Minister, facing the dispatch box. As soon as he appeared there was a great roar of welcome from the Progressive benches, and some of the excited Reds below the gangway jumped up and waved their hands, and made their greeting into a defiance of the Authoritarians on the other side of the House. "Sit down," screamed the Opposition: "Learn your manners." "Manners yourself," replied the Red from the corner seat below the gangway. Then the Speaker hushed the combat, and there was comparative peace again.

[1 January 1914]
Chapter XIX.
The Effect of Path's Speech.

The excitement of the House of Commons after Raston Path's speech was reflected in the morning papers next day, and political circles all over the country were agog. Even the ordinary non-political people who read speeches only at election time found something to talk about in the revolutionary proposals of the Home Secretary. No proposal for increasing taxation, of lightening of the burdens on working people, no penalising of dukes, no daft adjustments of the franchise could have stirred up people in the same way as the new scheme. The public were hit by the novelty of the thing. For the moment the question as to whether the change was advisable or inadvisable was not uppermost; a pleasant, stimulating surprise was in everybody's mind, and newness being the salt of political activity. Path and his Government reaped a harvest of comment and interest. Path had meant this to be the case, for it was part of his darting electricity that it communicated itself to others, roused approbation on the one hand and antagonism on the other, and left no one unstirred. There are dangers in this as well as advantages, so far as electoral chances are concerned, but the Home Secretary had weighed up the various considerations before he launched his project, and, indeed, had threshed them out pretty thoroughly with the Cabinet within the seclusion of No. 10, Downing-street.

Very few men, even among the noblest of the human race, are cold-blooded heroes, and Path was certainly not one of them, and one might take leave to doubt as to whether any active politician in a prominent position should rank himself among the self-sacrificing martyrs who are beacons of light on the road to progress. Grant that Path was perfectly sincere, grant that he was moved by emotions that did him credit, that he spent himself in the endeavour to give practical effect to his ideals; and yet he would have been more than human had he not calculated on the effect that the exposition of those ideals and the methods by which he sought to bring them into operation would have on the power an position of the Government and on the power and position of himself. One cannot divorce human motives. Path all his life had been struggling for the under-dog, but his very struggles had raised him to power and eminence, and these things bring in their train feelings and motives which are strangers to the obscure and lowly placed idealist. Who can tell what degree of conscientious conviction would suffice to drive a famous Cabinet Minister from office? Temptation which he knew not as temptation thrust themselves in his way, and it is an easy thing, perhaps, indeed, the right thing, that the Minister who sees his way to the accomplishment of various projects should persuade himself that for the sake of one principle it would be wrong to sacrifice the chances of carrying out many other principles; and if there mixes with his inclinations the desire to retain power not merely for his party but for himself, well then you must blame not the man but human nature. Path was as straight an individual as you could find in any average Government and he had that natural force which put him above the heads of a generation of statesmen, but withal he possessed the acuteness, the keen eye for effect, the swift judgment of ordinary people's impulses, which constitute a priceless possession to those who have to seen popular favour. That he was so well hated was in itself a gift, because it led to a loyal and fevered determination on the other side – a determination steadied and strengthened continuously by his luminous speeches, his personal courage, and his real decision to effect things instead of merely talking about them. He knew the uproar his new Bill would cause, and was not blind to the hostility which it would generate among large portions of the electorate, but he also knew that the dramatic effect of his move would be striking among his own people, particularly among the Reds throughout the country, and hardly less among the advanced Progressives, who would, he believed, drag along the more moderate Progressives. Something startling had to be done, because the swing of the pendulum in the constituencies was against the Government, and because the Authoritarians' campaign and Lodden's sedulous fight had undoubtedly knit together the Opposition, and had even unsteadied some of the Progressive elements. A sharp blow had to be struck, a rallying call provided, or there would be inevitably a continued disintegration of the Progressive forces. It is no good reckoning on the gratitude of the electorate for the achieved. Past history had proved that, and the only way to get another verdict is to set hand boldly to new work in the future and to rouse expectation. Achievement is nothing. So Raston Path took his risks and made the Government take them with him.

Astounded by the new announcement politicians did not, so to speak, get their breath for a few days, and even the newspapers, Authoritarian and Progressive, devoted more attention to the exposition of the actual plan of the Government, the gathering up of the proposals, with their practical effect, rather than to any violent measure of criticism or acclamation. Of course there were some opinions for and against in the papers, but it was not for a day or two that they gathered their full strength. In the street and in the workshop, however, the battle raged from the first, and there was no stint of comment and no hesitation among excited disputants.

The Reds throughout the country, it should be said at once, were delighted. Arrangements were set on foot for meetings to be held in various centres to deal with the new Bill. But the more moderate of the Progressive forces held themselves back a little, although it was plainly to be seen that they would be forced into line a little later by the aggressive enthusiasts. The Authoritarians were frankly staggered, for they had expected new taxation proposals – something on entirely new lines from the actual scheme. They quickly rallied, however, and expressed themselves overjoyed at the direct fight which Path's announcement was to bring before the country. They would have a clear issue, they said. "Government by navvies versus government by gentlemen"; that was the way they phrased the conflict, and they devoted themselves to battle in high spirits. The *Daily Light* was early to the fore, and in its vehemence gave no hint of the false forecast about Path's Bill which it had placed before the public some time before.

"It is impossible," said the *Daily Light* in one of its leading articles, "that the Government can have the idea of passing this Bill through Parliament before going to the country on it. Such an idea is inconceivable, even with this government. There must be a General Election in order that the country may give its opinion on this revolutionary scheme. Its vulgar, vote-catching proposals are such that the Constitution would be outraged if the Bill were passed with out a direct mandate from the people."

As a matter of fact the Government had another year to run before they intended to resign office, and although they wished to pass the Bill through all its stages, they could not hope to put it on the Statute Book, because the House of Lords would not fail to reject it, and this meant that two full years would be occupied in passing it through into law without the acquiescence of the peers. What the Government planned to do was to get the Bill thoroughly discussed in Parliament, and thus give opportunity for full and complete understanding in the country, and to do this before the dissolution, so that when the General Election came the surprise of the electorate should have worn off and the merits of the measure adequately appraised.

No Opposition worth its salt agrees to the plans of a Government, the first reason being that any Government which can choose the time for dissolution and an election would certainly decide on the period most convenient for itself and most conducive to its return to power. To Fleet-street this is the purpose of every Opposition. In this Bill of the Home Secretary's there might be found a weapon with which a chance blow could bring the Government to it knees and the Authoritarians were quickly in force.

A tower of strength to the Opposition was the fact that the moderate section of the Government supporters would undoubtedly be lukewarm about the Bill, if not directly hostile to it, and though it was possible they would be pushed into line by the forwards, it was also possible that by skilful work of the Opposition they might be detached from the main army, and might even help to bring it to defeat. Day after day there were meetings, consultations, and devices planned during the interval between the first reading and the second reading – a period of nine days.

While the first reading of a measure is only the formal presentation of an outline, and generally in the case of smaller Bills is allowed to pass without a division,[76] the second reading constitutes a debate on the principle of the Bill and provides opportunity for a definite pronouncement for or against that principle it is therefore, the crucial period for any measure. So far-reaching and important was Raston Path's scheme that the Opposition had not permitted even the first reading to get through by default, but had insisted on a division being taken against it and had cheered loudly when the division list gave a majority of only 25 in place of the usual Government 35 in favour of it. The difference was accounted for by some abstentions on the Progressive side and the illness of two stalwart Reds who were unable to be in their places. What would be the result of the second reading division was the question with which the newspapers stirred the country.

Gaunt, in his description of the scene in the House – he had been sent up to do a special pen picture – did not rise to the occasion in his usual impressionable way, and although nothing was said about him in the office there were no compliments for him, no acknowledgements of a masterpiece such as occasionally were sent out from Lodden's room after a big thing. His description – not to put too fine a point on it – was commonplace.

Gaunt in the gallery of the House of Commons that night was not the concentrated newspaper man who had made success for himself in the past, for over all the day there had been in his mind thoughts of Viola Cartlet and the crisis through which he had passed; doubts and wondering, some nervous anticipations. Not that he was thinking of these things when he was at Westminster, but they had disturbed his nerve; he was not unshaken and keen; and in a self-conscious way the edge of his enthusiasm for the interests of the *Daily Light* had been taken off. He was in a new atmosphere somehow, and it affected him even though he was looking forward to this night in the Commons and had strengthened himself for a big effort.

Other things reacted upon him. Impressions conveyed during Raston Path's speech at the Surrey Theatre trickled into his conscience and gave him moments of discomfort; and he remembered how he had stolen the first draft of the fictitious Bill and was not pleased at the thought of it; and recalled to himself his humiliating experiences in North London when he discovered Raston Path was just a kindly soul instead of a secretly immoral man. The verve which he would have put into his work was missing, and he was astonished and almost annoyed with himself as he looked down on that crowded gathering to find a sneaking sympathy with Path creeping up within him – a sympathy touched with admiration. Ruthlessly he put his feelings aside and endeavoured to present a picture of the debate which should make Raston Path seem a rather puny demagogue, but in the result his production was not powerful, was not even vivid, and he knew it very well himself, although he was not able exactly to state why. Now that events moved swiftly towards the climax of the second reading division he found himself harassed by doubts and by semi-inclinations, and realised within himself the joy of fighting as Path was fighting for ideals which whether mistaken or not, were at least unselfish. More than a suspicion was in his mind that, so far as the *Daily Light* and Lodden were concerned, Authoritarian convictions were prompted by self-help. And, indeed, he still thought that very likely they were right in general from the point of view of governance. But Gaunt was at heart a sentimentalist, and his work during the past months had caused him to think of matters which had never troubled him before, had driven him face to face with facts which were eloquent to such a man as he.

He remembered how Viola Cartlet had annoyed him with her superficiality, and, indeed, it was in some degree through her that Path's attitude towards life had made an impression on him. He saw as in a vision the mental standpoint of all the comfortable people in the country represented in the outlook of Viola Cartlet, and when that came to him he was for a few seconds as infuriated as Path himself. Nevertheless, he told himself, even as an emotionalist he could not accept the ideals of Path as a working formula for this hard material world, and he braced his nerves to carry out the work of the paper and defeat the operations of the Government. Moreover, the driving force in him, as in every other journalist like him, was the newspaper driving force. Ambition to shine in his profession, loyalty to his employer, keen enjoyment of his actual work; these things form a habit of mind as well as a habit of action and they frequently guide men along channels which would not be entered if the man had free direction and inclination.

[2 January 1914]

Chapter XIX – Continued.
Attitude of the "Daily Light."

Lodden found stimulating openings for attack in Raston Path's new scheme, and the *Daily Light* entered on its task with joyful avidity, in no way discouraged by the destruction of its previous forecasts – indeed, quite forgetful of them. The *Daily Light* was wise in its generation, for the memory of readers is as evanescent as that of party politicians. Let the dead past bury its dead – that is the motto of these modern times in Fleet-street and Westminster, consistency being treasured as a jewel only because of its rarity. And Lodden, sure of the hearty support of all the propertied classes in the country, gave a new twist to his scheme against Path, and lent his columns to ridicule as well as to denunciation, and held up to laughing contempt the weak-kneed and servile colleagues of Path. It was really a high time for the *Daily Light*, for while the Home Secretary's speech was a rallying cry for the Reds, it was no less a rallying cry for the Authoritarians. The other newspapers joined in the battle, and the Opposition journals, being the more powerful as well as the more numerous, did great work for their side. All over the country meetings were organised by the Opposition, because politics had now become very real to those who had hitherto regarded them as a respectable game, exciting only at intervals. Some of the more important Progressives left the Government camp. A good many of those who remained were not enthusiastic, but a substantial proportion, the majority, headed by the ardent Reds, acclaimed Path and his scheme to the skies, and went forth like missionaries to the great towns in the industrial districts to carry and develop the new gospel.

The Government pretended to have no doubts about the passing of the second reading, but the Opposition journals clamoured that in view of the prevalent discontent there was a good chance of defeating the Government. They ignored the fact that Governments with a majority of only 35 do not take any hazards that they can avoid. The most careful preparations had been made with regard to the coming division, and even taking into account the defections and allowing one or two votes lost by chance or malignity, there would still be a clear majority of 20 for the Bill.

Only once before the second reading did Viola Cartlet see Gaunt, and that was when she was with her husband, and she swept into vivacious talk about the political position as if nothing out of the common had occurred between them. He breathed relief. His emotions had been tossed this way and that way, his intentions went round like a weathercock, and it was with doubt and unsettlement that he accepted an invitation to dine with George Cartlet and his wife in Regent-street a week after his visit to Hampstead. George Cartlet was as natural as could be, and Gaunt was a little uncomfortable under his friendliness. As for Viola, she remained just as lively, just as charming to the eye, just as fresh and unconfined in her comments as she might have been to a well-liked brother. Embarrassment was not for her, and Gaunt for a little was staggered in spirit by it, but he recovered himself, or thought he did.

"A bit off colour to-night," said Cartlet, half-way through the meal.

"No," said Gaunt, in surprise.

"Well, you're deuced quiet; you don't seem to be eating much."

"Don't you see, George," said Viola, "don't you see what it is? He has been carried away by Raston Path. On the way to becoming a Red, aren't you, Marjorie?"

Gaunt smiled reassuringly, and said: "Well, you never can tell in these changing times."

"Go away, go away," said George Cartlet, "don't you get mixing yourself up with that crowd. Keep to the straight and narrow path."

"On the wide and easy one you mean," said Gaunt. "There's no martyr's blood in me."

"Oh, I don't know, Marjorie," said Viola; "once in a way you break out funnily. You can't tell how you're going to act. You know you let sentiment get the better of you in these political things, don't you?"

"I don't bar out sentiment."

"But you must have business as well," said Viola, with a sudden eagerness. "You must be practical. What we want its business men to run the country, not sentimentalists. Why wherever should be we?"

"Keeping me in the right road," said Gaunt to Cartlet.

"Aye, aye. I wonder if anyone will ever convert her to the other way of thinking."

"I wouldn't like the job," replied Gaunt.

"Do tell us, Marjorie," broke in Viola, "if there is going to be a General Election immediately. Won't it be nice if there is? Everyone will be sure to vote against Path."

"I wouldn't go as far as that. I think he'd get a good lot of votes. But as to the General Election, it cannot be very long delayed. What I fancy is that it will come towards the end of the year. You see, they won't pass this Bill into law. They'll get it through its various stages, and that will enable the country to examine it thoroughly and make up their minds about it. Then the Government will appeal on their record of things done and on their promise of future legislation, this being the particular proposal for the time."

"Well, that's all right," said viola. "There wouldn't be any doubt about the result if they did that. But what I am anxious about is, will the second reading be carried?"

"Oh, I think so," replied Gaunt.

"There's a great outcry against the Bill," said George Cartlet.

"Yes, but if the Government have prepared their ground pretty well they'll get through the second reading all right."

"If they don't?" asked Viola. "What if they should come a cropper?"

"I don't see it's possible for them to do anything but dissolve. I don't see how that can be avoided if they are defeated on the second reading of one of their important Bills."

"Oh, wouldn't it be lovely?" she said. "Can't we fix up something to make them defeated?"

Gaunt shook his head. "Can't do any more than is being done all over the country. Besides, I'm not sure that I want them to be defeated."

Cartlet lifted his eyebrows as he helped himself to another piece of bread, but Viola stared at Gaunt blankly. "What?" she said.

"I'm not sure that I want them to be defeated," he repeated. "I've had some doubt as to whether a good deal Path says isn't right."

"Good gracious," said Viola. "I told you so."

"Oh, don't make any mistake. I shall do what I can to 'out' him; that's my work – I'm on the *Daily Light*, you know."

"Well, I am surprised," said Viola. "Fancy you being contaminated even a little."

"Don't let us talk about it," said Gaunt, laughing. "I'm becoming quite heterodox. If we go on talking I expect I shall say some quite shocking things. I shall begin to think I really am a Red."

"What you want is a good fortnight's rest in the country," said Viola.

"Viola's cure for political heresy," remarked George Cartlet.

"Not a bad one, either," returned Gaunt, "if the fortnight was to be spent in the society of a stalwart like herself."

"Yes, that's right enough. She'd give you no chance."

You are not to think that Gaunt slackened his efforts on behalf of the *Daily Light* or of its campaign, nor are you to believe that he talked about his doubts in the office, for the genial cynicism of the reporters' room was not conducive to exchanges with regard to a man's moods or principles. Gaunt's article on his life among the poor in London had been fairly interesting, but had lacked the vitality of those done by his colleagues in other parts of the country – though the difference was not so marked as to call for any criticism, or, indeed, for comment. Gaunt himself realised more keenly than anyone else the deficiency in his work. He knew, too, that he had failed rather than succeeded in his picture of the House of Commons on the great night. Still, he was not troubled from the journalistic standpoint, because he knew as well as Lodden knew that the cleverest men on newspapers have their dull periods. It was four days before the second reading was due that Gaunt, in company with Lumley and Wansmuth, went down to Lodden's room for consultation with regard to tactics.

The Government was staking a lot on the coming second reading, and they knew it quite well, because not only would they be shaken if the Bill just scraped through, but if by any chance it were defeated even by the narrowest majority they would inevitably have to bring their period of office to a close and to go to the country. The authoritarian organisers were no less well aware of the fact. Lodden knew of it too, and was elated at the thought. Lodden was quite determined that with the second reading would come the hour for swift and successful action. He thought about various modes of action, discussed the matter with Wansmuth, and on one or two occasions had Gaunt in consultation as well. For a day or two nothing definite was fixed up, but the paper continued to publish carefully-worded criticism and no less carefully-worded appeals in order to quicken the impulse against Path's proposals, which was already manifesting itself among many of the comfortable middle class. Lodden felt victory in his veins, if the thing were properly handled. The situation as he saw it was this: that the Government might probably get a small majority for the Bill on the second reading; if by any chance they could be defeated the General Election which would result would inevitably return the Authoritarians to power. There was ground for his calculations, and, although the Government would have dismissed the proposition that the country might defeat them, they would nevertheless, in their hearts, know that they ran a risk.

Gaunt was uneasy in mind, for with fixed prejudices running through him he could sense the hard intention of Lodden to dislocate the second reading. He was annoyed with himself to find he was shrinking from the thing. Why he should shrink he did not know. But there was the disinclination. He could stand the open party appeals in the *Daily Light*; he could pass over even the open abuse of Path in the paper, because the Progressive journals were not above doing the same kind of thing on their own side; it was all in the game. But Gaunt had a kind of feeling that Lodden would not stop at this and that there would be some underhand effort, a real hard effort, to upset the second reading, and that Lodden would not be particular as to his methods and instruments. The fact that he himself had stolen a document from Path's room did not alter his feelings at all, for Gaunt, like a good many men of feeling, was illogical and unreasoning where his emotions were concerned.

Lodden, up at the Cartlets' house, talked freely about the advantage of securing an early General Election. "Some of my young men," he said, "are going to devise means for defeating the second reading."

"Is there any chance?" asked Viola.

"Oh, yes, there's a chance. It is only an outside chance unless something is done to help."

"I suppose," said George Cartlet, "that what you hope for are desertions from the Progressives, and that's why you are preaching away at these each day in the paper."

"Yes," said Lodden, thoughtfully. "It is just possible that that'll do it, but I don't think it's sufficient. Path's party don't think so, either. They're confident that there'll be just enough comfortably to carry the Bill."

"What can be done?" asked Viola.

Lodden shrugged his shoulders. "I suppose there is nothing to be done except to keep on telling the truth in the paper and trying to show up the whole thing. Of course, when the General Election does come there'll be a great turn-over."

"Yes," said Viola, " but the thing is to get a General Election quickly, before Path can do anything to trick people again."

"That's it," said Lodden. He did not seem very excited.

"What can be done?" asked Viola.

"Oh, a lot of things. If, for instance, a dozen Progressives can be kept away from the House on the night of the division it would finish the Bill. Just possibly they might be kept away by argument, but if that fails some of my young men are trying to devise means to – defeat them. Of course, I can't sanction any beguilement or anything of that kind."

"But that is what it comes to," said Viola. "If a dozen of Path's men could be kept away from the House that night the Bill would be lost?"

"Yes, that's so," said Lodden.

"Well, why not –"

"Oh, I can't go into anything of that kind," said Lodden, smiling. "I should have to reprove my young men if they suggested it. But you know what keen young fellows are; they won't be held in, and I have got a suspicion that they're at work now. Of course, I shan't approve of anything if it comes before me. That'd never do."

"No, I suppose not," said Viola, but she went on thinking about business.

[3 January 1914]

Chapter XIX – Continued.
The "Daily Light" Plot.

The next day she had tea with Gaunt, and was very full of the matter, though she was surprised that Gaunt was not at all enthusiastic.

"Can't be done," he said coldly.

"Oh, yes it can, Marjorie – it can be done. And think what a grand thing it would be if you would get this Government out."

"Would it?" asked Gaunt.

"Oh, don't' be silly. What's the matter with you this afternoon? Lodden talked to me about this yesterday evening. He declared he would not countenance any kind of plan to defeat the Government by getting their men away, but I know perfectly well his heart is set on it. It's only just his surface way of covering himself. I expect he mentioned it to me only because he thought I might be able to help."

"Dare say," remarked Gaunt. "I see you've still got him at your heels."

She paused and looked at him. "What's all that?" she asked.

"Oh, nothing. It just occurred to me, that's all."

"You silly, disgruntled old thing. Lodden's an interesting man; of course he is, but he doesn't matter really. Mind, I like this scheme of his to beat Path; I'd like that. I just hate that man, Marjorie. It's so funny about you and him."

Gaunt went away hopeless, knowing that Viola could never understand what he felt or realise the influences which were at work within him as within others. Path, of course was a closed book to her, and Gaunt simply shrugged his shoulders in despair.

The first he knew of the projected action with regard to the five Irish members came to him under the seal of secrecy from the news editor, Fore, who stated with his fingers on his lips that the plan had originated with some daring rising Authoritarian politicians and had been confirmed to the *Daily Light* and to the *Daily Light* alone.

"Of course, the paper must know nothing of the matter, because it would be a tremendous weapon in the hands of the Government people to be able to say that their chief opponent in the Press had descended to little less than kidnapping." But could not Gaunt, unofficially and without the knowledge of the chief, lend a hand, together, if necessary, with a reporter from Room 64?

"Where does the *Daily Light* come in?" said Gaunt. "We can't get a story out of it."

Fore winked at him – which was not a usual thing for Fore to do – and Gaunt immediately understood that the *Daily Light* was deeper in the plot than might appear on the surface.

"Our whole interest at the moment is to defeat the Government," said Fore, "and we've got to do it by hook or by crook. They're not particular about their methods, and we can't be either. We've got to 'out' Raston Path. That's the top and bottom of it. When he is 'outed' the *Daily Light* will celebrate its greatest triumph. Now do you see how we are interested in this job?"

"Yes, I see," said Gaunt, a little sullenly.

"Of course, this thing has been set on foot by some young politicians from the party office and they are quiet prepared to carry it out, but they'd probably bungle it, and if it were in the hands of the *Daily Light* men we should know that it would be carried out all right."

"Wansmuth and Lodden knew about this?"

"Oh, of course not," said Fore hastily. "They wouldn't soil their fingers with a thing like this. How could they?"

"Oh," said Gaunt thoughtfully, for he began to see that Lodden had planned a piece of daring dirty work which, if discovered, should not incriminate either himself or his paper. "Oh, these young bloods from the party headquarters!" he said.

"Quite so," said Fore.

"The paper will be mixed up in it if we're caught," said Gaunt.

"Why so? You and the other man, say Wrightson, won't blurt out that you are acting for the *Daily Light* if things go wrong."

"He's a masterpiece," said Gaunt.

"Who is?" queried Fore blandly.

"Why, Lodden."

"I dare say. Of course, he doesn't know anything about this."

"Oh, no," said Gaunt. "I suppose we ought to conceal it from him?"

"Yes," said the philosophic Fore, "and from everyone else, too."

"Well, what's the idea? Out with it."

"A careful reckoning up in connection with each of the members of the House has shown that the result will probably be closer than the Government at present expect, and if five of their stalwarts could be kept away from the House till after the division it is possible that they might be sufficient to turn the scale. In any case, their absence would go a good way towards it and other means might be brought to bear to make the matter certain."

"More to come!" said Gaunt.

"Well, well, don't bother about that; this is the thing we've got to attend to. You know that the Irish members – strong supporters of the Government – are not in attendance all the time in Westminster, but that they always muster in full force for a big division. Some of them come over from Ireland specially for an important occasion, and it's quite certain that a good many of them will be arriving on the day of the division. Follow that?"

"Yes, but I don't see what you're going to do about it."

"Well, they come across in groups, and Lumley, who, as you know, has had the entree to the Lobby for a good many years, has given us facts which make the thing seem easy."

"For goodness' sake, don't trust Lumley's plans."

"Oh, he's safe enough this time. It's only a question of facts, not of anything he's got to do. He says that on the last two occasions when there have been crises in the House ten to a dozen members from Ireland have arrived by the boat train at night and gone straight to the House. Some of them take taxi-cabs by themselves, others go by omnibus, but there is always a little party of four or five who pack themselves into a taxi-cab and go down together. There's Rafferty and Kilmain and Johnstone and O'Leary, together with Dick Murphy, the Whip, who went down this way last time. There may even be six, or possibly the party might be a little differently made up. But it's a kind of rule for a little group like that to travel down from Euston to the House together. See?"

"Still blind as a bat," said Gaunt.

"Well, if you look up the 'A.B.C.'[77] you will find the boat train from Ireland arrives at Euston at nine o'clock, and this gives them ample time to get down to the House before 10.30, the earliest moment at which a division can be taken."

"I'm getting a glimmer," said Gaunt.

"If by some extraordinary and inexplicable accident the driver of the taxi should take the wrong turning and drive straight out to the North of London, getting well away beyond Highgate into the country before, in the darkness of the night, his course was discovered, well, then, the motor-car might break down in some part where another could not easily be secured and the journey back to town could not very well take less than an hour, even if the wrong direction were discovered before the driver of the taxi had halted his car to find out what made it refuse to go any further."

"Nice for the driver of the car with five mad Irishmen round him," said Gaunt.

"I think it is even possible," said Fore, "that the driver coming to a stop might dislocate the machinery in some way and then make a bolt for it, footing across country before the gentlemen inside the vehicle rose to the occasion."

Gaunt's eyes sparkled. "It seems all right," he said. "Bit fantastic, but it'd be very interesting."

"Oh, exciting enough," said Fore, "but what we want is to stop the second reading of this Bill."

"There might be mishaps," said Gaunt, "before safety was reached with the taxi-cab; that is, safety with regard to the time."

"That would have to be risked, but I don't fancy there would be anything go wrong if the affair were properly handled."

"They'd break up the blooming motor-car," said Gaunt, "when they found out they'd been done."

Fore whistled softly between his teeth. "Yes, even so. Well, it's a great job we have in view, and the downfall of the Government might be cheaply achieved at the cost of a broken-up taxi-cab."

"I didn't know you had it in you, Fore," said Gaunt.

"Nothing of this must leak out," said Fore hastily. "Don't you let Lodden or Wansmuth know we've been talking about this."

"Oh, no," said Gaunt. "Wouldn't they be surprised!"

Fore looked up at Gaunt to see if he was smiling, but Gaunt was quite grave. "Well, what do you think about it?" said the news editor.

"All right. We can put it through if necessary. It will be a bit of fun. Dirty work, of course."

"Dirty be blowed," said Fore. "You don't seem to understand politics."

"Aye, aye," said Gaunt. "We'd better have a bit of dinner together to-night – you and I and Wrightson, to talk about the matter away from the office."

"Not a bad idea."

The excitement of the prospect dulled Gaunt's misgivings during the time he was in conversation about the adventure, and indeed had an influence over him throughout the day, but at night, while he was planning the actual arrangements, there was an uncomfortable little revulsion going on within him. His companions knew nothing of it. They would have laughed if they had.

Gaunt had moods which never before had come to him, and his reflections began to reach beyond the excitements of the day's work, beyond the surface satisfactions and success in his profession and he had some unsatisfied longings to which at first he could hardly have given a name. He found within himself a strain of something hitherto but faintly suspected. It was emotion of a sort, of course, but it was emotion which took him high, strangely opened his eyes, and spread before him in its sordidness the energies of his present work, and he wondered at himself and wondered at all the others who could be content with it. With a thrill he realised that there was a great new life to be entered, experiences to be gained there, which would make a new world. In these moments his personal ambitions, the desire for money, the struggle for freedom from wage-slavery, these things became as lead to him. The real gold was there if he put out his hand to grasp it. The planning and scheming and service of the *Daily Light*'s worship of success in every sphere, however achieved: the survey of these things scorched his spirit, and he perplexed himself about the dullness of all those clever men in not knowing that there was a higher world than the one in which they lived.

Meanwhile he went on with his daily occupation, simulating a heartiness for which he sometimes despised himself, but which he knew to be necessary if he was to draw his money at the end of each week. Gaunt was no hero; he would have been horrified at the mere idea of such a thing. His new feelings were indulgences which must not interfere with salary-getting – that is what he told himself frequently when his disgust at the underhand scheme against Path made itself felt. As the days went on he discovered that he was promising himself that some time he would give full play to his better side, and said his reformation should be carried out when it would cost him less. True, he had a horrid thought that happiness would escape him then; that now was the accepted time, that he should retire from his days and nights of uncertainty in full flush of benefit. He looked up at the stars at night and found comfort and encouragement in their eternity.

Seriously harassed with doubt was Gaunt as the day approached for the adventure with the Irishmen. It was just about this time that the first two of the young Authoritarian members fell sick in pursuance of the second part of Lodden's plan.

[5 January 1914]

Chapter XX.
Gaunt's Discontent.

The falling ill of Authoritarian members sprang from Viola, although the affair was but put on foot by Lodden; and Viola being very proud of her initiative was surprised and disappointed when Gaunt looked at her coldly during its revelation to him. Gleefully had Viola announced the sick list programme to Gaunt, for she felt that it was a manœuvre which his journalistic heart would respond to immediately. When he frowned at the narrative she took it to be jealousy of Lodden, and sought to rally him out if it, and when he came round to a kind of tolerant good humour she did not realise that he had reached the stage when he was bound to treat her like a child. For the sake of peace it was a good thing she did not realise this.

The contriving of Viola was built up on the careful day-to-day preparations of the Whips for the division on the second reading; the steady and regular counting of heads by the organisers in both camps with a view to eventualities on the deciding night. The Authoritarians had each hostile M.P. listed, with his whereabouts, the state of his health, his shade of opinions, his expressed decision, if any, to vote for or against Path's Bill. Similar careful notification was going on day by day in the Progressive office with regard to the Authoritarians. It was necessarily a chance process, because a good many members were fluctuating, some were unavoidably abroad, and a large number had as yet expressed neither approval nor disapproval of the measure. Every man, therefore, had to be watched. Viola knew all this, and one day she said to Lodden: "I suppose if one side knew for certain that various men on the other side could not attend the division it would give confidence?"

"Of course it would."

"It might even lead to miscalculation?"

"Possibly."

"Why not make it lead to miscalculation?"

"How?"

"Cannot it be reported that a certain number of our people are sick, and then have those same men turn up unexpectedly on the night of the division?"

"You ought to be in politics," said Lodden.

And so it happened that by means of certain twisting agencies a few days before the second reading debate misfortune attacked the ranks of the Authoritarians. In certain papers appeared the notification that Mr. Maclaird, member for one of the Glasgow constituencies, was down with a severe attack of influenza; and that Mr. Johnson, the member for Peckham, was under diagnosis for appendicitis. The public hardly noticed these items, but they were seized upon with pleasure by the Progressive organisers and carefully recorded. A hunting accident to Colonel Richardson in Leicestershire came next, and then the neuritis of Mr. Luddock, the Liverpool member. At this point the *Daily Light* referred to a touch of concern to the depletion of the Authoritarian ranks, and hoped that all its members would be well enough to be in their places on the fateful night. As for the Progressive organisers, they chuckled. By a coincidence, influenza seized Mr. Limpson, member for South Northamptonshire and Mr. Clowes, the Dorset member, on the same day; and the announcement of their indisposition was quickly followed by the statement that Sir Peter Muirhead, the young and newly elected member for Newcastle, had received from a sister suddenly stricken down in New York an urgent call to cross the Atlantic to her. The *Daily Light* took on a shade of melancholy over this, and declared that it was the stern duty of all members, at whatever personal cost, to be in their seats for the great division. "That is all very well," said the *Daily Messenger*, the Progressive organ, hardly able to conceal its delight, "but it cannot reasonably be expected that sick men should rise from their beds and endanger their lives in order to go down to the House of Commons and vote on a party project." Valiantly the *Daily Light* reiterated its call to arms. If some members were incapacitated all the more reason for the certain attendance of every other member of the Authoritarian side. The Progressive officials smiled compassionately among their own people and lessened the rigours of whipping in.[78]

The restlessness of spirit in Gaunt was in some degree due to temperament, and there were times when the idea of throwing up the *Daily Light* and all its advantages brought to him the touch of adventure which he loved. The suggestion grew upon him, though he would still have scoffed at the notion had anyone else put it forward that he was ready to give up material advancement for the sake of scruples of conscience. Nevertheless he had surveyed practical considerations, and to anyone who knew Gaunt this was very significant. His mother owned the house in which they lived at Beckenham, and was possessed of a small income, so that he had no need to worry specially on her account. So far as his own livelihood was concerned an avenue was open in the shape of outside contributions to various magazines and papers for which he had written from time to time, and on a moderate computation he could earn from £3 to £4 per week. He would be losing from the *Daily Light* £10 a week, with all the chances of advancement which lay open to the ambitious and determined young men closely under the eye of Archibald Lodden. The step, if he took it, would be decisive, irretraceable. He knew that. Much pondering did Gaunt give to the whole business. Sometimes he wondered how far his failures in this particular campaign were influencing his desire to leave the paper and then the doubts were swept away by his remembrance of the humiliating parts he had played in connection with Raston Path.

He thought of the cold-blooded planning of Lodden, his cunning pretences of political principles in the conduct of a great profit-making machine like the *Daily Light*, and then he remembered the coldness of Viola towards those out of her own little circle, her undeveloped interests apart from suburban bridge or tennis, and he shuddered at the though of the emptiness of it all. Increasingly there came to him a glow at the ideals of Raston Path, together with insurgent admiration for the man. Gaunt became ambitious, and felt himself fettered.

In the course of his *Daily Light* service Gaunt had never shrunk from an important assignment, but he had less and less liking for the kidnapping of the Irish members, as the time approached. Curiously enough, it was not the fear of failure that deterred him, nor the risks of the affair. These things were in the game. What oppressed him was the chance that he might be recognised. He had a rooted repugnance to being identified with these Authoritarian plans. He knew, his feelings being what they were, that he was a contemptible creature for taking a hand. Should the attempt miscarry he realised what would be the scornful anger and wrath of the Reds, and Progressives, and knew the condoning, laughing applause and enthusiasm which would be his from the Authoritarian army. Lip denunciation might come from the leaders, but they would not mean it. This prospect of Authoritarian applause was poison in Gaunt's mind, ruffled his days, and gave him indeed angry hours of reflection in bed when he ought to have been asleep. He tried to crush himself. He remembered that he was a journalist only, just a paid mercenary, that he was gaining golden opinions in Fleet-street – making rapid progress in his profession. His feelings burst through.

[6 January 1914]

Chapter XX – Continued.
An Interview with Lodden.

It was on the day before the second reading debate began that Gaunt determined on action, and set forth to Hampstead to interview Viola Cartlet. She had a telephone message that he was coming up, and she waited to receive him.

"I'm so glad you've come," she said, "it's really nice to have you here to lunch alone sometimes and you very seldom come up and see me of your own free will."

"I'm worried," he said, "I want to tell you about it."

She was tenderness itself, for Viola had deep sentiments for Gaunt which he did not understand and could not understand. "Dear boy," she said, "I'm so glad."

"It's about this political business and the *Light*," he said.

"Anything fresh?" she asked, her eyes sparkling for news.

He shook his head, "No, no. Things are going on all right and arrangements are made. That's what's giving me trouble."

"Trouble?"

"I know, Viola, you don't sympathise with me in this, but for months past I have been thinking differently on a good many things. Political matters, I mean, and I've come to have a great feeling for Raston Path."

"My dear Marjorie, don't be silly." Viola was much relieved, for politics struck no deep note in her. She certainly would not be able to realise that a man's will or conscience might be troubled on such a notion. She had feared that Gaunt was in personal trouble, and whatever trouble that had been she would have flown to his assistance; sickness, threatened perjury, disgrace in any shape or form, these things would have been almost welcome by Viola because they could have given her the chance of show him what she really felt for Gaunt, and what she could do for him, and would do.

"Politics –" She could have laughed but for the fear of hurting Gaunt.

"Yes," he went on, "I've been disturbed for a good while past, and some of my beliefs have been a good deal modified. Indeed, some of them have been turned upside down."

"Oh, I know you've got a kind of sympathy with these sentimental notions, but you're not going to allow that to worry you, are you, Marjorie?"

"I've done a lot of dirty work," he said. "I stole the false draft from the Home Secretary's room. I've written abusive things about him in the paper, and I carried out that offensive business about Miss Croxten to try to show him up as a rotten kind of chap."

"That's all right," said Viola; "you newspaper men have got to do all that kind of thing. See how he's gone for people from time to time."

"It's quite different," said Gaunt steadily; "quite different. I've pursued him, told lies about him, schemed to get him into trouble for the sake of my weekly money, and all the time he has been a white man."[79]

"You can't say that, Marjorie."

"I do say it," went on Gaunt doggedly, "and I say more; I say he is a great man. The fact that an institution like the *Daily Light*, which is simply a business out to make money, should devote the power it has built up to persecuting and trying to ruin a man like Path is simply revolting."

"I didn't know you felt that way," said Viola, with concern in her voice.

"Here are we, the lot of us, Lodden, Wansmuth, myself, and the rest, trying to trample this man in the mud, and all the time he is struggling for noble ideals, which in our crudeness and shallowness we cannot even understand. We haven't got enough nobleness. Don't tell me that he is selfish, working for his own end, and all that kind of cant. It's really horrible." Gaunt was pacing up and down the room. "I'm right up against it, Viola, and that's a fact."

"Poor old boy," she said. She did not sneer at him or laugh at him, and he was pleasantly surprised. He had not known how she would have received his downright confession, and he had come up, so to speak, to clear himself as well as to make an appeal to her. "I dislike Raston Path very much," she said; "sometimes I hate him. I don't know very much about these things that trouble you so. You ought to know, I suppose. Do you really think we are quite wrong, Marjorie?"

"Quite, quite wrong," he said earnestly.

There were a few seconds silence and then she said: "I'm sorry for you, dear; I know it must be wretched. I can't think you're right, though."

He smiled. "No, I don't expect you to."

"What has been in your mind, then, about the arrangements, Marjorie?"

"I feel completely rotten about the whole thing. Do you know what I've come to tell you? I've come to say that I'm not sure that I ought not to go straight to Path and tell him about the whole plot. I should have to pay for it by being kicked out of the *Daily Light* office, but I should have cleared my conscience, and I should have done a service to Path. I'm very anxious to do a service for him."

"What for?" she asked.

He flung out his hands with a gesture of despair. "Cannot you understand? Perhaps I haven't made it clear what I mean. I don't think I can say any more than what I have said."

"But, my dear, you mustn't go and do this. Think of what would happen. Why, the Bill would pass. I am sure it would, because apart from putting the Government on their guard and all that kind of thing it would produce a sort of reaction among our members."

"Well," said Gaunt gloomily.

"My dear, don't think about such a terrible thing. What does it matter? I tell you what – get through this business and then if you are unhappy look out for another position. Get on to a Progressive paper. You would be easy then."

"I don't seem to be able to make you understand what a sneak I feel. I've got to do something. I can't just sit still now."

Viola thought for a minute and then said, "You know I don't go very deeply into all these political things, but I feel you've got the wrong ideas, and I'm quite certain that one of these days you'll come round to the proper side again. Yes, I'm quite certain of that."

Gaunt shook his head. "Well, we'll see."

"But, my dear old boy, I can't have you miserable like this, nor yet go and do anything desperate which will hurt you. Don't you be silly. I tell you what; why not go to Lodden, he's a big man, and tell him what you feel? Perhaps he'll drop the thing."

Gaunt shrugged his shoulders. "Don't care about it," he said.

"He's quite a nice man," said Viola, with an attempt at gladness. "That's when you get to know him completely. I'm sure it would be well to go to him. Be guided by what he thinks."

"Oh, Lord," said Gaunt.

"Yes, I know that seems foolish, but do try it. Would you like me to go?"

"Oh, no," said Gaunt hastily. "That wouldn't do." He stopped for a moment's reflection. "Very well, the fat's in the fire for me one way or another, and I'll see if I can interview Archie."

He went down to the *Daily Light* with some of the weight off his mind now that he had decided on action. Seeking an interview with Lodden on "urgent business," he obtained an appointment for the afternoon. Lodden received him with uplifted brows, and Gaunt felt some how in the wrong atmosphere at once. The interview was short and to the point.

"I've something unpleasant to say, Mr. Lodden, but I know I ought to say it nevertheless, and so I've come down to see you."

"What is it?" snapped Lodden.

"This political business, this Raston Path attack."

"Well?"

"I've come to the opinion that we're playing a rather low-down game, and I have had more than my share in it."

Cold astonishment shone upon Lodden's face, together with a growing attention, and Gaunt thought he could detect in the recesses of those non-committal eyes the faintest flicker of a sardonic smile.

"It's all very well to attack a man," said Gaunt, "because we're an Authoritarian newspaper, but I think it's a mistake to do what we have done to carry on our scheme."

"Go on," said Lodden.

"I stole the document from his office, and we used it. Since then we've tried to blacken his character in every way we could. Do you think that's policy in the long run? I don't think it is. It will only hurt the Authoritarian cause. Now there's this kidnapping business, and this mock illness of the members who are going to surprise the Government on the division night. It doesn't seem to me to be playing the game."

"Conscientious young man, Gaunt," said Lodden, "quite right to express yourself. Quite right to say what you feel. I like a man who speaks out."

"Well, don't you think, Mr. Lodden," said the encouraged Gaunt, "that we might drop these schemes for the division night? It's really dirty work. Fight the Bill by all means, in the columns of the paper, but this treacherous beneath-the-surface business – well, I don't think we ought to do it."

"Aye, aye," said Lodden.

Gaunt was feeling much more confident now, and began to think that he had in some way misread his employer. He took a bold step.

"I've been talking the thing over with Mrs. Cartlet," he said, "because she's very strong on the side of the paper, and a very keen opponent of her brother-in-law. She agrees with what I say. She thinks we ought not to do these things during the next two or three days."

"Oh, she does, does she?"

"Even if the second reading of the Bill were carried, that doesn't mean it will become law," said Gaunt. "There will be a long fight before that, and it's perfectly obvious that the Government will have to go to the country before its final passage."

Lodden was looking at him rather abstractedly, and Gaunt paused for a moment.

"You've got a real white streak in you, Gaunt. I feared you had."

He spoke deliberately, reflectively. "You're a clever and useful man on the paper and I dare say you'll get on in time, but you are of no use as a commander in big emergencies. I've tried you, and what you now say shows that you have failed. The spirit of a sparrow, yes, the spirit of a sparrow. That's about the comparison."

Gaunt paled with anger. Lodden rose, and his voice deepened. "Let me hear no more of this nonsense, Gaunt, you can come off the job. Can't afford faint hearts on a thing like this."

"I am not the only one," began Gaunt.

"Don't talk to me," roared Lodden; "don't talk to me. As for Mrs. Cartlet's opinion, how dare you bring her name in? What's she to the *Daily Light*? She's a sister-in-law of Raston Path, the Home Secretary, and you presume to bring her opinion forward. Why, you must be mad."

With flushed face and a heart raging, Majority Gaunt found his way back to the reporters' room.

[7 January 1914]

Chapter XXI.
Nancy Takes a Hand.

Resentment and righteous indignation made Gaunt a very different person from the rather vacillating and undetermined man who had been unable to settle his course of action, and now there was in him a sort of raging exhilaration in the knowledge that he was being bourne towards a full revelation of the unscrupulous design to wreck Path and smash the Bill. Consequences did not trouble him so much, the result to himself began to appear a small matter in comparison with the defeat of Lodden. Whatever he might lose he would at least gain a measure of self-respect, would have the satisfaction of showing Lodden that even a colossus was not in invincible, and would also be doing something to wipe out the debt he owed to Raston Path. While he remained with the *Daily Light* it would be impossible to convince anyone, let alone the Home Secretary, that his thoughts and inclinations had turned sympathetically to those hitherto abominated Red doctrines; he could imagine how in the passing flicker of attention which Path might give to his protestations there would be shown that swift, contemptuous gesture with which Path met weakness or insincerity. Nothing of that kind could meet the bold relation of Lodden's preparations in time to put the Government on their guard to save the second reading of their Bill.

Gaunt's venture was a desperate one, but the thought of it warmed his heart after the response given to him by Lodden. The reflection that he would be throwing up his £500 a year salary – indeed, it might be £1,000 a year if he successfully carried the campaign through – did not trouble him at all. The *Daily Light* had become an incubus to him and Lodden was a monster. He lit a cigarette at the reporters' room fire with trembling hand, and felt pleased with himself at his stiffening determination to overthrow the whole machine. He wanted someone to talk to about it. Viola was out of the question, he knew what she would say; and he did not care to tackle the subject with his mother or sisters at home, because they would simply think him foolish in throwing up a good position. And so, as his mind ran over the two or three close friends, Nancy Kirk flashed upon him, and with his heart singing within him he decided to go down and tell her the story. She, at least, would understand. The brave little adorer of Raston Path – she would, he knew, be on his side, and all his nerves were a-tingle at the thought of telling her the story and seeing her face lighten up as she learned what he was going to do.

There was no time to be thrown away, and Gaunt, looking at the clock, saw that Nancy would soon be due to leave her office for home, and he put on his coat and set out straight away for the Borough. As he went along in the tram he began to plan out his action, for he must strike immediately to be effective. On the morrow at the latest – he was not sure it should not be that night – he must by one way or another secure an interview with Raston Path. That was the solution. Let him get face to face with Raston Path and tell him the position of affairs, and so far as the Government was concerned all would be well and the plot of Lodden would be made to miscarry. But Gaunt knew, none better, that promptness was called for; for even with the best arrangements the loss of a few hours might make all the difference between defeat and victory. He pictured in his mind exactly what he would do on the next morning.

Mrs. Kirk was alone when he arrived at Lant-street. She thought he had come in casually to see herself and the girls because he happened to be in the neighbourhood, and she said she was expecting Nancy in at any minute.

"I have come down to have a talk with Nancy about politics and things that have happened in the *Daily Light* yesterday and to-day."

Mrs. Kirk said "Yes," but did not ask for particulars, for these things were a little beyond her.

"You see, she knows a good deal about political affairs and knows all that is in the wind about Raston Path and so on, and I really want to tell her something and to ask her opinion about it."

At any other time Gaunt would have thought such confession strange, even unbecoming. He would have feared the inference Mrs. Kirk might have drawn from it, but just now it seemed the most natural thing in the world to come to Nancy for full explanation and discussion. He had passed the mental stage when images matter. As for Mrs. Kirk, she regarded Gaunt as rather a good-looking fellow quite beyond her, and nothing he said or did would have been out of place.

"She won't be long. Will you have a cup of tea while you are waiting?"

Gaunt had some tea and tried to chat with his hostess while he waited, and strangely enough he could hardly keep himself from telling some of the determinations in his mind to the non-understanding and amiable Mrs. Kirk. He did just refrain, but that was all. Afterwards he was glad about this.

Nancy came in with flushed face from hurried mounting of the stairs. The sight of Gaunt surprised but did not disturb her, and she took off her coat and hat almost as if he were a member of the family. Recent events had put them strangely on a level, and they both felt the difference. Nancy, indeed, had come to use conventional phrases to him.

"This is an unexpected pleasure, Mr. Gaunt," she said.

'I wanted to see you and talk about something important, so I just came along suddenly, without ceremony. Hope I'm not in the way."

"Of course not. Is it something urgent?" She was apparently prepared to put off her tea.

"Oh, no, no," said Gaunt. "I wanted to have a quiet half-hour's chat with you but it isn't at all pressing."

So Gaunt sat while she had her tea and talked disjointedly about several matters with her and her mother for 20 minutes or so, and Nancy began to see that what he had to say was to be said to her alone. Perhaps Mrs. Kirk saw this also, and then with some motherly mistake as to the purpose of his mission she put opportunity in his way.

"I'll be going out now," she said. "I've to do a bit of shopping in the High-street. I'll be back again in about an hour. Nellie's tea is all ready when she come in, Nancy."

When Mrs. Kirk had disappeared Gaunt lost no time. He said: "I don't know whether it will seem queer to you, Miss Kirk, but I have come down to tell you something about myself and what I am going to do to-morrow."

Nancy looked at him with serious, wondering eyes. He went on with a rush.

"I'm going to throw over the *Daily Light*. I'm sick of it. It's about this political business, and as you know all the story I've come down to tell you the climax. I want to know what you think about it, too."

Gaunt had never seen Nancy Kirk so surprised. Her mouth was open like a bow as she looked at him.

But all the time Nancy was pleasantly conscious that she found nothing strange in the fact of Gaunt's coming to her in the emergency; it was reasonable and right to her for reasons she did not visualise. She lent her interest to what he had to say as one who was concerned in the outcome. Her attitude was meat and drink to Gaunt. Somewhere deep within him was exultation that he had her to come to.

"All kinds of things seem to have been happening in my life in the past year," he said. "Before that I sometimes had flickerings of doubt as to whether the geniality and wit and material struggle of us journalists completely satisfied me, though, of course, it gives us an infinitely better time than the poor money grabbers have. I wouldn't change the job for anything if it were simply a question of earning enough to live on. We see all the interesting things of outside life, and we go through experiences which men in other occupations cannot possibly get. You have to be a solider, or in the navy, or go out exploring, or something of that kind to get even a part of our sensations. We have things spread out before us which millionaires can't buy.

"But I seem to have been a little different in the past year. When I was a boy and knew practically nothing of music (I don't know much now) and went to a concert I would sometimes come out feeling my horizon of life had been widened. I would have vague ambitions and would see phases of existence with wonderful possibilities, and they were all for me. These feelings would die away till I went to the next concert. Later, when I began to dive into books and began to like some poetry very much, I would come across passages which took me out of myself in a similar way. I have sometimes heard a preacher in church bring something of the same kind of feeling to me. All this was when I was quite young. In the struggle I had for a living this happy sort of feeling never came to me, and as I got on the romance and change of my work was enough, and I let the geniality and wit and good nature of Fleet-street grow into gods. These sentimental longings were not for me anymore. I had grown out of them. Do you understand?"

"I think that you and your friends are better men than you make out," said Nancy.

Gaunt shrugged his shoulders. "I expect if you knew more about us you'd alter your opinion. There are many fascinations, but they lure us on to losses we know not of. Yes they do. Is all this very much like sermonising, Miss Kirk?"

"Go on," she said, seriously.

"Well, I have had returns of the old youthful emotions in the past year; I don't quite know how or why – several reasons, I dare say; but there's the fact. I have had notions come to me that ought not to be in any work-a-day journalist's head. Of course, one meets different personalities and they influence one. That's a great factor, but here are other things as well. Everything seemed to work together. There were those dirty tricks I have had to play about politics and those articles and all that which made me think more about poor people. Doesn't this seem dull and stupid? It's true."

"I don't think it's stupid at all."

"Other people would if you don't. You won't think me foolish when I say Raston Path has rather got hold of me?"

Nancy nodded her head. "Yes, I know."

"I haven't been able to get that man out of my memory for months; then that speech at the Surrey Theatre finished it. What he was striving for knocked me on the head. How could one do anything but join him? It's incredible to me. I was turned about by it all. Yet I went on afterwards to try and ruin him."

"You did that for the paper?"

"It was all very sordid and rotten."

"But you had no choice. Of course you had no choice."

"Plenty of choice if I had had any courage. I knew I was wrong and I went on. Well, here I am now."

"Have you told anyone about this?"

"Oh bless you, yes. I've been to Lodden himself. And that's what brings me here really. I went to try and persuade him not to carry out a certain plot he has in hand for preventing the Government getting a majority for this Bill. Of course, I might have known what he'd say. He simply scoffed. They are all the same. It's a hateful business."

Nancy pondered for a moment. "One day, perhaps, you may be ale to get more congenial work. You are bound to get that if you try to find it."

Gaunt glowed within himself at the surprise he had for her.

"I feel much stronger on this matter than you know," he said.

"But there doesn't seem anything that you can do for the moment."

"Do?" he exclaimed. "Look at the situation. I don't think a man often gets such an opportunity as I've got to make a stroke for the things he believes in. What is the state of affairs? Think of this great profit-making clever man, Lodden, increasing his business, adding to his riches, by using politics as a pawn and scheming in cold blood to secure all the advantage he can for his papers by manipulating various policies or, when necessary, by ruining politicians. Remember this man, too, is always on the side – he has to be for his immediate purposes – of those who are rich and well-to-do and comfortable. Then there's the other picture: millions of people in this country in a weakened state and bringing weakened children into the world, because they haven't got enough food or shelter, or because they are huddled together like pigs in unhealthy dwellings or slums. Picture Raston Path, with all his failings, flashing forth as a king to do battle on behalf of these poor people against the great hosts of well-fed, arrogant, or at least comfortable persons. Lodden is on their side. Raston Path tells them it is their duty, even at cost to themselves, to see that the conditions are altered for these poor devils, men and women, who are born into a state of affairs for which they are not responsible and against which the majority of them are unable to struggle. You have the picture of Raston Path fighting by what means seem to him to be best (largely through politics) to progress step by step towards relieving these great wrongs, and you get him to the point where he is at present; in which he has one of his projects before Parliament with a good change of passing it. Lodden comes on the scene. He engages some of his minor people to foil Raston Path in this latest endeavour of his. Finding that a fight in the open is not likely to result in victory he fixes up hired assassins, that's what it amounts to, who by planned treachery shall stab him in the back." Mr.

Gaunt's face was flushed; he was leaning forward, his arm was thrust out. Open-mouthed, Nancy Kirk was listening to him. She had never seen Gaunt like this.

"Here am I with other colleagues engaged to do what? To kidnap members of Parliament to make other arrangements to deceive Path as to who will be present at the House at the time fateful for him. It's like a fairy tale, isn't it? And you say there is nothing I can do. Good Heavens. It looks to me that everything depends upon me. There's at least one man who can checkmate Lodden at the moment."

"You mean yourself?" said Nancy Kirk.

"Yes."

"You'll tell him the whole thing?"

"That's my idea. It's something to have lived for. What is in my mind is to go straight to Path, tell him what I think, and relate these arrangements. There will be time for him to counteract everything that Lodden has set on foot in relation to the Bill. He can stop the kidnapping, he can make provision to meet the unexpected arrival of the additional Authoritarian members for the division."

There was a light in Nancy's eyes he had never seen there before, for she seemed to look right into him, and he had a sense of mystery about it.

"You are the only person I can come and tell this to with any certainty of getting sympathy," he said. "I suppose it is very foolish of me, but I want at least someone who understands before I do anything."

"Mr. Gaunt, you have mistaken me. I think you are going to behave very, very wrongly."

"Wrongly?"

"You are going to upset all Mr. Lodden's plans and give him over to the enemy."

"Upset his plans? Oh, that'll only be a trifle to Lodden. It's very important to Path and myself and the Government, but it isn't very important to Lodden."

"I can't understand you," said Nancy.

The bewildered Gaunt looked at her for further explanation.

"I will tell you what I think," she went on. "Here are you, a trusted servant of the *Daily Light*. You have been put in possession of all their secret plans, bad and good, and you have carried out a good many of them in the past. You have suddenly got a flare of enthusiasm through your feelings and you want to go and give away all that has been solemnly entrusted to you. You tell me that a Pressman is like a soldier. Well, does a soldier go and become a traitor because he does to believe in the politics of his country? Does he go over to the enemy and say, 'These are my commander's plans; I give them to you because I don't think what he believes is right?' Oh, Mr. Gaunt, don't do this horrid thing. How could you think of it? You have been years at the *Daily Light*, and you have said how kind Mr. Lodden always was towards men when they were in trouble or distress, and what a wonderful man he was, and how he gives everybody good salaries and looks after them when they are ill. You have said yourself that you couldn't possibly have got on so well anywhere else, and you have had many hundreds a year out of him. You are pretty well part of the *Daily Light*. And now, through some feelings of your own, you want to go and throw them over and offer all these secrets to people who hate Mr. Lodden. You mustn't do it."

The staggered Gaunt tried to stop her. "But think of all that is concerned," he said. "Think of what Lodden is trying to do and what Path is trying to do. You must think of these things."

"I am thinking of what you are going to do," she said.

"I should pay for it. I should be kicked downstairs at once and have nowhere to go, and lose a big salary, and should have to scramble along as best I could afterwards. I should pay my price. Surely you can see what is in my mind?"

"Yes, yes," she said, "and it's horrible to me. You talk about the loyalty of you newspaper men and the honour they have among them, and all that. It's horrible. I don't care if Mr. Lodden is right or wrong. It will be wicked of you, wicked."

"I'll go," said Gaunt. He took his hat and went out into the street.

[8 January 1914]

Chapter XXII.
M.P.s' Race to the Commons.

Two days of tumultuous debate on the second reading of Path's Bill was over, and the third day, when the division was to be taken, was come. There would be a culmination of Parliamentary excitement, verbal duels, hours of criticism and declamation, and then at 10.30 at night, with the House crowded, there would be the closure of discussion and the rival parties would file into one or other of the two division lobbies and settle the fate of the measure.

Gaunt was not in the House; his work was elsewhere. Half maddened by Nancy Kirk's amazing opposition, he had formed a swift rebellious decision, and had flung himself into the *Daily Light* project wholesale, almost with ferocity. He found from Fore that Lodden only intended to deprive him of work in the campaign if he really desired to quit, and that if he wanted to go on he could do so (Lodden knew his man very well). And thus it happened that Gaunt, bitterly enough, fixed up a bargain with the proprietor of a motor which had the semblance of a taxi-cab and was with him at Euston to direct operations and see that there was no mistake. Three hundred pounds was reckoned as the cost of the venture if the car should be wrecked, and the driver was given guarantees for that sum. The *Daily Light* did not appear in the matter at all, and Gaunt made clear with malicious emphasis that those who had set the matter afoot were the Authoritarian officials. As it turned out, the affair was not nearly so costly as it might have been.

The Irish members fell into the trap right away and were easily induced by the disguised Gaunt in waiting on the platform (he was a special messenger sent down from the House to prevent mishaps) to enter the cab he had in waiting to take them off to Westminster. The plan was aided by the fact that the train was half an hour late, and the time for reaching the House cut down to a narrower margin. Away went the five members in the machine with the bribed driver to the North of London, and in their lively conversation among themselves they had travelled for a full 20 minutes before the unfamiliar aspect of the streets roused one of them to inquiry.

"Just a minute, sir," said the drive to the Irishman who had thrust his head through the open window, and he drove the taxi-cab up a residential street. He dropped from his place by the roadway, and while a couple of them were alighting from the cab to find out what it all meant he had lifted the bonnet which conceals the machinery and made some little adjustment inside.

"Going to get a spanner and some petrol, " he said. "Be back in two ticks." He hurried away from the questioning M.P.s and in a few seconds had disappeared round the turning. He was not seen again. He had been gone five minutes before the Irishmen suspected they had been tricked, and then their first idea was not to wreck the cab or revengefully to seek for the driver, but to get back to the House of Commons before it was too late. They knocked at the door of one of the houses and were told they were somewhere in the North of Hampstead, and that it would be fully a quarter of an hour before they could reach the main road. Cursing the easy carelessness which had made them the victims of an Authoritarian plot, they jog-trotted through various streets towards a thoroughfare where they might find some kind of motor – perhaps, indeed, a real taxi-cab – to take them along to Westminster.

It is not simple in a strange suburb to find a main road, even with the assistance of direction from occasional passers-by, and the allotted quarter of an hour was nearly twenty-five minutes before they came upon the tramlines of a well-lighted street. The blue lamp of a police station a few yards along gave them hope, and they dashed towards it for news of the nearest cabstand. The constable at the door said there was no cabstand for a mile, but sometimes a cab was to be found waiting for chance customers outside the Lord Pitcairn public-house, a few hundred yards further on. Alas! on their particular night there was no cab outside the Lord Pitcairn. The Irishmen bent themselves to the emergency and extraordinary efforts were made to secure some means of transit. Shops were knocked up, a fire station entered, and two motor-omnibuses stopped in the struggle to get back to the House in time. The mere thought that their situation might put the Government in danger was appalling.

"I shall track that driver down if it costs me a year's work and a thousand pounds in money," said Raffety, who was the head of a great whiskey firm, Raffety, Kilmain, and Murphy, grouped together on the kerb for five seconds after individual efforts in various directions, waited for Johnston and O'Leary, who were coming across the road after a descent upon the manager of a public-house, when they saw crawling along towards them in the distance the two lights which heralded a taxi-cab. It's slow pace told them no customer was inside. The truest prayer of thanks ever offered up by members of a religious race rose from that group of Irishmen. The taxi-cab was stopped, and the driver promised three times his usual fare for a speedy journey to Westminster. It was to be a real race, and the man was urged to set the speed limit at naught. Nothing but a miracle, they feared would see their names on the division-list that night. Quarter-past ten struck on a neighbouring church clock when they entered the cab, and they had about eight miles to cover through London streets in about twenty minutes, and on the face of it the thing was impossible.

Just one ray of hope cheered them. On a big night in Parliament, with a crowded House, with excitement thrilling the chamber, the preliminaries of a division take a little longer than usual. The hubbub, the thronging, put on a few seconds to the process which intervenes between 10.30, when the Speaker rises to close the debate and the moment when he rises again and order that the entrance doors to the division lobbies shall be locked. It might well be that the few extra seconds would give the members time to vote.

It was 25 minutes past ten as they came down Tottenham Court-road, and they saw then that they really had a chance. Give them a stroke of luck and they might yet vote in the division. It was one of those times when a tiny interposition of providence, occurring frequently in matters of no importance, would win them the race. Alas for human hopes. When help is needed an otherwise kindly Providence often withholds its hand. A block of traffic at the junction of Oxford-street pulled them up, and that notwithstanding appeals to the point-duty policeman – appeals made with all the fluency and point characteristic of Irishmen in difficulty. Of no avail were their hot words, and for over three minutes they were kept stationary while the tangle of vehicles unwound itself. Free at last, the cab started on its way, quite regardless of the law limiting pace, for the driver was by this time almost as keen as his fares. He went down Whitehall, with a rush, and swung into Palace Yard at a rate which made the policeman at the members' entrance turn a startled frown towards the incoming car. As it dashed towards him, however he took in the position. The clock stood at 10.37, and the division bells had been ringing minutes ago.

"All right, gentlemen," he exclaimed, wrenching open the door before the cab was at a stand-still. "I'll pay the driver. You get in as quick as you can."

"Fix it up, Brown," said O'Leary, as he and his companions tumbled out in a heap. They left the driver in the hands of the policeman and ran helter-skelter into the House. Dashing through the inner lobby with their overcoats on and their hats in their hands they made for the Chamber, where the speaker was still on his dais under the canopy, and where the benches were gradually filling up with a humming crowd of members who had already recorded their votes.

The junior Progressive Whip, with the tails of his frock-coat flying in the wind, was running by the side of the five members as they crossed the inner lobby. "For heaven's sake, hurry," he said, "it's a near thing. There's been trickery here to-night somewhere."

"More trickery than you think," gasped O'Leary as he ran.

It was touch and go. The Irishmen had to enter the Chamber from just behind the speaker's chair, and the door of the Government division lobby was at the other end of the House and an attendant stood ready to close it. The three bewigged clerks of the House, seated in a row beneath the chair of the Speaker, had their eyes on the electric device before them which gives the signal that the regulation period has elapsed. In an irregular group, forgetful of all decorum and wildly elated at having gained their goal in time, the five members came into view from behind the Speaker's chair, and entered a race down the floor of the House from the lobby amid the cheers of the Progressive members – a couple of hundred of them – who had already voted, and had found their places on the green benches ready for the announcement of the result.

[9 January 1914]

Chapter XXII – Continued.
The Fate of the Bill.

A stranger knowing nothing of Parliament would have felt the drama in the air. As the night had progressed and the speeches, bitter, eloquent, electric, had roused the House on both sides into fierce shouting matches, there had gone round a whisper that the Government was in danger of defeat. How or whence the whisper had arisen members in general did not know. It had been common knowledge beforehand that the Government would have to fight hard for a majority, but there was a pretty widespread understanding that they would be victorious – though the majority could not be large. Then, during the evening, there percolated over the benches a statement that through skilful generalship by the Authoritarians, or through bungling by the Government, the balance has swung round and very likely the Government might be defeated after all. The expectant turmoil when the Speaker cut short the debate and gave the word for the taking of the division yielded at least a column of copy to the descriptive sketch writers in the gallery. Cheers and counter cheers, personal recriminations, noisy appeals to the Speaker, evidenced the overcharged nerves, and the tumult was only lessened by the exit of members from the Chamber to the lobbies to record their votes. After the division commenced members began to file out though the lobbies and go into the House again to take their old places on the benches and wait until the figures should be known. They were stringing in from both ends of the House when the five members made their dash onto the floor from behind the Speaker's chair.

"Hear, hear," burst in a tremendous chorus from the Progressives as they saw the belated five.

"Too late, too late!" shouted the Authoritarians.

Under a storm of encouragement and derision the Irishmen tore down the centre aisle. Fate was against them. They had got abreast of the gangway which bisects the benches of the House when there came to them a sound which cut all their hopes adrift. "Ting, ting," went the tiny electric bell of the apparatus in front of the bewigged clerks. The Speaker rose.

"Lock the doors," he commanded in the rich, sonorous voice which enforces respect as well as obedience. The two leading Irishmen sprang in a frenzy over the intervening 30 yards between themselves and the division door, with their friends at their heels. The attendant, key in hand, looked at the oncoming men and glanced at the Speaker. The latter, calm and dignified, gave no sign. The attendant bent at the door, and all the House (silenced now at the crucial moment) heard the click of the key in the lock. The next instant the first of the five Irishmen had reached the door – too late. O'Leary, a dozen feet behind, flung his arms to heaven in his despair. A long-drawn "Ah-h" from the Progressive benches was drowned in the cheering of the Authoritarian, and the five Irishmen, panting with their exertions, went off moodily to the inner lobby to explain themselves as best they might to the Whips.

The shutting out of the Irishmen was a blow to the Progressives in an atmosphere which magnified every encouragement and made a disappointment seem a great affair. But as a matter of fact the chances were still on the Government side. A numerical advantage to start with, a keen organisation, together with the knowledge that defeat would lie in wait for any slackness; these things put the Government in a winning position apart from accidents. The failure of the five Irishmen, the inexplicable reappearance of scattered Authoritarian members who were supposed to be ill in bed or away on their travels, would narrow the margin to the point of danger, but in spite of all it was probable that the second reading would be carried. That was the Whips' opinion.

The Chief Whip of the Authoritarians was inclined to agree with this forecast. Not so his men thronging the Opposition benches, for they believed victory to be within their hands, and they were thrilling for the moment of the figures.

While the members were streaming in at each end of the House, leaders sat in their places on the two front benches facing each other, bearing themselves as calmly and unexpectantly as they could. The Authoritarian chief, with his arms folded across his breast, had his head cast back on to the top if his seat, and was gazing reminiscently into the roof, and at the other side of the table the Prime Minister showed a pinkness in his icy features which betokened an excitement unknown to himself. His eyebrows were elevated, and his forehead wrinkled laterally in a manner which indicated but mild interest in the proceedings, and with his hands resting one on each knee he tapped occasionally with his fingers as if he were touching the keys of a piano. Raston Path sat next to him, his slim figure bolt upright, as was customary with him in times of stress. In one hand he held a pencil and in the other a sheet of paper, and his hands were crossed in his lap as though ready for writing. It was just his habit, of course; he had nothing to write. He was frowning slightly in thought. His eyes were non-committal. Next to Raston Path was Sir Harry Venture, maintaining an aristocratical ease and indifference and showing it by reading with cold, intelligent face the order paper of the next day's Parliamentary business. All three knew the life of the Government, preserved as it probably would be by a narrow majority, might very well be doomed to an early death, by the narrowness of that majority. They had no thoughts for the destroying of their political plans, of the great ideals gone awry. The time was not one for humanitarians; fight was in the air. Tension stretched the whole assembly, and most strained of all were those who led the fight, who had brought the battle to an issue. In this moment eventualities were nothing to the leaders, least of all to Raston Path, the greatest fighter among them, for their thoughts were on one thing only – on victory. A majority of 10 would be victory, a good and stimulating victory, and that whistled through them, exhilarated them, made it hard to keep the masks in position on their faces.

The House had quickly filled up in every part, and over all was a growing stillness. Much longer than usual seemed the ticking off the names of the members in the lobbies, and as the seconds crept on and the House became more and more crowded, less and less noise was made. Presently even the whispering ceased, and there came a moment when it was even possible to hear the murmur of conversation from up in the Ladies' Gallery. Suddenly the block of members standing elbow to elbow on the space below the gangway at the end of the House were set in motion one against the other, and then were clove asunder. Two Whips were hurrying forward to their table with the figures of the Progressive vote in their hands.

They had almost reached the table when from behind the Speaker's chair at the other end of the House emerged two other Whips with the figures of the Authoritarian voting. The two Chief Whips met midway along by the side of the table, and in that chamber of silence 700 breathless people waited for the verdict. There was a moment's comparing of papers, and one of the bewigged clerks in attendance on the Whips filled in the two sets of figures on a formal sheet. His actions were watched with intensity. It would be his duty to hand the completed sheet to the Whip of the winning side. Very carefully, the clerk did the figures, then he took up the sheet and handed it to the Authoritarian Whip.

For a second there was a gasp of amazement, and then the storm broke. The Authoritarians shouting with joy leapt to their feet waving hats and handkerchiefs. Some jumped on the benches, and hurled fierce, derisive words across at Raston Path. The leaders on the Front Bench put their heads together in sudden, joyful conversation.

It was difficult for the Speaker to get sufficient silence for the announcement of the figures, but he did so at last. The four Whips, two on each side, formed up abreast on the floor of the House below the table, bowed low to the Speaker, advanced to the table, bowed again, and then the chief Authoritarian Whip read out the figures: –

> Against the Bill 320
> For the Bill 316

It was a hurricane this time, for there was no stopping the triumphant joy of the Authoritarians. A hundred men were on their feet shouting as many different calls. The staggered Progressives, recovering themselves a little, threw back taunts, but they could not hope to meet in volume the growing joy-song of the Opposition. Presently from amid all the uproar sprang up a single continuing chorus from the Authoritarian side, and in the course of seconds every member of the Opposition was joining it. The chorus consisted of the word "Resign!" It was shouted and screamed in a dozen different ways, but always was it the word "Resign!" The spreading volume of sound drowned intermittent retorts and gives from the other side. Victory was venting itself.

The Prime Minister and Path had a serious little whispered conversation, and then with Sir Harry Venture and one or two of the other Ministers they passed out of the House. Their disappearance was the signal for terrifying scorn, for exulting demands and defiances, and it was afterwards said the cries of the Opposition could be heard outside in Whitehall.

Down in the *Daily Light* office Gaunt, standing in front of the tape machine, saw the record of the division scenes and waited for the figures which showed that Lodden had been successful – that the Government was overthrown.

"Well, that's over," he said to himself, and went into the reporters' room to write one of two letters. With the strife at an end he felt relaxed. He had a sense of a burden lifted from him. He went home to sleep well that night. Fresh and strong next morning, he found that his bitterness of spirit was abated. His worst was done, and the task that now lay before him was comparatively easy. He had helped to compass the *Daily Light*'s purposes, and the matter had been well and truly finished.

Departure was the next chapter in his life, he knew that. Hidden forces and open forces had operated upon him, and he now fully and frankly accepted the fate that he must make new moves. Not in one thing only was he impelled, but in two or three. He must carry through a clean sweep. While each departure in itself would be painful, perhaps intolerably so, if it had come alone, the juncture of two or three made each conceivable. He had a sense of exultation. No fear was there and certainly no hesitation, and the inevitability of it all went through his nerves and brain and gave him calmness. Those who would in this crisis have judged Gaunt to be impulsive and to be driven by temporary sentimental considerations would have been completely wrong. A mass of weakness on the surface, Gaunt at heart had strength he knew not of. He could not even have told whence it arose. He was at the parting of the way. He knew without any possibility of doubt that it was a time of good-bye for him.

His treacherous and seductive companionship with Viola must be ended if he was to have peace, for he had known in the last week or two that he did not love her and that he had been coward enough to luxuriate in her passion while giving her but a faint reflection of it. She could not even be a friend, for in those things which are required for a friend she was quite lacking. Then there was Nancy, and the thought of Nancy gave him a dull pain. She had tumbled his house of cards, had shown him clearly that, despite a passing interest, she had been largely unaffected by his personality, that honest and good intent and some other abstract things were of greater importance to her than himself. He surged inwardly as he remembered how his impulses found no echo in her; how she was disgusted at his high handed treachery for a good purpose; and in his humiliation was the hidden fear that she was on the right track. She had grown upon him, this girl, and great had been the shock when he learnt, as he did, that no tender, loving look, no heart throb in her could ever be his. He cursed his forwardness to her on the first day they met, cursed his vulgar readiness with women, despised his ugly indulgences (even though he knew they would be bound to recur). He saw Nancy now with her youth and ignorance miles above him in the scale of knowledge. He had passed the point of revolt, and knew now he could not reach her, but even at the interview, when she had rebuffed him, some new determinations lit his soul, and the fact that she could never know them increased their potency. That interview with her had set his desperate thoughts clear before him. That he had achieved his first purpose and wrecked the Government was a solace. His spirit was high. He would go forth into the world again.

[10 January 1914]

Chapter XXIII.
A Memorable Dinner Party.

When Gaunt was on his way the following evening to make his last call on Mrs. Cartlet at Hampstead the evening papers came out with the expected news that the Prime Minister had announced in the House the King's intention to dissolve parliament forthwith. "The Press is mightier than the sword," he sneered, and wondered whether Lodden would be successful in winning the election which was to ensue.

Gaunt's thoughts flickered idly over his coming resignation and what Lodden would say about it. He would take it with a smile, Gaunt supposed, with an indifferent nod of his head. Of little account to him were the feelings of a reporter, or a dozen reporters, or all his staff put together. If Gaunt wanted any strengthening he would have had it from the knowledge that he mattered not at all to Archibald Lodden.

If Gaunt had been told that Lodden was dining at the Cartlets' on that very evening he would have smiled agreeably, for Gaunt had no nervousness in him when driven beyond a certain line, and the more unpleasantness there was for everyone concerned now the better he would like it.

He found it, however, difficult to dash into his mission when he arrived, for Viola met him at the door, happy, easy-mannered, delighted to see him.

"You didn't telephone to say you were coming. Suppose I'd been out? I am so glad you've come. I was afraid you would be too busy with all this political business, and I'd given up hope of seeing you for a day or two."

"I want to talk to you about one or two things."

"Well, you needn't be so serious. Come into George's room." She almost pushed him into her husband's study, talking the while.

"So you've managed to get your old Raston Path beaten? I'm so glad, Marjorie. You don't know how glad I am. I know you'll think I'm wicked."

They were in the room now, and she could see his face. "You're very glum. Oh, I'm forgetting." She put her hand on his arm. "I know how sorry you'll be about it all. You would far rather it had all come to nothing. But you had to go on with the thing. Poor old Marjorie. I expect it was beastly for you."

"Yes, it was rather rotten." He looked at her.

"Silly boy, you mustn't take it to heart. You only did what you ought to. I know what you think, but it will be for the good of the country. I'm sure it will. I've been talking to Mr. Lodden about it."

"On, you've seen him?"

"He's here now."

"Here?"

"Yes, he's come to dinner to-night."

"He has, has he?"

"George has got him in the drawing-room showing him some miniatures. He's interested in miniatures. We've been talking about the whole thing. He laughed over your appeal to him; he was most kind about it; he was, really."

"Confound him."

"He said he thought the more of you for telling him straight out what you felt. Oh, Marjorie, I'm so happy. Do you know, he's going to promote you. He's going to give you a big job. I don't know what it is, but your salary is going to be doubled. I'm just walking on air. Marjorie, say you're glad. Oh, I have looked forward to this. All your work is telling now. He says that. Your plans and organisation and your writing and all you have done for months past are having their effect. This last week it's all been plain sailing. Anyone could have brought it off after what you had done before. He says you've been the mainspring of the operation right up to the last."

"Liar."

"Oh, Marjorie, you ungrateful boy, after all he's said. You ought to have heard him. You have never met him here, though he knows you visit us. I'm going to take you in to-night. Won't it be ripping? He won't mind – he'll like it. You'll see him in a new light to-night; yes, you will."

"Well, I don't mind. Might just as well see him as not."

Viola could not understand Gaunt, but she realised that he must be depressed at all that had occurred – the thwarting of his inclinations and the part he had played against Path.

"Never mind, old boy, don't you think about these politics now. What I want to ask you is, can you come away at Easter with us?"

"Easter?"

"Yes. We're going to Brighton for four or five days. Won't you come with us? George will be delighted."

She looked in vain for the answering gleam in his eye. Gaunt was finding this task more difficult than he had thought.

"Don't know where I shall be at Easter."

"Oh, you can fix it up if you like, you know you can. Don't be nasty, Marjorie."

"Look here, Viola, I'm going to chuck the whole thing."

He had taken the plunge now.

"What?" she said, in frank wonderment.

"I'm done with the *Daily Light*."

"I thought ..."

"To-morrow I give Lodden a month's notice. I've come to tell you."

"Oh, my dear, don't – don't be silly. You are overwrought now. I know how you feel, I do indeed. You have only done your duty. You had to be loyal to your paper."

Faint surprise came to Gaunt at the nearness of her words to those of Nancy. He shook his head at her.

"It's no good," he said.

"Everything's over now. Your new work will be off politics. Lodden says so. Oh, my dear, don't be stupid."

"I can't argue, Viola; I can only just tell you the facts."

She looked at him for a moment, and then she said cheerily, "Well, now then, Marjorie, you just come in to dinner, and we'll see if your feelings are the same after you have heard what Mr. Lodden has to say. We won't talk about it any more now."

At dinner Gaunt found Lodden the affable guest who treated him as a friendly acquaintance, and if an occasional reference to the paper cropped up, Lodden's tone to Gaunt was one of genial companionship in a mutual enterprise.

"We really knew Mr. Gaunt before we knew you, Mr. Lodden," said Viola.

"Shows how my young men steal a march on me."

"They take advantage of you in more ways than one," said George Cartlet, smiling.

"Never know when I am level with them."

Gaunt said little all through dinner, and Lodden thought he was a trifle ill-at-ease, whereas he was simply rebellious. When coffee had been served, Viola made her audacious move.

"You know, Mr. Lodden, I, for one, appreciate Majority's scruples about Raston Path. I think it was rather hard of you to make him go through it."

Lodden sipped his liqueur. "We all have to do unpleasant things sometimes. Gaunt is not the man to shrink from them."

"I'm afraid he is," said Gaunt.

"Do tell him all about it," said Viola, addressing Lodden. "He's becoming quite a Red. Awful, I call it. But still, it must have been hard to carry on his work. I felt really sorry for him when Raston Path was defeated. What do you think of that Marjorie?"

"You are very kind," said Gaunt.

Lodden smiled. "It's well to have spirit when you are young," he said, and he looked at George Cartlet, who smiled in answer.

"Marjorie, you'll soon get over it," said Viola. "It's no good you looking so sullen. Another year and you will be as good an Authoritarian as ever you were. This is just a passing phase."

"Comes of your mixing with the lower classes," said George Cartlet.

Gaunt shook his head in polite dissent.

"Of course you will," said Viola. "I know you."

If the dinner had been a rather awkward period for Gaunt, it had been, all unknown to the others, a still more desperate time for Lodden. How were they to suspect it? This fascinating colossus, pleasant-mannered, of facile speech, with a mind which made fortunes in a month, with the power to break men like caged butterflies – this man was for once entirely shaken. The attitude of Viola was a surprise to him. He had heard of the friendly relations between Gaunt and the Cartlets, and knew of the mild interest Viola took in his reporter, had humoured her in it, and had promised, good-naturedly enough, to advance the young man.

No thought had he of the depth of her feeling. Now to-night he realised somewhere within himself a tremble at his discovery that she was wrapped up in Gaunt. Her words alone would not have told him, but he had a quick discernment not possessed by George Cartlet, and the dinner-time had shown him with painful clearness that the thoughts of Viola were given to this young man in a degree which he had never known in her. He had caught her looking at Gaunt when the latter was eating, when he was listening, when he was vacant-eyed, as well as when he was speaking. And always was there a shining light in her face. Like a beacon was the motive which possessed her, and that motive he knew all the time was Majority Gaunt. His own previous blindness had a salt unwelcomeness. He could hardly call himself a fool, but he saw he had fallen into the pit of a lesser man in an egotistic lack of imagination.

What was her husband thinking about? The man must be mad. Then the futility of his own position came upon Lodden, and almost for the first time in his life a silly, passing despair was at his heart. He was helpless and he knew it. Through all he showed no sign. None of the effervescence of Gaunt was his, none of the surface passion of Viola, and his eyes were placid and his fingers untrembling as he dropped pleasant non-committal remarks to the confident but unskilful probing of his hostess.

Neither George Cartlet nor Viola knew how near they were to dynamite. The emotions of buried years had surged through Lodden for months about this woman, and he had essayed with great striving to secure her, to make her think of him, to obtain some return, slight though it might be, of his infatuation. How little emotion she had to spare was clear as daylight now, and his heart was black and heavy. His despondency was all the greater from the suspicion, growing into knowledge, that her limited concessions had their origin in the interests of Gaunt. He had calculated that his wealth and position and power would help to dazzle her, and, now he learned that the reporter whom he could flick into the street with his finger was his conqueror. While Lodden's mind was working furiously his words were smooth, his brow untroubled, and Viola seeing a shade of reserve in him put it down to the fact that one of his staff was present.

As for Gaunt, he too, squirmed inwardly. The blind and kindly intentions of Viola helped him by hardening his purpose; and the good-humoured assumption of Lodden that his protest of a few days ago was just a sentimental freak, soon to be forgotten, kept his heart beating angrily. Restraining himself during dinner, he was longing for the moment now near upon him when he might show this group how they had misjudged him, show Viola that his convictions were of depth, show Lodden that one of his reporters was a man to be reckoned with.

[12 January 1914]
Chapter XXIII – Continued.
Gaunt Breaks With Viola.

George Cartlet and Viola went on toying with the explosive material at hand before them quite innocently.

"I suppose," said George Cartlet, "it really doesn't matter about a man's private opinions if he does his duty to the paper."

"Within limits," said Lodden, "within limits."

"Yes, I think that too," said Gaunt, mildly.

Viola saw no danger-signal in his tone and she joined in.

"After all, a barrister has to present the best case he can for his client whether he believes in him or not."

"Something in that," said Lodden, "but, still, on a newspaper you must have at least the chiefs sincerely working for their acknowledged ends."

"You see," said Gaunt, turning to George Cartlet, explanatorily, "journalism is not always so shallow as it looks."

He said it quietly; the Cartlets glanced at him in surprise; Lodden, with dull and unconcerned eyes, took a cigar from the box which was at his elbow.

"My young men are frequently bubbling over like this," he said. "They wouldn't be good men if they weren't. I like it even when they don't agree with me."

For a moment Viola was disturbed in mind, and then she came to the conclusion that all was well, and said, "I told you so, Marjorie."

"Yes," said Gaunt, "I think I know Mr. Lodden's opinions very well."

"Oh, but you don't," she said, "because you have been so worried about doing what was right, and there was no need all the time."

"Those foolish scruples are finished with now."

"They're not altogether foolish."

"On the contrary," said Lodden, "they are very praiseworthy."

"They were useless," said Gaunt, speaking to the Cartlets. "The time for them has gone by."

"Oh, no, not altogether," said Viola, who was beginning to feel herself at sea.

Lodden's eyes narrowed benevolently, and he watched Gaunt through the smoke of his cigar.

"When a man's scruples fail him," said Gaunt, "the man himself has failed. For the time at least, he is a back number."

"You're driving at something," said George Cartlet, "out with it."

"No," said Gaunt, "merely stating history."

He had a terrible machine-like deliberateness about him.

"It seems we're just beginning to know Gaunt for the man he is," said Lodden. "There's more in him than meets the eye."

Viola clapped her hands in front of her face like a child. Despair struck Lodden's heart like a stone as he saw the action. Gaunt paid no attention to her.

"Sensitiveness is a weakness in a newspaper man," went on Lodden, "but it's also a great strength. We know that, don't we, Gaunt?"

"I have never permitted myself much sensitiveness."

Lodden smiled indulgently.

"But I'm going to privilege myself a little in the future," he went on, steadily.

"Whatever do you mean?" asked Viola.

"Well, the work is finished. The *Daily Light* has got home, and Raston Path has been broken up."

Lodden shrugged his shoulders and turned a look of amused inquiry on the reporter, while the Cartlets were forced into seriousness by Gaunt's tone. They knew not what was coming.

"I'm finished," said Gaunt.

"Finished?" exclaimed Viola.

"Yes?" said Lodden.

"Finished?" exclaimed Viola.

"I go out of office with Raston Path."

"But you're not a Home Secretary," protested Lodden.

"No," said Gaunt, in an almost respectful way, "but to-morrow you'll get formal notice that I'm leaving the *Daily Light*."

"Interesting, but hardly suitable for the dinner-table," said Lodden.

Gaunt did not allow himself to think how perfectly right was this remark, but went on steadily, undeflected.

"I've schemed to get the Government into trouble. I've worked hard, have told lies, have slandered people, have plotted. I've had at least something to do with the result."

"A good deal, I'm glad to say," put in Lodden approvingly.

"The *Daily Light*, a great paper, has set out by lies and trickery to break a great man." Gaunt's voice had grown warmer. "I told you, Mr. Lodden, I thought Raston Path –"

"Oh, Marjorie, Marjorie," cried Viola, "don't go on now. Whatever are you saying?"

"Too much sensitiveness, too much sensitiveness," said Lodden, shaking his head regretfully to the company.

"He doesn't mean it, Mr. Lodden, indeed he doesn't. I know all that's in his mind."

Viola pleading for Gaunt was more even than Lodden could stand.

"I don't know," he said, "I think he does. Feminine influence, I'm afraid, Gaunt."

"Not mine," said Viola, hastily.

"Oh, no, Mrs. Cartlet. People he has met when on this political business. Too sentimental, Gaunt, my boy. I'm sorry, yes, I'm sorry."

"Sentimental?" said Mrs. Carltet.

"Come, Gaunt, let's have the truth," went on Lodden.

White and angry, Gaunt said, "This is foolish."

"The little girl devoted to Raston Path, the one who came to his rescue, I suspect her, you know."

The odiousness of Lodden appalled Gaunt. He believed the existence of Nancy Kirk was unknown to him. From the tail of his eye he could see Viola was leaning forward listening, and he said nothing.

"Oh, you young men, you young men. Well, we can talk about business tomorrow."

He turned to his hostess. "Forgive this intrusion of office matters. Funny how it cropped up. My foolishness somehow or other, I'm sure. I'll try to behave better in future."

Viola hardly heard him, though she had her eyes on him blankly.

"Have another cigar, Lodden?" said George Cartlet.

Lodden helped himself, and said, "I'll have to be off now."

Cartlet pressed him to stay, but Lodden regretfully insisted, pleading an early engagement in the morning. He shook hands all round in his pleasantest way, remarking to Gaunt. "Don't let your feelings carry you away, my boy. Think things over quietly before you do anything."

No sign gave he of the disillusionment that had been his that night. He was still the genial capable man of affairs. Yet he walked out into the night with his hopes broken, with the sure and certain knowledge that Viola loved Majority Gaunt, with the consciousness that he had been a tool in her hands for the sake of the reporter. No resentment was in him, only depression. His iron will tried to assert itself even in the gloom and before he had reached the garden gate he had decided that his last visit to the Cartlets had been made, that they must be cut out of his acquaintance, that the chapter was closed. He did not know the trouble he had left behind in the Cartlets' house, and would not have been the least interested if he had.

Lodden was hardly departed before Viola said, "I want to have a talk with you about this thing, Marjorie."

"Have it out with him in the drawing room," said George Cartlet; "I'll have a smoke. I want to look through this motor catalogue. Let me know how you get on with her, Marjorie. She's in a nervy mood."

"All right," said Gaunt, and he and Viola went into the drawing-room. The door was no sooner shut than she turned on him like a tigress.

"Has this girl been in touch with you?"

"What do you mean?"

"Has she really influenced you?"

"Not in the way Lodden suggested."

"She has, I know she has from what he said. You've been deceiving me. Have you seen her often? When did you see her last? Tell me."

She stood before him with her eyes blazing and scarlet in her cheeks.

"I saw her a few days ago. I haven't seen her frequently, but –"

"Why have you not told me? You have concealed it – yes you have. Playing with me as you have played with her. Oh, I know. No wonder your political principles are changed. I'm told she dotes on Raston Path. Marjorie, you're a wicked, wicked man! You pretend to love me –"

"I've come to talk about that."

She looked at him in a sudden quick silence, for intuition overwhelmed her with the truth.

"You love her?" she said.

"I've behaved like a coward to you and a traitor to George."

"Cant," she said sharply – "leave out the cant."

"It's time the thing stopped. This young girl has no feeling for me beyond friendship –"

"Oh, you beast!" Viola's voice was raised and she was past caring who heard it. And then she checked herself and said: "Do you mean that you don't love me any more – you don't mean that? You cannot! I know you do – I feel it in myself."

"You have always fascinated me, and do still, but –"

"Well, then, what do you mean and what are you trying to tell me?"

"I've found out I'm a scoundrel."

"Do you love this other girl?"

"I do love her."

The blow should have been stunning, but Viola had known for the last minute or two that it was coming.

"I've given you all my heart!" she panted. "You've been everything to me. You've told me you loved me, and then – and then this. I would have given you all – all; thoughts, body and soul."

"Let me go, Viola," he said, and turned to the door.

"You schemer, you brute! Good God, you don't love me! I can't believe it. You came here, you took everything, you let me work for you."

Gaunt fidgeted miserably towards the door.

"You want to go," she said. "I suppose you want to go to her?"

"Yes!" he exclaimed desperately.

She sprang forward at him.

"Devil!" she cried, and struck him across the face with her hand, and as she did this the door opened and George Cartlet walked in.

"What's all the row about?" he asked. "What's the matter, Viola?"

"Matter?" she said. "Ask him."

Gaunt still had a white mark on his cheek where she had struck him. He shook his head in a negative way.

"What has he done?" asked George Cartlet.

"Done?" cried Viola. "He just told me he's in love with some girl."

George Cartlet knew the trouble now, but all he said was, "Well, what of that? What's the matter? Why did you strike him? Pull yourself together, Viola. What's wrong?"

She sank on to the sofa, where many a time before she had sat with Gaunt.

"Wrong?" she asked. "What is wrong is that I love that man," and she extended her finger to Gaunt. And for the first time George Cartlet realised how infinitely unimportant he was in the scheme of things.

"Good Lord, you mustn't say that!" He went up and put his arm round his wife, and she pushed him away sharply. Then she dropped her face into her hands.

Gaunt stole quietly out of the room.

Five minutes later Viola lifted her tear-streaked face, and spoke to herself as though George Cartlet was not by her side.

"I don't think I can stand it," she said. "It's just like one's husband dying."

[13 January 1914]

Chapter XXIV.
Gaunt Leaves The "Daily Light."

The group of perverse, unseen gods who pull the strings in minor human affairs and upset well-founded calculations gave no chance to Gaunt of posing as a noble person and did not permit his new moods to end up comfortably with angels' benedictions. He had to be content with his own feelings, as it is well that it can be said of him that, for the moment at any rate, he was satisfied with this. Assuredly he could get no comfort from outside. His mother and sisters with plenty of affection for him thought him for once unbusinesslike and blind; his colleagues in the office said it was a pity he had thrown away his chances in a fit of temper; Lodden speaking to Wansmuth called him a womanish fool; and Nancy Kirk, well, she did not know of his action, and if she had would probably have misunderstood it. Opinion was therefore against Gaunt, good, sound, friendly opinion for the most part. And Gaunt was a man sensitive to opinion. He had no rhinoceros hide. Over and above this was the material fact that a lump sum of £10 a week (which would have been increased to £20 very soon) was thrown away for an uncertain £3 or £4 a week. In these hard times if you indulge your feelings you must pay the price. Possibly Gaunt got a spark of cheer in the knowledge that he was at last on the side of Raston Path, and it was well, therefore, for him that he did not hear the Home Secretary's remarks about him. They will be related a little farther on, and they show how frail is the comfort of rectitude. Altogether Gaunt from an outside standpoint was in a bad way and he did not blink the knowledge. It is, however, but just to him to say that he surveyed the whole of his recent story, looked upon its outcome, and in the balance found himself glad – a fact which revealed his general course of action as wise, far wiser than his critics could understand. Release, that was the great and tremendous recompense he found in the face of the opinion of his friends, release.

The man who sometimes does an unworthy thing, but from habit or temperament swings back to right-dealing like a compass needle to the north, loses no necessary self-respect, and may, indeed, gain strength from his lapses. Different, indeed, is he who, with excellent motives and a pleasant understanding, lets indulgent habits enmesh him. His sickly happiness is hard to break through. Gaunt, shaken as he was and lonely, felt relieved from the miasma which had begun to encloud him. Not by the unaided actions of his conscience had he obtained freedom; adventitious pressure arising from sources he knew not of had bent him to the effort.

The *Daily Light* was to be left behind him, the entanglement with Viola Cartlet was over, and his deep affection for Nancy Kirk must be stripped from himself. There was something miserably agonising for him in the last thought, but it steadied him, helped him, gave him a manlier view-point. At least he was without vulgar self-seeking, and if no ennobling joy had been given him there remained the fact that when the stings of severance were over he would be in clear air once more.

As an outsider he began to see how almost unconsciously he had used his recent changes of opinion to get the good will of Nancy Kirk, saw, too, that in all her ignorance and youthfulness she was in some ways his superior. With her had gone gladsomeness and peace. Once in a way temptation would steal on him in the shape of a deep-seated hope that he was perhaps not altogether finished with her, and that in coming days she would think differently of him, and realise some appeal in her personality, but quickly these shadowy thoughts would be blown away by the memory of her attitude on the last meeting, its damping friendliness, its entire absence of the acuter sentiments. He laughed unpleasantly to himself as he recalled his self-flattery as to his knowledge of feminine instincts. The cold, but invigorating, east wind was sweeping through Gaunt's soul.

He turned himself to determinations for the future, his work for other papers, the one or two certainties in the way of weekly contributions, the speculative efforts in the form of stories – in all a widened field, far less regularly lucrative, but with unending possibilities. Already he had put in train his energies, had written two editors, seen two others, had mapped out a serial, arranged for some weekly articles. Difficulties would flock upon him, he knew that, and he carried no thought of big success. He bore himself erectly, his eye was more reflective, there was in his manner a quiet deference to events which surprised himself.

So far as politics were concerned, if he had not purged himself he had gone some way towards it, and found in his present affairs the proper outcome of commingled delinquencies. Gaunt had a vague thought that all the influences about him had been working to this end. A fastidiousness – squeamishness the reporters' room would have called it – made him enjoy this freedom of action, this release from doing things which might be right in the eyes of good Authoritarians, but which violated his new feelings. He could survey public forces as well as private forces with the calmness and judgment of a detached looker-on, and he had a sense of ease.

Spending the four weeks of his notice in non-committal work, Gaunt was untouched by the office preparation for the General Election, but he watched the fight in the country with keenness and found relaxation from personal matters in expectance of the result. Raston Path and his followers held great meetings and stirred strong partisanship in the great industrial districts, but it was doubtful whether the Reds made any headway in the country as a whole. The Opposition had the finest cry given them for a generation in this proposal to make "labourers rule the country," as they phrased it. Not all Path's contradictions, not all the explanations of Ministers, not all the persuasiveness of working men's organisations could get rid of the popular idea that "government by gentlemen" was to be finished with. Raston Path did great things in making his plan seem reasonable, showed that abolition of "government by gentlemen" would under one interpretation be a very good thing for the common people, yet as a matter of fact and accuracy he did not propose that any such change should be carried out.

Lodden thrust home without mercy. Scalding ridicule for the Bill through letterpress and cartoon was backed up by a steady blackening of the Government and the continuous presentation of Path as a braggart and windbag. Sometimes in the course of his speech Path would make a slip in a narration of some facts, and the *Daily Light* would be on the mistake with a shriek of joy. The error would be twisted, magnified, illustrated. "So this is the kind of man who wants power to revolutionise England. Why, he is not even correct in matters which require no investigation. What are his contentious statements worth?" Columns of extracts from old speeches in which he had personally attacked opponents were displayed in large type as evidence of his vulgarity, and his "financial dealings" in regard to Government contracts were splashed on the principal page in different form from day to day. Once, indeed, the *Daily Light* so far forgot a self-denying ordinance as to make an illusion to a closed topic. "We have shown up the public character of the Home Secretary, and the country now knows what kind of person will be put in power unless the Authoritarians are victorious. We have said much; more remains behind. Neither as a politician nor as a man is Mr. Raston Path to be trusted."

Gaunt went to Fore, the news editor, about the passage.

"This must be a reference to the Croxten affair," he said. "Can you tell me if that's what is meant?"

"Some of us think that he managed to deceive you on that occasion," said the evasive Fore.

"Oh, you do, do you? Does Lodden think so?"

"Don't know about that," replied Fore.

"So this is the next little game, is it?" said Gaunt. "I want to say this, and you had better convey it to the proper quarter; that if there is the slightest attempt to dirty Path's name in that way it will be so wicked that I shan't stand on ceremony, but shall go straight to the *Daily Measure* and tell them all my experiences, and of the dastardly dishonesty of the *Daily Light* after it had convinced itself of the man's innocence."

"That's strong language," said Fore.

"I'll make it stronger when I deal with the matter in the *Daily Measure*," said Gaunt.

Fore, as in duty bound, related Gaunt's protest at the editorial conference in the evening, and Lodden was decisive on it.

"The man's a danger," he said. "He must go at once. Pay him what money is due for the rest of his notice and send him off to-day. Hear that, Fore?"

"Very well," said Fore.

So Gaunt at six o'clock that evening shook the dust of the *Daily Light* building from his boots and stepped out into the street a free man. His shackles were gone now, and he took his mother to the theatre that evening and felt happy in a subdued way. Lucky for him he did not know what comments on himself had been made at Whitehall earlier in the day by Raston Path, or he would certainly have been without rest or peace.

[14 January 1914]

    Chapter XXIV – Continued.
    The General Election.

"Between ourselves, Path," said Sir Robert Furley, the chief agent, "I don't think we shall pull it off."

"Oh, I don't know. There's big opposition, but we've got the bulk of the people with us."

The chief agent shook his head. "Well-meaning and far-seeing people in politics do not recognise that the majority of electors, whether they are well-meaning or not, are by no means far-seeing. Is that heresy? Can't be helped. It's a fact. People instinctively resist changes in their lives, even when they are convinced that the changes will be beneficial. It's the same with the country as a whole. You can persuade them, you can convince them, and then they will go and vote against you, because instinct and prejudice ruled them at the last moment."

"One has to be a pessimist to be an effective election agent of a party."

Sir Robert Furley smiled.

"No, only I have no room for illusion in my work."

"Probably we shall come out of it better than you think," said Path.

The agent shrugged his shoulders. "Reports from the country are not promising and you know what London will be like. Of course, the papers have been able to make the running against us with a Bill like this."

"Perfectly outrageous, some of them. The *Daily Light* is beyond words."

"They're unscrupulous, but they're clever," said Sir Robert.

"They've got a chap named Gaunt who's been doing most of it in the *Light*."

"But Lodden is the evil angel."

"Oh, yes, but Gaunt is a clever, daring young blackguard who has been working much of it."

"I've come across him once or twice. Did you see the *Light* this morning?"

"Yes, same old clap-trap."

"You don't mind what they say about you."

"Oh, that's not it. The point is that, knowing the truth about Mrs Croxten as they do, they deliberately in the leading article this morning bring up the old scandal."

"I shouldn't have thought even that the *Daily Light* would have gone so far as that."

"Incredible, it really is. I am perfectly certain that this man Gaunt did it. Lodden is at least a big man."

"Don't trouble. No one will pay heed to it after the election."

"I don't know about that, Furley. I've a good mind to stop it. If they give me a chance for a libel action I shall take it."

"Better still – get the story republished in the *Daily Measure*."

"Not a bad idea. Perhaps I'll have a go at it when we get through with this fight."

Nancy Kirk heard some of this conversation, but it was not to be expected of her that she should interfere, that she should have courage to say a word when these two important men were talking. Since the affair at Finsbury Park, Raston Path had always exchanged a friendly word with her on coming into the Progressive office, and when the facts of her intervention were known she had been warmly commended by Sir Robert Furley. Perhaps the increase in her weekly salary which followed was in some way connected with all that happened. It is quite certain that the increased confidence and trust which the chief agent extended to her followed directly on the announcement by Path of her initiative and courage. She was now part of the organisation, so to speak. At the same time she retained an elemental shyness, and she certainly was not in a position to break in upon a conversation between the chief agent and the Home Secretary.

Her friendly associations with Gaunt gave a sting to the misconceptions of Path. What crossed her mind was that she might subsequently be able to tell Gaunt about this, and let him find out means to put Raston Path right in his judgment. She did not reckon, however, with the line of thought which had been set up in Sir Robert Furley's mind, and she found an unexpected opportunity in comment after Path had left.

"Let's see. You spoilt this man Gaunt's game up at Finsbury Park, didn't you? Have you heard anything about him lately?"

"Yes, I saw him a week or two ago. I saw him just before the division on the Bill in the House."

"Trying to get something from you, was he?"

"Oh, no, quite the opposite."

"Opposite? What do you mean? Did he come to tell you something, or were you trying to get something out of him?"

Then with some doubts and many hesitations, Nancy Kirk told Sir Robert Furley the story of Gaunt's visit to her, what he had proposed, and how she had dissuaded him. Perhaps Nancy would not have had the courage for this but for the injustice which had been done to Gaunt in the conversation she had just heard. She had to force herself to get through the story. She need not have feared, for Sir Robert Furley was a hard man only on the surface. He looked at her thoughtfully over his eyeglasses for a second after she had finished, and then he said "You're a little brick!"

"I didn't like to hear Mr. Gaunt blamed," stammered Nancy.

"Oh, that won't hurt him," said Sir Robert. "I dare say he deserved it for other things. Still, he ought not to be kicked just now, if only for the sake of his attempt to do the right thing."

"I know – I think he would be glad if Mr. Path knew the truth."

"I'll tell Path when I see him," said Sir Robert. He turned to the papers on his desk and said; "Well, now, we must get on with some work. There's not too much time to spare for sentiment when you are the chief agent of a big political party."

The first results of the elections were pretty evenly balanced, and not till after three or four days' polling[80] did signs of the Authoritarian wave become manifest. There could be no doubt about it then. Authoritarian victories were creeping in from the Midlands, from the West, even from the North. The prophecies of Furley looked like being justified, and by the time the election was three-parts over it could be said with some certainty that the Authoritarians in the new House of Commons would have a majority of 50 or 60 members, and it was at this point there came one of those freakish strokes of fate which blot out the careful devisings of long sighted men. The Prime Minister, who had been speaking at intervals throughout the campaign, was the object of special attention from a band of militant suffragettes, who interrupted his speeches, sought to waylay him on his travels, and generally to do mosquito work[81] wherever an opportunity occurred.

It was in a meeting at Cambridge that one of these ladies managed to alter the course of the General Election. Turbulence had marked a series of questions to the Prime Minister with regard to his inaction on women's suffrage, and his grandiose evasions cheered by the audience in general had set the women in the back of the hall in a ferment. One of them, a middle-aged, clever, angular woman was almost frenzied. There was a good deal of noise and disturbance, and in the midst of it she was heard declaring she was ready to die for the cause. She was standing on a chair, and those near her saw that she had taken from the recesses of her dress a small revolver. Events afterwards showed that she had no intention of hurting anyone, and certainly had no desire to do the Prime Minister a serious injury. But she was almost beside herself in her endeavour to make a sensation, to show that she and her friends were in earnest and to make evident the real rage at the non-committal skill of the government, and the declared hostility to their movement by the Prime Minister. She waved the revolver about screaming out some hysterical words. Flourishing wildly her weapon, she endeavoured to direct it above the people assembled on the platform and to fire the bullet over their heads. In the exciting second or two during which she was seen with the pistol in her hand, there was the hot belief that she intended to shoot someone on the platform, and a very natural belief it was. When she pointed it vaguely towards the front of the hall no one who saw her doubted that she intended to hit the Prime Minister.

The whole thing was over in about ten seconds, and though people were struggling towards her to pull her down she had achieved her purpose and discharged the revolver before she was dislodged. The amazing thing was that she did exactly what people thought she was intending to do, and, mistaken as they were in her purpose, ninety-nine people out of a hundred of them could never doubt that she came to the meeting with the deliberate intent to fire on the Prime Minister. The bullet struck him just below the shoulder, and he stood for a moment with his hand on the table at which he was speaking, as though trying to understand what had happened, and then his knees became shaky and he half-turned to the chairman on his left and eventually collapsed in a heap.

The woman was with difficulty secured from the clutches of the crowd by a strong force of police, and it was found that she had herself narrowly escaped death, one of her arms being broken, her face battered, and serious injuries inflicted on her back. In the hospital, indeed, it was a race between the two invalids, and, as a matter of fact, both eventually recovered about the same time.

That shot which brought down the Prime Minister at Cambridge had an astounding effect on the elections. There is in the British people an elemental quality which for the want of a better name might be called respectful fair play, a quality which transcends political feeling, and gives the nation a part of its individuality. That instinct was violated by the attack on the Prime Minister. The badgering to which he had been subjected for weeks, although little was said about it, had been looked upon by all sides as derogatory to the dignity of the head of the State. Even the Authoritarians, perhaps with a side-glance at what would be their lot when they came into office, condemned it vigorously. Now came the disaster at Cambridge, which shocked all the moderate opinioned people of the country, and, indeed, to be truthful, roused resentment and horror among a good many of those who ranked themselves as the Prime Ministers opponents. Particularly strong was this feeling among Parliamentarians, who, whatever their differences on other points, knew him to be a straightforward English gentleman of dignity who worthily upheld the position of chief adviser of the King before the other nations of the world.

The effect on the polls was immediate. A cynical Red said that nothing better could possibly have happened for the cause. In an unreasoning way people went to the polling stations to record their votes not so much for the Bill of Raston Path, or against it, as to show their indignation at the way the foremost statesman of the country had been struck down. The poor Authoritarians were in despair. They made haste to rectify the impression against themselves, and shouted loud from the platforms their horror at what had occurred and their sympathy for the injured leader. It was no good, and, indeed, the chief organisers knew it to be no good. The voting was now with the Progressives. The Cambridge outrage had swung popular sympathy completely round. Only the impregnable strongholds of the Authoritarians were held by the opponents of Raston Path, and victories for the Reds came tumbling in in dozens. Red and Progressive majorities were increased, Authoritarian majorities were swept away, and in three or four days the advantages gained by the Authoritarians were wiped out. The close of the General Election left the Reds and Progressives with a new majority of 35.[82]

The Progressive leader was in bed with his injury, and thus it came about that the King sent for Raston Path, and asked him to form a Ministry. The wheel had gone the full circle. The revolutionist was in power. Raston Path proceeded with his work and restored most of his recent colleagues to their old places. The Authoritarian journals, while accepting the fact that a Progressive Ministry was in power again, with a Red as its chief, argued, and with much reasonableness, that the country had not endorsed the Red programme, and that it would be impossible, in view of the elections as a whole, for Raston Path to proceed with the passing into law of his now famous Bill. They could not perceive the political upheaval of six months ahead, due to causes hardly regarded at the moment; could not foresee that another election would be upon the people before the year was out. Meanwhile Raston Path yielded nothing, admitted nothing, but proceeded with his task of building up the Ministry afresh with the deliberate intention of putting through his proposals.

Abstract political matters were for the moment in the background, owing first to the attack on the Prime Minister and the chance that even now he might not recover from his wound, and, secondly, to the wonderful rise of Raston Path and the drama which had set him at the head of the Empire. The personality of the man touched all minds. Let us see what the *Daily Light* had to say in its first leading article on the day after the King had summoned Raston Path to his counsels and asked him to become Prime Minister: –

"Through a series of occurrences which we need not now enter into, the Government of the country has again been given over to the Progressives, and Mr. Raston Path, who has already achieved prominence, has been entrusted by the Sovereign of these islands with the tremendous responsibility of presiding over the Government. We have steadily fought the party which is again in power, and we have opposed the public work of Mr. Raston Path in many directions. It will probably be our duty to do so again. At this hour, however, in common with our political opponents, we desire to congratulate a distinguished man on reaching the highest post the British Empire has to offer. That he will worthily uphold the dignity and traditions of his great office we have no doubt. Mr. Path, from whose general political conclusions we differ entirely, is a man of great qualities, and has fought his way to the front, proved himself a leader, and may safely be trusted with the immense responsibility thrown upon him. He is now, in the eyes of the world, the representative of the British nation, and in such a position we shall consistently support him in so far as his actions do not cut across national interests. It is the proud boast of Britain that political differences do not prevent the recognition of great qualities on the part of opponents.

"We shall never be accused of having fought the present Prime Minister unworthily. Strong as has been our comment on his politics, we have carefully avoided any personal references. We may, without mock modesty, look with satisfaction upon our attitude, and our careful avoidance of anything that might reasonably be called personal abuse. In this connection it gives us much pleasure to state that we are able to dispel once for all the suspicions current some time ago about the past life of Mr. Raston Path. A romance in his life was hinted at. We have been to some trouble to ascertain the facts, and that episode reflects nothing but credit upon the distinguished statesman whom the Sovereign yesterday honoured. In our news columns will be found a full narrative of the touching story, and no person, be he Progressive, Red, or Authoritarian, but will feel regret that Mr. Path has suffered anything from calumny in respect of an episode which shows him up as a generous man softened by the memory of an incident touched by pathos and tragedy."

[15 January 1914]

Chapter XXV.
Gaunt and Nancy Kirk.

One might suppose that in the course of time Gaunt would have made it his business to see Nancy Kirk again – this for a certain subtle, regretful pleasure, a delicate self-indulgence – for sentiment was deeply cored in Gaunt. This does not mean that he had hope. One of the lessons he had learnt in dealing with women was that a man under a rebuff or suffering from a woman's indifference made his case no better by importunity. He would not have pestered Nancy Kirk for worlds; if she did not care about him instinctively, nothing he could say would change her. A woman's passion cannot be engendered by devoutness or tender care. He indulged himself so far as to send her the following letter: –

> Dear Miss Kirk, – I know you will forgive me for my abruptness in running off on the night I saw you, for I was disturbed, and your advice came to me as a great surprise. I realise now that you were right. This is to say I have left the service of Mr. Lodden. I carried through my duties and did what I could to help the political work on the *Daily Light* up to the point which led to the overthrow of the Government. After that I resigned. I am now away from the office altogether. Literary work will engage me for the present. I look forward to having a chance of another talk with you some time in the future. Meanwhile, may I wish you all kinds of luck and happiness – Yours very sincerely, MAJORITY GAUNT

That was a very straight, right kind of letter, and Gaunt sent it as a kind of good-bye to satisfy himself and without any idea that it would come as a surprise or have any special effect on Nancy Kirk. In actual fact it brought her amazement, pleased amazement. His frank relinquishment of hope with regard to her, together with his tribute to her advice, and finally his severance from the *Daily Light*, flooded her with a new peaceable assurance in him. The outer dross was coming away – though for long she had had glimpses of the real gold. On the way to the office next morning it was with a little shock that she found herself surmising by what means it would be possible to meet Gaunt again. She could not keep her mind on her work during the day. Will it be believed when I say that in a quiet quarter of an hour after tea she wrote the following not to Gaunt: –

> Dear Mr. Gaunt, – I was glad to get your letter. Won't you come and see me some time soon? – Yours sincerely,
> NANCY KIRK

Gaunt, though without delusions on the message, was happy to get it, and in the evening he went round to Lant-street.

Nancy was smiling and natural, but Mrs. Kirk and Nellie were a little restrained now that he had left the *Daily Light*.

"I've got two upper circle tickets for the St. James's Theatre," he said.

"Do you want to go to the theatre?"

"Not in the least. But I thought I had better equip myself in case you did, that was all."

There was a stoppage of the conversation for a few seconds.

"I wonder if your mother and Nellie would care to go?"

"Rather," said Nellie; "wouldn't you, mother?"

Mrs. Kirk agreed, as she did to most things that Nellie suggested.

"Then we'll have a walk," said Gaunt.

"Shall it be politics or journalism?" said Nancy, smiling as she put on her coat.

Gaunt looked at her and his heart throbbed. "Neither," he said.

Down in the street they discussed what they should do and they decided to take a tramcar down to the new art gallery that had just been opened near Camberwell-green.[83] "Quiet there," he said. "We can find a seat in one of the small rooms, and we shan't be disturbed for an hour if we want to talk so long."

A different girl was Nancy on the journey down from the one whom Gaunt had known before, for she chatted light-heartedly on many things, and he, curiously enough, had difficulty in answering her.

"You're silent to-night," she said, as they alighted.

He smiled and said, "Isn't it a relief? Usually I do all the talking."

She did not answer this, and they were in the roomful of pictures before the next exchange occurred. Some discerning remarks on one or two of the pictures came from her, but he paid no heed.

"Let's go over into the small water-colour room," he said. "There's a seat in the middle of it and we can sit and pretend to look at the pictures while we talk, and no one will overhear us."

"Is there much to say?" she asked.

He put her in her place on the seat before he answered her, and then he said, "Not very much, but what there is is important."

She raised her eyebrows, and then she sat there with her hands on her lap and one of her gloves removed. Gaunt found his words awkward and unkempt. He blundered on for a few seconds. She did not face him, but looked reflectively straight ahead of her at a picture opposite.

"You've had a good deal to do with my life since I met you, more than you know about. I want to tell you of myself before I go away."

"Yes, I am glad," she said.

"When I came to Lant-street three weeks ago I was upset by what happened, and afterwards I began to be afraid I shouldn't see you again. I thought I would like to, and that's what really made me write to you."

Nancy kept a brave, untroubled, pleasant face, and her eyes now were sympathetic, for she knew what was coming because Gaunt was speaking with gaps between his words and he could not hide his agitation.

"May I speak about myself?"

"Yes," she said simply.

"There can't be any sort of misunderstanding. You know the truth and I know the truth. I have come to see you to-night to tell you that I love you, knowing all the time you don't love me."

He had a hard job to get the words out, and his difficulty was increased by the agitation in her face. The sorrow for him in her gentle heart made him desolate.

"Before we separated altogether I thought I would like to make one or two things clear to you. I can't bear to drop out – just the same kind of fellow you've always known."

Nancy slowly turned her eyes on him with understanding, for she was feeling this interview more than Gaunt knew.

"I'm just going to tell you plain out my feelings. I want to say this – oh, I know I've got nothing to gain by it – that you have been the best and most potent influence that has touched me since I've been a grown-up man. I couldn't go away without telling you that. Afterwards I shall be happier because I've told you."

Nancy half-nodded her head to show she felt all he said.

"Once I thought I'd got over your first dislike of me, but I realised the night you upset my plans that you couldn't go very far with me. I knew what I wanted was out of the question. Well, it's all over now. I know you can't love me, but I should be very miserable if you took away some wrong impressions about me.

"I know it's no compliment to be loved by a chap like me. Oh, I know that, Miss Kirk. But don't go and think too badly of me. I'm not going to whitewash myself, don't be afraid. I'm going to try to tell you the truth to-night. The day we first met in the Progressive office I felt your distrust of me – yes, I did. You were perfectly right. You knew me at once. I've been a pretty bad sort of fellow so far as women are concerned ... Flirted, well, yes, I've flirted – if that word is sufficient. It will serve. For a good many years I've been a man who played about with women.

"Sometimes women have frivolled with me, been just as bad as I have; perhaps worse. But on the whole I've been the one responsible. Even an ordinary chap can make a woman fond of him if he sets out on the job. I mean not every woman, but a woman now and again. I have been as rotten as anybody could be. That's all. Beginning to place me now, Miss Kirk, I suppose?

"Oh, I wasn't an absolute villain – haven't got the fibre for that. And I have frequently had at the back of my head that some day among these experiences I would find a woman I would give everything to marry. Foolishly enough, I thought that when I found her she would be quite willing to marry me.

"I'd a funny kind of feeling when I saw you first at the Progressive office up at Westminster. I couldn't sort it out exactly. There was freshness and newness about you, something different – I can't express it. It's almost weird when I look back. It's wonderful, though. I suppose you thought I lit up at contact with a pretty girl, and that's want made you standoffish. Perhaps I did. Very likely I did it mechanically. I remember I tried to get you to come out to tea. I dare say this seems silly piffle to you. I can't help it.

"I went home that night feeling I had made a discovery in you, a kind of spiritual discovery which I had been seeking for years amid a mass of unspiritual things. There was a message about you which went straight to all that was best in me. It reached me afterwards every time I met you; it reaches me now. I don't know what it is, and I don't suppose I ever shall. It isn't your hair or eyes, or speech, or your walk, or your manner, nor in any one thing of you; but there it is, and every part of you has some portion of it. When I see someone who looks rather like you in the street from a distance I get a funny little thrilly feeling in my throat. Well, that's the beginning. I dare say you thought me a pretty awful person that first day."

Gaunt stopped for a moment, and Nancy raised her eyes to his and said gently, "I would like to hear all that you have to say, and then I'll tell you what I think. I do hope you won't be hurt then."

"I trust you will believe this of me, Miss Kirk, that amid all my sins I never had one unworthy thought of you. Nor for one moment did I cease to extol you in spirit. You were always a beacon of goodness to me in the midst of sordid things and people, and selfish, vulgar thoughts of my own. It would have been impossible to hold for a single moment the idea of badinage with you, or joking conversation or flirtation. You can believe it or not of a man like me, but it's perfectly true that I should have shuddered at the idea. So far as I was concerned you were in the clouds. I knew you were instinctively against me, and knew how right you were too. It just so happens that you need not have had any fear of me, but your instinct was right all the same. Well, I am nearly at an end now. Steadily you have grown more wonderful. I realise now that you are something outside and beyond my life. It will always make me happy, though, to think that I came to you and you told me what you thought of things – I mean about this political business. The one little evidence I can bring of my sincerity is that I followed your advice."

Nancy nodded her head. "Yes, you did," she said.

"You hadn't got the least idea of it, but you made me feel differently about a lot of things. I hated you should know I told lies and used trickery in my work. Queer, wasn't it? Then everything about you was kind of illuminated. When I saw you walking along the pavement it lifted me up and made me feel for the moment just in heaven. I dare say I seem a fool. Any day that I was going to meet you I woke in the morning trying to get my senses together as to why I felt so happy. When I got to know you better and found out about your life, I saw what a small, miserable outlook mine was. It's easy to run oneself down, but you've got to feel as I have felt about you and to have known your life and to have talked to you in order to understand how selfish and narrow I have seemed to myself. I think Raston Path owes you some part of his new convert."

"Always while I live," said Gaunt, "your memory will be an influence with me, and I dare say there will be times when I shall ask myself if you would like this or that to be done before I fix things up. I'm afraid I am not very religious, or anything of that kind, Miss Kirk, but I know if there is a heaven the greatest gift it has given me, or could ever give me, is the acquaintance I had with you. I have seen all kinds of things differently. I dare say I shall be bad again, but whenever you come back to my mind there will be a good influence at work."

Gaunt pulled himself up with a touch of bitterness. "Oh, aye, you see I'm becoming quite a saint."

Pain came into Nancy's eyes, and he flinched under it.

"Oh, I'll be no better or worse than the majority of men," he said, " but I can see my way ahead so far as one side of life is concerned. I mean this business about politics and work, and I shan't deviate there. You don't want me to go into the whole business." He smiled a little. "I think you have more to do with my change of feeling than you'll ever know. There's one other thing. I told you just now I was a woman hunter, and all that, but so far as the moment is concerned I wouldn't have felt clean enough to have come and talked to you if I hadn't cut that out of my life, at least for the time being. I have buried some days about which you know nothing."

"Viola Cartlet," said Nancy, looking at him straight. He nodded. She paused for a little.

[16 January 1914]

Chapter XXV – Continued.
Capitulation.

"Now hear me for a moment," she said; "when I saw you at the Progressive office that day, I had for the fraction of a second some revelation about you which was very pleasing, and which has come back to me and remains with me now. But at that time, after the first glimpse, I saw you as a pleasant, smooth-tongued young man, with an eye for a pretty girl. I think I saw some of the things in you which you have talked about now. Is that harsh? Well, you want me to speak the truth, don't you? I mistrusted you, I did very much; but I couldn't get you out of my mind. I grew to distrust you still more when I found I couldn't get you out of my mind."

"Couldn't you?" said Gaunt, with wide-open eyes.

"I soon knew in my heart," said Nancy, with soft, unwavering directness, "that you were the most remarkable man I should ever meet in all my life." She looked at him still softly, but with confidence, for she knew she had reached a curious moment.

"I have heard what you have said," she went on, "and now it's my turn to make a confession." Gaunt was almost breathless. He certainly could have found no words to speak. He remembered afterwards that he could hear his own heart beating, something which had never happened to him before.

"I know how seriously I ought to take your sins about women. I dare say it's wicked of me, but I don't care. What does it matter? Perhaps I'm going into misery." She stumbled with her words.

Gaunt had taken her hand from her lap, and was holding it tremblingly in both of his. They had both an excitement in which it was hard for both of them to speak coherently. One or two casual visitors to the picture gallery gazed at them with a moment's curiosity and passed on uninterested in the sight of a couple of lovers.

"You don't mean – you can't mean –"

"Oh, I do, I do," she said, with a moan of relief.

Gaunt bent forward, shaking with excitement. He took both her hands in his. She made a great effort and looked him straight in the face.

"You want me –"

"What you –"

He had drawn her to him and her head was on his shoulder.

"If you want me," she repeated, softly, "I will come."

"Oh, Nan, Nan," he said, and held her to him. She put her upturned face to his. Tremblingly he kissed her soft lips.

Presently Gaunt said, "You will really marry me, Nan?"

Her eyes were on his, and she replied very seriously, "Yes."

"Will you marry me soon?"

"To-morrow, if you want me."

* * *

Archibald Lodden was surprisingly interested when he heard a few days later from Wansmuth in conversation that Gaunt was engaged to be married almost immediately to Nancy Kirk. "That's good," he said.

"Tried to play us a dirty trick," said Wansmuth.

"Not at all, not at all," said Lodden. "He had courage. He believed things. You may say he's a fool, but perhaps he isn't so much of a fool as you are, or I am. Don't you make any mistake about Gaunt. Of course, we had to turn him down. He'll do something yet, that man."

"Oh, I don't know," said Wansmuth, "he's a fool to marry when he's out of a job."

"Not he," said Lodden, "he's doing exactly the right thing. I suppose he's got no money, though."

"Shouldn't think so," said Wansmuth.

Lodden touched the bell on the table and his secretary came in.

"Write me out a cheque for £100 for Gaunt," he said, and then he drew a sheet of his private notepaper towards him and scribbled:

> Dear Gaunt, – Enclosed please find a little wedding gift. With all good wishes for much happiness – Yours, A. Lodden.

Though Lodden did not go to the quiet little wedding at St. James's Church, Beckenham, Raston Path did, and Sir Robert Furley as well.

Gaunt and Nancy travelled down at once to a bungalow at Crowborough[84] where he was at work. In the train Nancy said to him:

"I didn't think it was possible to be so happy and live."

"I wonder if I shall keep you happy?"

"Don't fear," she said. Perhaps she had a better knowledge of herself and him than he had.

It only remains to be said that Viola Cartlet scoffed about Gaunt's marriage, and referred to his wife as "that little servant maid." Nevertheless, Viola had been hard put to to keep her composure though all the hours of the wedding day. As the weeks went by the blow did not seem so heavy, and within six months her husband was chaffing her about her new admirers. Once her sister Hilda mentioned Gaunt.

"Not a bad fellow," said Viola, "but rather conceited and bound up in himself. Every thought of his life was comprised for him in politics and journalism. He was rather interesting for a time. I'm glad he's gone now, though."

But if you could have got down to the bottom of a locked drawer in her room you would have found an old tennis jacket belonging to Gaunt, a pair of gloves, and a photograph. She secretly took them out and looked at them every time his birthday came round, and there were always tears in her eyes.

'Pat', 'Living Retired. An Unconscious Tragedy' (1914)

"Hello Sam, thar't dressed up an' gon' eawt i' good time. Wheer as't bin'; or 'appen thar't nobbut gooin'?"

"Nay, Dick, owd lad, aw'm just coming whoam fro a trip ta Southport."

"Ta Southport? Wod's taen thee to Southport? I su'd ha' thowt as Blackpoo' wur moor i' thy line."[1]

"Weel, tha sees. Aw've bin payin' a visit to owd Jem Buckley; he's livin retire theer."

"Ay, aw heer'd as he'd med brass enoof, an' hed gon' a-livin' retire, but aw didna' know as he'd gon' ta Southport."

"Ay, but he hes, an' a grond place e's getten; tha never see'd such a foine stack o' furniture as he's bought i' o' thy puff."[2]

"Some foak hes a' th' luck i' this warld."

"Nay, nay, tha 'noas Jem wur olez a sticker at wark. He's addled o' he's geeten.'

"Weel, thee an' me's never bin 'slackers,' hev we, Sam?"

"Noa, Dick, aw connot say as we hev; but we've boath on us taen a bit o' pleasure on th' road, like. We've getten a 'obby apiece; tha likes mekkin' fishin-rods, an aw liken a bit o' gardenin'."

"Not th' on'y bit o' owd Adam i' thee, eh, Sam?"

"Neaw, then, noan of they owd buck; tha 'noas wot foak s'ud do as live i' glass heauses."

"Weel, wot abeawt Jem Buckly an' thi trip?"

"Weel, Dick, we con't ston' heer a' th' day stoppin' th' traffic; which way ar'ta gooin', an' aw'll tak' thee agate."[3]

"O' reet, come on an' let's heer thi tale."

"Weel, Jem met me at th' station an' he did seem some fain ta see me; aw'd never thowt as he's set sich store o' me afore."

"'Appen he's getten sick o' th' quality a' ready, an wur fain ta see a common chap ageon."

"Aw'll tell the w'ot, Dick, some o' these days summat 'll o'ertek thee."

"Iv it's summat good aw durn't care a pot dog!"

"Tha'll be piked up i' little bits, blown oop wi' tho own wit."

"Ger on wi thi tale; aw owt ta 'noa as it's noa use sparrin' wi' th' loikes o' thee."

"Weel, here goas fur another stert. After we'd had a bit o' a refresher, Jem said as we'd hev a torn on th' front while his missus med th' dinner; he'd med me promise as aw'd stop while this mornin' soas we could hev a good crack at neet –."[4]

"Aw thowt as they's 'appen keep a sarvant lass as they're livin' retire, Sam?"

"Tha'rt wos nor a Belle View parrot,[5] Dick, blest if tha're not – stickin thi motty in everythin'."

"Aw on'y wanted ta noa!"

"Weel, aw mud as weel tell thi furst as last and stop thi gab. They did hev a sarvant at furst, but Jem's missus sacked her i' good time – said as ther' worn't wark for two on 'em an' hoo hedn't coom to Southport ta sit wi' her honds i' th' front on her."

"Aw could name some women as 'ud be glad o' th' chonce."

"Ay 'appen tha could an when they'n hed a spell o' doin' nowt they'd be fain ta start ageon, loike Jem's missis. Aw tell thee, Dick, wark's as nat'ral as natur', and we're a' on us better fur doin' a bit o' summat, if it's nobbut ta keep us eawt o' mischief."

"By gum, Sam, tha'll finish thy days i' th' pulpit, way as tha'rt going on."

"There's wos places nor pulpits, but theer's some folk as aw 'noa as loikes ta empty a barrel, an' then ston on th' top on it ta do they're spewtin'."

"Snuffed ageon! Ger on abeawt Jem."

"Wheer wur aw? Oh, after we'd hed a stroll we went in to th' dinner. Mrs. Buckley wur fair in her glory, up to th' eyes cookin' an bustlin' abeawt th' kitchen. Hoo said as hoo wur fain ta see me – 'appen aw'd stor Jem oop a bit, as he scroped abeawt like an owd rooster as couldn'd find a shelter fro' th' rain."

"Weel, aw never!"

"After we'd hed a rompin' dinner, Jem showed me reawn'd th' gardin. Neaw aw' 'nowed as Jem wur no moor than a hen gard'ner –."

"A hen gard'ner, Sam?"

"Ay – seeds put i' greawnd one day, and' scrat oop th' next."

"That's a cobbed[6] 'un!"

"Aw axed Jem abeawt his gardin, and he said as he paid a mon fur lookin' after it. 'An' w'ot does tha do?' aw ses. An' he looked o'reawn'd an then he whisper't loike, 'Nowt.' 'An Sam,' he ses, 'aw'm dom-weel sick o' mi job. Aw'm sick o' trailin abeawt an crackin on as aw loike it. Mon, aw'm noan gradely tired when aw go to mi bed, same as aw use bein'."

"'Why doe'na tak th' missis eawt?' aw ses. 'Th' missis,' he says, 'is olez too busy since hoo sacked th' lass; hoo tells me to ger eawt o' th' road an' hev a nice walk while th' dinner's ready. Hoo's as merry as a grig[7] cleanin' an dustin' reawms as we never use, an bakin' an' sich loike."

"'But, Jem, con tha do nowt?' aw ses, fur, Dick, th' look i' his een went fair through me; it wur loike a little choilt looks as getten lost, an' doesn't 'noe w'eer it lives.

"'Noa, Sam,' he ses, 'tha sees aw never had a 'obby o' noa sort; aw wur olez keen on th' brass, olez hed a fancy for carpin'. Tha noas aw never hed a pint wi noan on ye, never spent a tanner on a footba' match, nor noa jollification o' noa sort –'

"'But,' aw chips in, 'tha'z getten w'ot tha wanted – lots o' brass, an' tha'rt livin' retire.'

"'Ay, Sam,' he ses, 'an' aw wish to goodness as aw'd never done it. But come lad, aw mun show thee th' inside or o' th' fat u'll be in th' fire wi' th' missis.'

"Weel, Dick, he took me i'th' parlour – 'drorin-reawm' he co'd it. My! But it wur foine! Theer wur a Brussills carpet on th' floor, an' on th' top o' that wur w'ot he co'd a crumb cloth, tho' aw'll wager a mouse 'ud ha ta starve i' theer. He lifted one corner o' th' crumb-cloth to show me th' carpet. On th' top o' th' cloth wur a strip o' oilcloth reachin' fro' th' fire-place ta da dur, ta tread on. On th' chimbley-piece wur a great pair o' lusters, them wi' glass danglers; these hed white covers on. Jem he ta tek one off ta show me; an it wur th' same wi' every blessed thing, grond fallals an' o' covered oop. An' aw wondered loike who'd wear 'em eawt when owd Jem wur gone; fur, betwixt thee an' me, Dick, at rate as he's gooin', ther's nowt laft fur him ta do but dee!"

'Poor owd Jem! An ta think as aw begrudged him!"

"Ay, lad, aw see nowt i't' front o' me but scrattin' t' th' finish, but aw wodn't change shops wi' Jem Buckley. Foak as drops one job s'ud hev another ready ta pick oop wi' w'en they gan'ower rubbin' they stert a rustin', an' rust hes a way o' eatin' in. So long, Dick; aw'm leavin' tha heer. Thee an' me hes no need ta be frit; we're noan shapin' fur livin' retire."

W. O. Pitt, 'The Last Dinner' (1914)

"More steak, Bill?"

"Thanks, it's prime. I don't suppose I'll get steak like that where I'm going.'

"Where *are* yer going, Bill?"

"Dunno, Lill. If you're set on finding out, you arst old K. He's sure to tell yer, if yer put it to him straight."

"I believe you'd have your joke if the house was burning down."

"Well, I ain't going to get downhearted to please ole Kaiser Bill,[1] anyhow."

"If it was only him an' his sort I wouldn't mind. Oh, Bill, do you remember that Mr. Holz that was over here with the German unions? I was only looking this morning at the photo he gave us; him an' his pretty wife and the sweet, little, fair-headed girl, Gretchen. It's him an' the like of him you're fighting."

"Too late to think of that now, old girl. Hope I'll shake hands with him when it's all over. But it's fighting time now."

"But why must it be? If we women had our way –"

"Yes, if women had your way. Remember the strike at the works last year? Why, you an' your mother wanted me to 'blackleg,' an' said I had nothing to get an' all to lose. An' when it was over didn't little Mrs. Duff say the few extra shillings we got her man an' the rest of them made all the difference between living an' starving?"

"She cried in my arms, Bill, an' she said 'If it wasn't for good, brave men like your husband –'"

"That's enough of it. But who was right, me or you an' your mother?"

"Seems to me you're always right. But it's cruel hard on us poor women."

"Got any pudding?"

"Course, ole gingertop. Got your favourite apple-pie. My word, the apples is good and cheap this year."

"Takes a good cook, too, to make apple-pie like this, Curly. I wish you was coming with us."

"You'll take care of yourself, won't you, Bill?"

"S'far as my duty as a soldier permits. Chuck it, will yer? ... Sorry if I spoke cross, Curly, but that's the part I can't bear to think of, being away at a time like that."

'Oh, I'll be all right with mother. An' there's a little saved. An' what with the firm behaving so fine an' all, there's no need to worry about me. I wish all poor wives was left as well as you're leaving me, so long as you come back."

'Oh, I'm coming back all right ... An' if I don't, see he runs straight. Make him join the union an' stick to his mates, an' –"

"Him! Hark to the man! As if there was no such thing as a girl in this world."

"Sure there's no need to tell you how to bring up a girl. Make her like yourself, an' she'll do."

"My old man!"

"Who's that knocking at the door?"

"Only mother. She's coming along to the station with me to see you off."

"No, she's not, nor you neither. That's no place to say good-bye. Home's the place for that."

"Hallo, mother, what's your news?"

"Only about Tom. Says he won't be long after you, Bill."

"Oh, mother, not Tom, too?"

"An why not? My son can help his country as well as your husband. And see, Bill, ere's a pouch o' tobacco from me an' the girls an' a pipe from father. He says he only wishes he could go over with yer an' see them pore little Belgians right.[2]

"I'll bet he does, the old sport. Thanks, mother, you an' all of yer."

"How soon do you go, Bill?"

"Now. Forward! Quick march! Come here, Curly! There – an' there – an; there. Now half-a-dozen to pass on to young you-know-who. Buck up, old girl."

"Ain't you going to kiss me too, Bill?"

"O' course. Look here, mother, it don't need no words o' mine for you to know what I'm leaving behind with you. This girl is all you told me she was on our wedding day and a sight more. Take care of her for me. Cheer her up when there's no word from me. You know I'm one part of John French's big surprise packet for Kaiser Bill.[3] Next address, Berlin."

"But you'll write, won't you, Bill?"

"I suppose a card or so, but this is no letter-writing trip I'm on. She knows where to write for a letter to reach me."

"Good luck, Bill"

"Good-bye, Curly. Mind, no news is good news. And beefsteak an' apple-pie for dinner the day I come home."

"Bill! My Bill!

JUSTICE

Tom Quelch, 'His Reward', *Justice*, 30 December 1911, p. 7.

Victor Grayson, 'The Lost Vision. A Spring Fantasy', *Justice*, 4 May 1912, p. 3.

Edward Hartley, 'Mr. Prowser-Wowser', *Justice*, 28 June 1913, p. 2.

Edward Meyer, 'It Can't be Done! A History of Impossibilities' (from the *New York Call*), *Justice*, 6 August 1914, p. 8.

Justice (1884–1925) and the Social-Democratic Party (SDP) continued the call for socialist unity in Britain, and during the 1911 SDP conference they passed a resolution to establish a 'United British Socialist Party', officially named the British Socialist Party at the founding conference later that year.[1] The conference report for 1912 claimed a membership of 40,000, but this was probably an exaggeration; the figure had dropped to just over 15,000 in the conference report for 1913. Harry Quelch (1858–1913), who had edited *Justice* since 1886, fell ill in 1912 and was replaced as editor by Henry W. Lee (1865–1932) in 1913. This was not the only major change to affect *Justice*: the Twentieth Century Press, formed in 1891, which owned *Justice* and was organized by the executive council of the SDF in the names of Hyndman, Quelch and H. R. Taylor, went bankrupt in 1912 after a libel case and was replaced by Twentieth Century Press Ltd. *Justice* continued until 22 January 1925, when it merged with a revived *Social Democrat*. This periodical continued to be published monthly from February 1925 to its final issue in December 1933.

Although *Justice* did not carry any further serializations during the period covered by this volume, it did continue publishing short stories, the inclusion of which had been revived in the period covered by Volume 4. There were a number of anonymous stories published as well as one-off stories by authors such as Francis Welland (n.d.), Labour Councillor W. G. Veals (n.d.) and Tom Quelch (n.d.), the son of Harry Quelch and a delegate from the British Socialist Party at the Communist International in 1920. Edward Hartley (1855–1918) also continued to publish short stories, although not as prolifically as before. During this period he was secretary of the Clarion van movement before touring Australia and New Zealand in 1912–13, but he lost a great deal of support by leaving the SDP to join the pro-war British Workers League. For Hartley's full biographical details, see the headnote for *Justice* in Volume 4, p. 136; and for Victor Grayson (b. 1881), see the headnote for the *Clarion* in Volume 4, p. 2. Edward Meyer has not been identified.

Notes
1. C. Tsuzuki, *H. M. Hyndman and British Socialism* (Oxford: Oxford University Press, 1961), pp. 173–5.

Tom Quelch, 'His Reward' (1911)

Old Peter Dunn turned slowly into the Park.

As he hobbled along, leaning heavily upon his stick, his face twitched nervously. He was evidently laboring under some deep emotion. In his weary eyes was a gleam of satisfaction.

At length he reached one of the seats overhung by trees whose leaves had turned a tawny yellow, for it was October. A pale autumn sun shone from a dappled sky. The weather was dry and crisp, and occasionally a shrill wind whistled through the trees.

Nestling to the end of the seat, turning his coat-collar up over his ears, and holding his stick between his legs, old Peter made himself as comfortable as he possibly could.

That day was a great event in Peter's life, a day of wassail and huge delight.

And he had come to the Park to dwell upon it for half-an-hour in calm enjoyment.

That day was his birthday – and this birthday was one out of the ordinary.

He had just popped his white old head through the crust of the seventieth year. He had reached the allotted span of life, and he was proud of the fact for more reasons than one.

But it was when he realized that from now on until the shadows claimed him he would be entitled to the Old Age Pension[1] that his pride almost reached bursting point. His shrunken bosom swelled, his eyes gleamed.

That morning he had been to the Post Office, satisfactorily proved his claim after laborious preliminaries, and received the first five shillings.

Since then little surges of delight were continually arising within him.

"At last," he kept murmuring to himself, "I have got my reward."

And in the dusky evening of his life those five silver coins seemed to glitter like five silvery moons.

Sitting there he represented the typical toiler who, by dint of hard work and considerable roughing-it, has managed to wade thorough a tumultuous existence without the aid of the Poor Law or the prison. He was worn and gnarled, bent almost double; but there was a quiet dignity about his red, puckered face that told of pride and independence.

For sixty years had Peter worked – sixty hard, long, blinding years. He began when he was but ten years old – now he was seventy.

He was by trade a carpenter. And each week-day of all those years had seen him sawing, planing, hammering, measuring, except during several grim and tragic periods of unemployment.

His industry had been singularly fruitful – for other people. There was hardly a town of any importance in the country that did not contain some portion of his handiwork. Sometimes it was on houses, at other times on public buildings and public-houses, and even on churches, that his energy and skill had been expended.

Now he had finished.

"He could no longer find masters to employ him. Unemployment, even with his solidly-built reputation in the trade, had come, as he began to age, upon him more and more frequently, until at last he had abandoned – on that very day – the pursuit of work altogether.

Yes, he had finished; and now he was about to enjoy the reward of all those years of industry, of unflagging drudgery.

To Peter there seemed unlimited possibilities in those five shillings.

He began to ponder over what he should do with them – how he could most advantageously lay them out.

First of all there must be half-a-crown for the room in which he was to live; he could not possibly get one for less.

Then he would want clothing and coal, for winter was coming on, besides bread and butter, sugar, tea and milk. However much he scraped, it was necessary to have a dinner sometimes, and that would involve expenditure on meat and vegetables.

It was very tantalizing. There seemed such a heap of things to buy with that half-crown. No matter how much he retrenched, his demands always exceeded his means.

If he dispensed with any new clothes, and rubbed along with those he already possessed, he would still have to pay to have his shirts washed.

In the first flush of enthusiasm he thought of having his meals in a coffee-shop but when he found that it would not pan out to a week of dinners – to say nothing of breakfasts and teas – he gave it up.

The more he contemplated the more the potentialities of his reward diminished.

A sad, helpless kind of feeling came over him.

Leaves were continually dropping from the trees and rustling around his feet. The wind grew more boisterous. The pale sun receded into fleecy masses of cloud. The air, keen and penetrating, caused the old toiler to shiver.

At length he struggled to his feet. He had spend his half-hour of calm enjoyment on this day of wassail and huge delight, and two heavy tears ran the course of his wrinkles as at last he muttered: –

"It'll have to be the Lump[2] after all."

Victor Grayson, 'The Lost Vision. A Spring Fantasy' (1912)

On a sunny day at noon in the early spring, a young man loitered in the shade of a green-budding wood; all around him the stately trees were putting on their verdant robes, and the filtered sunshine wrought a carpet of curious and beautiful design for him to walk upon. The earth was wrenching itself from the cold clasp of winter; the air throbbed and trembled with the ecstasy of awakening life, and the pregnant earth seemed to heave with the bitter-sweet yearning of maternity.

A song was singing in the young man's soul. His eyes beamed with the light of joyous vision. He was sharing Nature's dream of coming glory; in his heart fresh shoots of hope were springing; he bathed his spirit in the gladness of the world's new birth. From sheer joy of existence he shouted aloud, and a thousand birds responded with an anthem of confident and forward-looking faith.

The young man had a priceless dowry that only Nature can bestow. He was strong, lithe and handsome; he was conscious of all the richness and beauty of the earth; the wonderful universe was his – and he knew it! His path was bright primroses, and his sleep would be canopied by myriads of lustrous, mystic stars. Flowers, too, were coming – thousands of beautiful flowers – to fill the air with their fragrance; and in return for his loving labour Nature would give forth its bounteous tribute of food things to feed and clothe his graceful body. Somewhere in the world's quiet places there was preparing for him a tender, lissome mate who would bear him robust children, and he would watch them grow up in the sunlight as he was growing now. He lay down and embraced the warm kindly soil with the grateful reverence of a child for its mother.

He was indeed blessed above his fellows. With lilting step the young man fared forth from the wood and returned to the "hum and shock"[1] of mankind. Boldly he trod the sinuous mazes of the social labyrinth, and beheld with truthful, fearless eyes all there was to behold. He saw the rows and rows and rows of putrid hovels where starved and hopeless slaves breathe out tired and paltry lives; he watched these dens at sunrise spawning forth their semi-human contents into the congested reek of mean streets and alleys; he saw the dirty children – sweet little flowers of humanity soiled and bruised in the bud – he saw these in their tens of thousands stewing in the foul cauldron of grime and crime and poverty; he saw their little skeleton arms and hands grasping at the disease-fouled air as they yielded back to nothingness the meaningless fragment of their lives.

He saw broken-hearted mothers bending over little graves, and heard cries of anguish as they gave to Moloch[2] other bairns to glut his maw; he saw their parched, milkless breasts and their backs bent and distorted with inhuman toil; he saw them cooped for long hours in sultry factories, and being done to death in accursed sweating dens; he saw the daughters of the poor with rouged cheeks and leering eyes, plying their debased bodies for hire in the public thoroughfares; he saw them in the death agonies of unspeakable disease, in hospitals provided by the kindly rich.

He saw men tramping the streets in rags and misery, begging in vain for employment for their hands; he saw the tears steam down their hollow cheeks when the little ones asked for bread; he saw them in the workhouse wards and the prison cells, being drilled and bullied and damned by the disciplined flunkeys of their own class. He saw the workers toiling patiently in the mines and the mills, and he saw them shot and bludgeoned at the masters' behest when they tried to increase their pittance. He saw all the horror and squalor of the veritable hell upon earth which is known as "the workers' lot."

* * *

Other sights also the young man saw. He saw the fat and insolent plutocrat lolling in idle and superfluous luxury; he saw him strutting truculently in mansions whose bricks were compounded of the wage-slaves' flesh, and whose mortar was their blood. He saw their fleet motor-cars and their floating castles, their priceless wines and dainty viands, their bejeweled wives and expensive concubines. He saw crafty lawyers – out for gold – and ambitious politicians – out for place – sitting together in the seats of the mighty – protecting the Constitution. He saw the whole tangled mass of lies, cunning, cant, chicane and fraud which buttresses and sustains the vast structure of privileged tyranny.

* * *

The young man returned to the wood and considered these things he had seen. Rain had fallen, and the tears of the sighing trees fell quietly into the sodden earth; the wet branches drooped as with dismal disappointment; the birds were singing, but their song was a wistful threnody; the air was pervaded with melancholy tenderness. The young man wept for that he was born into a world of strife and sadness. His sight of the ways of men had shown him Spring as Winter in disguise. Near by him a mighty tree was being slowly strangled in the merciless embrace of its creeping parasite; tiny insects were destroying the green leaves

– thus preparing themselves to form a future meal for insects of stronger and subtler growth. A spider was patiently spinning its gossamer web to snare the feet of the trusting fly. Here in the wood, as in the world, were paupers and criminals and idle rich; the prevailing law was the pitiless "law of prey"; the teeth and claws of nature were red[3] with the blood of the mangled weak. The young man shrank back from this revelation of universal horror. He felt helpless and hopeless in the face of life's sinister mystery.

But as the sun shone suddenly through the trees, he ceased weeping, and a strange light kindled in his dark blue eyes. He seemed to be listening to far-distant voices, to be watching the world's chaos swinging into ordered harmony. The birds burst forth again into a song of hope. With head erect, clenched fists and shoulders squared, the young man walked resolutely back into the human battle-field.

For he had found the Vision.

* * *

It is winter in the wood, and an old man picks his way with feeble steps through the winding avenues of bare trees. His skinny yellow fingers are encircled with costly rings, and he is clothed in the manner of those who command great wealth. There is something hard and repulsive in the wrinkled face, the mouth has a sordid droop, and he stares at the ground with bleared, expressionless eyes. He would seem to be seeking something, this old man, for now and again he mumbles to himself in a husky, quavering voice, and peers inquiringly about him on every side. At an old dead tree he pauses, and with trembling hand plucks a spray of ivy from its decaying bark. As he holds it in his fingers the crafty lines of his face seem for a moment to disappear and his dull eyes moisten with reminiscence. He is trying to recall to memory a day in an early Spring of long ago, when the great road stretched in front of him right up to the celestial heights, and his soul had caught the sudden gleam of the ideal. He remembers the first few battles with greed; the glamour of power, the cunning deals, the attainment of riches – and now he realises that though he can *buy* anything, he can truly possess nothing!

So the old man goes doddering sadly through the wood, staring about him with pathetic appeal, as if he thought he might find again the Vision that he had – somehow, somewhere – lost.

Edward Hartley, 'Mr. Prowser-Wowser' (1913)

New Zealand trains are not very fast, and New Zealand railway journeys are a wee bit wearisome.

In going from Wellington to Auckland most of the passengers drop off and stay overnight at some hotel, finishing their journey on the second day.

A gentleman in one of these trains began to praise them, and pointed out the speed (?) at which we travelled. I told him that when at home I could receive a wire calling me to London 200 miles away, pack my bag, get some lunch, and be in the centre of London in less than five hours.

"Oh!" said he, "I wouldn't travel on a train like that! I'd be afraid!"

It is, however, possible to have a conversation, and there is certainly plenty of time. It was on one such journey when, after reading, and looking out of the window at some striking scenery, which, however, had a tinge of sameness, that there entered the carriage a gentleman who had asked questions at a meeting I had held, and who afterwards came and spoke to me, and said how pleased he had been with both the address and the answers.

He saw me at once, and, taking he adjoining seats for himself and companion, introduced me to one whom we will call Mr. Prowser-Wowser.

THE SELF-MADE MAN

Mr. Prowser-Wowser was a man to whom the word "smug" is most appropriate. A smug complacence literally oozed out of him. Life for him was obviously prosperous. His neat grey suit, his soft grey hat, his plump white hands – in fact, his whole appearance said, "Look at me! I've done well!"

He was the kind of man who would be an excellent husband; a good, kind father, if his children were submissive and obedient, but who would not brook much opposition; and in business matters be much like "Scrooge," a tight-fisted hand at the grindstone.

Still, life as a whole had been so good to him that this streak of hardness had not been over-developed. He would have been a real good fellow if he had not been so prosperous.

We talked for a while about general matters. Then the strike at Waihi[1] was mentioned. My first acquaintance said, "You know Mr. Hartley is a Socialist."

"A Socialist," said Mr. Prowser-Wowser, with something like astonishment. "A Socialist! Why, Mr. Hartley seems a very sensible man."

I laughed and said: "Yes, that is why I'm a Socialist. All sensible men who have considered the subject are Socialists. Some are either loth or afraid to admit it; but if they understand they know it is true, and they know it is inevitable."

"Well, now! I'm not a Socialist, yet I've been called a sensible man."

SOCIALIST AND SENSIBLE!

"Do you know what Socialism is? Have you studied it?"

"No. I've never had time."

"Are you opposed to Socialism?"

"I certainly am!" And he was very emphatic.

"And you don't know what it is!"

This brought silence for a while, and his friend's eyes twinkled.

"May I ask why you are a Socialist, Mr. Hartley?"

"Because I'm tired of the present system."

"Oh, the present system is all right." And Mr. Prowser-Wowser looked himself over and regained his self-possession.

"It may be all right for you and me, but it is not all right for the great mass of the workers."

"Oh! they seem to be all right generally. But what's wrong with the system?"

"It's so unfair! The hardest, the most dangerous, and most disagreeable work gets the least pay; the easiest and most pleasant work the biggest and better pay; and when you get to the gentleman he does nothing at all, and gets the best income of the whole lot."

WHAT IS HARD WORK?

"Come, now! It depends on what you call hard work. Would you say that a judge's work was hard work?"

"Not very hard. Which would you rather be, a judge or a policeman?"

This rather startled him, but after a pause he said: "A judge, certainly!"

"Why?"

"Oh, I suppose for several reasons; but it would be much pleasanter."

"Exactly so! Now, I think one miner is worth all the lawyers and parsons in a country."

"What about the teacher? I suppose you would call him a worker?"

"I never mentioned the teacher; but I want no mistake made about my opinion of him. I count the teacher the most important man in the community."

"Then you will include the parson in the most useful men."

"I don't think so."

"Why not? What's the difference between the teacher and the preacher?"

"A vast difference! One teaches something he knows all about, and the other talks about something he knows nothing about. What can the parson know about Heaven?"

"He knows as much about it as you do." This somewhat stiffly.

"Probably; but that may not be very much. I don't know much about Heaven and the future life."

"No. But he may know as much, or even more."

"Not more! He cannot! Speculations we may have about future life and places; there can be no knowledge."

"But you admit he knows as much about these things as you do."

"Exactly! But I know nothing, neither does he."

"Well, he can tell you a good deal about these things."

"Likely! That is easy enough. I could tell a lot of what I think about a future life; but it is all speculation what I think and fancy. I can give you no proof; neither can any other man."

THE WAIHI STRIKE

This finished the conversation for a while. Then the talk drifted back to the Waihi strike. Both these gentlemen were opposed to the strikers. I find most people who ride in first-class carriages usually are opposed to all strikers.

I pointed out that even if the men were wrong there was not justification for the masters. Their profits were big enough to give the men both better wages and better conditions.

"But the men have both good wages and good conditions. A member of our church worked there for several years, and he told me about the place and its workings."

I had discovered that Mr. Prowser-Wowser was the main financial supporter, and practically the head of a Methodist church.

"Did he tell you the enormous profits that had been made? Did he tell you the men's wages averaged less than £3 a week?"

"No. He probably didn't know. But surely these people are entitled to the results of their brains and capital."

"Of course they are! Only the profits are not due to their brains and capital."

"Really, Mr. Hartley! You astonish me."

"Perhaps so. I don't want to astonish you. I want to convince you."

OUR FOOLISH TALK!

"But you talk so foolishly."

This is the usual way when people have no answer to Socialist arguments. They generally suggest that we are fools. I paused, and he continued:

"To say that the profits are not made by brains and capital is mere rubbish." Here his smug self-complacency was almost irritating.

"Of course, something is due to the working men," he added, grudgingly. "But most of the wealth is made by the brains and capital of the managers and shareholders. Even you will admit that, Mr. Hartley."

"I shall not. I shall maintain that the real wealth production is done by the workmen. The previous wealth-production of the workers, which we call capital, is useful, and so are the brains of the managers, when they've got the right kind of managing brains; but the real wealth-making is done by the men who work."

"But this is ridiculous. What could you do without capital?"

"What could you do without labour?"

"Well, nothing, of course; neither can you do without capital."

"Yes, we could do without capital, though we don't want to do without wealth."

Here he got impatient, and said he'd "no time for hair-splitting." I don't like hair-splitting, and was tempted to follow him, but refrained, and said, "Labour has produced the capital."

"Nothing of the kind."

CAPITAL AND LABOUR

"Yes. Abraham Lincoln put it very well when he said, 'Labour is prior to and independent of capital. Capital is the fruit of labour, and could not exist if labour had not first existed.'² All the capital in the world is the stored-up labour of the working men, past and present."

"Hear, hear! Bravo!" said both Mr. Prowser-Wowser and his friend. "I'm glad you admit that capital is stored up labour."

"I must admit that. The trouble is that one man generally does the labour, and the other man stores it up."

"I'm not so sure about that. But do I understand you to say that it is not the brains and capital which are the main things in the production of wealth? Of course, the workmen help, but the main things are the brains and capital of the rich men."

"I deny that altogether. The workman could manage without the capitalist, but the capitalist cannot do without the workman."

"Really, Mr. Hartley." This in a tired tone, as who should say, "There is nothing more to be said."

I took up the newspaper. "Have you read this? The output of gold in the Auckland Province is nearly £200,000 less than in the same period last year. This fall-off in production is mainly due to the unfortunate dispute at Waihi."

"I don't quite see what that has to do with the argument."

"Have any of the Waihi managers died at Waihi?"

"Not that I've heard of."

"Have any of the shareholders withdrawn their capital?"

"No! but many of them would like to."

"Then you admit that with the same brains, the same capital, and the same managers, the output of gold is £200,000 less. Why should that be if the gold production is due to the brains and capital of the rich men?"

A SILENCER

Mr. Prowser-Wowser was quiet for several minutes, the said: "After all, Mr. Hartley, the shareholders don't get very much!"

"Don't they? Not at Waihi? Why, the capital is less than half-a-million, and the dividends are paid at four-and-a-half millions in 21 years."

"Now, Mr. Hartley, that is just where you are wrong. I know what I'm talking about. I've invested a fair sum in the Waihi Mine and lost money."

"Oh, no!"

"Really, sir! Do you mean to say that I don't know my own business? I tell you I've invested money in the Waihi Mine and lost by it."

"Very well. I tell you that if you invested money in the Waihi Gold Mining Company you have not lost any money. As the dividends paid are four and a half millions sterling, and the paid-up capital under half-a-million, if you got original shares, so far from having lost money, for every pound you put in you will have had nine pounds out, and still have your pound invested."

"Oh, quite so! But, I didn't get original shares."

INVESTMENT AND GAMBLING

"Then you didn't 'invest.' You've been gambling in shares."

His face was a study.

"Gambling! Gambling! What do you mean? I'm very much opposed to gambling of any kind. It is sinful."

"Perhaps so. Yet if you didn't get original shares you didn't invest. And if you've been speculating in shares, it's gambling, much like horse-racing, you know."

"Not at all, sir! Not at all. Buying shares is a very different matter."

"As you say, not at all! You put your money on the wrong shares instead of the wrong horse, that is all. Yet it's gambling, all the same."

This finished Mr. Prowser-Wowser. He glared at me for a while, then sank back in his seat, and a few minutes later slowly arose, and, reaching his handbag, sought other quarters, without even bidding me "Good-day."

He was mad, and I don't think he's forgiven me yet. I don't think telling the truth always makes friends.

Edward Meyer, 'It Can't be Done! A History of Impossibilities' (1914)

CHAPTER I.

(Stone Age.)

Stone Hammer; Look at that crazy gink over there.

Sheep Skin: Wot's he up to?

S.H.: Oh, he's loony. He says it's nonsense to run after deer in order to capture it. He says he can take a hickory stick, a strip of raw hide and another short stick with a sharp stone on one end and a feather on the other end and then send that second stick after the deer and get him! Can you beat it?

S.S.: Gee! He must be a nut! Whoever heard of such bunk? Why, it's against all the laws of nature and human precedent! Don't we know from experience that the only way to get a deer is to run after him and catch him? Hickory stick! Sharp stone! Oh, fudge!

IT CAN'T BE DONE!

(But it was done.)

CHAPTER II.

(Later On.)

First Moss Back: Waddye know about that fool blacksmith?

Second M. B.: What's the idea?

First M.B.: Why, the blamed idiot says he is going to build an iron tube and put a black powder in it and then shoot a lump of lead a hundred times as far as we now shoot an arrow from a bow! Ain't that the limit?

Second M. B.: Why, that fellow must be as crazy as they make 'em! Whoever heard of such a thing? It's against all reason and logic.

IT CAN'T BE DONE!

(However, it came to pass.)

CHAPTER III.

(A previous date.)

Tree Dweller: Are you hep to the fool stunts that yap across the lake is up to? Cliff Dweller: Why, no. Put me wise.

T.D.: Why, the condemned simp says it's all foolishness to straddle a log when you want to paddle your way across the lake. He says the sensible and scientific thing to do is to burn the inside out of that log, and then sit down inside the log instead of on top of it.

C.D. It's a safe bet he's bughouse, all right. Haven't we and our ancestors always straddled a log when crossing the lake? Now comes the bloke and tells us we ought to sit inside the log instead of on top! Oh, piffle.

IT CAN'T BE DONE!

(But the canoe arrived.)

CHAPTER IV.

(Some time later.)

First Fisherman: I've had my laps on that cuss down in the cover. Wot's doin'? Second F.: Aw, he's off his nut! He's got the dope that he's goin' to quit paddlin' his canoe; got an idea in his think tank that he will put a big stick up in this boat and hang a hide on it and make the wind take him where he wants to go.

First F.: Why, the poor mut. Does he think he can get away with that? Don't we know from experience that the only way to move a canoe is to paddle it? A sailboat! Oh, phsaw!

IT CAN'T BE DONE.

(But she sailed.)

CHAPTER V.

(Later yet.)

First Bonehead: Get wise to this guy. He's got an idea that he can put the kibosh on the steam that comes from hot water, and then bottle it up in a machine and make that machine work! Get that? Isn't he bughouse?

Second B.H.: You bet he is! Why, there is no weight, or power to steam! It floats in the sir, as light as a fog! Power from steam! Nothing to it!

IT CAN'T BE DONE!

(But the engine turned over.)

CHAPTER VI.

(Further on.)

First Colonist: Say, there is a darned fool over at the Hudson River with a little ship he calls the Clermont,[1] and he had the fool idea in his bean that he can do away with sails and make the steam engine do the stunt.

Second C.: Do tell! Hasn't he any better sense than to know that while the steam engine has a limited usefulness on land it is impractical and a failure on board ship? Take it from me, the Clermont will never move!

IT CAN'T BE DONE!

(But the Clermont did move.)

CHAPTER VII.

(Still later.)

First American: Say, this fellow Langley[2] in Washington, D.C., is dead wrong. The idea of him saying that a human being could learn to fly.

Second A.: Right! It's beyond the bounds of human possibilities to fly. Moreover, it is sacrilegious to fly. If the Lord ever wanted us to fly He would have created us with wings.

Human beings ever fly? Never!

IT CAN'T BE DONE!

(But they do fly now.)

(Historian's Note.)

Several hundred thousand chapters of the world's history are omitted from this work for the sake of brevity.

What the writer desires to point out is that in the progress of mankind a never-failing series of cycles has taken place. Here is what has happened in a regular rotation: –

One day, Ignorance says; "It Can't be Done!"

Next day, Intelligence does it.

The following day Ignorance says of something else: "It can't be done!"

The day after that Intelligence makes Ignorance back up by doing the very thing that "could not be done!" And so we find it down through all ages, Ignorance trying to hold humanity in darkness and Intelligence lifting mankind out of intellectual night into clear daylight – into ever brighter light.

To the non-Socialist who may happen to read the foregoing the writer wishes to point out that the Ignorance which says the interests of Labour and Capital are identical is the very same Ignorance which says "Socialism is impossible."

On the other hand, it is the extremely superior Intelligence of twenty million (20,000,000) Socialists in the world to-day who say that the interests of Labour and Capital are absolutely opposed to each other. It is this same massed Intelligence that says we are even now about to realise the fulfillment of this "beautiful dream" which would always "remain a dream!"

Now, Mr. Non-Socialist, which way are you betting? Do you back Ignorance to win?

If so, I place my money on Intelligence and give you heavy odds.

And, by the way, if you want to meet up with the highest grade of intelligence on earth to-day just cultivate the acquaintance of the Socialists. They have the history of humanity's evolution at their finger tips.

They and they alone understand why present conditions are as they are. They (the Socialists) and they alone know how to make the future as it should be – and will be.

When anyone tells me (not knowing what they are talking about) that Socialism is "impossible," I think of the "impossibilities" Ignorance has set up all through the ages, and which Intelligence, with unerring aim, has every time wiped away like a set of ten pins on the bowling alley. Then at this point I get real busy brushing the cobwebs out of the cranium of the gink who impersonates a phonograph reproducing a record recorded in his brain by the flutes – "Socialism is impossible!"

LABOUR LEADER

J. Keir Hardie, 'Nellie', *Labour Leader*, 27 January 1911, p. 53.

I. O. Ford, 'In the "Good Old Times"', *Labour Leader*, 11 August 1911, p. 509.

Herbert Morrison, 'Lord Santa Claus, G.E.R., M.P. A Drama in Ten Minutes', *Labour Leader*, 6 October 1911, p. 634.

Herbert Morrison, 'The Weaker Vessel and the Strike', *Labour Leader*, 20 June 1912, p. 396.

J. Zimmerman, 'Stitch, Stitch, Stitch', *Labour Leader*, 11 September 1913, p. 4.

'Casey', 'Alice in Sunderland. A Baffling Mystery', *Labour Leader*, 18 June 1914, p. 5.

The editorship of the *Labour Leader* (1893–1987) passed from J. T. Mills (n.d.) to Archibald Fenner Brockway (1888–1988) in 1912. Although the *Daily Citizen* became the official daily paper of the Labour Party, the *Labour Leader* continued and remained tied to the ILP; it published under a number of different titles until 1987. The increase in the amount of fiction included in the periodical under the editorship of J. T. Mills was continued under Brockway, although the preference was for short stories. The only lengthy piece of fiction serialized during the period covered by this volume was Upton Sinclair's (1878–1968) 'The Convict', which was published between November 1912 and January 1913. Of the authors included in this selection, only J. Zimmerman cannot be identified. Biographical details for Isabella Ormston Ford (1855–1924) can be found in the headnote for the *Labour Leader*, Volume 3, pp. 163–4.

The most famous of the authors is James Keir Hardie (1856–1915), who came to politics through the mining trade unions of Lanarkshire. He worked in the mines from the age of eleven, before moving into trade union work and journalism in 1879. Originally a Liberal, Hardie met Robert Cunninghame Graham (1852–1936) during the Lanarkshire miners' strike of 1887, and through Graham he was introduced to Tom Mann (1856–1941) and Friedrich Engels (1820–95). Hardie fully embraced labour independence after he was rejected by the Liberal Party for the 1888 Mid-Lanark by-election, when he stood unsuccessfully as an independent Labour candidate. He had launched his own periodical, the *Miner*, in 1887, which was re-named the *Labour Leader* from 1889 before ceasing publication in 1891. Hardie was elected the independent MP for West Ham South in 1892 and caused a sensation when he arrived at Parliament dressed in ordinary tweeds and a deerstalker rather than the usual morning dress. After becoming chairman of the ILP in 1893, he restarted the *Labour Leader* in 1894 as a weekly publication. He lost his seat in the 1895 general election and became chairman of the LRC in 1900. Returned to Parliament in 1900 for Merthyr Tydfil and again in 1906, Hardie was one of the few who knew of Ramsay MacDonald's (1866–1937) pact with the Liberal Party on the fielding of candidates at elections. He took an anti-war stance on both the Second Boer and First World Wars and withdrew from politics as hostility against his opinions grew and affected his already poor health.

Herbert Stanley Morrison (1888–1965) entered politics through the National Union of Clerks; he joined the ILP in 1906 and then the SDF (the Social-Democratic Party from 1908) before returning to the ILP. In 1912 he took a job as a travelling salesman for the *Daily Citizen* until the paper folded in 1915, and he was voted secretary of the London Labour Party the same year, after the death of Fred Knee (1868–1914). He became Labour mayor for Hackney in 1920 and entered the London County Council as councillor for Woolwich in 1922. He was part of the Labour Party National Executive Committee and party chairman between 1928 and 1929. Morrison was elected to Parliament as MP for South Hackney in 1929, was Minister for Transport in 1929–31, and was the leader of the London County Council between 1934 and 1940. He was Minister for Supply during the wartime coalition government, lord president of the council and deputy prime minister in the 1945 Labour government (despite an attempt to topple Attlee), Foreign Secretary in 1951 and deputy Leader of the Opposition between 1951 and 1959. He became Baron Morrison of Lambeth in 1959, moving to the House of Lords, and became president of the British Board of Film Censors in 1960 until his death in 1965. His grandson is Peter Mandelson (b. 1953), the architect of New Labour.

'Casey' is the pseudonym of Walter Hampson (1864–1932), railwayman, poet and author of *Who Are the Bloodsuckers* (*c.* 1907), his famous dialect work *Tykes Abrooad* (1911) and *Awheel in Wharfeland* (1918). He was editor of the *Clock Almanac* from 1917, after the death of John Hartley (1859–1915), until his own death in 1932.

J. Keir Hardie, 'Nellie' (1911)

Nellie was a bulldog. Her master was a bachelor, and Nellie and he lodged together in a room over an eating-house in the East End of London. Nellie's master, in addition to being a bachelor, was also a shop assistant, and 40 years of age. Fatal age. I don't know whether his hair was becoming grey, or his eye dim, but at last he found himself out of work, and in due time came to the conclusion that life and he had no longer any use for each other, and so he committed suicide.

One morning the servant girl of the eating-house downstairs carried up his breakfast, but finding no response to her knocks at this door, except the growling of Nellie, she left the tray outside, and then proceeded with her duties until dinner time. When dinner time came she took up a second tray, and was astonished to find that the breakfast tray was still outside the door and untouched. She knocked again, but still the only response was Nellie's growl. Somewhat alarmed, the girl reported what had happened, where upon an attempt was made to open the door, but the voice of Nellie from within warned the would-be intruders of the reception that was in store for them. Finally, the police were sent for, and they proceeded to make an attempt to break down the door, but by this time Nellie was in a state of fury which there was no misunderstanding, and so the police very wisely desisted. Clearly Nellie was an Anarchist, and the proper thing would have been to send for some hundreds of policemen, a squadron of sharp shooters, a field gun, and a fire brigade, together with of course, a Home Secretary. Instead of which the policemen contented themselves with boring a hole in the door, and peeping through.

The sight that presented itself was that of the body of the shop assistant lying in a pool of blood on the floor, his throat gashed from ear to ear. In front of the body sat Nellie, showing her teeth, and uttering low but menacing growls. The hole in the door was enlarged, Nellie becoming more watchful as the operation proceeded, and an attempt was made to induce her to drink some poisoned milk. But the dog was not to be seduced from her watch by the body of her dead master. A piece of meat tied to a string had no better result. And so the hours passed, the policemen outside, the dead body on the floor within, with poor Nellie whining over it, licking the dead face, and determined to guard it against all comers.

Finally, late in the evening a piece of poisoned meat was obtained, and thrown in front of the faithful creature. For over 24 hours she had tasted nothing. She looked at the meat, she looked at the dead Shop Assistant's body, she was very hungry, and, without for a moment talking her faithful eyes off the hole in the door, she cautiously crept forward to where the tempting morsel lay, ravenously swallowed it, and in five minutes she too lay stiff and dead beside her master.

She was only a dog, and presumably had no soul to be saved, but she was the only God-like thing in all that horrible tragedy. A great Christian Government ruling over a great Christian nation, in which wealth abounds to an unlimited extent, knew nothing of the Shop Assistant, and could do nothing for him. The policemen who guard our lives and our property would have been in duty bound to run him in had they found him taking bread wherewith to stay the cravings of hunger. Our civilization our law, the whole organization of our society, were all helpless, heartless, or powerless.

The Coroner, with his twelve good men and true, who sat on the corpse, brought in a verdict certifying that the man had committed suicide during a fit of temporary insanity. They had heard the letter read in which he told of the terrible drudgery and monotony of his daily toil, of his starvation wages, and of his being out of work. They had not a word to say about the employer who overworked and underpaid the man, nor of the system which, when it had sucked body and brain dry, cast him aside as a useless cumberer of the ground. He was "insane," because he preferred to die at once by his own hand, rather than starve to death by inches. The one thing that cared for him was Nellie, and she was only a dog, and could do nothing for him save love him in life and guard him in death. His one regret on leaving life must have been the parting from his sole companion Nellie. There are thousands of these lonely souls in London and elsewhere, slaves of the desk, of the counter. Few of them have even a dog for companion. Heaven help them.

The man in his solitary life needed fellowship, human sympathy, and human help, and the one creature who, in life and in death, was faithful and loyal and devoted to him was Nellie. One pictures the hours these two spent together, how joyously Nellie would listen for his footsteps ascending the wooden stair after his day's drudgery behind the counter was ended, the evening walk together through the crowded streets in the cool night air, the frugal supper together and then, perchance, while he smoked his pipe and read his book, Nellie would lie contentedly by his side, enjoying that fullness of companionship which communion of soul alone can give. Then came that awful evening when, after a farewell caress, Nellie saw something happen to the man she loved so much, and one can picture her through all the long hours of the black night sitting by the body, looking into the glazed eyes, seeking to attract their attention, and wondering why he lay so cold and so still. Somewhere at the back of Nellie's brain, perhaps, there would be the vague undefined feeling that never again would his kindly hand stroke her, or his eye light up with affection at her approach, and in her own dumb fashion, Nellie resolved that no sacrilegious hand would be laid upon him whilst she had strength to guard and protect him. That those who had neglected him in his life, those who were responsible for his death, should not be allowed to come near him. Faithful Nellie! God grant that human heart may be as tenacious to its trust, as faithful in its loyalty as was poor four-footed, soulless, heroic Nellie.

I. O. Ford, 'In the "Good Old Times"' (1911)

It was a hot Sunday morning in August, and the train crawling along, as only Sunday trains can crawl, seemed to be as much exhausted with the heat as we were in our third-class compartment. The incline was steep and the engine puffed slowly and languidly as we wound amongst the narrow wooded ways.

The mills were standing silent and smokeless in the sunshine, which, in this Lancashire manufacturing district, is real sunshine only on Sundays and holidays. The outline of the hills behind stood out for once clear and beautiful against the blue sky, instead of blurred and darkened by the black clouds usually pouring out of the tall slender chimneys.

Presently we passed one valley narrower and darker than any of the others, too narrow to be reached by even this morning's sunshine, and at the farthest end I caught a glimpse of an old half-ruined mill. It was a gloomy place, and in the days before the railway came past it, must have been tolerably inaccessible. One or two cottages stood near the railway end, and behind the mill the hills rose up, steep and bare.

"What a strange looking place; somehow it looks as if that mill had a history," I said, speaking to the person sitting opposite me. He was a dreamy-looking man, of middle age or more, with a pale, thin face, and stooping shoulders – and he was tormented by a perpetual cough.

"Ay! you may well say so," he replied. "It's a place as I cannot abide to look at. No one will use yon mill now, or touch it, and it's only right as they shouldn't, for if ever there was a hell upon earth, that place was one."

There was a ring of passionate earnestness in his voice which quite startled me, and made me forget some of my fatigue, and the breathless heat of the carriage.

"My father used to tell us what he'd heard from his father about it, and I never look out o' t' windows i' this part, for it's all cursed, all of it. And it's ruin and desolation too, for the smoke is killing everything that's beautiful, everything that God made. There's only left them ugly towns wi' nought but streets and gas lamps – nothing left to set one thinkin' on God as made us, and made them hills and valleys. But, perhaps you don't believe in God? There's so many Atheists about now, and I don't wonder as there is ..."

I told him I wasn't an Atheist and that I agreed with all his remarks about the wickedness of destroying the world's beauty, and I begged him to tell me about that particular mill.

"Ruin and desolation it is," he went on, his grey eyes looking as if he was beholding some vision, "they take our health and strength from us" – his cough tore him for a moment – "and they take our souls, too, for they leave us nought to see that lifts us up to the things of spirit. Damn the whole crew of them, I say, and I only hope He will damn 'em."

The other people in the carriage roused up at this and began to listen, too. One fat, cheerful man, began to laugh.

"Come now, mister," he said, "you must remember that 'where there's muck there's money,' as the saying is."

"Where there's muck there's money!" retorted my friend, "and I'll show you for why I say it. Look at yon mill we've passed. In the years before there was Factory Acts,[1] and they – t' employers – could do just as they pleased; they used, as you'll know, to buy childer or get 'em wi'out buying,[2] worst and cruelest o' t' lot. It was where they sent t' youngest uns, for it was out o' t' sight and not easy to come to, so no one knew what went on there. T' childer as went there was mostly never seen nor heard of again. Grandfather told my father as how he'd as a lad many a time seen carts going up there full o' childer crying their very hearts out and some too young to cry or know anything, but sitting starved and silent, little uns of four and five even – and some not right in their heads, either, as they got for naught – and cripples.

He stopped a moment for breath, and I saw the tears were standing in his eyes. A thin, sad looking woman in black, with a chubby baby in her arms, began to cry.

"They'd do it now, missus," he said, turning to her, "them devils would, if they could. They try summat like it, with the young girls as they pay starvation wages to." The woman nodded her head at him and wiped her eyes.

"But that mill," I urged, "what of it?"

I saw a discussion was imminent with the fat man and a mission preacher, who was shocked at my friend's language, and I wanted to hear the story of the mill before I got off the train.

"Is it haunted?"

"Ay, for sure it is, or so they say; for though it was said to be closed because t' water power wurn't good enough after they made yon new reservoir, and because t' road wur bad for cartin' t' stuff away. I never believed it wur aught but because of t' wailin and cryin' which you can hear any still night up there, and such a sound o' sobbin' in one room at t' back – and there's some queer lookin stains on t' floor there too, folks say no washing takes 'em out – it wur all that as set everyone again t' place. Grandfather lived in one o' them cottages we passed, and he used to go up there on errands, and sometime wi' t' letter, an' 'e got to know some of t' childer a bit – though he had to speak to 'em on t' sly like, they was kept that close and never went out except a bit in the dinner time into t' mill yard which had a high fence round it. There was one lad in particular 'e'd got to know and which 'e oftentimes talked about. 'E was a lad of may be seven or eight years old, with a crooked leg, and 'e used a crutch to hop about with. He had t' saddest lookin' eyes and t' saddest little face as ever was; father said grandfather used to cry whenever he talked about 'im. 'E was a workhouse child, and once when grandad got talkin' to him through a hole in t' fence, 'e told 'im as 'e'd never had no father nor mother, no one 'ad ever been kind to 'im as 'e could remember, 'e'd never played at no games, 'e'd worked as long as 'e could remember aught. They dursen't speak to one another only a word now and again, but all t' same them lads got to love each other. Willie, that was 'is name, wur that gentle, grandad said you had only to look at 'im to love 'im. My grandfather would be eleven or twelve years old then, and was a big strong lad for his age. Well, one cold winter's day, when t' snow wur lyin' on t' ground – and it can lie deep up yon valley, I can tell you – grandad went up to t' mill i' dinner time wi' a little pup in his pocket as 'e 'ad just got and was main proud of, and naught would satisfy him till 'e'd shown it to Willie. He reached t' little hole in t' fence and looked through it for Willie. T' lad see'd him and came hoppin up, and grandad showed him t' pup and let it lick 'is face. 'E never see'd such a smile as Willie gave, 'is face lit up all over, 'e wur that pleased. 'I'll give it thee,' whispered grandad, and he began pushin' t' little dog through t' hole, but Willie, he nearly screamed: "Tak' him away and be sharp, for yon man" (meaning t' overlooker whom they called Tom, or oftener, 'Bloody Tom,') 'e'll kill 'im if he catches sight of 'im. I've nowhere to keep 'im, I've no place to myself, and t' childer is that cruel, too, Tom makes 'em so – bring 'im up now and again for me to see," and 'e kissed t' pup's little wet nose as it was pokin' out at 'im, and it's little tail a-waggin' that hard.

"All on a sudden t' bell began ringing for work, and Tom came out with his strap, shoutin' at t' childer to be quick in. Only Willie were out, t' others were trying to warm theirselves near t' engine house. As grandfather dragged t' pup into his pocket it gave a squeal and Tom heard it.

"'Run, run,' whispered Willie, but 'e wouldn't; he hid hisself behind a barrel and waited, for his blood wur up, and he wur always one fur fightin', wur grandad."

The fat man nodded his head approvingly. The mission preacher looked pleased, and then hastily closed his eyes, as if in disapproval.

"'What's yon squealin'?' shouted Tom, 'it's thee, young crooked legs, is it? I'll give thee summat to squeal about ...' – 'e never could abear Willie for 'e knew all t' other childer liked him. He laid into t' little un something shameful, and when he fell down into t' snow on his face t' blood were fair runnin' down 'im. Seein' as 'e didn't stir nor call out Tom kicked 'im. Still he gave no sound, so Tom turned away; 'Crooked legs isn't wanted here,' he said with a laugh, 'they cost more than they're worth.' He thought as t' little un wur dead, and so he wurn't going to waste this time over him. When 'e'd gone and t' yard wur empty grandfather came out from his hiding place, and by breaking away t' fence a bit more he made a hole big enough for him to get through. He crept up to Willie and turned him over and laid t' pup down beside him and it began lickin' his face and whining. Willie opened his eyes, and such a smile came into them when 'e saw t' dog beside him as made grandfather burst out cryin' like any girl, he told father – and he and Willie kissed each other. The next minute 'e wur dead, Willie wur."

There was a pause, and the fat man blew his nose and spat noisily out of the window.

"Some one found him lying beside Willie cryin'," the weaver went on, "and he was turned out pretty quick, but not before he'd given them a bit of his mind. Father said as 'e wur reckoned the finest swearer in the countryside, wur my grandfather, he knowed more words and could put them together better nor anyone round, and through 'e wur only a lad, 'e wur fine at it even then, and 'e give it 'em strong. 'E told as 'e fair terrified 'em all! 'E told 'em as 'Bloody Tom' would be in hell before long. 'E'd had a vision about him – happen you don't believe in such things," he said, turning to the preacher, "but they's true I can tell you." No one spoke, and he went on: "I have visions too and they are like what grandad had. 'E saw Tom lyin' dead and a terrible look on his face same as if 'e wur mad wi fear; not fear o' men, for he never felt none o' that, but fear o' summat far more terrible. Grandad said it wur like a sight o' hell in his eyes. And it came true just as 'e 'ad told it all. Six months later, out on t' hillside behind t' mill one dark hot summer's night 'e were found lyin' dead, and the look on his face wur that dreadful! There'd been a thunderstorm that night and 'e wur struck by lightning as they said, though some said as 'e'd been murdered. No one ever rightly knowed my father said. And after that sickness broke out amongst t' childer, and they died like flies and were just buried anyhow, shovelled into t' ground in batches. And then folks began stirring a bit about Factory Acts and such – and the mill began to go down, and wur closed. And now, there aren't a many who care to go past it at nights. I've even heard as lights are sometimes seen in t' windows, though all t' flooring is either gone or is fair rotten, and the sound o' childer cryin' is something to make you creep, they say.

"And the puppy, you ask? Well, grandad set more store by that dog than 'e ever did about any of his own family. He called him Willie, and his grave is down in the garden by one of them cottages, and on it is the words "Here lies Willie's friend." My father could just remember him as an old dog sitting always beside grandfather's chair and lookin' as sensible as any human critter. But I believe as animals 'as souls,'" and he looked across at the preacher.

My station was in sight, so I only heard the beginning of what promised to be an endless discussion of the nature of the soul. The last words I heard as the train moved away were from my friend: –

"Now, which was more fit to have a soul and go to Heaven, Tom or yon pup, 'Willie's friend,' as licked t' dying' lad's face? Tell me that."

Herbert Morrison, 'Lord Santa Claus, G.E.R., M.P. A Drama in Ten Minutes' (1911)

I.

(*Scene.* – A luxuriantly furnished bedroom at night. The only light is the light of the moon shining through the windows. A gentleman – old in years, but young in mind – is just settling down in bed. He is Lord Santa Claus.)

LORD S.C.: Ah ... thank heaven I am in bed at last. This has ben a trying day for me ... A trying day. To be cross-examined by that Henderton[1] man; to be tripped up by him on the question of the Glass Trade in relation to Tariff Reform and recognition – all this after I had been denouncing paid agitators. Just fancy! *Me* being cross-examined by a one-time iron-founder; and being made to admit that the Socialist workman has more brains than my Dear, Dear, Contented Working Man ... I'm a fool, that's what I am. A damn fool.

But I love my workmen, provided they always *are* mine. And I feel sure they love me ... That is, I think they do ... Of course, there are many ... But they must, they must. Confound the dogs, they *shall*. But this won't do, Santa, my boy. I suppose I am getting old and bad tempered. Santa mustn't get cross. No, he must sacrifice himself for the sake of his Dear, Dear Contented Working Man. *He* doesn't get in the ... way of a ... decent div.[2] Good old ... dividends. But these crafty ... agitators. Damn 'em ... Good old Kings Lynn[3] ... Ah ... Good old ... old ... (*He sleeps*).

II.

(*Scene.* – An office at Union House, Mr. J. Billiams – General Secretary of the Amalgamated Railwaymen[4] is sitting writing at the table. There is a knock at the door.)

Mr. J.B.: Come in. (*Office boy enters.*)
   O.F.: Gentleman would like to see you, sir. Mr. Grate Eeston, his name is.

Mr. J.B.: Tell him to wait. I'll ring when I want him.

O.F.: (*Entering in response to the bell, thirty minutes later*): Your bell rung, sir?

Mr. J.B.: Tell that man to come in.

Mr. G.E.: (*Entering*): Good morning, sir. (*No response*) Ahem. Good morning, sir.

Mr. J.B.: (*Still writing*) Morning. Wait a minute.

Mr. G.E.: (*After reddening, biting his lip, and accepting the inevitable*): Very well.

Mr. J.B.: (*Head down, looking over his spectacles – even as Mr. G.E. did in better times – five minutes later*): Well, what can I do for you?

Mr. G.E.: Oh – er – I – I am Mr. Grate Eeston, you know, General Secretary of the Amalgamated Society of Railway *Shareholders*.

Mr. J.B.: H'm. Think I've heard your name somewhere before. What do you want?

Mr. G.E.: Well – er – I've called to see if you've any objection to us having a dividend this year ...

Mr. J.B.: (*Cocking his head in the air and looking through his spectacles, his expression not being dissimilar to that employed by Mr. G.E. in former times*): Dividend? Good God! *Dividend*? Why, you had a dividend last year, man. Heavens, what are our shareholding classes coming to? Dividend, two years running? Certainly not!

Mr. G.E.: I would respectfully submit, sir, that even shareholders must have something to live on. And dividends are our only method of getting a living.

Mr. J.B.: Don't be impudent. You must either be polite and respectful, as becomes a shareholder's position, or you can clear out. This is the result of recognising your confounded Union. I told my Executive what the result of that would be. You'd have got no recognition if I'd had my way. Our shareholders would have been contented and loyal enough, had it not been for you agitators of the A.S.R.S. You fellows ought to be hanged, and the shareholders put under military law. Fortunate for you the Liberals are in power; if Mr. Austen Chamberlain had been Prime Minister ... But there, he's not. Don't imagine we've got no influence with the Government; we can cripple its party funds. We'll smash you and your Union yet, sir.

Mr. G.E.: Surely we've a right to combine, sir?

Mr. J.B.: You've no rights at all, except those we care to give you. The sooner you understand that the better it will be for you. Besides, you've only got 25 per cent. of the eligible shareholders in the Amalgamated Society.

Mr. G.E.; I am instructed to ask if you could not possibly manage 1 per cent. dividend this year, sir. It would be so little to you and such a lot to us, you know, sir ...

Mr. J.B.: That's quite impossible. Quite. Do you know what it would cost the industry? No, of course you don't. Don't care either. Well, 1 per cent. would cost £600,000. Six hundred thousand pounds. See? And the industry won't stand that, you know.

Mr. G.E.: I'm afraid it will be very difficult for us officials to keep our members in hand if they don't get 1 per cent. There is much unrest among railway shareholders.

Mr. J.B.: Well, if they don't like it, they can invest their money somewhere else.

Mr. G.E.: But they can't; nobody will buy railway shares.

Mr. J.B.: Oh well, you leave your members to us and the Government. The police and military, the forces of law and order, will see to them. Think of the food supply. If that were endangered, shareholders would be among the first to suffer. You people have no gratitude. None whatever. Think of the things we've done for the benefit of our shareholders. Have we not created sick and pension societies for you? Have we not taught you thrift by allowing you to pay into these institutions? And have we not provided you with tracts on the simple life? Base ingratitude! Oh *what* are our shareholding classes coming to?

Mr. G.E.: Well, tracts on the simple life won't feed us. Anyhow, sir, we *have* to lead the simple life, quite irrespective of the tracts you gave us.

O.F. (*Entering*): Your bell rang, sir?

Mr. J.B.: Show this man out.

III.

(*Scene.* – As in I., except that Lord Santa Claus is sitting bolt upright in bed, shouting at the top of his voice; his arms are flourishing in the air; he is severely perspiring; and his eyes are flashing as in the excitement of battle.)

Lord S.C.: Socialists! Confiscators! Robbers! What about the shareholders' hard-earned savings? What about he widows and the orphans, eh? You Trade Union Dictator ... Don't you go out, Mr. Grate Eeston ... Don't go! Don't. (*He wakes up.*) Lord! What a dream. Thank heaven *that's* not real!

Herbert Morrison, 'The Weaker Vessel and the Strike' (1912)

I.

It was night, and Mr. and Mrs. Jack Robins were in bed, asleep; their three children slept in another bed in the same room – the stately home of the Robins only consisted of two rooms in one of the tenement houses of the East. London's terrible, magnificent East.

Had you been there, you would have heard Mr. Robins repeatedly murmur in the dulled voice of sleep: "Don't talk to me ... We got to live, we 'ave ... wife and three kids. *Am* I a blackleg? ... Can't 'elp your troubles; we ain't going to starve, *we* ain't ... Wife and three kids ..."

And, in tones of sadness and self-reproach, the voice of Mrs. Robins, thus: "Bill on strike; my *brother* Bill ... the b— masters trying to make 'im go back ... ... blackmailing 'im ... starvation of his own wife and kids."

"My ole man – a blackleg ..."

Had you been there some half an hour later you would have seen that they were both awake; they were not talking, they were thinking, thinking hard. She was thinking about the strike; about brother Bill and the masters; about her husband – a blackleg! As for Jack, his soul was troubling him. His blackleg soul ... He hated the greed and cruelty of the masters as much – perhaps more – than any ticket man;[1] in his heart he believed the strikers to be right – absolutely right. But Jack was not a smart, courageous, Trade Union man; he was just a coward – a moral coward! He was not honest with his masters, nor with his fellows, nor with himself. He was dishonest; he was morally corrupt.

So they lay, musing for a space, the one not knowing that the other was awake.

Then – "Jack," said Mrs. Robins, nudging him, "Jack!"

"Yes, mate ..."

"This ... this 'ere strike."

"Well?"

Sitting up, putting a hand on either shoulder, and looking deep into his eyes: "*You ain't going to blackleg no more!*"

"Oh," rejoins Mr. Robins, with a touch of indignation, "ain't I? And 'oo says I ain't?

"*I* says you ain't! Blacklegging's *dirty* work, Jack ... And you're my ole man. See?"

Pause, so that Jack may have time to see.

After which: "Well! *You* ain't getting no flash ideas into your 'ead at all, are you? My Gaud! Like a blooming suffragette[2] ... How are you going on for grub and that if I don't work? You got a banking account? Cos I ain't!"

"I'm ready to do my share of the suffering," said she, quietly.

"What about the kids?" was the prompt interrogation.

"Ah, that ain't so easy, Jack! I been thinking about them, and I see it this way. All being well, those kids'll grow up; they'll know more than what we know, Jack – they come along later ... When they grow up, the likes of us won't put up with the rotten time we're putting up with; they'll kick against it! And our kids'll be among the kickers – I'm seeing to that. Do you think it'll please them to remember that their ole man was a blackleg? ... They'll cuss the likes of you; they'll feel you've put a blot on their characters; they'll say you wasn't a good father, 'cos you never joined your mates to get more wages, so that they could be brought up better. *That's* what about the kids!"

Pause.

"Never saw it that way before, mate."

"I didn't till this morning."

"Y'know, I'm not proud of being a blackleg; I felt I couldn't look at the Union men straight in the face, but I couldn't see you and the kids 'ungry. Now you've rounded on me! ... 'Ave I got to join the Union?"

"You got to join the Union. I shan't feel ashamed of my ole man, then!"

Pause.

"Kiss us, mate ..."

They kissed.

And they had never kissed quite like that before.

II.

Mr. and Mrs. Bill Wright were in the room of their two-roomed tenement which served as kitchen, dining room, smoking room, and study, in addition to being the nursery of the two Master Wrights. The whole family was "at home."[3]

Had you been there, you would have seen that they were all unhappy and unsettled. Mrs. Bill was in a distinctly bad temper, and Mr. Bill was obviously conscious of the disturbed state of her mind; husbands get to know these psychological moods – so do wives! Bill was standing looking out of the window into the mean street below; he "smoked" an empty clay,[4] and was prepared for a row. The Masters Wright were breakfasting.

"'Ow much longer are you going to stand staring out of that window?"

"Any 'arm in that?"

"Well, there ain't any *good* in it, anyway!"

"What would you like me to do then?"

"Oh, do what you like!"

"That's what I *am* doing!"

"Well, it won't bring any money home, will it?"

"Go on, *go* on! Now we're orf, mum!"

"You ought to be saucy, *you* did. If you was a man and a real 'usband and father, you'd go out to work. That's what you'd do!"

"'Ow can I, when there's a strike?"

"Strike be damned! They got a notice up at the docks, wanting men. Go and work!"

"And be a blackleg!"

"That's better than letting your wife and kids go short ... You and your Union, and our leaders, and your meetings, and your rights! My word, wasn't I a fool to get married to a man like you!"

"You wasn't the only fool ..."

"*Very* clever! ... Now then, you, Georgie, 'ave you finished your breakfast?"

"Yes. Didn't want much finishing! Dry bread and tea; we used to 'ave dripping[5] on the bread."

"Well, that's your *father's* fault. Can't afford dripping now; sticking up for the rights of labour won't stand dripping, my son! Go on, you two kids, get orf to school."

They get.

Mrs. Bill clears away the breakfast things, breaking a plate and cursing in the process. Then she goes out of the room, shutting the door with a furious bang.

And had you seen Bill's face just then, you would have observed a tear trickling down his cheeks ...

Poor, brave Bill!

J. Zimmerman, 'Stitch, Stitch, Stitch' (1913)

"'Ah many pair 'as you done?"

The question was asked harshly, the speaker stitching away for dear life on a pair of trousers. Her words were more than a question, for their tone exhorted the girl to work more quickly.

"Fifteen," answered the girl listlessly.

"Wot!" exclaimed Mrs. Adams, and stopped the mad flight of her needle to look at the pile yet to be done. "Gawd 'elp us! On'y fifteen pair done an' the 'ole lot mus' be in the shop fus' fing i' the mornin'. Lumme, we mus' buck up."

She quickly resumed her work and stitched away at a more maddening rate than before.

After a slight pause the girl stole a glance at a clock standing on the mantelpiece, and said:

"Oh dear, it's gorn 'arf pas' nine."

"'As it?" replied Mrs. Adams, indifferently, and then grasping the girl's hint, she continued, "W'y 'cors it as. I fergits. But yer ain't goin' 'ome, I carn't let yer. Yer knows yersel' this lot mus' be done else I don't git no more work orf the shop."

"Muvver's ill an' I says ter 'er as 'ow I'd be 'ome 'arf pas'," the girl said, still stitching away as fast as her weary hand could move.

"Wot kin I do? This 'ere lot mus' be done, yer know," Mrs. Adams said helplessly.

"But me muvver's ill, an' there ain't nobody ter look arter 'er, as me bruvvers gorn on the night shif'," the girl said, almost crying.

"It means losin' the shop, an' I git no money if the work ain't in fus' fing i' the mornin'. I tell yer me rint's a minth be'ind an' I'll git chucked aht if it ain't p'id Mond'y. An' the kids is starvin'."

Mrs. Adams spoke rapidly, almost to herself, and in this gloomy survey of her circumstances she forgot the girl's remark. Suddenly she looked again at the pile of unfinished trousers and said, almost fiercely:

"Come on, hah, we've got ter buck up an' git 'em done," and she summoned strength from some mysterious source and stitched away in a greater frenzy than ever.

While they were talking they did not notice that one of the two children had fallen asleep upon a pile of trousers from which he and his brother were clearing stitches. For Mrs. Adams' two children, aged nine and seven, were forced to help. They sat in a corner and put the trousers they had done under the bed; the garret was too small for room to be found for them elsewhere. A gas-bracket was fixed in one of the walls. Mrs. Adams and the girl sat right in front in order to make the most of its by no means brilliant light, and by so doing threw the greater part of the room into shadow. Only slight rays stole through the space between them, and by their light the children had to pick out stitches. Long practice had made them adepts and in spite of their tender years they were of real help. And now, at half-past nine at night, they were sitting in the densely-oppressive atmosphere; one picking stitches and the other huddled on a heap of trousers asleep.

"Well, an' ah's the kiddies gittin' on? Do th'y warn't ter git done?" Mrs. Adams bantered, trying to treat this hard work lightly, as if it were a pastime, and not a tragedy.

"A' doin' of 'em, mummie," answered the younger.

"'Ullo, w'y don't Tom answer? I b'lieve 'e's the eldes' an' I fink 'e's yer guv'nor, too, ain't 'e? So mind yer don't come it, 'cos yer didn't oughter speak w'en your boss's arst somethink."

But the child, trying to divert her attention, cried, "Mummie, I ain't arf 'ungry."

"'Ere, y'ar, talkin' agin! Nah w'y don't Tom speak?" Mrs. Adams continued, with a somewhat heavy humour. "Bet 'e's gorn dumb, or does 'e warnter go on strike?"

But the sleeping child slept on, and the wakeful one said nothing for fear of incriminating him.

"Hah, Tom, buck up; carnt yer speak?" continued Mrs. Adams, beginning to think she would really have to lose a second to see what the child was doing.

"'E's sleepin', mummie," said the younger at last.

Mrs. Adams jumped up, exclaiming, "Wot, sleepin'!" and rushed over to wake him.

"Nah, wyke up Kidde, do," she shouted, albeit tenderly, as she shook the child. "There's a goon 'un, dear; an' 'elp yer muver. We'll soon git the blarsted lot done an' I'll buy yer a kyke. Nah come along, an' be a good 'un an' buck up."

While Mrs. Adams was coaxing thus, there was a tap at the door, and before she could answer, a well-dressed man stepped in.

"Oo are you?" she demanded, and stood up alert, apprehensive that the stranger boded no good.

"All right, Mrs. Adams, you needn't be alarmed, I'm only the factory inspector."

"The wot?" she almost shrieked.

"Sh, don't be frightened," the inspector said, without being in the least disturbed, for he was accustomed to all kinds of reception while on his duties.

"'Ah did yer know I lives 'ere? This ain't no workshop an' I ain't got no rules."

The inspector took no notice, but asked the girl her age and other particulars. Noticing the children, he said:

"You'd better put them to bed. They look tired enough."

Mrs. Adams stood by helplessly, while he jotted down sufficient details to enable him to apply for a summons. At last he said, as he closed his notebook, "I'm afraid you'll hear more about this, Mrs. Adams."

"Wot? So yer means ter summons me, do yer?"

"It's a serious case," he replied.

"Ain't me starvin' kids an' me serious?" asked Mrs. Adams derisively. "Me rint's a month be'ind an' aht I goes if it ain't p'id jolly quick, I kin tell yer. Ain't thet a serious kyse, or wot clarsy nyme yer might like ter call it? Lumme, d'yer fink I does it fer me 'elth, d'yer fink it's me 'obby?"

"I'm sorry, Mrs. Adams, but I must do my duty."

"Carn't yer let us orf, jist this once?" she sobbed, her mood changing from derisive anger to despair as she realised it *was* a serious case – for *her*. "Nah, carn't yer?"

Tom, now thoroughly awake, saw by his mother's tears something was wrong, caught hold of his brother, went over to her, and added his non-comprehending tears to hers. Mrs. Adams kept repeating, "me poor dear kids, Gawd 'elp me."

The inspector was silent. He looked around and seemed racked by some great doubt. At last he said in despair.

"The case is down in my book. I must do my duty," and left the room hurriedly.

He was glad to get away, for the scene was painful to his feelings as a man, and liable to divert him from his duty as an inspector.

The trousers were finished by the morning. Mrs. Adams and the girl worked without a break – and the children picked stitches between their involuntary naps.

* * *

"Are my trousers done?" asked Mr. Smith, officially known as Mr. Inspector.

"No-er-no, sir," the assistant answered.

"You promised them faithfully, and I've got an important engagement this afternoon."

"Er – very sorry, sir, but the truth is we're rather busy jist now," and turning to the cutter, he whispered, "It's that blarstid Mrs. Adams. She's late agin; we'll 'ave ter give 'er the bullet."

"Look here! You promised the trousers, and I want 'em," said Mr. Smith, vexedly.

The assistant tried to excuse himself, but could only be feebly apologietic beneath Mr. Smith's righteous indignation.

Suddenly Mrs. Adams entered in a tremendous hurry with a parcel in her arms. As the assistant caught sight of her he shouted, forgetting, in his anger, a stranger was present, "At last, damn yer! No more bloomin' work *you* git."

But Mrs. Adams stopped dead; she stared at the inspector aghast, unable to speak or move. She could only stare.

"Wot are yer standin' like a stuck pig for? Carn't ye budge? Nah then, git a move on. 'Ere, give us the parcel and wyte dahnstairs." And he took the parcel from her and hustled her out of the shop.

"So that woman made my trousers, did she?" asked the inspector, who was not insensible to life's little ironies.

Such a question was unusual from a customer, and the assistant pretended not to understand.

"Look here," Mr. Smith continued, "I'm a factory inspector and I visited your work-hand's place at ten last night. I know she must have worked all night to get the trousers done. I didn't suspect mine were among them."

"H'm, is that so, sir? Sorry, but we put ahr work aht an w'at 'appens ter it ain't ahr business," replied the assistant jauntily, with an elaborate affectation of polite interest, which was a covert sneer at the inspector's assumption that *he* was interested in Mrs. Adams' hours of labour.

"As I'm to blame for making her late I hope you won't sack her. I don't mind telling you, but as a matter of fact, I wanted these trousers to wear in court when reporting her case. But I'll do what I can to save getting her into trouble."

The assistant promised not to sack Mrs. Adams, his manner still politely insinuating that he thought the inspector a bit of a fool to trouble about so insignificant a creature.

Mrs. Adams had another "coppin' from the shop," as she expressed it, but she was used to that. She could not understand why she didn't get the sack, and wonders what made the inspector forget his summons. But she still frequently works all night, helped by her children and the sickly girl.

And the inspector tempers law with mercy, although he feels mercy is crueller than the law, for it perpetuates the evil conditions the law was established to remove.

But what can he do? He has seen the irony of it all; why should he summons Mrs. Adams and not himself?

The episode of the trousers has taught him that someone ought to inspect the inspector.

'Casey', 'Alice in Sunderland. A Baffling Mystery' (1914)

> The author deeply regrets this week's article. The truth about it is that he stayed two hours at the Pentecostal Convention[1] held during Whit-week[2] in Sunderland, and on his arrival at the well-known health resort of Jarrow[3] the daughter of his hostess recited "The Mad Tea Party" from *Alice in Wonderland*. Unfortunately, the two events became mixed – not the author – hence the mystery. He hopes his many friends and enemies, likewise Lewis Carroll, will forgive him.
> – WALTER HAMPSON ("Casey")

Alice was beginning to get very tired. Her mother had taken her to hear the Pentecosters. Her head ached with the uneven singing, so she finally crept to a door at the back of the hall and wandered away in the dark.

Suddenly she felt herself falling and falling, until she lost consciousness.

She was awakened by a voice she thought she recognised. "Who has followed us up here?" it asked.

"Why, it's the Mad Hatter!" said Alice. "Please, where am I?"

"You should not say 'Where am I,' but 'here ma I,'" corrected the Mad Hatter.

"But where's here?"

"Oh, here is where – where you are, you know. Still, it does not matter much because you are not now."

"I don't understand you."

"Well, it isn't really necessary now, you Izzer Deadun."

"What is that?" cried Alice, thoroughly alarmed.

"You Izzer Deadun from Sunderland. You have left it far behind."

"Well, thank heaven for that."

"Don't be so heavenly thankful, you might wish yourself back again on earth."

"Rubbish," said Alice, "I am quite tired of listening to those Pentecosters straining discordant unisons thro' their neezy noses. It's too slow."

"Ah," said the March Hare, chiming in, "let me assure you you've jumped from the frying pan into here. We Eternitists sing more hymns in one year than your Earthistes do in a billion."

"Great Scott," said Alice.

"No, no, not Scott, mostly Wesley and Newman.⁴ How do you suppose we'd get thro' Eternity if we did not sing hymns?"

"Ark at 'is science!" said the Mad Hatter, chiming in. "Eternity is not a turnstile or a railway tunnel. You can't get thro' Eternity. It has no beginning, nor no ending. It is all over again."

"But how can it be all over again, if it never began?"

"Treason," yelled the Dormouse, waking up. "She's axing questions."

"Well, if I can't ask questions, I want to go."

"I knew it," sang the March Hare.

> She wants to go, she wants to go,
> She wants to go right down to Dixie.⁵

"Why, that's not a hymn, that's a song," said Alice.

"Ha, ha, ha," laughed the March Hare, "your knowledge is not worth an old song. Don't you know a hymn is simply a song of praise about Dixie."

"Don't bother with her," said the Mad Hatter.

"And don't you bother with hymn," retorted Alice.

"You are simply arguing about a trifle," chimed in the Dormouse.

"You'll be whipped shortly," said the March Hare, "and you'll find that no trifle."

"Ridiculous," yelled the Mad Hatter. "How can you whip a Wasser or an Isnot?"

"She's a saucy little baggage," yelled the March Hare.

"'Ark at 'is science!" laughed the Mad Hatter. "She is neither a saucy baggage nor has she any. She Izzer Deadun, and an Izzer Deadun is a ghostess; no legs, no arms, no nothing."

"Certainly," said the Dormouse, "she does know nothing."

"Is a ghostess a kind of spirit?" queried Alice.

"So to speak," replied the Dormouse. "A ghostess or ghost is a kind of spirit level. Something on the Astral plane."

"Well," said Alice, "if the Astral plane is anything like Annfield Plain,⁶ I prefer to be excused. But I can't make it out. First I am an Izzer Deadun, then a ghost on a spirit level; bless my soul what am I? I do not understand."

"Guddle, Goddle," roared the Mad Hatter. "You are not supposed to understand. No one understands – except – except those who do. And what's the use of these things, for you haven't a leg left to stand on. That is as plain as the nose on your face."

"You're a nasty pasty, calling my nose plain."

"You really 'ave no nose," said the Mad Hatter, "spirits 'aven't."

Alice put her hand to feel – I mean she would have put up her hand if she'd had any.

"You've quite confused her," said the Dormouse. "When he said you had no nose, dear, he used it as a figure of speech. He used figures of speech, while honest John uses speeches of figures."

> Tell me not in mournful numbers
> That the soul is dead which slumbers
> Like a Burnsian speech[7]

"I am getting still more confused," said Alice.

"Well, you cannot know these things anyway," said the Mad Hatter, "it's all a mystery."

"What, a kind of Maskelyne and Devant?"[8]

"In your case," said the March Hare, "it's a kind of Feminine and Devant. This place is inhabited by spirits who never ask questions."

"Bother," said Alice, "I dunno where I are. First I'm an Izzer Deadun, next I'm a ghostess, then I'm a spirit. Bless my soul, I'm a sausage."

"Treason. Blasphemy. Lay hands on her," said the March Hare.

"Don't be silly," said the Mad Hatter, "there are no hands here, they're all on earth. What do you mean by saying spirits and souls are sausages?"

"Well," said Alice, humbly, "on earth the sausage is a mystery."

"Chuck it," said the Dormouse, "tell us a story."

"I do not know any stories."

"Great expectations!" hissed the March Hare. "I'll tell one myself. There were once three nice little girls who wanted to be angels."

"What's an Angel?" asked Alice.

"Axing again," said the March Hare.

"An Angel is a composite nebula with wings fixed too high for aeroplaning and not low enough for floating," said the Mad Hatter. "For further information study the old masters."

"Ha, ha! Caught yer," said the March Hare. "How can she study when she has no head for study?"

"You lost yours long ago," roared the Mad Hatter. "It's your fault," he said, glaring at Alice, "you've tried to upset our most cherished beliefs."

"Rubbish," said Alice. "All beliefs were cherished until brighter, purer, and better beliefs upset them."

"I am quite sure you've lost *your* head," said the March Hare.

"Why?" queried Alice.

"Because spirits have none," said he, triumphantly.

Alice knitted her brow – at least she would have done had she possessed one – when suddenly she felt herself shaken, and a well-known voice rang in her ears –

"Wake up, darling. Come and have some tea and toast.

"Bless you, dear old mummy, I wouldn't swap you for a million souls."

"Hush, darling," said mother, quite shocked, "You mustn't say such things."

SOCIAL DEMOCRAT

'Optimus', 'The May-Day Festival in the Year 1970' (translated from the Vienna *Arbeiterzeitung*[1]), *Social Democrat*, 15 April 1911, pp. 189–92.

May Westoby, 'Shamed', *British Socialist*, 15 November 1912, pp. 524–8.

Schalom Asch, 'Behind the Wall', *British Socialist*, 15 December 1913, pp. 573–6.

The *Social Democrat* (1897–1913) maintained its internationalist perspective during the period covered by this volume. This interest in the international socialist movement continued after the periodical was renamed the *British Socialist* in January 1912, when it aligned with the British Socialist Party formed at the end of 1911. It was published under that title until its demise in December 1913 and was edited by H. W. Lee after Harry Quelch retired in April 1913 through ill health.

The *Social Democrat* published only one short serial during this period (William Henry Caudle's (n.d.) 'Slaking Lime', September–November 1913) but continued to include short stories, often by international authors. Of the stories selected for publication in this volume, 'Optimus' is the only author who has not been identified. May Westoby (n.d.) published poetry, was the author of *Through the Ivory Gates* (1901), and edited *The Young Socialist – A Magazine of Justice and Love*. Schalom Asch (1880–1957) was a prolific Yiddish author who was born in Poland but became a naturalized American citizen. Some of his work was recorded on disc for Folkways Records, a label founded by his son, Moses Asch, who also recorded socialist musicians such as Woody Guthrie and Pete Seeger.

Notes
1. The *Arbeiterzeitung* workers' newspaper was founded in 1889 by Vicktor Adler (1852–1918), leader of the Social Democratic Party of Austria.

'Optimus', 'The May-Day Festival in the Year 1970' (1911)

On April 29, 1970, the "Volkstribüne," official organ of the Socialist administration for the district of Lower Austria, published the customary order of the President that all work should cease on the First of May. Only such work as was necessary for the festal celebration of that day was to be allowed, but even with regard to the latter the President's message desired that the decoration of the streets and the preparations for the festival should, as far as possible, be carried out on the preceding day.

On the morning of the First of May the great garden city of Vienna, which now extends from Stockerau to Mödling,[1] lay in deep repose. The many bright-coloured little houses, in Cotta style,[2] each surrounded by a small green garden, had been already decked out the night before with red flags, and so it was half past six o'clock – the sun had long ago risen brilliantly – before the first of the green blinds in the workers' little one-family houses were drawn up.

Already the evening before the young people had planted flag-staffs between the blooming chestnut trees, and many hundreds of red flags were already waving merrily in the breeze. The regular roads were strewn with freshly mown grass, and in every district – from Stockerau to Mödling – a large platform was erected in the principal square, with a small platform and speakers' desk opposite to it, which was also to be used by the conductor of the district orchestra.

At 7.20 a.m. the motors from the milk co-operative and other food supply stores, which from old association still kept the name of "hammer-works," ran through the workers' cottages, and deposited in the breakfast receptacle which is built into the front of each house the necessary provisions for the festal day, milk, eggs, bacon, or fish, fruit, vegetables, coffee, cigars, etc., according to the orders given the preceding day at the food centre. At 8 o'clock smoke was already rising from the chimneys of all the pretty houses, and whoever entered any of the clean, white-washed halls was met by an aroma of fresh coffee and newly-baked bread. And at this time many a housewife might be seen going up and down the garden with large scissors choosing the peonies and tulips which were destined for the festal board.

At 8.30 500 bands of music marched through every division of the garden city, except, of course, the inner quarters, on feast days resembling cities of the dead, which are exclusively given up to workshops, factories and offices. The underground railway, which takes one in 4 to 6 minutes from, for instance, the St. Viet garden city to the factory quarter of Brigittenau,[3] rests to-day. But at certain headquarters of each district one can – after previously giving notice at the traffic centre – have one of the motors which stand there, which indeed one must drive oneself, in order to do which it is necessary to have passed the chauffeur's examination, a thing which is, in general, done by one member of each family. There is, however, no very great demand for them, most of the comrades preferring to pass the day with companions in the same district, to which they have been drawn in order to be near the friends of their choice.

The silver trumpets of the bands bring jubilation, noise, movement, confusion into the quiet garden city streets. In a twinkling the battalions of the "Youth" were drawn up, and, headed by the bands, marched rank after rank to the platforms on the public place. The orchestra played historical battle songs from the old departed times of oppression, and the choirs of youths chimed in with clear voices. By 9 o'clock everybody was on their feet; 800 platforms in all the great squares were crowded, and from millions of throats now rose a real true hymn of the people into the stir, a song of joy and of labour, a pæan of youth and strength, a song sung by awakened mankind in its own honour.

Then all became still.

An old man mounted the tribune (the procedure was the same at all the centres of festivity) and spoke: "Comrades, brothers, fellow citizens! Let no man to-day forget the times of struggle! You rosy-cheeked youths, from out whose eyes life sparkles, you know not how black and threatening it was, here on earth, even as late as 60 years ago. You never knew the horrors of exploitation, the misery of those who had deadened themselves with drugs, the hopelessness of those who were utterly weary. We elders, who were witnesses of that dread epoch, we are dying out. But yet to-day I remember with a shudder the days of the horrible tenements in the narrow alleys of the large towns, of the neglected children roaming naked about the streets, of the torture of unemployment and of dependence on an employers – that life led by millions of proletarians, which was no life, or would not have been if it had not been spiritualized by the burning desire to destroy that world of oppression! You, who are growing up in light and sunshine, in the strength and fullness of a free life, think of the hell of capitalist society whose portals we have successfully broken down."

The words, spoken with trembling lips by the old man, were listened to in breathless silence.

Then a young woman, slender as a girl, in a long flowing robe which showed the chaste beauty of her noble form, mounted the platform and spoke with impressive nobility of manner, without undue heat and yet full of life: "Comrades, sisters, brothers! The words of the fatherly veteran have sunk into our hearts. We know, indeed, that there was once a time of the madness of possession. We know that the soul was once fettered by the demons of selfishness. We know it, but we can no longer fully realize what it was. For how is it possible that human beings themselves should have maimed their own souls and bodies? How was it possible that thousands should slavishly serve one? How was it possible that, instead of becoming strong and free in light and air, well cared for and well educated, men should pine in pestilential air, in ugly homes, untaught and half-starved? At that time man only knew *himself*, and that made him small! We know that man and man, flower and animal, the blade of grass in our garden and the stones on which we tread, are all parts of the same world, and only he who feels himself at one with all creation, he alone is worthy to be our brother. Whoso finds himself anew in others, whoso has conceived the great law of fellowship, he who will not tread down a blade of grass unnecessarily, whose glance caresses every child, he who feels and knows that is taking place in the soul of his neighbor, he is rich. To the slave of the vanished state of society his possessions formed a world, to us the whole world had become a possession!

No applause was heard. No evil look fell on that proud figure. But a thousand youthful, sparkling eyes looked at each other, filled with the noblest emulation to become prominent in the service of the whole.

Music struck up. The youths sang. The crowds then went leisurely home. In the group in which the old man walked someone pointed over to the factory district. "Yes, indeed," the old fellow related, "the factories then were not worked by electro-dynamos as now; there was infernal black smoke in almost every workshop, and our hands were covered with soot; and where was there ever a chance that a gifted workman might study or ever leave the factory to be admitted to other social work? When his strength failed him – well then ..."

But the old man had now reached his goal. They led him to the gate of the palace which bore the inscription "The Castle of Peace." Such places 60 years ago, miserably arranged, were known as "poorhouses" or "alms houses."[4]

The middle of the day was passed by each one in is own family circle. On each table was a beautiful bouquet. After dinner the old people lay themselves down in hammocks, the young ones went into summer-houses, taking with them this or that book from the central library which supplies every citizen daily, as gifts or loans, with the books he desires. The little ones ran to the great public playgrounds.

At 3 o'clock trumpet blasts called once more to the feast. Now the masses made a pilgrimage to the 50 great arena buildings, the people's theatre, in which to-day festive performances, free to all, were held. The great orchestras played, glorious voices sang hymns of freedom, and at last the rising of the curtain disclosed the stage. Goethe's "Faust,"⁵ still as ever the symbol of struggling humanity, was performed. Breathless stillness in the whole arena, a hundred thousand human beings feeling the words: "Wer immer strebend sich bemüht, den können wir erreten."*

It is evening; the inner districts lie in darkness, but in the garden city quarters there are lights shining from many thousand houses. From the Kahlenberg⁶ thousands of rockets ascend flaming through the sky; on the Danube boats with bright red lamps are sailing. From the gardens before the houses sound violins and flutes; the children sing till they are tired. No drunkard reels through the peaceful streets. From the "Castle of Rest" may be heard the voice of a happy old man. He is weeping for joy.

* "Whoever struggles with difficulty himself to redeem, him can we save."

May Westoby, 'Shamed' (1912)

Beatrice and Percy Tonson, fortunately released from office drudgery during the same week, had decided to spend it delightfully at Deal.[1] And since civilization, and what we deem its comforts, demands for us a roof to shelter beneath, they had engaged rooms at a boarding house as suitable to their restrictive means as they had been able to find through advertisement.

Anxious not to miss a moment of the pitiful holiday thought sufficient to recuperate their energies after a year of more or less mean and entirely uninteresting toil – that last degradation of the afore-mentioned civilization – they had arrived at Deal in the forenoon, and were now seated side by side occupying the places reserved for them at one of the two long tables which were only uncovered when clean cloths were laid down, once a week. It was tea-time, for at Barnley House this meal was not conducted on the more aristocratic lines considered de rigueur by more fashionable – and better paid – hostesses, but was taken in the dining-room like other meals.

In the exact centre of each table was an epergne[2] filled with fading flowers, which were only changed in company with the tablecloths. Flanking these on either side alternately and at equal distances from them and each other were plates of mediumly thin bread and butter, and glass dishes containing biscuits or segments of cake. Disregarding the rule taught to most of us in our infancy, in which politeness prescribes to us to blunt the edge of our appetite on bread and butter, the guests of Barnley House were apt to eat cake first. This was doubtless because they knew from painful experience the wrong way was yet the only one of satisfying one's taste for sweet things. The result of such knowledge was often an undignified scramble, which never failed to shock Beatrice and annoy Percy, who had been well nurtured by a refined mother.

Amid the clatter of unmusical voices a phrase here and there detached itself. Someone would remind Miss Gracely, who presided, that she did not care for sugar, while someone else earnestly requested to be accommodated with:

"My tea very weak, you know, please, Miss Gracely"; or,

"Two lumps for me, *please*"; or even,

"As strong as you like to make it, thank you, Miss Gracely."

Gradually everyone was, for the moment, provided with tea, and conversation, pending the passage of cups to be refilled, took a less strenuous turn.

"Wonder," asked a languid youth, impartially, "how the old strike[3] is getting on?"

"I'm sure I don't know," responded his neighbor, the belle of the boarding-house; "there's so many nowadays,[4] you can't take much interest in them. Life is too short."

"It's the Labour Unrest, you know," a thin, dark woman said in a manner she considered wittily epigrammatic.

"Labour unrest be blowed," contributed the rubicund father of a family, who sat amidst them at the top of the table directly facing Miss Gracely; "if I had my way I'd hang, drown, or imprison every blessed striker there is. Why," he continued, empurpling himself, "I know a young woman who's had to put off her marriage just because her fianceé's father has lost so much money lately. I did hear how much – master lighterman[5] or something, you see. What do you think of that? And all for a lot of lazy brutes who aren't satisfied with four or five pounds a week."

There was a varied chorus of shocked surprise, amidst which Beatrice Tonson was understood to inquire why, if the strikers earned the wages stated by the last speaker, there were anxious only to be given 30s. per week.

No one being able to answer this satisfactorily, the rubicund one took refuge in a sneer: –

"So, you're for these strikers, young woman, are you?" he asked unpleasantly.

"Certainly," she replied; "I am on the side of anyone who fights against injustice and slavery."

"And so am I," added her brother, Percy. "Why should masters be allowed to break their agreements any more than the men?"

"I don't know what we are coming to," said someone, inevitably, and someone else answered disconsolately, "And I'm sure I don't."

The heavy father disregarded these interpolations. Shaking his head and the forefinger of his left hand at Beatrice and Percy, he said impressively: –

"I do believe you young people are Socialists!"

There was a cessation in the redistribution of teacups. Everyone, excepting Miss Gracely, looked at the brother and sister anxiously, curiously, or scornfully, as their natures dictated.

Beatrice had flushed long ago, and now Percy's fair skin was dyed scarlet, but he looked up doggedly.

"Yes, we are both Socialists," he said proudly.

"There, what did I tell you?" their interlocutor appealed to the company. "That's what the country is coming to. To be over-run by a pest of Socialists. You *never* know where you're going to meet them now." He was complacently unaware of his own boorish rudeness: "A lot of pale-faced, red-tied, atheistical loafers!"

"I think you are making a mistake," began Beatrice, timidly, although she was very angry, but was interrupted by their tormentor: –

"What you want, of course, if for everything to be divided up. Oh, yes, I know what your sort want! And, suppose we did divide up everything to-day, where would some of us be next week?" (Oh! time-honoured query.) "Why, just as good-for-nothing and penniless as these helpless unemployables are now"

"Socialists," cried Percy Tonson, shortly, "don't want things divided up."

"Oh! they don't, don't they? Then what the deuce do they want?"

"They want everyone to be healthy and comfortable, and to have time to think of things," answered Beatrice.

"Bless my soul, so do we all. Only you can't do it by robbing people and blowing them up with dynamite. If everyone worked and no one loafed the world would be well enough. Look at me!" – and he clapped his chest proudly – "I began as an apprentice, and –"

A diversion was created here by the entrance of a tall, dark man of about thirty. Two girls pushed back a chair that had stood empty between them.

"We have saved your seat, Mr. Bertram," one of them said, coquettishly.

"You are very kind," he replied as he sat down, and turning to Miss Gracely: "Am I too late for a cup of tea?"

"Not at all, Mr. Bertram; I have just had a fresh supply," she replied, graciously.

"Loth to leave that nice young lady we saw you with this morning?" inquired the gentleman at the end of the table, with instinctive good taste.

Mr. Bertram looked at him coldly: "As I think you observed, Mr. Potter," he replied, slowly, "it *has* been too hot to-day to hurry overmuch" – he turned to Miss Gracely again at once – "even for the sake of tea, which is an attraction as if anything could be in this sultry weather."

Mr. Potter, foiled of the full display of humour he had intended to delight the company withal, returned to the original theme of interest, to the intense discomfiture of the two Socialists, who had welcomed Mr. Bertram's entrance as a saving grace. For, like many others, although they felt Socialism to be the one thing needful for society, and understood it themselves after a rather muddled fashion, they were not capable of explaining their faith to others, or even of clearly answering the most commonplace objections which crop up surely as their belief is discussed among people with different views, or with no views at all except the one that the newest creed must be the worst ever evolved from the busy brains of men.

"I suppose you two," began Mr. Potter, nodding his head elegantly towards them, "after you have got your share of the wealth other people are to disgorge for your benefit, would have us all numbered and ticketed like – er – like well, like convicts?"

"Disgorge is at any rate a good word as you used it then," said Percy, who had been struck by its aptness.

Mr. Potter, as purple now with triumph as before with rage, threw up his head with a loud laugh.

"Caught you that time," he announced. "Thought you said you didn't want us to divide anything up?"

"We don't," reasserted Beatrice, hotly; "nor do we want anyone numbered, or anything like that. Under Socialism people will have more freedom than they have now."

"How do you make that out, then?"

Beatrice hesitated, uncertain what to reply, an Percy came to her aid as best he could: –

"We shall all be able to do as we like, and not have to work so long, and –"

But Mr. Potter was again overcome with uproarious laughter.

"Live like blessed dukes," he declared noisily, "*and* princes. Goodness me! *What* times we *will* have when none of us have to work!"

"But, under Socialism *everyone* will have to do some work," Percy protested, fuming and yet helpless to take advantage of his opponent's ignorance.

"Everyone, strange as it may sound to those who consider work degrading, will want to work, and actually enjoy it," put in Mr. Bertram, unexpectedly.

Beatrice and Percy looked over at him gratefully. Eyes generally were withdrawn from them and fixed on him. Mr. Potter voiced their owners' thoughts when he said in surprise: –

"You don't mean to say *you're* one of them?"

"If you mean, am I a Socialist, I am glad to tell you that I certainly am. But I may not, therefore, be what you think me."

"Would it be troubling you to tell me what you think Socialism really is?"

"Not at all, sir, not at all."

Several people here rose and went out, desirous not to lose any more precious time within doors. Miss Gracely also rose.

"Perhaps you would not mind finishing your interesting discussion in the garden or the drawing-rom," she said, "because I think these tables should be cleared."

Mr. Potter got up as she was speaking; so did the rest, but when she had finished he cried out: –

"Just half a moment, Miss Gracely. It won't take me two ticks to give you my opinion of Socialism. It just means turning the world topsy-turvy in order to make the rich poor, and the poor rich. And after that we shall all have to do as we're jolly well told, like children at school, or suffer the consequences." He waved his hand towards Mr. Bertram: "There you are sir, as short as I could put it."

Mr. Bertram led the way from the dining-room into the strip of front garden where a few chairs stood, and those who followed settled themselves comfortably as he said to Mr. Potter: –

"I have heard your sentiments in many different forms before. May I tell you what most Socialists mean by Socialism?"

"Delighted," exclaimed the gentleman questioned, with a wink at the others that made Beatrice long to slap him.

Mr. Bertram, ignoring the evident irony of Mr. Potter's delight, quietly and ably explained the basic beliefs upon which the theory of Socialism rests, and as quietly and ably answered every objection put forward by his audience. Mr. Potter, although he blustered to the end, was palpably defeated, and two other people said, the one grudgingly, the other heartily: –

"I certainly have not understood so much about Socialism before. It gives one a different view of it."

Beatrice and Percy were intensely relieved, and both ready to worship their rescuer. Nor were they offended when, on a better acquaintance, he suggested to them that it would be as well for them – as, indeed, for all other Socialists – not only thoroughly to understand their creed themselves but to be prepared to answer the objections of others to it.

"You will find yourself in less awkward positions," he said, "and you will spread our glad tidings instead of merely fixing people in their old ideas by an insufficient explanation of what ours really are."

Percy objected half-heartedly that they had not much time, and were usually tired in what of leisure remained to them.

"Don't, Percy," cried Beatrice, hurt; "you are only saying that to excuse us. If our Cause is anything to us, surely we can devote a little time to understanding it. Only we have not thought about it in that way."

"Half-an-hour a day and a few good books to read and talk over together will do wonders," suggested Mr. Bertram, cheerily.

"We can manage that all right," Percy agreed.

And they forthwith occupied themselves in making a short list of books which explained Socialism.

So their week's holiday was of value in more ways than one.

Schalom Asch, 'Behind the Wall' (1913)

In the middle of the plain stands a huge black fortress, surrounded by a broad, mighty river. At eve, when all is still and sinks into silence, the waves murmur ...

Within the fortress every floor was filled with prisoners. During the day it seemed to be a dead building, a catacomb, the cavities of which were peopled with living, healthy, human beings. The convicts were sleeping on their sacks of straw, or gazing fixedly at the cornice of the stove or some similar object till they were nearly mad.

But towards evening the place came to life. Everywhere knocking began on the walls, and, thanks to the secret alphabet, long conversations were held. Every now and again a heavy step in the corridor plunged the whole house into silence. But, hardly had the warder passed by before all the knocking began again, even more vigorously.

The prisoners got accustomed to their speechless existence. They could now only talk with their fingers, and were at last able to guess by the knocks the character of their neighbour and even his social position. Sometimes, indeed, the desire assailed them to see, to speak a little – just to use once more a sleeping organ, to see if it was still able to fulfil its function.

One evening, when the whole prison was engaged in lively conversation, a fresh, youthful, merry laugh was suddenly heard – the clear voice of a young girl. The prisoners started. Something quite unusual was evidently happening, and the knocking on the walls ceased, the prison lay wrapt in silence. But the merry laugh, which warmed like the sunshine, sounded a second time between the walls ... strange ... as though the dead began to speak.

She was hardly more than a child, she who laughed there. When they brought her away from her mother's house she had not in the least realised the seriousness of her case. She had risen proudly, and followed the gendarmes in a romantic attitude. After such an adventure she expected something very wonderful, something in which she would be the heroine. But once alone between the four walls, loneliness laid heavy hands around her heart.

For a long time she cried silently to herself. Then she got better, and began to feel like a heroine. With clenched fists she raised herself on her couch and presented her chest as if it were about to be pierced by the bullets of the soldiers. Then she suddenly remembered that she was alone, and burst out sobbing like a child.

The warder hurried to the spot and cast an irritated glance through the spy-hole. As the eye appeared at the little opening, the young girl could not help a burst of laughter. When he saw her – the only female prisoner – the soldier was touched, and laughed too. But then his sense of duty got the upper hand, and when he spoke again he spoke in a rough voice, and put on his bearish manner.

Thus was the discipline once broken in the gloomy building. Soon the news spread through the whole prison that a young girl had arrived. How did it get about? Once she was fastened up in the cell, they could no longer hear her voice. Only the knocks of the secret alphabet penetrated through the walls. Neither could she be seen for she was taken alone for her walks. But they probably recognised her as a woman by her step when she passed along the corridor.

Then, too, she was musical, and in order to console herself for having to do without her piano, she sat down, the very first day, in a corner and beat with her foot the rhythm of her favourite songs. The convicts in the dark cells heard her above their heads, recognised the rhythm, and hummed the divine melody to themselves.

The whole gloomy building seemed changed by the presence of this fair creature.

In the neighbouring cell lay a young man. The dungeon walls had already robbed him of eight months of his life, but had not succeeded in stifling his fiery heart. He only felt that it was asleep in his breast. After getting up in the morning, he used to lie down again on his couch and think for hours of scenes from his childhood which now smiled at him as in a dream. Thus the energy which dwelt in him was lulled to sleep. It was a matter of indifference to him whether the sun shone outside or whether the rain came down in torrents. And yet it needed but a breath to awaken his heart once more.

He heard through the wall the step of the young girl, and when in the evening twilight she beat the rhythm of a Chopin nocturne, he became lost in sweet dreams. The saw a young wood in the first days of Spring. Here and there a glint of sunbeams between the little trees … A deserted castle reflected in the blue river, a young girl wandering beneath the pines. Wrapped in mystery, she steps softly between the trunks – she comes from a strange land and wanders into a strange world …

He had already tried to talk to her through the wall: with his fingers he confessed to her his love.*

---

* This is not at all improbable. Russian political prisoners have been known to communicate their inmost thoughts by these means.

"Who are you? I feel that you are young and beautiful, and I love you ... I am as strong as a lion. When night comes I will break down the wall and come to you. I will hide you in my breast like a little bird, and will flee with you far, far away ..."

She listened to the beating of his fingers, but without understanding it, for she did not know the secret alphabet. But she had at least the feeling that behind the wall a heart was beating which belonged to her, and that a voice was there calling to her. And she often laid her ear against the wall to listen, and to try to make out this mysterious language. Sometimes she knocked too, as though her fingers could speak.

Often, too, as night fell, she lay down on the floor close to the wall, and knocked to find out if he was at the same place on the other side of the wall. Thus they waited, and with his fingers he sang songs to her through the wall and told her of his love.

Though she did not understand them, yet the knocks touched her to her heart. She pressed her forehead against the wall.

One day something suddenly happened which sent a thrill of horror through the whole of that dreadful building. One of the convicts had discovered that a gallows had been erected in front of the prison.

Like rain dripping into the gutter the sound of knocking on the wall sighed on the whole night long through the prison. First it passed from wall to wall, then from floor to ceiling. They exchanged advice and comforted each other, asked questions and said farewell. That nocturnal beating was as the beating of the wings of the death-angel against the walls. At last the sounds gradually died away. Each prisoner in his own cell thought once more of his own life.

But during the night the knocking of the young girl's neighbour had assumed a strange tone. His fingers trembled as if in fever. Surely he had something serious and urgent to communicate. His knocks became faster and faster ... Then silence, as though a shudder passed over him. She divined that he was pressing his face against the wall; that he was giving her kisses through it; that he grew frenzied and began scratching it. But she could not tell what secret he was trying to confide to her.

Outside the wind wept and raved and rattled at the little iron shutters and moaned through the bars. Never had the young girl's cell appeared more dreadful to her.

She had already knocked several times, to call her neighbour; but he remained silent, as if angry with her. Then she became sulky and threw herself down on the bed. An unbounded sadness crept over her. She would have liked to go again to the wall and call him, but she waited that he should come first.

An uncanny stillness lay upon the prison. The knocking had quite ceased ... nothing was to be heard but the far-off stop of the sentry. At last horror got the better of her, she sprang up and ran to the wall. She knocked, sought, begged, and even hurt her face against the rough stones.

"Answer me, what are you doing?" she murmured. "What has happened? O, I am so frightened! Answer! Give me an answer! ..."

SOCIALIST

Eugene Sue, '"Stop Thief!" The Proletariat and Slummery (An Incident of the Revolution of 1848, told by Eugene Sue)', *Socialist*, April 1911, p. 63.

Tom Anderson, 'Mary Davis; or the Fate of a Proletarian Family. A Lesson Given to the Glasgow S.L.P. Socialist Sunday School', *Socialist*, January 1912, p. 34.

The *Socialist* (1902–24), subtitled *The Official Organ of the Socialist Labour Party*, was first published in Edinburgh and then in Glasgow from 1912 until its demise. Priced at one penny, it was published monthly and then quarterly. The *Socialist* was edited by James Connolly (1868–1916) in 1902, George Yates (n.d.) in 1903–4, John Smith Clarke (1885–1959) in 1913–14, John William Muir (1879–1931) in 1914, Neil Maclean (1875–1953) and George Harvey (n.d.) (the exact dates for Maclean's and Harvey's editorships have not, so far, been identified, other than they held the chair respectively between 1914 and 1919), and Arthur McManus (1889–1927), who co-edited with Tom Bell (1882–1924) in 1919–20. According to the *Warwick Guide to British Labour Periodicals, 1790–1970*, the *Socialist* was started by a pressure group within the SDF in Scotland, which went on to form the Socialist Labour Party in 1903. A Marxist-leaning publication, it carried no serials during the period covered by this collection and only a few short stories, and mostly favoured poetry.

Of the two authors included in this selection, Tom Anderson has not been identified, but Eugene Sue was the pseudonym of Joseph Marie (or Marie-Joseph) Eugène Sue (1804–57). Sue was a French author most famous for his serialized works *The Mysteries of Paris* (1842–3) and *The Wandering Jew* (1844–5), both of which were inspired by his socialism.

Eugene Sue, '"Stop Thief!" The Proletariat and Slummery (An Incident of the Revolution of 1848, told by Eugene Sue)' (1911)

Suddenly the cry: "Stop thief!" "Stop thief" resounded in the middle of the road, and a man who was running away as fast as his legs would carry him was seized by four or five working men in blouses and armed with guns. Among these a rag-picker, with a long white beard, but still strong, was conspicuous. His clothes were in tatters, and although he carried a musket under his arm he did not remove his pack from his shoulder. He was one of the first to seize the runaway, and now held him firmly by the collar, while a woman, running toward the group and panting for breath, cried:

"Stop thief! Stop thief!"

"Did this fellow rob you, my good woman?" asked the rag-picker.

"Yes, my good man," she answered. "I was standing at my door. This man ran up and said to me, 'The people are rising; we must have arms.' 'Monsieur, I haven't any,' I answered him. Thereupon he pushed me aside and went into my shop, despite all I could do, saying: 'Well, if you have no arms, I shall take money to buy some. So saying, he opened my till, took out of it thirty-two francs that I had there, and a gold watch. I tried to hold him, but he drew a knife upon me – fortunately I parried the blow with my hand – here, see the cut I got. I cried for help and he fled."

The culprit was a good-sized, robust, and well-clad man but of ignoble countenance. Hardened vice had left its indelible impress upon his wasted features. "It is not true! I stole nothing," he cried in a husky voice, struggling to avoid being searched. "Let me go! What does it concern you, anyhow?"

"That may concern us considerably, my young fellow," answered the rag-picker, holding him firmly by the collar. "You stabbed this poor woman after robbing her of her money and a watch in the name of the people. Keep still! This demands and explanation."

"Here is the watch for one thing," said a workman after searching the thief. "Can you identify it, madam?"

"I should think so, monsieur! It is old and heavy."

"Correct," replied the workman. "Here it is, madam."

"And in his vest," said another workman after searching another of the thief's pockets, "are six hundred sou pieces and one forty sou piece."[1]

"My thirty-two francs!" cried the tradeswoman. "Thank you, my dear men, thank you."

"That part being settled, my young fellow, you must now settle scores with us," proceeded the rag-picker. "You stole and meant to commit murder in the name of the people, did you not? Answer!"

"What is all this pother about, my friends; are we engaged in a revolution[2] or are we not?" answered the thief in a hoarse voice and affecting a cynical laugh. "Well then let us break into the money boxes!"

"Is that what you understand by a revolution?" asked the rag-picker. "To break into money boxes."

"Well?"

"Accordingly, you believe the people rise in revolt for the purpose of stealing – brigand that you are!"

"What other purpose have you, then, in insurrecting, you pack of hypocrites? Is it perhaps for honour's sake?" replied the thief brazenly.

The group of armed men, the rag-picker excepted, who stood around the thief, consulted for a moment in a low voice. One of them noticing the door of a grocery store standing ajar, went thither; two others went in another direction, saying:

"I think we would better tell Monsieur Lebrena of this affair, and ask his opinion."

Still a fourth whispered a few words in the ear of the rag-picker, who answered:

"I think so, too. It would be no more than he deserves. It may be a wholesome example. But while we wait send Flameche to help me mount guard over this bad Parisian.

"Halloa, Flameche!" called a voice, "Come and help father Brilri hold a thief."

Flameche ran to the rag-picker. He was a true Parisian gamin.[3] Wan, frail, wasted away by want, the lad, who was gifted with an intelligent and bold face, was sixteen years of age, but looked only twelve. He wore a dilapidated pair of trousers, and old shoes to match, and a blue sack coat that hung in shreds from his shoulders, for a weapon he carried a saddle-pistol. Flameche arrived jumping and leaping.

"Flameche," said the rag-picker, "is your pistol loaded?"

"Yes, father Brilri. It is loaded with two marbles, three nails, and a knucklebone – I rammed all my toggery[4] into it."

"That will do to settle the gentleman if he budges. Listen, my friend Flameche – finger on trigger, and barrel in vest."

"Tis done, father Brilri."

With these words Flameche neatly inserted the muzzle of the pistol between the shirt and the skin of the thief. Seeing that the latter tried to resist, Flameche added:

"Don't fidget; don't fidget; if you do you may cause Azor to go off."

"Flameche means his dog of a pistol."

"Frauds that you are!" cried the thief, carefully abstaining from moving, but beginning to tremble, although he made an effort to smile. "What do you propose to do? Come now, be done with your fooling! I have had enough of it."

"Wait a minute!" interjected the rag-picker. "Let us converse a spell. You asked me why we are in insurrection. I shall satisfy your curiosity. First of all, it is not to break into money boxes and loot shops. Mercy! A shop is to a merchant what a sack is to me. Each to his trade and tools. We are in insurrection, my young fellow, because it annoys us to see old folks like myself die of hunger on the streets like a stray dog when our strength to work is no more. We are in insurrection, my young fellow, because it is a torment to us to hear ourselves repeat the fact that, out of every hundred young girls who walk the streets at night, ninety-five are driven thereto by misery. We are in insurrection, my young fellow, because it riles us to see thousands of ragamuffins like Flameche, children of the Paris pavements, without hearth or home, father or mother, abandoned to the mercy of the devil, and exposed to become, someday or other, out of lack for a crust of bread, thieves and assassins, like yourself, my young fellow!"

"You need not fear father Brilri," put in Flameche; "you need not fear – I shall never need to steal. I help you and other traders in old duds to pack your sacks and dispose of your pickings. I treat myself to the best the dogs have left over. I make my burrow in your bundle of old clothes, and sleep there like a dormouse. No fear, I tell you, father Brilri, I need not steal. As to me, when I insurrect, by the honour of my name! it is because it finally rasps on me not to be allowed to angle for red fish in the large pond of the Tulieries[5] – and I have made up my mind, in case we come out victors, to fish myself to death. Each one after his own fancy. Long live the Reform! Down with Louis Philippe!"[6]

And, turning to the thief, who, seeing the five or six armed working men coming back, made an effort slip away:

"Do not budge, mister! Or, if you do, I shall let Azor loose upon you." Saying which he tightened his finger again on the trigger of his pistol.

"But what is it you have in mind to do with me?" cried the thief, turning pale at the sight of three of the working men another, coming out of the grocery he had just stepped into, brought with him a poster made of brown paper on which some lettering had been freshly traced with a brush dipped in blacking.

A dismal presentiment assailed the thief. He struggled to disengage himself and cried out:

"If you charge me with theft – take me before the magistrate."

"Cannot be done. The magistrate is just engaged marrying his daughter," explained father Brilri calmly. 'He is now at the wedding."

"Besides, he has the toothache," added Flameche, "he is at the dentist's."

"Take the thief to the lamp post," said a voice.

"I tell you that I demand to be taken to the magistrate!" repeated the wretch, struggling violently to free himself, and he began to shout:

"Help! Help!"

"If you can read, read this," said one of the working men, holding up the poster before the thief. "If you cannot read, I shall read it for you:"

"SHOT AS A THIEF."

"Shot?" stammered the fellow, growing livid. "Shot? Mercy! Help! Assassins! Murder! Watchmen, murder!"

"An example must be set for the likes of you, in order that they may not dishonor the Revolution!" explained father Brilri.

"Now down on your knees, you scoundrel!" ordered the blacksmith, who still had his leather apron on. "And all of you, my friends, get your guns ready! Down on your knees!" he repeated to the thief, throwing him down to the ground.

The wretch sank upon his knees in a state of utter collapse and terror that, crouching upon the pavement, he could only extend his hands and mutter in an almost inaudible voice:

"Oh, mercy! Not death!"

"You fear death! Wait, I shall bandage your eyes," said the rag-picker.

And letting down his sack from his shoulders, father Brilri took a large piece of cloth out of it and threw it over the condemned man, who, on his knees and gathered into a lump, was almost wholly covered therewith. Soon as it was done, the rag-picker stepped quickly back.

Three shots were fired at once.

Popular justice was done.

A few minutes later, fastened under his arms to the lamp post, the corpse of the bandit swung to the night breeze, with the post attached to his clothes –

"SHOT AS A THIEF."

(From "The Galley Slave's Ring," the nineteenth and closing story of Eugene Sue's famous series of historic novels, published under the collective title of the "History of a Proletarian Family Across the Ages," by the New York Labour News Company, and translated by Daniel De Leon,[7] Editor of the *Daily* and *Weekly People*).

Tom Anderson, 'Mary Davis; or the Fate of a Proletarian Family. A Lesson Given to the Glasgow S.L.P. Socialist Sunday School' (1912)

Comrades, Girls and Boys, and Grown-ups, –

The lesson[1] I am going to give you to-day is in the form of a story, and the story is about a young woman – her name was Mary Davis. She was the daughter of a coal miner.

This is a true story, and it happened fully twenty-five years ago.

Two miles east from here is the mining district of Lanarkshire, and it was there that Mary was born and brought up.

Mary had two brothers, Tom and James, and they were both miners.

We had been companions from our school days, and I was a regular visitor at their house from my boyhood up till I became a man of many talents, and I want the girls and boys here to remember, and to be on their guard, when they hear their teachers in the day schools tell them of the great men and women in history.

We have a text, which you all can repeat, but which possibly you cannot understand quite clear as yet. It is: "The Great are only Great because the Workers are Wage-Slaves. Let us organise." This little incident of Tom Davis will help you to understand what I mean.

Old Tom Davis was a coal miner, – a wage slave. If you had met him coming home from the pit, just as you were coming home from school, you would have seen a big burly man, with a very black face; his clothes were coarse, his jacket, trousers, and vest were all begrimed, just as his body was, by his occupation. His master, I am sure, would never have allowed him to come into his house with such clothes on. He, to his master or his master's friends, would not be a great man; he, to them, would only be a common miner. Yet he was a truly a great man. The great men you are told about by the lackeys of the master class live in big houses and have servants to attend to them, they own a great deal of wealth, and you are told stories about them and of their greatness, to cloud your brain and make you servile. Do you know, that if you are told a lie often enough you will believe it,[2] and these stories of the great men you are told about are not true, but your fathers and mothers were told the same stores that are being told to you, and they believed them all their days to be true. Nearly all the workers believe them to be true. It is only the revolutionary worker who knows them to be false, and the master class is afraid of these men, lest they should be able to explain to the workers the true position.

Now, let me ell you something about old Tom's talents, or his greatness. We called him "old Tom," not that he was very old – he was only forty-five – a younger man at that time than I am now. Well, he was a splendid violinist, one of the best reel and strath-spey[3] players in the district. Many and many a time has he played at the marriages of the miners and others, just for the love of playing. He was a good quoit player,[4] and at the local flower shows he took prizes many a time for his flowers. He was an authority on dogs, birds, and poultry, and as a debater on politics and history he was looked upon as a master. And he was only a coal miner. His name does not appear in any of your history books. That would never do. Your father's masters would not suffer such a thing to be.

Now, let me give you a description of the Davis's home. The Davis's lived in a room and kitchen house – it was called a "butt and ben," that is, the room went off the kitchen. That was the usual kind of house occupied by the miners, and it is the same to-day. This "butt and ben" of the Davis's will always live in my memory. It appeared to me a palace in the true sense. The floor was so well scrubbed that it always looked nearly pure white, the polished parts of the grate were always very bright, and the old-fashioned sweay,[5] with its large chain links, I think I can still see hanging down into the center of the fire. The set of "cans," a marriage present of years ago, adorned the shelf, and on them were inscribed the names of Tom and Mary his wife. On the right hand side of the fire hung the old "waggity we-clock,"[6] with its brass chains and brass weights. The old style kitchen dresser, with its display of plates, was always to my mind a work of art. There were two beds in the kitchen: we call them built-in beds. The coverings on them were pure white, with an embroidered border, the work of Mary the mother. This "butt and ben" was a marvel of order and brightness. The walls were colour-washed, the bottom part pale green, the top and ceiling pure white. A few pictures adorned the walls, but none of the pictures were of saints, or of kings and queens. The pictures were a few photographs of the family, of a prize canary, and of some prize flowers. And in the room was a good-sized bookcase packed with books.

The Davis family did not go to any church; this at that time was a great sin. Many a time have I heard old Tom laugh when a busy-body from the church would call to see if he would send his family to the church. He would as his visitor *why* he should send his children to the church, and the visitor would say, that they might be saved. "Man," Tom would say, "I am astonished at your simplicity." He would then rise and go to the room and bring a few books from the bookcase. Then he would ask his visitor if he had read *that* (Gibbon's "Decline and Fall of the Roman Empire"[7]), handing him the work. This always closed the conversation, the visitor always preferring to go away without saying any more on the question.

Sunday was a great day in Davis's house. Breakfast was at nine o'clock, then all the topics of the week were discussed at the table; dinner at two o'clock was the same, the only difference being, one or two men folk (friends) would be there, and the discussion took a wider range. Supper at six was on the same lines.

Mary Davis at this time was a young woman of eighteen years of age. She worked in a weaving factory. She was a fine, bright young woman, tall, and of good appearance. She was a born rebel and a strong supporter of all her father's views. She had tried on several occasions to improve the conditions of labour in the factory, but the results were so small that it daunted her spirit; still she headed every revolt that was made to secure improvement. One day, as she was engaged at her looms, the manager's son came along to where Mary was working. He had heard a great deal about this rebel woman and he wanted to inspect her. He stood behind her, and, being the son of a rich man and a boss, he put a hand on each of her shoulders. Like lightning the daughter of the miner wheeled round, and with a shuttle which she had in her hand struck him across the face. The young snob was upset. He was smarting from the blow, and he turned round as if to strike back, but when his eyes rested on the brave woman standing ready for him, he shewed the white feather.[8] There was great excitement in the mill all the afternoon, for the news spread like "wild fire." All the women (and there were nearly 1,000 employed in the mill) were inwardly delighted.

When Mary reached home that night – the news had arrived before her – there was a big crowd standing at her home to see her. To Mary the incident was nothing; she considered it her duty to do as she had done, and she said had she not done it she would have been a coward. In the Davis's house that night a concert and dance took place in honour of Mary. Next morning Mary turned out to her work as usual, but he gatekeeper had strict orders not to admit her, and as she entered the gate, this white servile wage-slave, according to orders, stopped her, and said, "You are not to start work here again."

"Brave man," said Mary, "noble slave, go now and lick your master's feet; and for so doing you will be allowed to work all your days in the mill," and with that she turned and walked home.

Some time after this incident the miners were on strike, and a meeting of the men was being held on a piece of common land near the town. Mary went to the meeting; her father was chairman, and the principal speaker was a young man – John Sneddon, a rebel of his time – and he was Mary's lover. There was a big crowd at the meeting. After the chairman had spoken, he called on John Sneddon. This young man's speech had a great effect on the miners; he was one of themselves. He put the case clearly before them, and asked, "Are you going to give in?" "**Never,**" was the unanimous reply. There were several policemen, along with several of the highly paid lackeys of the coal masters, moving around the meeting, and it so happened they halted just where Mary was standing, and one of the lackeys said, "Listen to that fool Sneddon." Mary was so enraged that she turned on the man and struck him. The police seized her, then a free fight ensued, in which the police and the lackeys came off "second best."

During the night the arm of the law visited Mary's house, and she was dragged from her bed and taken to the office. After a delay of several weeks, she was tried and found guilty, and sentenced to three months' imprisonment with hard labour.

A great fete was arranged for the day on which Mary was liberated. The largest hall in the district was taken, and Mary and John Sneddon were married. The event was one of the greatest ever known to have taken place in the district. For years after it served as a date; "It was on the night on which John Sneddon and Mary Davis were married," was quite a common saying.

For the next few years the Davis's and the Sneddon's had to move all round he district to get work, for Capitalism makes you pay for it, if you attempt to assert your manhood, and this is one of the great levers that makes many of the workers cowards. It is not that they have not the desire to fight, and they know that they should fight, but they are afraid of the starvation of their women and children. They go back to their work defeated men, they hope that their fellows will soon give in, and that the strike will be settled, and that it will soon be forgotten, and they endeavor to make themselves believe that there was some excuse for their going back. That their fellows will excuse them for "blacklegging" is their one anxious desire. They know they have been "Rats," but they feel that the loss of their manhood is a great price to pay to get bread, and in silence they curse their fate, and their one desire is, that some day may come, in which they will join with their fellows and fight like men, and so the hope of this keeps them from sinking.

Time, however, brings changes. Old Tom suggested to his sons and John Sneddon that they ought to try their old district again, for it was in that district the greatest part of his life had been spent: his boyhood days, his days of love, courtship, and marriage; there his children were born; there his old "butt and ben" awakening memories of the happy days spent in it – the old man yearned to go back, yes, even to go back and work in "Number 3 Pit." And back they went. They all started in "Number 3 Pit." The men in the pit were well pleased to see their old friends back. These are good men, the manager said to himself, and they have had a good lesson. So there they worked. Nothing of any importance cropped up during the next year or two, and the family were all back again into their old way of living, spending their spare time as they did in the good old days.

One beautiful afternoon in June there was a great stir in the street the Davis's lived in. No one could tell what was wrong, till, late in the afternoon, the news came – there had been an accident in No. 3 pit. Then the frightful truth was known. A "fall from the roof." Everyone was afraid to say who was hurt. But the news leaked out – "the Davis's." At the mention of these names many an eye became moist. Still, no one was sure. It was an anxious time. The crowd in the street began to open out, some men were coming. They were middle-aged miners, and they were walking with their eyes cast downward. They were coming to the Davis's house, to break the news and condole with the bereaved ones. These men walked as if they were blind; their comrades were killed, how would they break the news to the women? Their hearts were full, they knew their duty, and so they walked, knowing not how. Not one in the crowd attempted to speak to these men, theirs was a holy mission; rather did they stand aside reverently, with a slight bend on the body, as a mark of great respect and sympathy. The miners entered the house, while the crowd stood in silence. They knew, from experience, that it was death; no one spoke. They waited, and in a short time the miners came out, with their heads bare, and a glance at them told that these strong hewers of coal had been shedding tears. The three men halted on the step of the door, and one of them said: "Tom Davis and his two sons, and also John Sneddon, have been killed by a fall from the roof." The miner said no more. The crowd was speechless. "It is terrible," was the expression on all lips. Terrible, children, yes, terrible, the price the workers pay for their bread.

Three days afterwards, the remains of the four men were buried in the old chapel graveyard. All the pits in the district were idle, and hundreds of the miners attended the funeral. They came just in their ordinary clothes. The four coffins were carried by the miners shoulder high, and Mary Davis, her mother, and old John Sneddon and his wife, were the chief mourners. The cortege was four deep, and it extended to a great length. They walked from the house to the graveyard, which was fully a mile. There was no priest at the funeral; Mary and her mother desired it so. Old John Sneddon was asked to officiate, and for the memory of the dead, he was only too pleased to do so. His words were few. Just before the coffins were lowered, he said, "Friends, four brave men have been killed, whom we all knew. Let it be the duty of us all to cheer those who have been left, and if we do that, we will have done our duty, and we shall have nothing to fear. Those who are gone had no fear, they were good fighters; their battle is ended, let us continue it in their spirit is my earnest appeal to you all."

Mary and her mother bore up well under their great misfortune but the blow was too great for the old woman. By the close of the year she had also passed away, and was laid beside her husband and her sons in the old chapel graveyard.

Mary was back again working in the factory. She was a different woman. She seemed as one who was waiting and waiting. She had one girl, who was now twelve years of age, and the child kept her in life.

The women in the "pass" in which Mary worked had a grievance against their tenter or "overseer,"[9] and they approached Mary to be one of a deputation to go to the manager to state their case. Mary was silent, till one of the women said, "Are you afraid, Mary?" She looked up and said, "Of whom? I will go." The deputation was successful in getting what they wanted. It was a paltry matter.

The following week after this, the "tenter" came to her and said, "You will have to leave on Saturday, Mary." She looked him straight in the face, and said, "If I leave on Saturday, I *will kill you before next Saturday*." The man turned white, he was afraid of this woman. He went, however, and got another "tenter," and brought him down to where Mary was working, and said to her, "You might just repeat what you said to me a few minutes ago." Mary laughed and said, "What are you joking about?" The "tenter" was foiled, and Mary was allowed to work away, he being afraid to pay her off.

Some months afterwards Mary left and went to work in a mill in the North of England, where a friend of hers had gone. Just at this time the Labour Movement had taken birth in this country. Mary became one of the pioneers. She began to live again as in the days of old, but the master class or their lackeys always watch these brave, outspoken people, and the master class is the same the world over. Starvation and death they mete out to any one who may rebel against their rule. This woman became known to them; she must go. She was hounded from one factory to another. One poor, brave, penniless woman capitalism meant to kill, in quite a legal way.

The pity of it all was, the workers for whom she worked so hard were blind and servile slaves. The promise of a little bit of extra bread kept them quiet. They did not see that their bosses were giving them a trifle, so as to keep them sleeping, as it were, and they were using many of the weaker ones among them, through their lackeys, to speak ill of Mary. Mary was forced to look for work elsewhere, so she decided to move on to the great City of Death – London. She had decided to walk all the way, – nearly 200 miles, – so the two started. It was Mary's expectation that she would find some work for her daughter and herself in some of the smaller towns they passed through.

It is very strange, girls and boys, and yet it is true, when men or women get crushed down, when they feel they are sinking, all the hope and love of life leaves them. The great capitalist society disowns them and calls them wastrels, their once fellow wage-slaves give them the cold shoulder, just as the masters do. The world is against them; wage-slaves are of little value, and so they sink and sink, and then they have no labour-power that any one will buy, they are of less value than rags thrown into the ash pit, and yet at one time they were as you now are, cheerful girls and boys, full of life and joy and love. So I would counsel you to have mercy – you who are just entering into womanhood and manhood, you so full of life and vigour, hope and love; you who think that the world is beautiful and the road is smooth and plain, and nothing but happiness in front. You have not met as yet the vulture Capitalism, your young minds have not yet grasped its power, you are chained to it, but you do not know it yet, and you laugh, and are merry, as you should be at your age, but what awaits you when you reach thirty years of age? The same lot as your comrades in chains – hardships, trials, suffering, pinched and wan faces, love gone, poverty eternally hunting you, hope gone. And the young slaves come along, and they are laughing and singing, and they are dreaming the dreams you used to dream. Little comrades, this is a true picture, and there is only one hope left to the wage slave to keep him alive and above water, and that is to become a rebel, to sound the slogan of the Class War, to consecrate his life to the organization of his fellows, so that they may be organized into one vast industrial army, to take the means of life into their own hands, and so kill this vulture Capitalism.

It was harvest time, and Mary and her daughter got work with a farmer. The work to them was hard, but they kept at it. The folks whom they worked along with were plain, simple, country people, full of sympathy and kindness, cheerful in nature, and ever telling simple stories of the district and its people. Capitalism had not as yet got those people into its tentacles and debased them; they lived in a different world from the industrial wage-slave, and so with the work and the people Mary's spirits began to revive, and by the end of the season she was feeling quite at home. Being only an odd hand taken on to assist at the harvest, with its finish she had to go. So once more the two of them faced the Great North Road. And on the same road many hundreds of industrial slaves have trod. Many a brave man and woman have walked as Mary and her daughter walked – knowing not the end. They had walked well on to the outskirts of London without being able to secure any work – they were not alone. They met very many people on the road, many of whom were on their last walk, for soon, very soon, that little power they had to labour would be gone for ever. This they knew, and could not help. They marched on, and when the darkness of the night set in a few of them passed over to walk no more. No one knew, no one cared; useless wage-slaves – dead – the best thing that could happen to them; and they were buried, not for love, but for fear of pestilence. And capitalists sit securely in their mansions, surrounded by all the luxuries of the world, self-satisfied.

Mary was successful on the outskirts of the great city of death; she got a job in a laundry to work a steam mangle. Her experience as a weaver induced the boss to give her a job; she also looked a fine, healthy slave, and likely to be steady, judging from her appearance. Here she and her girl worked till near the end of the busy season, but just before its close, they had been working all night to finish a large order. They were on their last hour, when one of the sub-foremen (a man who had a grudge against Mary) who was carrying a large basketful of clothes in front of him, knocked against Mary as he was passing her. She was feeding the roller at the time, and her hand slipped and caught in the rollers, and was fearfully mutilated. The brave woman uttered not a sound, the machine was stopped at once, but too late, the arm could not be saved. An ambulance was sent for and she was taken to the hospital. A worker's arm is nothing, another worker can be had with two arms, and another was willing to take the place of Mary, who had left to get the right arm taken off above the elbow. The nurse who had care of her was struck by her remarkable appearance and fortitude, and as she grew better she began asking Mary questions. Mary for a long time said nothing, she could not be induced to speak; she had made up her mind to die – to end it all. But the nurse won her sympathy, and Mary told her the story of her life. "I have a little book." She said, "it is in our lodging; my girl shall bring it to-morrow. In it I have entered the principal events of my life since I was fourteen years of age, up till I came here; and I want you to keep it for me, and should anything happen me, send it on to the address given on the first page." The nurse promised to do so, and she also got Mary's girl a place in the hospital. A few weeks after she was better, she was visiting her daughter at the hospital, and a deputation from a town in the North of England was being shewn through it. Mary was standing in the corridor as they passed, when one of the deputation stopped, stared, and said to her "Are you Mary Davis or Sneddon?" She answered, "Yes." He said, "I thought so," and passed on. This angel of capitalism, at the luncheon given in their honour that afternoon in the Board Room, told the story of the dangerous woman Mary Davis, to suit his class interests. All the other angels at the feast were agreed on the suggestion by the angel from the North, that this woman and her stock should be removed from all respectable society.

Some one may say, such is not the case; they, I am afraid, know little of these men. They will call themselves Christians and make a pretence of worshipping the meek and lowly Nazarene, but on the Monday some of them will got to their factories and make little brass gods to send to the heathen, at a profit, – for profit is greater than all the gods ever created, and they would shed the blood of the nation to retain these profits.

Why, then, do you think, they would scruple at killing one woman and her child. Look at the death roll of Labour's Army, a 1,000 workers are nothing, 10,000 are nothing. It is, how do they stand? They, with mock solemnity, send condolences to the widows of the murdered miners, when it happens to be a batch of 200 or 300 killed at one time; when they are killed by the dozen they say nothing, it is not worth taking notice of.

If it were to serve their purpose they would turn the army on the works to-morrow and kill them by thousands, yes, by tens of thousands, if it were required.

If the workers were to become class-conscious, (a sufficient minority of them), and put up a good fight, these men would then shew their hands, blood would flow in every street in the kingdom. These men know not any thing that is sacred, except their class interests. Religion, family, love, honour, friendship, courage, home, or country, none of these things count to them; their type is the lowest, despicable type the human race has evolved.

Their class is all they know, everything is justified by that standard, and if you tried, as an individual, or as an association, to stand up for your rights, WOE UNTO YOU. Look at the fearful position of the wage-slaves to-day in any modern factory. They are given on starting work a small brass token with a number on it, slave number 22. He takes it off the board in the mornings as he enters the factory gate and puts it in a box. He has no option, he is not John Smith or Tom Scott, he is number 22; when the boss enters he looks at the board to see if all the slaves have started; if any numbers remain on the board he gets the time-keeping slave to take a note of them, and the slave or slaves must appear before him and tell him WHY they were not at their work.

Some years ago I was working in a large joinery factory, where nobody but craftsmen slaves were employed at "test work" (work that must be done in a certain time or else the slave would be paid off). I was the shop delegate, and I called the other shop delegate a wage-slave; he was very angry and denied it, and wanted me to prove it. The other craftsmen slaves got interested in our discussion and they raised their heads from their jobs to listen. Just as they were all leaning forward so as to better catch what was being said, the door at the far end of the building opened with a bang, and the master of the slaves stepped in. Transformation of transformation, every craftsman wage-slave had bowed his head in double quick time. I shouted to the men near me, and especially to the wage-slave who was on the other side of the bench to me (with whom I had been discussing), *"Raise you heads, you wage-slaves, raise your heads: be men."* But, no, the man at the far end of the shop was still standing there, they could not raise their heads; they had not the power. Such is the power capitalism has over the worker to-day.

But when a brave woman like Mary Davis defends herself against the master class, many, very many, of the workers marvel and say it is not true. They say to themselves, how could she do it? They feel they are too well bound. Take courage, take courage, it can be done, once you get started on the way. The chains that bound you in the past are useless, they can bind no longer.

I have given you a short description of the workshop to prove that Mary Davis's case is not an isolated one.

Mary's end was drawing very near. She and her daughter decided to try the centre of the big city. Mary was not living now, she was an automaton. She was also a woman now without an arm, and women in the big city are very cheap.

No one can tell how very cheap they are. You can buy them for a few pence, yes, even for less than that; you can buy them for a shakedown of straw if you happen to own a small attic in any back street. They are not human beings now, these women; if they were, they would be revenged, and then die. But the paid hirelings of capitalism have drugged them from their birth, and even in the degradation they keep on drugging them, that they have no will power of their own.

Mary and her girl wandered about for a week or two without hope. Footsore and weary, they arrived late one night at Trafalgar Square, the hub of the great city. They were hungry and the girl wanted to beg from some passers-by, but the mother would not hear of it; her proud spirit arose within her; it was nothing to die, why beg? At last she turned to her girl and said, "Go and ask the workmen in the trench for a piece of bread." It was then near midnight, and the workmen were making a big trench across the street, just at the Strand, for a main sewer. They were labourers, big, burly men; they had come from the sort of men that ordinary craftsmen despise. They were men of open countenance, men you could ask for a match or a pipeful of tobacco and get it. They were merry at their work. It was to these men Mary sent her girl to beg. The girl approached the first navvy, and said, "Could you give my mother a bit bread?" The man lifted his head and looked at the bright girl and then casting his eyes to the Square, he saw the form of a woman there. "A bit bread, my lass; yes, my lass, with pleasure." His coat was lying by on a mound to turned clay; he got his coat and took from his pocket his supper – it was wrapped in a red cotton handkerchief, and as he was opening it, the other navy next to him said, "I will give a bit, too, Bill, there is no need of your giving it all." And these men, at the very bottom of Labour's rank, shared their supper with an outcast woman and her child, simply because they asked for it. It is the poor, children, who help the poor.

That night the world knew Mary Davis no longer. Less than 200 yards from the Square is the river Thames, and in its icy embrace Mary Davis, the woman of large heart and soul, gladly found rest.

SOCIALIST REVIEW

D. C. Parker, 'Elsie's Day', *Socialist Review*, December 1911, pp. 313–16.

R. C. G., 'The Patriots', *Socialist Review*, January 1912, pp. 374–9.

Eileen Hynes, 'Barky: A Sketch', *Socialist Review*, July 1913, pp. 395–400.

The *Socialist Review* (1908–34), subtitled *A Monthly Magazine of Modern Thought*, was first published monthly and then quarterly in London by the ILP. The periodical did not include a note of its price on the cover as most other periodicals did, nor does the *Warwick Guide to British Labour Periodicals, 1790–1970* list its price.

All the serial fiction published in the *Socialist Review* during the period covered by this collection were French fictions by authors such as George Sand (1804–76), Theophile Gautier (1811–72) and Victor Hugo (1802–85), and all were translated by Jacques Bonhomme (n.d.). Although fiction was included, the favoured literary genre was poetry. Eileen Hynes has not been identified, but D. C. Parker (n.d.) was also the author of an article entitled 'Music and Socialism' in the *Socialist Review* (1909), while R. C. G. is presumed to be Robert Bontine Cunninghame Graham (1852–1936). Graham's full biographical details can be found in the headnote for *Justice* in Volume 3, pp. 145–6.

D. C. Parker, 'Elsie's Day' (1911)

Elsie's day began approximately at 7 a.m., when she roused herself and looked at the faded wallpaper, the grotesque faces upon which had been sneering at her these five years. There was no particular reason why they should sneer for she was a tidy little person. It always took her an hour to dress, set her things to rights, and clean her room, an operation which was invariably brought to an end by a smart pull which left the window open about six inches. Then she went to breakfast.

Elsie did not say much, but this does not mean that she had no ideas, or was sheepish. Far from it. A person with a greater sense of comradeship or a more generous social instinct it would have been hard to find. But some of us go through life with stifled secrets and beauties buried in our breasts because in our neighbours there is no receiving station to catch the note. You cannot expect a flower to raise its tearful eye in a coal pit, and so Elsie, at breakfast was wisely silent. Her mother presided had, in a pathetic fashion, tried to be amiable. Having hurried to bring all the dishes together in due time for Elsie and the lodger, and losing her temper every day over the effort, she was hardly a person to be contradicted at eight o'clock in the morning.

The lodger was a young man full of negative virtues and with a vast variety of hideous shirts and socks. His notion of enjoying himself was that of the hundreds of young men whom one meets with in a large city. Not openly bad, he had no capacity for great or essential things. He was a born trifler, a minus sign. He would go on tinkering with everything he touched until, perhaps, death found him lounging somewhere with a cheap cigarette and the back number of a magazine, and stopped his trifling for ever and ever.

It was not a gay trio, and out of this harsh atmosphere Elsie marched every morning towards nine o'clock, very smart and methodical. Her expenditure, like her salary, was small. Her occupation that of a typist. At the end of her half-hour's tramp she turned into the offices of Bickersmith & Co., there to be swallowed up for the remainder of the day in a counting house. Bickersmith & Co., were quite big people. Mr. Bickersmith himself was said to make £10,000 a year, and his father had left him a fortune.

No one in the office was a sweet as the honey-comb. People think nowadays that, in order to be business-like and smart, they must be rude and cantankerous. The other typists were, like Elsie, kept busy all day. But there was one beam of sunshine in her commercial life, and it was the fact that one person was drawn to her and she to him. This individual was the office-boy. If you have ever been in an office you must know that everybody bullies. Bickersmith, with all his money, with his motor-car and beautiful wife, bullied the heads of the departments. The heads bullied the juniors, and the accumulated volume of bullying always reached Tomkins.

Now there is no more selfish and callous creature on God's earth than a healthy boy, and Tomkins's nature was so hard that a rhinoceros's hide would appear like the finest Japanese silk by companion. But Tomkins was a human being, and the continual threats and reproaches which were hurled at him opened a capacity for sympathy which seldom exists in a careless, happy youth. To him it seemed a shame that a little creature so amiable and delightful as Elsie should have to tick at a dead machine everlastingly, and so, when there was a Royal procession or a Lord Mayor's show and Tomkins was trying to boss at one of the windows,[1] he always reserved a corner for Elsie, and pointed out the celebrities (who were never what he labeled them) to her.

Elsie's leisure was partly spent in looking at shop windows. A person with her financial resources can only look – not buy. Those in high places have shop windows of their own. Freak banquets, mad dances, expensive and sensational caperings – these are for the rich. Elsie had to content herself by looking at Russian sables[2] and buying packets of pins. Two hats did her for a year, and these she trimmed herself with sixpenny ribbons, which made quite a brave show. She wore her costume seven days a week and for ten or eleven months in the year. Making most of her own meals and the little mending which always had to be done filled in some more of her time. An occasional walk in the park on Sunday among perambulators and soldiers gave her much needed fresh air and exercise.

And then there were the long moments of solitude. A woman who is lonely suffers an hundred agonies which the busy world has not the time to notice. She often thought of many things, and the thoughts sunk down and settled into her little soul. She would look at the fine, strong, hairy fellows in the school playing-field at the end of the row, and then turn away, she could not tell why; but their enjoyment and buoyancy filled her with an unutterable sadness. Perhaps she went to church – herself. There she felt more lonely than ever, for she heard great talk of brotherhood and fellowship. That was a language which an employee of Bickersmith & Co. could not be expected to understand. Besides, she had no fine clothes and was a little awkward in her manner, and it was a curious experience to pray with so many fine people. And when the preacher talked as though everything were just as it ought to be it seemed to her like an attempt to make a gasometer picturesque.

People often looked at Elsie. She was really interesting, whether fresh in the morning or tired at night. Her potentialities were great. In another sphere she might have become a notable figure, but she was stunted and dwarfed by her surroundings and unsympathetic tongues. She was bullied by circumstances. In another age she might have been a strong, free woman dancing along the sands of a western isle, her fair hair tossed by the wind of the sea. As it was she resembled a Jericho root[3] which had never been blown to its proper soil.

* * *

To where she disappeared nobody ever seemed to know or care. It was noticed that for some time she had not come back in the evenings, and was not to be seen stitching and mending at her little window. Things went on just as before, but one wonders how many lonely souls there are like hers. It is a far greater trial to be alone within reach of comforts and luxuries than to be the only inhabitant of Juan Fernandez.[4] Those who think that slavery is abolished and that the heathen only lives abroad should look near at hand. To do him justice, the lodger missed Elsie. Like most unreflective people he only appreciated a thing when it was taken away from him. But her mother's tongue was more scorpion-like than ever. Where had Elsie gone? Would she return? No one could supply an answer. She had melted away, had perhaps been spirited off by one of those grotesque figures who had for so long inhabited the wall-paper.

R. C. G., 'The Patriots' (1912)

I.

The good citizens of Cheriton Park boarded the 8-14 a.m. on the morning of the 2nd of April, feeling, like thousands of good citizens in England that morning, a little amazed at their lack of enthusiasm. The Declaration of War had been so hotly discussed the night before, and so keenly apprehended during the previous fortnight, that the grim formality as set forth in the cold print of their morning papers did not stir them as it should have done. Individually they were rather oppressed with a sense of anti-climax. After the violent protestations, loud indictments, prophecies and plans made at club, fireside, or garden-gate on the previous night, each had become aware in the morning, that while the Nation might be doing great things as a whole, they were all singly rather negligible factors; and they felt an ill-defined resentment at their littleness.

As soon, however, as they had herded into their third-class "smokers"[1] and got together in their accustomed gangs, a sense of collective responsibility fell upon them. Mr. Henry Stokes, aggressive and fluent, as usual, re-opened the subject. "'News of the Fleet,'" he cried, scanning his journal – "by Jove, I should think *so*. 'News of the Fleet'! my word, it ought to be off their coast by now. Bottle 'em up, I say. Hope they've given old Jimmy Heresford[2] supreme command. He's the man we want, eh?"

The conversation started out in all directions.

"What's this about the Dravia frontier?"[3] asked John Sandys, rhetorically, deep in a corner of his *Chronicle*.[4]

"You know," pursued Mr. Stokes with expert confidence, "that's where you Terriers[5] will get a chance – we're bound to send troops over."

"Yes, but they'll be regulars," replied Fred Gabriel, who was cuddling a rifle encased in brown canvas: "didn't the Sergeant say so last night?" he asked a fellow Territorial, who was similarly distinguished by a weapon.

"Yes, but we've got mobilisation orders. God! I hope we get a knock."

"Down at the Hall last night?" enquired Mr. Stokes, with the air of a minister consulting an Inspector-General.

He was answered in the affirmative. The conversation then flagged, until the adventurous Mr. Stokes, in a loud and unctuous tone, revived it.

"Well, gentlemen, I wonder what our friend in the corner has to say?"

The individual alluded to had not yet spoken. He was tall and dark, of neat but undistinguished dress. His face, alone of all those in the compartment, was contracted with the lines of thought and discontent. He eyed the company morosely.

"Well, I suppose you've got what you wanted," he said bitterly, but not aggressively.

"'What *we* want,'" cried Gabriel. "Of course you rotten Socialists go and make it all the worse for people who have got some patriotism left – what *we* wanted! Huh!"

But old Mr. Livingstone took up the sermon.

"Do you mean," he asked, eyeing Grant sternly, "that in a crisis like the present you would give at those who are preparing to sell their lives for their country?"

The words struck the right note. Their thoughts and intentions, before contemptuous and semi-jocular, now became serious. In the old days things had seemed too far off to quarrel with Grant about them. But now the reality was at hand, and the restraint born of a hundred motives fell away and left each hot at heart and dully resenting Grant. Davis, who sat opposite him, suddenly leaned forward, and said in a voice that did not seem to belong to a man who was a poor little clerk: "Look here, Grant, we don't want to hear any more of your ideas. We've heard quite enough of them. Some of us rather take this war seriously."

Little weedy Davis, insignificant father of a drab household in Cheriton Park, spoke for fifty millions of souls, ordered tall ships sailed by stern men, and long battalions rolled up behind him. The image grew on them – their great country; half-assimilated lumps of English history; Drake, Nelson and Wellington; the glorious past – only Grant was outside the magic circle, at a vanishing point, with his impious ideas and irritating personality – Grant, the Socialist, the damned.

They had never taken him seriously before; they used to be too polite, or too cheerful, or too frightened to be rude, but now, as the train rolled into Queen's Cross, he sat glowering on them and they in their turn glowered back.

II.

Cheriton Park was on the lines that the defenders had drawn round the capital. The invaders had rolled up the fields to the suburb-edge, but in a preliminary attempt to rush the houses they had lost heavily in crossing the Park and the allotments, and had retired into the Park and open country beyond. The defenders' lines were drawn at the end of the blind turnings, where the roads ended in the countryside or were closed with barriers of timber, barbed wire, and builders' débris.

Most of the city offices were closed, and there was nothing left for men to do but to volunteer for enrolment, assist in some minor capacity, or prowl round in search of news. Already famine had manifested itself; already the folk that felt hungry first had shown their mettle, and two isolated outbursts, one near Paddington and one in the East End had been put down with bloodshed.

Grant was eyed and suspected by other non-combatants in Cheriton Park. Many of the citizens had volunteered, the rest took stock of Grant. He certainly was no patriot – had he not expressed his views upon the war? But was he actually a traitor? Wherever he went, he met with nothing but averted faces and silence. His few friends had retired into the city and left him in isolation.

A dull fire burnt in his heart and a sickening dread that the forces of organized Labour would not rise. He had never belonged to any Socialist body, and so was deprived of the opportunity of learning how the cause he loved was faring and what it was planning. Day after day he waited in vain for the glorious moment when he could take the newspaper containing the news of the General Strike and thrust it into Stokes' or Johnson's face and say: "Look, you bloodthirsty Imperialist, you can't have your game of soldiers any longer!"

At length a rumour got abroad that Black, having defeated the invaders' Southern army at their base, was advancing to relieve the capital. A week of sickening apprehension went by – hope and dread – culminating in two days of heavy firing to the North-West and continued movement in the enemy's lines. In Cheriton Park it was known that an attempt was to take place on the Saturday morning to join forces with Black. The sortie was made from that part of the lines. Through all the day men waited in Cheriton Park, ever asking the same question, ever wandering after news, ever apprehending the faintest bugle call.

Evening fell and then, somehow, the news began to pass abroad that Black had been defeated, was retiring North, and the sortie was retreating badly cut up into the capital.

Then, as the few lights that were permitted began to illumine the unkempt roads and shattered masonry, the flotsam of the sally began to flood back. All the non-combatants thronged the streets to greet it. Grant heard the tumult and went out beyond his gate to watch. The streets were full of people, and for a time he was unnoticed. All around him he saw nothing but the anguish and dejection of defeat, wrought to a breaking-point by the sight of the shattered regiments as they trailed past with all the hideous signs of carnage upon them.

Suddenly he found himself the focus-point of looks distorted with despair and baffled hopes. Ominous murmurs broke out around him. Several of his old companions of the 8-14 – his neighbours – were to hand. The press of the crowd increasing, he tried to get away, but was forced roughly against Johnson. The latter turned:

"Get away, you damned traitor, you!" he cried, passionately thrusting Grant back.

Grant tried to work his way through the crowd, a rising tide of feeling in his heart. But Johnson would not let him go. He caught him roughly by the sleeve.

"Look at those poor fellows – look at them! and many a better man than you, dead! I suppose you're gloating, you scum!"

The violent grasp of the infuriated man, and the jar of his childlike bafflement and melodramatic patriotism suddenly unlocked Grant's lips. He swung himself clear and forced his way to an open space.

"Men of England," he cried, but his utterance was drowned in a wave of savage cries. His voice rose above it. "You don't know what you are doing! You are being betrayed, murdered by the Government for the sake of the rich and the worthless. How can you stand by and let these brave fellows be butchered for a sham and a lie?"

Someone struck him in the back with the butt of a rifle. He fell heavily, to rise gasping painfully. At last the words came: –

"Cannot you rob the rich of their prey; cannot you defraud the scheming governments that lure you to destruction with lies? Cannot you say: 'There shall be no war?'"

A tumult of oaths and cries stormed round him; he was struck again and again. He won clear and faced his persecutors: –

"Throw down your arms! You don't want this war. You have been drugged by the Press and the diplomats. You have thrown away our happiness for financiers and contractors. Oh, cannot you end it?"

He flung himself towards the soldiers with outstretched hands: –

"Throw down your arms," he cried again.

But someone cried "Ugh! you traitor," out of the darkness, and thrust him through the chest with his bayonet.

He fell writhing, and was for a long time trampled under foot by the crowd recklessly hurrying after the soldiers. In blind, unreasoning excitement and passion, it swept down the road towards the hospitals and lines, and no one heeded Grant, who was lying, dead, in the roadway.

Eileen Hynes, 'Barky: A Sketch' (1913)

On Westminster Embankment the plane trees rustled pleasantly and sooty sparrows hopped from twig to twig and chirped; they formed the treble of a natural symphony, to which the roar of the County Council trams and the whizz of passing motors added a bass. The pavement was wet from the last shower, and the river, swinging along in front sent up to a thousand indifferent nostrils that individual Thames smell, at once sticky and clinging, which is the combined result of water, weed, and a city's dirt.

Barky sniffed apathetically. He sat perched humbly on the edge of a seat, stooping forwards, with old, claw-like hands clutching at his trousers: from his wrinkled face, fringed with grey stubble, faded blue eyes looked out on the world with the anxious expression of a child expecting a blow: in his dulled brain an impression of injury mingled vaguely with a sense of shame. It seemed to him that each home-going passer-by remarked as he went, "Look! Barky is going to sleep on the Embankment! Barky has come down to that! Barky is no longer a respectable man!"

His hands twisted nervously and showed as they turned the cicatrised spot on the inner side of the right palm which marks the cobbler. He had stuck to his last until three months previously, when his employer had dismissed him for failing eyesight, and since then he had earned a precarious livelihood by selling penny toys in the streets. On ordinary days he cleared eightpence, which was sufficient to pay for his bed at a common lodging-house[1] and leave him fourpence for food; but to-day it had rained until seven o'clock, and who stops in the rain to buy trifles? Yesterday had been bad too, only threepence, and it was this combination of ill-luck that had brought Barky to the Embankment.

At the opposite end of the bench was a tramp, apparently in a semi-somnolent condition, flaccid, unwashed, and with that peculiar musty appearance that comes from wearing the same clothes night and day. Barky gazed at him with tremulous disapproval. It was a great come-down to be sharing a bench with a tramp; but the very greatness of the come-down yielded a kind of lachrymose satisfaction.

A young clerk came and sat down between Barky and his unsavoury neighbor to tie a bootlace, and the tramp, as if suddenly galvanized into life, sat up and begged. "Spare a copper for a pore man, sir! I ain't 'ad nothin' to eat since lars night –"

The clerk produced a penny. "Can't you get work?" he asked sympathetically.

This simple question seemed to effect the tramp considerably. His whine changed into a resentful monotone. "The worl's very 'ard on a pore bloke!" he declared, and Barky looked up; that sentence expressed his own feelings absolutely. "*They* don't work," asserted the tramp, jerking his head backwards towards the users of passing motors, "and I don't want nothink but ter be let ter sleep where I like; I cun pick up fags and a bit o' scrand[2] as I go along, and I don' want nothink else –"

"Beer?" suggested the clerk.

"Naow! Beer turns my belly. Always 'as done. Wot 'arm would it do them, if we got a bit o' sleep? It's very 'ard on a pore bloke!"

The clerk rose and hurried on to the tram terminus, and the tramp turned to Barky. "'Tain't much as we wants!" he grumbled.

Barky felt himself bound to protest. "It's different when you've been used to live respectable," he objected. "It's quite different when you've always lived respectable."

A woman had slipped into the seat vacated by the clerk. She was young and consumptive, and her attire consisted mostly of a rusty black skirt in the last stages of dissolution, a strangely-shaped snuff-coloured shawl, and a battered travesty of a hat. She seated herself briskly and her eyes were cheerful enough.

The tramp seemingly possessed of a desire to demonstrate his principles, and finding Barky unsympathetic, addressed himself to the woman beside him. "It's orl right if you cun sleep stan'ing like 'im"; he pointed with his thumb at a motionless figure, standing as if looking over the wall at the water below. "'E's bin sleeping there this 'alf 'our! But I carn't do it. Like a bloomin' 'orse! 'Tain't natcher! Wot 'arm would it do them, if we got a bit o' sleep?"

"I cun sleep 'most anwyeres," said the woman cheerfully, "but I once knew a cove as couldn't an' 'e felt it crool." She stood up and waved her arm gaily to a man standing with his back to the balustrade, looking along the now crowded benches. "Room 'ere, Dandy!" she called out.

The man slouched up grinning. His shirt collar was tied with a bow of green ribbon and the same vivid hue was repeated in his socks which showed through his boots in places: the rest of his costume was corduroy, which made him look like a working man. He sat down by the woman. "Well, Jane, fancy 'avin' the pleasure of seein' you!" he observed gallantly. "Where've you 'opped from?"

"'Ose got socks?" she retorted derisively.

"Found-'em-in-aredge," explained Dandy complacently and proceeded to open out the contents of his bundle which contained a mixed selection of meat, bread, potatoes, and fish. "'Ave some?" he suggested hospitably.

"I could do with a bit," owned the woman.

Barky with a sudden sigh turned away from the sight of the food. The tramp had tucked his bundle under his head and relapsed into his former condition of inertness.

Barky leaned forward and felt under the seat for the carpet-bag which contained his stock-in-trade, some twenty children's balls made of paper covered with coloured string and attached to pieces of elastic. The bag felt wet and a sudden fear contracted his throat. He peered anxiously under the seat and saw a gleam of water. There was some irregularity in the paving, and the rain had lodged in the hollows. With trembling fingers he unfastened the bag; then his face grew grey and he sat gazing blankly at a sodden, discoloured mass.

The water had soaked through. One after another he turned the balls over, sopping and out of shape; some dropped to pieces as he handled them: all were ruined, unsaleable.

He sat staring, vaguely trying to realize what had happened.

If he had nothing to sell he could not live; unless he went into the House:[3] but his brain refused to conceive such a desperate condition.

In a kind of dream he caught scraps of the conversation of his two neighbours. "Where's the kid?" – "With Jim." – "Wo'th a couple of bob a day, that kid was!"

The evening was closing in, and lights began to flicker over Westminster, sending sickly yellow rays on to the plane trees. The embankment lamps shone with increased lustre, and in the fighting lights the dolphins who support them changed their usual expression of irritating stupidity for one of bland benevolence. Barky looked at the lamp near him with frank admiration for it as an artistic production. "Wunnerful!" he muttered. "Wunnerful!" Then the extent of his loss dawned on him again, and he subsided into a bland, bewildered silence.

The tramp had fallen asleep, and so had Jane. Dandy was smoking peacefully. Presently Barky's eyelids drooped, and he fell into the light, uncertain slumber of age.

He awoke to feel a heavy hand on his shoulder and a deep voice in his ears. "Wake up, my man! You know you can't stay her any longer! Wake up!" A bull's-eye lantern flashed in his eyes.

He sat up blinking, conscious of confused yellow light against a black background and the Titanic form of a policeman standing by him. He was alone on the bench, so the others had evidently gone. The policeman flashed his lantern in his face. "Come, wake up! And get along! Where's your card?"

His "card" to Barky was his insurance card. Of the "visiting card" of the homeless, he had as yet no knowledge. He began to apologise feebly. "I bin out o' work three months. I 'ad it up to then all regerlar, but I aven't in able to keep it up –"

"I didn't mean your insurance card. I meant a ticket for the casual ward." The policeman became suddenly sympathetic. "First time you've done this, isn't it?" He was fumbling about his person. "I'll give you one for an Army shelter.[4] That's better than the ward. They'll give you some food and a bed, and maybe they'll find you a job if you ask them. Goin' round with the wood or something." He thrust the card into Barky's hand. "Know where to go? Just by the station, through the arches."

Barky clutched his "stock" and then recollected its ruin and a full flood of misery swept over him. The policeman's words had conveyed little to his fogged brain; only the lowering vision of the House had become more imminent. He rose tremblingly, gripping his bag and walked aimlessly in the direction pointed out, shuffling slowly with leaden footsteps that echoed in the silence.

From the Strand came the sound of distant hubbub and the noise of the river was insistent in the night. Barky, conscious of deadly weariness, came to another bench. It was not to be resisted: his feet refused to carry him further: he sat down. The policeman, watching, followed him up.

"Now what's the use of that?" he demanded with mild exasperation. Barky looked up with scared eyes, "Get along now!" said the policeman. "It won't take five minutes," he added good-naturedly.

Barky got up and shuffled on. Despair had lent him obstinacy. When he reached the next bench he sat down again, and again the constable came up, while Barky peered with glowering apprehension. "I don't want to do it!" said the policeman with sudden indignation. "It's not my fault! But the inspector will be around in a minute, and then I'll have to take you in charge. You must move on! And look here," he became almost persuasive, "there's only one more seat this end. Don't go and sit down on that! I'll only have to turn you off. Now you'll go right on, won't you?"

"Yes," said Barky. "I'll go." His old eyes gleamed dully. He got up and the policeman having watched him pass the critical point, turned away. "It does seem a shame," he muttered. "What's he done to get that? Nothin' but work all his life!"

The dolphins, now lighted only from above seemed to scowl as he tramped by. From behind him came the sound of a faint splash. "Mother o' God!" gasped the man and spun round.

There was no sign of the feeble figure that had been silhouetted in the glaring artificial light: all was blank and deserted. Rushing to the parapet, the policeman looked over, then he ran to the life-buoy, whistling for assistance. All the futile procedure was gone through with the usual futile results. Barky had moved on.

EDITORIAL NOTES

Cartmel, 'Jeshurun's Great Kick'

1. *napper*: the head.
2. *dordums*: a dialect term for which no translation has been found.
3. *Brer Rabbit*: a traditional American trickster character with origins in African and Native American storytelling. Brer, or Br'er (meaning brother), Rabbit lives by his wits and overcomes adversity, although not always by moral means.
4. *bum-bailiffs*: a derogatory term for bailiffs of the lowest order.
5. *Just look at them in Australia ... defyin' the whole world*: The European rabbit was originally introduced to Australia in 1788 but did not spread. In 1859 twenty-four wild rabbits were released near Geelong for hunting, and those rabbits bred, spread and multiplied into pests. The annual costs of rabbit damage runs into hundreds of millions of Australian dollars, and a number of viruses, including myxomatosis and rabbit haemorrhagic disease, have been introduced into the rabbit population in attempts to control numbers.
6. *scut*: short erect tail; *OED*.
7. *snek*: usually meaning a latch or catch on a door or gate, but used here to indicate an addition to his name – presumably a legal qualification – that allows him to pass judgment on others.
8. *lesson at the goose*: saying grace before carving.
9. *gargles*: gargoyles.
10. *a grandsire or a triple*: traditional methods of church bell ringing giving different speeds of pealing and number of bells: grandsire, grandsire doubles, grandsire triples, etc.
11. *Jeshurun*: a poetic name for Israel. Deuteronomy 33:26: 'There is none like unto the God of Jeshurun, *who* rideth upon the heaven in thy help, and in his excellency on the sky'.
12. *Jimmy Denny*: There is no listing for 'Jimmy Denny' in the Football League players' records of 1888–1939 or in the records of the Rugby League for this time. The emphasis on Jimmy Denny's kick suggests that the game named here as 'football' is in fact rugby, as a footballer's kick would be taken for granted while in rugby the ball is kicked only for conversion.
13. *hogshead*: a large cask usually for storing liquids; *OED*.
14. *Alexander Selkirk*: (1676–1721), mariner, castaway and probable inspiration for Daniel Defoe's (*c*. 1660–1731) *Robinson Crusoe* (1719).
15. *on tick*: on credit; payment deferred until a later date.

16. *kicking strap*: a strap to prevent a kick, usually applied to horses. Young Strickland wants the rabbit hampered in the fight.

Blatchford, 'The Perpendicular Recruit'

1. *Hunstanton*: a coastal town in Norfolk on the Wash. Blatchford and his family moved to Heacham on the north coast of Norfolk after he withdrew from the *Clarion*. His friend Harry Lowerison had founded a school in the area.
2. *Ramchunders*: Blatchford's name for the 103rd Dublin Fusiliers, the regiment he joined after enlisting with the army.
3. *a thing of beauty and a joy for ever*: the first line of John Keats's (1795–1821) *Endymion* (1818).
4. *amadhauns*: omadhaun, in Irish English, Manx English, Newfoundland, meaning an idiot, a fool; *OED*.
5. *pultan*: Anglo-Indian slang for regiment. The Fusiliers had recently returned from service in India when Blatchford enlisted.
6. *Rooshions ... with us*: an allusion to Matthew 26:11: 'For ye have the poor always with you; but me ye have not always'. The verse, Christ's response to his disciples' criticism of a woman preparing him for burial by pouring on him costly perfume which could be sold to aid the poor, is paraphrased to suggest a permanent and inevitable threat to national security by Russia and Prussia.
7. *Erse*: refers to Scottish Gaelic and its speakers, sometimes – as here – used to refer to Irish Gaelic; *OED*.
8. *wax vestas*: matches produced by the Swan Vesta company, founded in 1883.
9. *ring-tailed*: an Anglo-Indian term for new recruits to the British army.
10. *loot wollah*: lootie wallah, Anglo-Indian term for a band of marauders or robbers; *OED*. Cashman is accusing the recruits of stealing his bread.
11. *Morar*: a town in the Gwalior district in the Indian state of Madhya Pradesh. Gwalior was first occupied by the British in 1780 and was important in the British defeat of the Indian Rebellion of 1857–8.
12. *pipeclay-box*: Pipeclay was used not only to make tobacco pipes but also for whitening and polishing leather, particularly in the British army; *OED*.
13. *Oh, what will ye do ... seas beyond*: 'What Would You Do Love?', a traditional Irish song.
14. *Salpeens*: usually salapeen, an Irish dialect word for someone untrustworthy; in this case Ryan accuses all Englishmen.
15. *stand fornnist*: No source has been found to explain this word, but in this context it appears to mean 'stand against', to fight.
16. *goose-step*: either a basic military drill, balancing on one leg and swinging the other backwards and forwards, or a straight-legged march; *OED*.

Lyons, 'Unearned Increment'

1. *"Christian Commonwealth" ... "Gasfitter's Gazette"*: *Christian Commonwealth* (1881–1980), subtitled *Organ of the World-wide Progressive Movement in Religion and Social Ethics*, a weekly London publication; *Pelican*, possibly the *Pelican Record* (1891–present), a magazine edited by members of Corpus Christi College, Oxford; *Gasfitter's Gazette*, not identified. The narrator has an eclectic reading taste covering religion, an Oxford alumni magazine and a trade paper.
2. *Rest Cure establishment*: a psychiatric hospital. The rest cure was a 'cure' for psychiatric disorders developed by Silas Weir Mitchell (1829–1914) and famously criticized by Charlotte Perkins Gilman (1860–1935) in *The Yellow Wallpaper* (1899).

Suthers, 'A Coster's Funeral'

1. *Plumstead*: an area of southeast London.
2. *Cabinet Minister's Marconi explanation*: the scandal of insider trading of shares in the Marconi telecommunications company that broke in 1912. A number of high-ranking members of Herbert Asquith's (1852–1928) Liberal government, including David Lloyd George (1863–1945), were reported to have bought shares in the company just before it was to be awarded a large government contract. The French newspaper *Le Matin* was sued by Sir Rufus Isaacs (1860–1935) and Herbert Samuel (1870–1963) on the grounds that the paper accused the men of buying shares in the English Marconi company when they had bought shares in its American branch. No member of the government was found guilty of insider trading, but an atmosphere of impropriety surrounded those involved.
3. *Mrs. 'Enery 'Awkins*: the music hall song 'The Future Mrs. 'Awkins' (1892) by Albert Chevalier (1861–1923). The narrator is admiring the women in the working-class districts of Elephant and Castle and Old Kent Road, as the future Mrs Henry Hawkins is described as 'a daisy'.
4. *Woolwich*: to the west of Plumstead.
5. *Arsenal men*: The Royal Arsenal was situated in Woolwich and conducted research into armaments and explosives for the British armed forces from 1671 until its closure in 1994.
6. *in the midst of death we are in life*: a reversal of the phrase from *The Book of Common Prayer*: 'In the midst of life we are in death'.
7. *Algit Station*: Aldgate station.

Anderson, 'Who Killed Downie? An Aberdeen Legend'

1. *sacristan*: the sexton of the university's church.

Dilnot, 'The Public Spirit of Mr. Josiah Grub'

1. *North Hyben*: a fictional area. Dilnot also published *The Tyrants of North Hyben* in 1904 and *The Worthies of Hyben* in 1915.
2. *New Kent-road*: In southeast London, the New Kent Road was originally formed as a shortcut taken by monks travelling from Canterbury to Walworth Manor in the eleventh century, and made permanent when the Archbishop of Canterbury made his home in Lambeth Palace. The road was immortalized in the song 'Wotcher; or Knocked 'em in the Old Kent Road' (1891), written by Charles Ingle (Auguste Chevalier, n.d.) and his brother, Albert Chevalier.
3. *traveller*: a commercial agent who travels from place to place soliciting custom; *OED*.
4. *Band of Hope*: a temperance organization founded in 1855 to educate children about the dangers of alcohol. The organization was phenomenally popular, and by 1905 there were three and a half million members, both adults and children.

Starr, 'The Aerial Armada. What Took Place in A.D. 2000'

1. *Goodwood*: a racecourse in Sussex, north of Chichester.
2. *Alhambra matinée ... Maud Allen species*: 'Alhambra' was a popular name for theatres in Britain in the nineteenth century. Maud Allen (1873–1956) was born Beulah Maude Durrant in Toronto, Canada and was a popular music hall entertainer. She was renowned

for her scanty costumes, and her 'Salome Dance' was excluded from some performances in her national tours as it was deemed licentious by some theatre censors.
3. *Leicester-square*: an area in London associated with the theatre. The Alhambra Theatre stood in Leicester Square from 1856 (originally opening in 1854 as the Royal Panopticon of Science and Arts) until its demolition in 1936.
4. *Nore observation station*: The Nore anchorage in the Thames Estuary was the location of a naval mutiny in 1797, following the Spithead mutiny at the anchorage in the Solent. The power of the British navy has been superseded by the power of the air force.
5. *dirigible*: a balloon or airship; *OED*.
6. *chewing-gum*: Chewing gum had been used in various forms for centuries, but the use of chicle, imported from Mexico, in the 1860s produced what is recognized as chewing gum today.
7. *Ouida's guardsman*: Ouida was the pseudonym of author Marie Louise de la Ramée (1839–1908). The reference to the guardsman is to the character of Hon. Bertie Cecil in *Under Two Flags* (1867), a member of the Life Guards who carries out many heroic acts under the name 'Louis Victor' after having faked his own death to save the honour of his brother.
8. *I mean billiards*: an allusion to Francis Drake (1540–96) playing bowls at Plymouth Hoe while the Spanish Armada was sailing towards England. Drake is supposed to have waited to finish the game before setting off to defeat the Armada.
9. *financiers and Bourse thieves*: A bourse is a meeting place for merchants and the name of the French equivalent of the Stock Exchange. The biggest danger to Britain comes from capitalists and moneymen.
10. *promissory note*: a written promise to pay the bearer of the note the sum stated; *OED*.
11. propria forma: in proper form, in a form legally binding.

Derrick, 'The Making of a Red'

1. *Portuguese ... Seven Sisters-road*: Overfishing of the native British oyster (*Ostrea edulis*) in the nineteenth century led to legal protection of the species (the adage of not eating oysters during months without an 'R' refers to the protection of the species during the spawning months of May to August), and shellfish farmers turned to the cultivation of imported species. The most popular were the American Blue Point oyster (*Crassostrea virginica*) and the Pacific or Portuguese oyster (*Crassostrea gigas*), the latter first cultivated in Essex in 1922. The working-class area of Seven Sisters in London is the place where Gaunt sells these alternatives to the native oyster because oysters had been a staple of the working-class diet during the nineteenth century. As oysters grew scarce they became an unaffordable delicacy, and therefore the cultivated (and less tasty) alternatives were offered to the working class while the native variety became the preserve of the rich.
2. *trim beard ... square-cut*: Facial hair began to fade from fashion in the early twentieth century as beards and moustaches were found to harbour bacteria and innovations were made in shaving equipment. However, for those who cultivated beards, the fashion was to trim them in either pointed or square cuts.
3. *America Cup*: The America's Cup is an international race between two yachts – the defender, the club that holds the cup, and the challenger. The America's Cup, founded in 1851, is the oldest sporting event in the world. The cup was held by the New York Yacht Club for 132 years (itself a record) until the Australian team won in 1983. Lodden's ambitions, therefore, would seem lofty if not unattainable.

4. *Privy Councillor*: A Privy Council member is a former member of the House of Parliament or the House of Lords who advises the monarch on the exercise of the royal prerogative in common or civil law. The title can be spelled 'Councillor' or 'Counsellor', but the Privy Council Office prefers the latter spelling, which emphasizes the role as one who gives counsel. Lodden aims for one of the most influential positions in British government.
5. *Trendane Castle in Sussex*: a fictional castle. This aim suggests that Lodden has an ambition to live as an aristocrat; the self-made man is challenging the historic power of the aristocracy.
6. *Beckenham*: Now a borough of Bromley in the southeast of London, Beckenham had been a village on the outskirts of London in the mid-nineteenth century; after the advent of the railway, the area became attractive to wealthy businessmen, who built their villas in the area. As London encroached the exclusiveness of the area declined, and the journalist's residence there in 1913 suggests an aspiration to the rapidly fading gentility.
7. *Confucianism or Theosophy*: Confucianism is a system based on the teachings of the Chinese philosopher Confucius (551–479 BC), whose social philosophy emphasized personal responsibility, self-restraint, kindness and compassion towards others, and respect for Heaven, and whose political philosophy argued that leaders should practice these tenets and govern by example. Theosophy is the knowledge of divine nature through material nature, which gives a more profound understanding of divinity than empirical investigation can provide. Both systems promote universal brotherhood, something that Lodden is as uninterested in as he is in any political ideology. Neither the spiritual nor the ideological has any bearing on the materialist Lodden.
8. *Southern Counties Militia*: Militia in this sense refers to a body of civilians armed and trained to act as an army. Lodden is making his managing editor aware that the paper could flex military might as well as intellectual and ideological might.
9. *new Children Act*: The Children and Young Persons Act 1908, passed by the Liberal government of 1906–14, allowed the prosecution of abusive parents, restricted the sale of tobacco and alcohol to minors, banned the employment of children in dangerous trades, and founded the juvenile court system to try and incarcerate young offenders separately from adults. The act was part of the Liberal Welfare programme, which also introduced pensions in 1908 and national insurance in 1911. The *Daily Light*'s praise could be interpreted as support for the programme.
10. *('The characters ... living persons.)*: This disclaimer appears at the end of every instalment but will not be repeated throughout this transcription.
11. *the elder Pitt*: William Pitt, the first Earl of Chatham (1708–78), Whig politician and Prime Minister in 1766–8. Pitt the politician had cultivated his reputation as the 'Great Commoner', but his acceptance of the peerage destroyed that image. His ministry was beset by political difficulties and Pitt's poor health.
12. *Reform Bill*: The 1832 Reform Act, known also as the Great Reform Act, extended the British franchise beyond its limitation to the aristocracy to include owners or tenants of property with a rental value of £10 per annum or more. Charles Grey, the second Earl Grey (1764–1845), was appointed Prime Minister in 1830 at the age of sixty-six, bringing a manifesto for franchise reform to the new government, whose ministries were headed primarily by aristocrats. He was returned to Parliament in the general election of 1831 on a wave of support for reform. The Reform Act was followed by the abolition of slavery in 1833, which Grey had been working towards since 1806. Venture's political antecedents have been associated with the people despite their aristocratic positions.

13. *80 years ... Reform Bill episode*: This dates the action of the fiction to 1912, which contradicts the narrator's earlier claim that the cause of the leak to Raston Path was unknown 'Even now, after the passage of years'; in Chapter VI, Path's proposed bill would come into being on 1 January 1920.
14. *The Bill*: possibly an allusion to the difficulties passing socialist-based bills such as the 1911 National Insurance Bill, which required an employer to contribute a set amount for each employee. For example, an employee over twenty-one earning between 1*s*. 6*d*. and 2*s*. per day would contribute 1*d*. per week, and Parliament would contribute 1*d*. per week, but the employer would be required to contribute 5*d*. per week. For an employer of large numbers of workers, like Lodden and his Authoritarian supporters, this made a significant impact on their profits.
15. *foolscap*: shortened term for foolscap folio, a sheet of paper usually 8½ by 13½ inches in size, half the size of the full foolscap, which is usually 17 by 13½ inches – hence folio, meaning a folded sheet. This was one of the British imperial measurements of paper used before International Standard paper sizes (A2, A3, A4, etc.) were adopted, and which is still used for legal documents in Britain, Canada and the USA. The term foolscap refers to the watermark used in the early manufacture of paper of this size.
16. *snooker-pool*: snooker's pool, a game played on a billiard table combining pool and pyramids; *OED*. The game grew in popularity at the end of the nineteenth century and is now known simply as 'snooker'.
17. *feminist*: The word is not used in the modern sense of one who supports equality for women, but rather in the sense of one (usually male) who appreciates the female form and character.
18. *Hampstead*: a very wealthy area of London, northwest of Charing Cross. It is known for its intellectual and artistic residents. The irony of Authoritarian Viola Cartlet's residence in this area is that the general political leaning of many of its famous residents was to the left, including, at different times, Henry Mayers Hyndman (1842–1921) of the SDF, Sidney (1859–1947) and Beatrice (1858–1943) Webb of the Fabians, James Ramsay MacDonald (1866–1937) of the ILP and first Labour Prime Minister, and Aneurin Bevan (1897–1960) of the Labour Party and Minister of Health responsible for building the National Health Service in the 1945 Labour government. The many left-leaning politicians and intellectuals who lived at Hampstead gave rise to the term 'Hampstead liberalism'.
19. *heaven and earth ... reporters' room*: a re-wording of Hamlet's statement to Horatio when explaining his encounter with his father's ghost: 'There are more things in heaven and earth, Horatio, / Than are dreamt of in your philosophy'; *Hamlet*, Act I, scene v. Fore uses the quotation to point out that it is not only journalists who can be inquisitive and manipulative.
20. *the war*: presumably the 'Roumanian War'; see below, p. 357 n. 23.
21. *Salvation Army*: a Christian Methodist movement founded in 1865 by William (1829–1912) and Catherine (1829–90) Booth in Whitechapel, London. The Salvation Army, whose members were organized in a hierarchical fashion similar to that of the army, sent men and women into urban slums to convert the inhabitants to Christianity. There was also some relief work carried out to alleviate some of the sufferings of poverty, but generally the socialist movement was critical of the Salvation Army for elevating the soul above the body's material sufferings and therefore distracting the poor from working towards social, political and economic change. See, for instance, the exchange between Henry Hyndman and John Law [Margaret Harkness] in *Justice*, March 1888, after the publication of her novel *Captain Lobe: A Story of the Salvation Army* (1888; republished in 1890 under the title *In Darkest London*).

22. *the poor we have always with us*: Matthew 26:11, Christ's reply to the disciple's dismay at the expensive perfume used on Christ, which could have been sold and the money given to the poor: 'The poor you will always have with you, but you will not always have me'. The quotation is often used to justify the presence of the poor in wealthy societies.
23. *Roumanian War*: possibly a reference to the Russo–Turkish War of 1877–8, which threatened to disrupt British imperial power in South Asia, but the following description of the national mood towards British military power suggests the fervour surrounding the Second Boer War in South Africa.
24. *My country, right or wrong*: originally coined in 1816 by Stephen Decatur (1779–1820) in post-revolutionary America as a toast: 'Our country! In her intercourse with foreign nations, may she always be right; but our country, right or wrong'. The phrase has subsequently been used to justify blind and unquestioning patriotism. The author G. K. Chesterton (1874–1936) criticized the statement in the sixteenth article, 'A Defence of Patriotism', in the series 'Defences' published in the *Speaker* in 1901 and published as *The Defendant* in 1902, arguing: '"My country, right or wrong," is a thing that no patriot would think of saying except in a desperate case. It is like saying, "My mother, drunk or sober." No doubt if a decent man's mother took to drink he would share her troubles to the last; but to talk as if he would be in a state of gay indifference as to whether his mother took to drink or not is certainly not the language of men who know the great mystery.'
25. *execrated ... public platform*: Meetings held to criticize the British government and armed forces involvement in the Second Boer War were similarly stormed and broken up by jingoistic mobs. Biographies and autobiographies by and about pro-Boer socialists such as James Keir Hardie and non-socialists such as W. T. Stead record the violence aimed at critical speeches and anti-war groups such as the Stop-the-War movement.
26. *gangway*: 'The gangway is a set of stairs which divides the benches on each side of the House of Commons Chamber. The benches "below the gangway" are generally where the minority parties sit'; from 'Glossary', *www.Parliament.uk*, at http://www.parliament.uk/site-information/glossary/below-the-gangway/ [accessed 24 September 2012]. That Path is 'below' the main parties should signify his reduced power, but the challenge to the established parliamentary parties emanates from 'below', just as the challenge to the ruling aristocratic and bourgeois power is emanating from the classes 'below'.
27. *pawky*: artful, sly, shrewd; *OED*. The leader of the Progressive Party is shrewd enough to recognize the importance of having Path on their side in the Commons debates.
28. *History of Rome*: There are a number of histories of Rome that Viola might be referring to, but it is probably not the one published by the Liberal-minded Thomas Arnold (1795–1842) between 1838 and, posthumously, 1843. It is possible Viola is referring to Edward Gibbon's (1737–94) *The History of the Decline and Fall of the Roman Empire* (1776–88), which blamed the decline of the Roman Empire on its corresponding decline of civic responsibility, with the Christian focus on an afterlife undermining the motivation for progress. Gibbon's reasoning on the decline of Roman power was often used as an argument against the selfishness and greed of capitalism and as a prophecy of its decline in similar ways to that of the Roman Empire. Viola, though, is pointing to the history as an argument against socialism, presumably equating the barbarian hoards who overran the Roman Empire with what she imagines is the violence of the 'Reds'. The careful exposition of Viola's political understanding as based on the opinions of others suggests that she has not read Gibbon's work.
29. *billiard match between Stevenson and Grey*: a series of professional billiard matches between the Australian George Grey (n.d.) and the English champion H. W. Steven-

son (b. 1874), which were played between January and March 1912. The *Daily Citizen*, unlike most British socialist periodicals, carried sport reports.
30. *turn the other cheek to the smiter*: Matthew 5:39: 'But I tell you, Do not resist an evil person. If someone strikes you on the right cheek, turn to him the other also'. Raston Path refuses this conservative Biblical advice. For Path, and socialists generally, change must come through challenging the powerful.
31. *Mount-street*: an exclusive road in Mayfair, London, that runs from Hyde Park to Berkeley Square. Lodden's residence in this area is an indication of his wealth.
32. *right-about*: meaning to turn an angle of 180 degrees, used figuratively here to indicate a dismissal; Gaunt would be 'turned around' and sent away from the paper's offices.
33. *dainty imperial*: a small goatee-style beard.
34. do bon ton: meaning to have good style and breeding; Lumley's manners will allow him to move in the circles of power.
35. *Don Alfonso*: Don Alfonso XIII (1886–1941), the last king of Spain, who ruled from his birth in 1886 until the proclamation of the Second Spanish Republic in 1931. He left Spain and lived the rest of his life in exile in Rome, but he did not abdicate, and his grandson, Juan Carlos (b. 1938), is now the reigning monarch of Spain.
36. *P.A.*: the Press Association, founded in 1868 to act as a collating service for gathering news around Britain.
37. *investments ... stock he held*: perhaps a reference to the Marconi scandal of 1912; see above, p. 353 n. 2.
38. *Gladstone, Beaconsfield, Salisbury, and Asquith*: William Ewart Gladstone (1809–98), Liberal politician and Prime Minister in 1868–74, 1880–5, 1886 and 1892–4; Benjamin Disraeli, Earl of Beaconsfield (1804–81), Conservative politician and Prime Minister in 1868 and 1874–80; Robert Arthur Talbot Gascoyne Cecil, third Marquess of Salisbury (1830–1903), Conservative politician and Prime Minister in 1895–1902; Herbert Henry Asquith, first Earl of Oxford and Asquith (1852–1928), Liberal politician and Prime Minister in 1908–16. Lodden's even-handedness, listing equal numbers of Liberal and Conservative 'great men', may appear to demonstrate an apolitical stance, but it also indicates both parties working for the benefit of the wealthy employers, fearing the threat posed by Labour in the person of Raston Path.
39. *flap-doodle*: nonsense; Burton imagines Path will prove the *Daily Light*'s exclusive exposure as the overblown sensation he knows it to be.
40. *Conan Doyle's, "The Song of the Bow"*: Sir Arthur Conan Doyle (1859–1930), best remembered as the author of the Sherlock Holmes series. 'The Song of the Bow' was published in 1898 as part of Conan Doyle's collection of verse *Songs of Action*, and it was set to music by George John Learmont Drysdale (1866–1909). The poem celebrates English global power (What of the mark? / Ah, seek it not in England) and the might of the English army (The bowmen – the yeomen, / The lads of dale and fell).
41. *spick and span*: The phrase generally means to be smart, clean and new; Viola has made a special effort with her appearance for meeting Gaunt.
42. *Our special commissioners ... bettering matters*: a similar undertaking to the survey carried out by *Justice* in 1885 and published in 1885–6. Hyndman records in his first autobiography that 'we entered upon an investigation, exclusively conducted by the Democratic Federation, as to the condition of the people in the working-class districts of London, in order to determine how large a proportion of the wage-earners were receiving as their weekly remuneration an amount of payment insufficient, under the conditions in which they lived, to keep themselves in proper physical health for the work they had to do'; H.

M. Hydman, *The Record of an Adventurous Life* (London: Macmillan and Co., 1911), p. 330. Hyndman goes on to claim that Charles Booth's detailed investigations were motivated by a desire to contradict the claims published in *Justice*: 'Mr. Booth ... assured me that he felt quite certain we were wrong, and then told me that he himself intended to make, at his own expense, an elaborate inquiry into the condition of the workers of London' (p. 331). Both Booth and Lodden are proven mistaken in their assumptions about the poor.

43. *box-makers' strike in Southwark*: a fictionalized treatment of the 1888 Bryant and May matchgirls' strike. The *Daily Light*'s position on the strike is similar to that of newspapers such as the *Times*, which opened a report of a meeting of the striking women with an interview with owner Theodore Bryant, who claimed that the workforce were well paid; see the *Times*, 9 July 1888, p. 6.

44. *model dwellings*: Model dwellings were a philanthropic answer to the problem of the London slums in the 1870s–90s. Housing trusts such as the Peabody and philanthropic companies such as the East End Dwellings Company cleared slums and built apartments that were supposed to be healthier and better for the inhabitants. A caretaker would often supervise the buildings, and philanthropic ladies would collect the rents while monitoring the behaviour of the tenants. Margaret Harkness and her cousin Beatrice Webb were rent collectors at Katherine Buildings in East Smithfield for a time, and although Webb criticized what she saw as a lack of decency and comfort for the sake of low rents and sanitary homes, the buildings were some improvement over the slums. The role of the lady rent collectors was not only to collect money but also to ensure decency in the building and to 'civilize' the poor. Nellie's position as a tenant in a model dwelling suggests that she is poor but respectable.

45. *Sydenham*: a district in southeast London where the Crystal Palace was rebuilt after its removal from the 1851 Great Exhibition site at Hyde Park. The presence of the Crystal Palace made the area fashionable, and notable residents included Eleanor Marx (1855–98) and W. G. Grace (1848–1915). Gaunt's dwelling places him in a comfortable area, but one not nearly as wealthy – or as intellectually liberal – as the Cartlets' Hampstead.

46. *district visitor*: possibly a reference to the people who were employed to collect the rent from tenants living in model dwellings; see n. 44 above for information on model dwellings.

47. *Kennington Park*: previously Kennington Common, where a large Chartist demonstration was held on 10 April 1848. The land was made a park in 1854, and 'its status as an ancient commons was reduced to that of a Royal Park'; this has been called 'a colonisation of working class political space' by Stefan Szczelkun in 'Kennington Park, Birthplace of People's Democracy', at http://bak.spc.org/kenningtonpark [accessed 31 October 2012]. The 'vulgar' music halls and taverns surrounding the park vied with the 'rational recreation' of the bandstand inside the park as working-class entertainment, and a young Charlie Chaplin played in the park while his father drank in the Horns tavern. Viola is once again placed in an area of left-leaning liberalism.

48. *Westminster to the Obleisk*: not the Obelisk, also known as 'Cleopatra's Needle' and which is located on the Thames Victoria Embankment, but St George's Circus in Southwark. The St George's obelisk was designed for the junction in 1771, was moved to the park in front of the Imperial War Museum in 1905, and did not return until the late 1990s.

49. *a fortnight as an out-of-work*: There were many social investigations carried out during the latter part of the nineteenth and early part of the twentieth centuries where investigators would immerse themselves into the lives of workers or the unemployed. Mary Higgs (1854–1937) published *Glimpses into the Abyss* in 1906, having already published *Five*

Days and Five Nights as a Tramp among Tramps in 1904 under the pseudonym 'A Lady'. Her investigative work – following that of James Greenwood (bap. 1835–1927), author of *A Night in the Workhouse* published in the *Pall Mall Gazette* in 1866, and Jack London (John Griffith, 1876–1916), author of *The People of the Abyss* (1903) – involved dressing as a tramp to report on the experience of the female tramp. Walter Besant's (1836–1901) *All Sorts and Conditions of Men* (1882) was based on such investigations. For a socialist fictional approach, see Charles Allen Clarke's 'The Red Flag' in Volume 4, pp. 147–254.

50. *Wandsworth*: Wandsworth Prison was opened in Wandsworth, South London, in 1851 and today still houses category B prisoners (those not dangerous but likely to escape). Oscar Wilde was one of its former inmates. Mr William Guggins, like many, assumes the unemployed are criminal.
51. *Elephant and Castle ... Newington-causeway*: a short walk, but Lant Street is beyond the causeway.
52. *New Oblisk ... old*: possibly a reference to the clock tower that replaced the obelisk in 1905.
53. *New Cut*: a street in Lambeth and Southwark now known as the Cut. The market held in the New Cut every Friday and Saturday was one of the largest in Victorian London and was noted by Henry Mayhew (1812–87) in *London Labour and the London Poor* (1851; 1861–2) as having been reduced in size by police regulation.
54. *Ostend rabbits*: a large breed of rabbit originally imported from the Netherlands. The Ostend rabbit would be used as a food source; the stall owner's comment on them not keeping long either refers either to the rapid decay of unrefrigerated meat or to the cost of feeding the rabbits if kept live.
55. *Portuguese ... blue points*: see above, p. 354 n. 1.
56. *Haroun al Raschid*: 'The Night Adventure of Harun al-Rashid and the Youth Majab' is one of the stories of *The Book of One Thousand and One Nights*, or *1001 Arabian Nights*. Harun al-Rashid was Arab Abbasid Caliph who ruled from Baghdad in AD 786–809. The night adventure tells the fictitious story of his incognito travel through Baghdad, and his surprise at finding a magnificent palace in the unpretentious byways of the city. Raston Path would be unlikely to find anything resembling magnificence in the ordinary London suburb of Finsbury Park, nor is the area so poverty stricken that it would be of any interest for social investigation into the extremes of poverty in the city.
57. *Tolstoyan Christian*: The author Leo Nikolayevich Tolstoy (1828–1910) held strong Christian beliefs on the importance of Christ's teachings and pacifisms. To Tolstoy, Christ's teachings were to be applied directly to life and should be taken as law; therefore his pacifism advocated no retaliation to violence, no matter what the attack. Raston Path is no pacifist, relishing the political battle, but his motives and goals are honourable and for the benefit of society, not merely for his own self-aggrandizement.
58. *Government Whips*: Within the British political system, each party allocates a member to act as 'whip' to ensure that MPs follow the party line. There are no official sanctions for those who do not follow the party other than the withdrawal of the whip – meaning to suspend the Member from the party – but the whip's role is to convince compliance with party policy. Path's personal issues will be of interest to the whips, who would be concerned about the effect of the revelations on the party as a whole.
59. *chief agent*: A political party agent's role is wide-ranging, but Path will speak to his party agent for advice on dealing with the media and producing press releases.
60. *Stevenson's "Vailima Letters"*: Robert Louis Stevenson's (1850–94) *Vailima Letters: Being Correspondence Addressed by Robert Louis Stevenson to Sidney Colvin, November 1890–*

October 1894 (1895). Stevenson's letters describe his final years of living in Samoa, the Samoan landscape and history. Nellie's selection of this book suggests her interest in both literature and the world outside of her own experience.

61. *Then Gaunt talked to her of books ... by Nellie*: the range of reading undertaken by Nancy suggests her intellect and in some ways her political leanings. William Makepeace Thackeray's (1811–63) *The History of Henry Esmond* (1852) is the history of the fictional Henry Esmond, supposedly the illegitimate son of Viscount Castlewood, during the reign of Queen Anne and the English revolution. Alfred Lord Tennyson's (1809–92) *Idylls of the King* (1859–85) was a series of long narrative poems of the Arthurian saga regretting Arthur's failure to establish human perfection in the world. In Charles Lamb's (1775–1834) *Essays of Elia* (1820–3), Elia was Lamb's pseudonym and the fictional narrator for the Letters published in the *London Magazine*, which drew on his own experiences. The essays were collected and published in 1823 and followed by *The Last Essays of Elia* in 1833. Mrs Henry Wood (Ellen Wood, 1814–87), author of the best-selling sensation novel *East Lynne* (1861), was a prolific writer whose reputation was overshadowed by *East Lynne*; she had fallen out of favour by the end of the century. *Waverley* (1814) was Sir Walter Scott's (1771–1832) first novel, *Ivanhoe* (1819) was a later novel, and *The Fair Maid of Perth* (1828) was one of his last. All are historical novels, set during the Jacobite Rebellion, the reign of Richard I, and the reign of Robert III of Scotland respectively. James Matthew (J. M.) Barrie's (1860–1937) *Margaret Ogilvy* (1896) was an autobiographical account of Barrie's poor childhood through his mother's experience. Nancy's preferences are wide-ranging, encompassing both high (Tennyson) and popular culture (Wood), and show a leaning toward stories or accounts of ordinary working people and pre-industrial settings. Nellie's preference for cheap novels suggests she is not interested in literature.

62. *stringent to severity ... creature comforts*: from Benjamin Seebohm Rowntree's (1871–1954) study of poverty in York, *Poverty: A Study in Town Life* (1899). The calculations Raston Path refers to in his speech are also taken from Rowntree's study, which sets out a definition of absolute poverty.

63. *Practically the whole of this class ... I never tells him*: This extract and the household budget in the following chapter are lifted directly from Rowntree's chapter 'The Standard of Life' in *Poverty: A Study in Town Life*.

64. *the tiny ones ... same town*: These figures are taken from Rowntree's chapter 'Relation of Poverty to Health' in *Poverty: A Study in Town Life*.

65. *sixty years*: probably a reference to the 1867 Second Reform Act, which doubled the British electorate and enfranchised a significant proportion of working-class males. It was highly contested and resisted by some politicians, to the extent that the road to reform, after the Chartist movement petered out in the early 1850s, saw many governments fail to pass and implement reform legislation. The indeterminate chronological setting of Derrick's fiction makes this the most likely piece of contested legislation.

66. *breaking up the British Constitution*: Constitutional arguments were put forward in opposition to the extension of the franchise in the discussions leading to the 1867 Second Reform Act. The British Constitution is famously unwritten (the only other, at the time of writing, being Israel), which, constitutionalists argue, gives greater freedom for change in adapting to modern issues.

67. *thirty-pounds-a-year house*: the property's rental value. In 1913 Herbert Asquith's Liberal government proposed a bill to make manhood suffrage universal and not restricted to the occupiers of property worth a rental of £10 per annum. The bill failed because the inclusion of female suffrage had been ruled out of order by the Speaker. The occupier

of the house visited by Raston Path is, therefore, in a relatively comfortable position compared to the minimum voting requirements and the poverty experienced by Gaunt and the Kirks.

68. *His sweetheart died ... Miss Croxten died*: This revelation contradicts the claim made on 6 December that her father was a widower at the time of Path's relationship with Miss Croxten.
69. *Theirs not to reason why*: 'The Charge of the Light Brigade' (1855) by Alfred Lord Tennyson: 'Theirs not to reason why, / Theirs but to do and die'. Gaunt devolves responsibility for his actions by claiming to be unquestioningly following orders, as the soldiers of the Light Brigade did when ordered to charge at Balaclava during the Crimean War. This is more than a little disingenuous, as Gaunt had laid the plan without Lodden's knowledge.
70. Westminster Gazette: Liberal newspaper published from 1893 to 1928, owned by George Newnes and influential in Liberal political reporting.
71. *casteth out fear*: 1 John 4:18: 'There is no fear in love; but perfect love casteth out fear: because fear hath torment. He that feareth is not made perfect in love'.
72. *Trilby hat*: a soft felt hat with a narrow brim and indented crown; *OED*. The hat is named after the eponymous character of George Du Maurier's (1834–96) phenomenally popular novel published in 1894.
73. *with point*: meaning an appeal to the Speaker of the House of Commons for clarification. The MPs are making a detailed scrutiny of administration and policy.
74. *Distinguished Strangers' Gallery*: The strangers' gallery in the House of Commons is a viewing area where members of the public not associated with the House or with the Members can watch proceedings. Distinguished strangers – ambassadors, peers' family members, foreign diplomats and others – have seats in a gallery separate to that for the general public.
75. *dispatch case*: sometimes called a dispatch box (and to be distinguished from the wooden lectern mentioned later from which government ministers deliver their speeches), used to carry ministerial papers. The most famous dispatch case is the red budget box carried by the Chancellor of the Exchequer on budget day. The case carried by Path is the visual signal of the imminent reading of the new bill.
76. *division*: A division in the British Parliament is the physical dividing of the members into Aye or No lobbies, through which their support or opposition to a bill is registered. A vote on a bill will be registered by members calling out their agreement or opposition, but if a vote is close – as it is here with a majority of only 25 out of 650 – a division will be called to determine the passing or failure of the bill. Each member's name is recorded as they enter the lobby; this is the division list.
77. *A.B.C.*: The ABC railway guide, first published in 1853, gave times and destinations for rail travel to and from London. Unlike that produced by George Bradshaw (1801–53), it was not a national railway guide.
78. *the rigours of whipping in*: The party whips – who are responsible for making sure every member capable of voting for the side of the party will be in attendance and voting along party lines – are now more confident of passing the division and less rigorous in their efforts.
79. *been a white man*: meaning he has played fair and straight. The origins for this phrase are unknown, but there is a clear imperial tone to the association of whiteness with fair play. The unacknowledged opposite is that non-white people are generally assumed to be devious and cunning. Rudyard Kipling's (1865–1936) poem 'The White Man's Burden' (1899) asserts the social, cultural and political superiority of white, Western society

above non-white, non-Western societies and therefore the necessity of the white man to take responsibility for 'civilizing' the non-white.
80. *three or four days' polling*: Until 1918 British elections were held over the course of a number of weeks. For instance, the period for the election when the Liberal government was returned to power in 1910, and which remained in power until the Liberal/Unionist/Labour wartime coalition government was formed in May 1915, was held between 3 and 19 December 1910. The first single-day election was held on Saturday, 14 December 1918, when the Liberal/Unionist wartime coalition was returned again.
81. *mosquito work*: Mosquitos are carriers of a number of diseases, some of which are dangerous to human beings, and they can pass life-threatening diseases to humans without any danger to themselves. The suffragettes are threatening the political life of the Prime Minister without any danger to their own cause.
82. *majority of 35*: In the British Parliament a majority government would be formed by the party who had won 326 seats or more. A majority of 35 is enough to form a government but is not a comfortable margin.
83. *art gallery ... Camberwell-green*: possibly a reference to the South London Fine Art Gallery on Peckham Road, which opened in 1891.
84. *Crowborough*: a town in East Sussex, southwest of Royal Tunbridge Wells. In the late nineteenth century it was renowned for its healthy atmosphere. Gaunt and Nancy leave the unhealthy metropolis – both physical and psychological – for a new start in a healthy area.

'Pat', 'Living Retired. An Unconscious Tragedy'

1. *Southport ... thy line*: Southport and Blackpool are both Lancashire coastal resorts that were popular in the nineteenth and twentieth centuries. Blackpool was especially popular with the Lancashire working classes, while Southport was associated with the middle-class visitor. Jem Buckley's financial success is signified by being able to afford to retire to Southport rather than Blackpool.
2. *puff*: life, the span of life.
3. *tak' thee agate*: accompany you to your place of destination.
4. *a good crack at neet*: so they would be able to enjoy themselves without care; crack as a derivative of the Irish 'craic', meaning fun or entertainment.
5. *a Belle Vue parrot*: Belle Vue Gardens at Gorton, southeast of Manchester city centre. One of the attractions at the Gardens was a collection of caged birds, including parrots. The point here is that Dick keeps interrupting in the same manner as a parrot squawking, always having to get a word (motty) in the story.
6. *cobbed*: There are a number of uses for the word 'cob' in Lancashire dialect and in this context it means to excel or surpass; Sam's description of Jem's gardening technique tops all.
7. *merry as a grig*: Grig is dialect for either a cricket or a lively child, the sense being that Mrs Buckley is in her element because she still has her work, while Jem has been severed from his.

Pitt, 'The Last Dinner'

1. *ole Kaiser Bill*: Kaiser Wilhelm II (1859–1941), emperor of Germany. He succeeded his father in 1888 and took a militaristic approach to German global presence. He abdicated on 9 November 1918 when it became clear that Germany was losing the war, and he spent the rest of his life in exile in the Netherlands.
2. *see them pore little Belgians right*: The escalation to war after the assassination of Archduke Franz Ferdinand of Austria-Hungary on 28 June 1914 was caused by a series of complex pacts between the European nations. Britain was ultimately drawn into the war by Germany's invasion of Belgium as the quickest way for the German army to march on Paris. This triggered the 1839 Treaty of London in which Britain pledged to defend Belgium's neutrality.
3. *John French's big surprise packet for Kaiser Bill*: The German invasion of Belgium and France and the German declaration of war on Russia triggered a French–Russian pact as well as the Britain–Belgian treaty. Britain, France and Russia entered the war against Germany within the first four days of August 1914.

Quelch, 'His Reward'

1. *Old Age Pension*: The payment of a state pension to retired workers was implemented by the 1908 Old-Age Pensions Act as part of the Liberal government welfare reform. The five shillings collected by Peter Dunn tells us that he is either unmarried or widowed as the allowance for a retired couple was initially seven shillings and sixpence. The pension was paid through the Post Office to avoid the shame and stigma associated with other unemployment institutions such as the Poor Law.
2. *the Lump*: the workhouse.

Grayson, 'The Lost Vision. A Spring Fantasy'

1. *hum and shock*: George Gordon Lord Byron, *Childe Harold's Pilgrimage* (1811), Canto II, stanza XXVI: 'But midst the crowd, the hum, the shock of men'.
2. *Moloch*: a person or thing that demands costly sacrifice; *OED*.
3. *the teeth and claws of nature were red*: Alfred Lord Tennyson (1809–82), *In Memoriam* (1850), stanza LV: 'Tho' Nature, red in tooth and claw'.

Hartley, 'Mr. Prowser-Wowser'

1. *the strike at Waihi*: a six-month mining strike at the goldmines of Waihi. On 12 November 1912 escalating violence aimed at strike-breakers culminated in gunfire, the storming of the miner's hall by police, and the death of striker Fred Evans by beating.
2. *Labour is prior to ... not first existed*: from US President Abraham Lincoln's State of the Union Address, 3 December 1861.

Meyer, 'It Can't be Done! A History of Impossibilities'

1. *Clermont*: the first practical and commercially viable steamboat, designed and built by Robert Fulton (1765–1815) and Robert R. Livingstone (1746–1813) in New York in 1807.
2. *Langley*: Samuel Pierpont Langley (1834–1906), pioneer of aviation.

Ford, 'In the "Good Old Times"'

1. *Factory Acts*: A series of parliamentary acts were passed during the nineteenth century to improve working conditions within the factories. The earliest acts concerned the limitation of children's work in the factories, starting with the 1802 Act that imposed a maximum eight-hour working day for children between nine and thirteen. The final Act of 1901 raised the minimum working age to twelve. Subsequent Factory Acts (1937, 1959, 1961) consolidated earlier acts.
2. *buy childer ... wi'out buying*: In the late eighteenth and early nineteenth centuries, trafficking destitute children for factory labour (and other trades and services) was widespread across Britain and the Empire. See J. Humphries, *Childhood and Child Labour in the British Industrial Revolution* (Cambridge: Cambridge University Press, 2010) for further details.

Morrison, 'Lord Santa Claus, G.E.R., M.P. A Drama in Ten Minutes'

1. *Henderton*: possibly a reference to Arthur Henderson (1863–1935), member of the Parliamentary Labour Party and the ironfounders' union. Henderson was chairman of the PLP in 1908–11 and party secretary during Ramsay MacDonald's (1866–1937) time as chairman and treasurer.
2. *decent div.*: a decent dividend; a significant return for shareholders from the profits of a company.
3. *Kings Lynn*: The Great Eastern Railway (the 'G.E.R.' of the story title) was formed in 1862 and had controlled the railways in East Anglia until the formation of the Midland and Great Northern Joint Railway in 1893; the GNJR took over the line serving King's Lynn (and other towns and cities) in 1889. The GER had a reputation for carrying out improvements and works on the cheap, including increasing capacity in carriages by cutting carriages in half and inserting a section. These were called bogied carriages.
4. *General Secretary of the Amalgamated Railwaymen*: the Amalgamated Society of Railway Servants, founded in 1871. In 1913 it merged with the General Railway Workers Union and the United Pointsmen and Signalman's Society to form the National Union of Railwaymen.

Morrison, 'The Weaker Vessel and the Strike'

1. *ticket man*: a member of the union.
2. *suffragette*: a female supporter of the women's suffrage movement, especially the militant parts of the movement; *OED*. The term, although now used generally to refer to supporters of the female vote, was a derogatory term at the time and separated the militant 'suffragettes' from the more peaceful 'suffragist'. Mr Robin's use of the word implies he is not used to his wife's forthright demands.
3. *"at home"*: an ironic use of the middle- and upper-class practice of being prepared to receive guests. Mr Wright is 'at home' because he is not at work, being on strike.
4. *an empty clay*: a clay pipe, the cheapest material for a tobacco pipe.
5. *dripping*: congealed fat and juices from cooked meat. The consumption of dripping suggested the family used to be able to afford meat – a sign of comparative wealth for working-class families – but that their food range has been significantly reduced during the strike.

'Casey', 'Alice in Sunderland. A Baffling Mystery'

1. *Pentecostal Convention*: Pentecostalism is a revivalist branch of Protestant Christianity that practises radical evangelism and which emerged in Britain and America during the late nineteenth and early twentieth centuries. The annual Sunderland Convention was organized by Alfred Boddy (1854–1930).
2. *Whit-week*: Whitsun is the seventh Sunday after Easter; Whitsuntide is the week following Pentecost, the seventh Sunday after Easter, and a religious holiday for Christians. The holiday was celebrated in the north of England with towns organizing walks or parades of Sunday school children through the town, brass band displays and competitions to herald the beginning of summer. The Whitsun holiday is a relic of feudal society when the lord would allow his serfs time away from work.
3. *Jarrow*: a town in the northeast of England associated with shipbuilding. It is most famously associated with the 1936 Jarrow March, when men walked from Jarrow to London to protest against unemployment.
4. *not Scott, mostly Wesley and Newman*: Sir Walter Scott (1771–1832), poet and novelist; John Wesley (1707–91), founder of Methodism, who published a large collection of hymns entitled *A Collection of Hymns, for the Use of the People Called Methodists* (1780); John Henry Cardinal Newman (1801–90), part of the Oxford Movement of the 1830s and 1840s that believed High Church Anglicanism to be one of the branches of Catholicism. The March Hare takes Alice's exclamation to differentiate between the secular poetry of Walter Scott and the hymnal poetry of the churches.
5. *She wants to go ... down to Dixie*: a rewording of Irving Berlin's (1888–1989) 'I Want to Be in Dixie' (1912): 'I want to be / I want to be / I want to be down home in Dixie'.
6. *Annfield Plain*: a mining village in County Durham, to the west of Sunderland.
7. *Tell me not ... Burnsian speech*: a critical reference to the speeches of John Burns MP (1858–1943). Burns was elected to Parliament in 1892 as an independent labour candidate along with James Keir Hardie. Burns lost the support of the socialist and labour politicians and members when he gravitated towards the Liberal Party, accepting a position as president of the Local Government Board in the Campbell-Bannerman (1836–1908) administration in 1905.
8. *Maskelyne and Devant*: former watchmaker John Nevil Maskelyne (1839–1917) and his friend, former cabinet maker George Alfred Cooke (1825–1904), were stage magicians and illusionists who have been credited with devising some of the most famous illusions, including levitation. After the death of Cooke, Maskelyne formed a partnership with David Devant (1868–1941), a partnership that became even more successful than Maskelyne and Cooke and lasted until just before Maskelyne's death. The mysteries of religion and of stage magicians are all the same to Alice.

'Optimus', 'The May-Day Festival in the Year 1970'

1. *Stockerau to Mödling*: villages to the north and south of Vienna. The prediction is for Vienna to have grown in size to encompass these two villages, a forecast that has not yet been achieved in the early twenty-first century. Vienna was a socialist stronghold, and the city elected the Social Democratic Party to power after the First World War. Its left-wing politics earned it the name Red Vienna. The author hopes that the strength of Vienna and its socialist politics will grow to greater importance in the twentieth century.

2. *Cotta style*: a small land measure containing eighty square yards; *OED*. The houses have space and land surrounding them, differentiating the socialist attitude to planning from the pre-socialist period described by the old man, who recalls the overcrowded slums of capitalism.
3. *Brigittenau*: an area to the northeast of Vienna's city centre. There is a clear geographical separation between work and home.
4. *"poorhouses" or "alms houses"*: a building for housing the poor and needy often funded by individual philanthropy.
5. *Goethe's "Faust"*: *Faust: A Tragedy* (1808; 1832) by Johann Wolfgang von Goethe (1749–1832). The line is from Part II Act V, where Faust has died – as the contract with Mephistopheles demanded – when he attained a moment he wanted to last forever. This came as he imagined a free land: 'I willingly would such a throng behold, / Upon free ground with a free people stand'. Faust is taken by angels and redeemed in Heaven despite his contract with Mephistopheles.
6. *Kahlenberg*: a mountain in the Wienerwald, or Vienna Woods, on the edge of Vienna and a popular tourist destination.

Westoby, 'Shamed'

1. *Deal*: coastal town in Kent, eight miles northeast of Dover.
2. *epergne*: a table ornament in branched form used to hold small dishes for dessert or, in this case, vases for flowers.
3. *strike*: the National Coal Strike of 1912 for a minimum wage for all men and boys working in the pits. The strike was organized by the Miners Federation of Great Britain to put an end to complicated locally set policies on payment for mine work. The strike began at the end of February, with miners beginning the strike at different times according to their notice, and ended on 24 March 1912. The strike was not entirely successful for the miners but the Minimum Wage Act was passed, although this was still liable to local settlements.
4. *there's so many nowadays*: The period 1911–14 was one of significant industrial unrest as trades, including miners, dock workers, railway workers and even school children, demanded fairer treatment.
5. *master lighterman*: one in charge of a group of lightermen, men who worked on a flat-bottomed boat or barge used to unload ships that could not be docked at a wharf; *OED*.

Sue, '"Stop Thief!" The Proletariat and Slummery (An Incident of the Revolution of 1848, told by Eugene Sue)'

1. *sou piece*: a historical French coin with a low value, worth the twentieth part of a livre or franc; OED
2. *revolution*: A series of revolutions swept Europe in 1848, and the French events ended the Orleans monarchy and elected Louis Napoleon as president of the Second Republic.
3. *gamin*: a street urchin, a neglected boy; *OED*. Brilri goes on to give Flameche as an example of the children who are without family or home.
4. *toggery*: Usually used as a term for clothing (clerical toggery, official toggery etc.), Flameche uses it here to describe his collection of small items used for shot in his gun.
5. *Tulieries*: the Tuileries Garden, originally created by Catherine de Medici (1519–89) as the garden for the Tuileries Palace in 1564, opened to the public in 1667 and made

a public park after the French Revolution of 1789–99. Despite it being a 'public' area, the Tuileries Garden is still kept as an ornamental park when children like Flameche are starving.
6. *Louis Philippe*: Louis Philippe I (1775–1850), king of France in 1830–48 under the July monarchy; he abdicated in February 1848 in favour of his grandson, Philippe, Comte de Paris, and fled to England in disguise.
7. *Daniel De Leon*: (1852–1914), American socialist, influential member of the Socialist Labour Party and editor of its newspaper, *The People*, from 1892 until 1914.

Anderson, 'Mary Davis; or the Fate of a Proletarian Family. A Lesson Given to the Glasgow S.L.P. Socialist Sunday School'

1. *The lesson*: This lesson is given to the Sunday School of Glasgow's Socialist Labour Party (SLP), a Marxist group with a strong membership in Clydeside.
2. *told a lie ... believe it*: 'A lie told often enough becomes the truth'; Vladimir Ilyich Lenin.
3. *reel and strath-spey*: reel, a traditional Scottish dance of four or more participants; strathspey, a lively dance or reel, the music to accompany the dance; *OED*.
4. *quoit player*: a game played by throwing rings of flattened iron, rope, rubber, etc. at a peg placed in the ground; *OED*.
5. *sweay*: I am unable to find a definition or suggestion for this word, but the context suggests a mechanism for holding a cooking pot or pots over the fire.
6. *waggity we-clock*: possibly a colloquial term for a dutch clock, a wall-mounted clock with exposed pendulums.
7. *Gibbon's "Decline and Fall of the Roman Empire"*: Gibbon's *The History of the Decline and Fall of the Roman Empire*; see above, p. 357 n. 28. Mr Davis is intimating that the same situation is being repeated in Western capitalist countries as the rich eschew moral and ethical responsibility to society as a whole, focusing only on the acquisition of money. This is compounded by their insistence that workers look to the afterlife for their reward.
8. *shewed the white feather*: a symbol of cowardice.
9. *"pass" ... tenter or "overseer"*: pass, passageway or corridor between the looms; tenter, either someone who stretches out cloth to dry after dying or someone who oversees (or tends) machinery; overseer, someone in charge of the workers in a specific area or room of the mill. This scene describes the hierarchy among workers in the mills, as an employee in charge of the machinery (spinners, weavers) would sub-contract part of the work to others, their wages being paid out of the spinner's or weaver's wages. Charles Allen Clarke describes this sub-division of labour and the double standards of the unionized weaver or spinner when dealing with their own employees through the experiences of Jim Campbell in 'The Red Flag'; see Volume 4, pp. 159–60.

Parker, 'Elsie's Day'

1. *boss at one of the windows*: boss, to make to project, or to manage, control, direct; *OED*. Tomkins wants to be noticed by Elsie.
2. *Russian sables*: fur from the sable made into coats and jackets. Elsie can only look at expensive garments and must content herself with meagre purchases.
3. *Jericho root*: Jericho is the city held by the Canaanites and destroyed in Joshua 6, but it is more likely that this phrase has a horticultural origin. The Rose of Jericho grows from a seed that, when conditions become harsh, retracts from the soil and is moved by desert

winds until a more conducive location is happened upon. The phrase suggests unfulfilled potential, and Elsie's disappearance is suggestive of her removal from harsh conditions in the hope of better ones elsewhere.

4. *the only inhabitant of Juan Fernandez*: The Juan Fernández Islands are a remote group of islands in the South Pacific, where Alexander Selkirk (1616–1721) was marooned for four years.

R. C. G., 'The Patriots'

1. *third-class "smokers"*: During the early years of British rail travel, there were separate carriages (and at stations separate waiting and dining rooms) for first-, second- and third-class passengers. By the end of the nineteenth century and the early years of the twentieth, rail companies, with dwindling first-class passengers, ended the expensive first-class carriage and renamed second class 'first' while third class became 'second'. The Scottish and north-eastern railway companies were the first to change the class system, so the reference to third-class passengers may be a referential hangover from the three-class era or used to emphasize the commuters' position in relation to the other passengers. There would be designated carriages, or parts of carriages, for those wishing to smoke on the journey. The carriage is occupied by the ordinary lower-middle-class commuter.
2. *old Jimmy Heresford*: a fictional general, possibly a reference to William Beresford, whose command of troops in southern Spain led to the disastrous Battle of Albuera in 1811.
3. *Dravia frontier*: a fictional battle line.
4. Chronicle: The *Daily Chronicle* (1872–1930) was a Liberal newspaper that supported British involvement in the First World War.
5. *Terriers*: members of the Territorial Army, civilians who train as though part of the regular army but are not full-time members of the armed services. The TA was founded in 1907 as a defensive corps, but members were given the opportunity to volunteer for overseas service in 1910. During the First World War more than seventy TA battalions volunteered to serve in France.

Hynes, 'Barky: A Sketch'

1. *common lodging-house*: also known as a doss house or kip house; a private house where a bed – or a shared bed – could be bought for between four and sixpence a night.
2. *scrand*: scran, a nautical term for food or food rations; *OED*.
3. *House*: the workhouse.
4. *Army shelter*: The Salvation Army began its social work in the 1880s by providing shelter for London prostitutes, and shortly after opening shelters for men. The shelters were not run on such harsh grounds as the workhouses, providing the opportunity for men to develop new skills to enhance their opportunities for employment. See also above, p. 356 n. 21.

SILENT CORRECTIONS

Derrick, 'The Making of a Red'

p. 43, l. 26	intend] intended
p. 53, l. 22	moment] moments
p. 144, l. 16	made] make
p. 145, l. 39	Let's] Lets
p. 154, ll. 27–8	accretion] accretion of
p. 196, l. 24	Chapter XIX.] Chapter XIX – Continued.